The Soviet Writers' Union and Its Leaders

D1572048

SRLT

NORTHWESTERN UNIVERSITY PRESS
Studies in Russian Literature and Theory

SERIES EDITORS
Caryl Emerson
Gary Saul Morson
William Mills Todd III
Andrew Wachtel
Justin Weir

The Soviet Writers' Union and Its Leaders

Identity and Authority under Stalin

Carol Any

NORTHWESTERN UNIVERSITY PRESS / EVANSTON, ILLINOIS

Northwestern University Press
www.nupress.northwestern.edu

Printed in the United States of America

10   9   8   7   6   5   4   3   2   1

Library of Congress Cataloging-in-Publication Data

Names: Any, Carol Joyce, 1952– author.
Title: The Soviet Writers' Union and its leaders : identity and authority under
    Stalin / Carol Any.
Other titles: Studies in Russian literature and theory
Description: Evanston, Illinois : Northwestern University Press, 2020. | Series:
    Studies in Russian literature and theory | Includes bibliographical references and
    index.
Identifiers: LCCN 2020020751 | ISBN 9780810142756 (paperback) | ISBN
    9780810142770 (cloth) | ISBN 9780810142763 (ebook)
Subjects: LCSH: Soi͡uz pisateleĭ SSSR—History. | Soi͡uz pisateleĭ SSSR—Officials
    and employees—Biography. | Literature and state—Soviet Union—History.
Classification: LCC PG2920.S68 A59 2020 | DDC 891.706047—dc23
LC record available at https://lccn.loc.gov/2020020751

For Peter and Andy

Contents

Acknowledgments

I DOUBT THAT I have fully expressed my gratitude to the colleagues, friends, and loved ones who offered their knowledge, insights, encouragement, and patience during my long years of trying to understand Soviet literary life. I am not sure I know how to tell them how important they have been. This book would not exist without them.

Evgeny Dobrenko, Caryl Emerson, and Peter B. Brown read the manuscript at various stages and gave me invaluable suggestions. My colleagues at Trinity College, John Alcorn, Thomas Harrington, Samuel Kassow, Sara Kippur, David Rosen, Mark Silk, and Erik Vogt all generously took the time to read and critique an early version of my work. Janet Chang provided me with direction in researching the psychology of group behaviors and responses to authority. Vera Terekhina and Alexei Chagin of the Institute of World Literature, Russian Academy of Sciences, gave me invaluable assistance with archival access. Alexandra Smith, Boris Lanin, Pyotr Aleshkovsky, and Ilya Venyavkin shared their reflections, pointed me to important sources, and energized me. Gary Saul Morson offered me much needed encouragement.

The generous research policies of Trinity College have been instrumental in bringing this project to fruition. My work was also made possible by the cooperative spirit of the staff at the libraries and archives in Moscow and Saint Petersburg: The Russian State Archive of Literature and Art, the Russian State Archive of Social and Political History, the Central Archive of Social Movements in Moscow, the Russian State Library, and the Saltykov-Shchedrin Library.

Some of the material from chapters 3 and 4 has appeared in, respectively, *Russian History* 35, nos. 1–2 (Spring–Summer 2008): 199–214, and *Taboo Pushkin: Topics, Texts, Interpretations*, ed. Alyssa Dinega Gillespie (Madison: University of Wisconsin Press, 2012), 378–401.

I hold in my memory Andrei Pliguzov, who warned me of the magnitude of what I was getting myself into, and Lidiia Libedinskaia, who helped me see into the intricacies of personal relationships among writers in the Stalin years. My deep appreciation goes to my editors at Northwestern University Press, Trevor Perri for his uncanny sleuthing, and Maia Rigas, for her cheerful willingness to go the extra mile.

My treasured husband, Peter B. Brown, generously helped me through every stage of this book, sharing his encyclopedic knowledge of Russia, assisting with minute clerical tasks, and cheering me on. He also had the trying experience of putting up with my less pleasant moments, of which there were many, during my sometimes fitful work on this project. He had to sense when to walk on eggshells and when to prod. I am able to appreciate that more in hindsight than I did at the time. To him, and to our son, Andrew Brown, I dedicate this book.

Note on the Text

THIS BOOK USES a modified version of the Library of Congress transliteration system. The masculine adjective ending has been simplified to a simple *y*; the soft sign has been omitted except preceding a soft vowel, where it is rendered as *y*; and a *y* has been inserted between two soft vowels for easier readability. *Y* also replaces *I* at the beginning of names beginning with я and ю; ё is always rendered as 'yo'. Commonly known names are given in the form most familiar to English speakers.

Titles of Russian books and periodicals are referred to by their English translations, except for newspapers and magazines that are known to English speakers by their Russian title: *Pravda, Izvestiia, Krasnaia zvezda, Literaturnaia gazeta, Novy mir, Znamia*, and *Zvezda*.

Abbreviations

AFPD   *Aleksandr Fadeev: Pis'ma i dokumenty; Iz fondov Rossiiskogo Gosudarstvennogo Arkhiva literatury i iskusstva,* comp. N. I. Dikushina (Moscow: Izdatel'stvo literaturnogo instituta im. A. M. Gor'kogo, 2001)

AG   Arkhiv Gor'kogo, Institut Mirovoi Literatury imeni Gor'kogo

APVS   *Andrei Platonov: Vospominaniia sovremennikov; Materialy k biografii,* comp. N. V. Kornienko and E. D. Shubina (Moscow: Sovremennyi pisatel', 1994)

FP 1973   Aleksandr Fadeev, *Pis'ma, 1916–1956* (Moscow: Sovetskii pisatel', 1973)

LF   *"Literaturnyi front": Istoriia politicheskoi tsenzury 1932–1946 gg; Sbornik dokumentov,* comp. D. L. Babichenko (Moscow: Entsiklopediia rossiiskikh dereven', 1994)

LG   *Literaturnaia gazeta* (Moscow, 1929–)

MMN   T. M. Goriaeva et al., eds., *Mezhdu molotom i nakoval'nei: Soiuz sovetskikh pisatelei SSSR; Dokumenty i kommentarii,* vol. 1 (Moscow: Rosspen, 2011)

NLP   *Na literaturnom postu* (Moscow, 1926–32)

ONI 1   L. V. Maksimenkov, "Ocherki nomenklaturnoi istorii sovetskoi literatury (1932–1946)," pt. 1, *Voprosy literatury* (July–Aug. 2003): 212–58

ONI 2   L. V. Maksimenkov, "Ocherki nomenklaturnoi istorii sovetskoi literatury (1932–1946): Stalin, Bukharin, Zhdanov, Shcherbakov i drugie," pt. 2, *Voprosy literatury* (Sept.–Oct. 2003): 241–97

PT   *Pisateli i tsenzory: Sovetskaia literatura 40-x godov pod politicheskim kontrolem TsK,* comp. D. L. Babichenko (Moscow: Rossiia molodaia, 1994)

PVSSP   *Pervyi vsesoiuznyi s"ezd sovetskikh pisatelei, 1934: Stenograficheskii otchet* (Moscow: Gosudarstvennoe izdatel'stvo "Khudozhestvennaia literatura," 1934)

RGALI   Rossiiskii gosudarstvennyi arkhiv literatury i iskusstva, Moscow

Abbreviations

RT   Stanislav Kuniaev and Sergei Kuniaev, *Rasterzannye teni* (Moscow: Golos, 1995)
SF   *"Strana filosofov" Andreia Platonova: Problemy tvorchestva*, vol. 4 (Moscow: IMLI RAN, "Nasledie," 2000)
SL   *"Shchast'e literatury": Gosudarstvo i pisateli, 1925–1938; Dokumenty*, comp. D. L. Babichenko (Moscow: Rosspen, 1997)
SLNE   *Sovetskaia literatura na novom etape: Stenogramma pervogo plenuma orgkomiteta Soiuza sovetskikh pisatelei (29 oktiabria–3 noiabria 1932)* (Moscow: Sovetskaia literatura, 1933)
TPS   Gennadii Kostyrchenko, *Tainaia politika Stalina: Vlast' i antisemitizm; Novaia versiia*, 2 vols. (Moscow: Mezhdunarodnye otnosheniia, 2015)
TS   *Tvorchestvo i sud'ba Aleksandra Fadeeva: Stat'i, esse, vospominaniia, arkhivnye materialy, stranitsy letopisi* (Moscow: IMLI RAN, 2004)
VKI   *Vlast' i khudozhesvennaia intelligentsia: Dokumenty TsK RKP(b), VChK-OGPU-NKVD o kul'turnoi politike; 1917–1953 gg* (Moscow: Mezhdunarodnyi fond "Demokratiia," 2002)
VP   *Vtoroi plenum pravleniia Soiuza sovetskikh pisatelei SSSR, mart 1935: Stenograficheskii otchet* (Moscow: Gosizdat "Khudozhestvennaia literatura," 1935)
VSP   *Vtoroi vsesoiuznyi s"ezd sovetskih pisatelei, 15–26 dekabria 1954: Stenograficheskii otchet* (Moscow: Sovetskii pisatel', 1956)

xiv

The Soviet Writers' Union and Its Leaders

The Writer-Cadre Oxymoron

PRIVILEGE AND FEAR are a potent mix. Suppose the first of the Great Purge show trials coincided with the good news that a private apartment was ready for you after years in a cramped, damp dwelling that threatened your family with tuberculosis. This was precisely the timing when the new writers' apartment building on Moscow's Lavrushinsky Lane was ready for occupancy in August 1936.[1] Soviet writers were a privileged caste, with access to a closed distribution system of goods and services unavailable to most of the population. Their literary production was a service that warranted preferred living quarters, food, and paid resort vacations. Such at any rate was the quid pro quo that Stalin devised when he created the Writers' Union.

As Nadezhda Mandelshtam points out, accepting one of those apartments was a practical decision, not a moral one.[2] But the Writers' Union was a control mechanism that distributed material benefits in a culture of deprivation and fear; and when moving into a desperately needed apartment coincided with a sensational trial verdict, it could color political and moral perceptions. That these benefits were often not luxury items but essential groceries and living space that lifted the recipient out of dire poverty only heightened their potency to co-opt.

The business of the Writers' Union was not literature but writers as human resources. It had three primary functions. These were to communicate party policies to writers through organized discussions; to ensure the creation of a literature about the young communist nation by subsidizing writers' travel to factories, collective farms, and construction projects; and to reward cooperative writers with apartments, quality foodstuffs, supplemental income, and paid working vacations. A fourth, covert function was to feed information on writers to the security services—the Writers' Union has even been described as the literary wing of the secret police.[3]

What writers most wanted from the Writers' Union, however, it did not offer. It did little to facilitate readings of works in progress where writers could receive colleagues' feedback. Nor did it give writers a voice in literary policy. It could not do so, because even its own officials had no hand in it. Policy was made higher up, by the Politburo and party secretaries in consultation with the Agitation and Propaganda Department (an office that underwent many changes in name and structure; for simplicity, I refer to it throughout as Agitprop).[4] Agitprop officials reported directly to the Central Committee secretaries (usually numbering four or five), who worked through this office. Policies and pronouncements were handed down from the secretaries or Agitprop officials to the head of the Writers' Union, who disseminated these policies among the membership. The notorious characterization of writers as "engineers of human souls" is only the most famous example of literary policy being made outside literary circles and at the highest level of party governance. Socialist realism, the official "method" of Soviet literature, also originated in private, behind-the-scenes conversations dominated by Stalin. The lengthy discussions of it sponsored by the Writers' Union were not self-initiated but a response to a pronouncement from above. Writers attempted to take ownership of socialist realism by redefining its ideological boundaries, but they would always be trumped by Agitprop. Gerrymandered out of policy making, the Writers' Union was merely an end-use tool for implementing decisions taken by Stalin and the top leadership.

The relationship between writers and the regime has frequently been characterized as an alliance from which both stood to gain. Stalin, having decided to make literature the vehicle for spreading a new nationwide culture, needed writers as much as they needed him.[5] The shared goal was a heroic literature that would prove a worthy descendant of the great Russian classics, inspiring readers at home and abroad to follow the Soviet advance toward social justice. Soviet books would model a mind-set and behavior for the communist age. The path to this collective literary project was cleared with the union's creation in 1932, when existing groups of like-minded writers were dissolved on the grounds that Soviet writers had come to share a single, demonstrably Soviet literary aesthetic.[6] The new union's credibility depended upon writers' belief in its mission; so Stalin and his Politburo set out to woo the nation's writers.

Many writers, especially communists but also some nonparty writers, certainly saw themselves as allied with the party leadership. They were eager to write the books that would seed the popular imagination with new heroes and mythologies for a new culture. So the notion of alliance provides an important corrective to a simplified view of top-down control.

Nonetheless, this book tests and narrows the idea of alliance. Two points should be made at the outset. First, except for Maxim Gorky, no individual writer was indispensable to Stalin. Certainly Stalin needed writers, but he thought of them in socio-literary categories and generally courted

4

writers in groups rather than as individuals. He tailored his message by constituency: ideologically sophisticated communists; naive party enthusiasts; sympathetic, left-leaning nonparty writers; old intelligentsia nonparty writers; novice writers. Second, any alliance was largely destroyed by the Great Purge of 1937–38. When it came to individual writers, Stalin's principle in cultivating them as allies was "use and discard." To take one of many familiar examples, the prominent writer, journalist, and envoy Mikhail Koltsov reported on the Bukharin show trial in March 1938, received honors over the next several months, and was arrested in December.[7] Writers owed their allegiance to Stalin, but not the other way around. Intellectuals who, like Koltsov, hoped to achieve a "transnational fraternity of leftist intellectuals,"[8] in Katerina Clark's phrase, ultimately could not achieve their vision.

The relation of the state to its writers was not so much ally as patron. Writers were dependent on the state for a living and a readership. Pierre Bourdieu's sociological model of Gustave Flaubert's France is useful in considering the Soviet case as well. Soviet writers had to position themselves in a force field created by the interplay of literature, ideology, party politics, and social profiling.[9]

These matters of alliance, patronage, and the official ideologizing of literature lead to another question that has occupied scholars of Stalinism: how much individual agency did writers have? Certainly, as Katerina Clark has argued, writers like Koltsov and Ilya Ehrenburg were not simply agents of Stalin but were acting out of conviction in a moment of "headiness."[10] Writers sometimes approached Stalin with policy suggestions and personal requests, occasionally displaying a startling degree of entitlement.[11] Stalin on occasion granted these requests, burnishing his reputation for magnanimity and building up his psychological advantage.

The degree to which a writer might exercise agency in this force field was constantly shifting. Writers' Union control mechanisms were both hard and soft, direct and indirect, punitive and incentivizing. They were administrative and bureaucratic; material and economic; and not least, psychological. Writers found strategies for physical and creative survival. Often they followed party directives, whether out of sincere belief, opportunism, or self-protection. Less often they resisted. In between were various shadings of calculated behavior, including reluctant obedience, weak or partial compliance, avoidance, and hidden misgivings or dissent. When the formalist critic Boris Eikhenbaum relinquished the study of poetics in 1928 and turned his attention to "literary milieu" (*literaturnyi byt*), he was responding to a shift in the literary force field. No longer was a writer's main concern to discover how to write, said Eikhenbaum. A more urgent problem had arisen: how to be a writer. He meant that each writer now had to decide how to behave.

What choices were involved in exercising agency? It was a Stalinist version of the Bourdieuvian question.

In the 1930s, Eikhenbaum's question became still more pressing. The Writers' Union started out in 1934 with 2,200 members. Twenty years later that number had risen to 3,700,[12] a figure that understates the true number of writers who were added, since not only natural deaths but also arrests of writers had to be offset by new memberships. In the thirty-five years from the revolution to Stalin's death, some 2,000 writers were arrested, of whom three-quarters were executed or perished in labor camps.[13]

We all like to believe in our own independence in standing up to authority, and yet we are often less courageous than we imagine. Under nationwide political terror, independence and courage are the province of heroes. Yet documents record the courageous efforts of some writers to argue with authority. Inside the Writers' Union presidium and secretariat, outspoken writers were a minority, but almost never were they entirely absent, even when a stenographer was taking down their every word. Nonparty writers in the presidium, like Vsevolod Ivanov, Boris Pilniak, Viktor Shklovsky, Nikolai Tikhonov, and Yury Tynianov, took a pragmatic approach, avowing their support for the party's goals and arguing that the party would be more likely to achieve them with a friendlier literary policy. Some loyal communist writers made largely the same case. Party leaders consistently disparaged or ignored these proposals. Perhaps the question we should ask is not how much individual agency writers had but how it paid off in measurable results.

How we exercise personal autonomy, and to what effect, are questions that arise directly from a study of the Writers' Union, and they are a central concern of this book. I have structured my study of the union around the men Stalin chose to lead it. This book explores their interactions with those "below," which is to say the country's writers, whom they were charged with overseeing, as well as those "above," their own overseers in the upper echelons of the Communist Party hierarchy. In doing so, it exposes the interdependence of literary policy, communist morality, ethical debates, party infighting, and the personal psychology of key actors.

Stalin selected his literary cadres with a social typology in mind.[14] Each personality was suited to a particular *nomenklatura* role. At the same time, Stalin was mindful of character traits he could exploit—a lust for power, an extreme sense of communist duty, a reluctance to abandon a cherished utopian dream, an uncritical susceptibility to Bolshevik propaganda, or various combinations of these, distorted by a murmuring undercurrent of fear.[15] He matched personalities with the policies he was about to unroll. Ivan Gronsky, an energetic and savvy party activist, was suited to the Writers' Union's initial phase, which required party guidance but also letting writers feel invested. Gorky, who combined literary prestige with an inspirational aesthetic, was the perfect figure when it was time to persuade writers to embrace socialist realism. Vladimir Stavsky, a proletarian and rabid party enthusiast, was ideal for the Great Purge.

Aleksandr Fadeyev's more moderate temperament made him a good choice to replace Stavsky when the purges wound down. Fadeyev's predilection for reasoned argument, his debating skills, and the pride he took in self-discipline were suited to a particular sociocultural need, that of serving as the respectable public face of a coercive and destructive literary policy. Fadeyev's deeply internalized sense of party duty made him useful through many policy shifts and accounted for his longevity at the head of the Writers' Union. Vladimir Yermilov, nicknamed the scourge of Russian literature, also figures prominently in this study in his role as chief literary critic and a close friend of Fadeyev's. A natural bully and virtuoso phrasemaker, Yermilov found his social role waiting for him in the abusive journalistic practice of the party press.

All except Gorky were party members, cadres who dedicated themselves to following party directives in service to a greater cause. The word "cadre" in English has a sterile bureaucratic ring; and English has no good equivalent for the Bolshevik use of this term. One might choose the word "functionary," suggesting a faceless official in a bureaucratic machinery. Used in the plural or in reference to an entire cohort, it might be rendered in English as "personnel," suggesting employees of a corporation or government agency. "Human resources" edges closer, a company term that points both to individual employees and the use to which they are put. But while Bolshevik usage could sometimes have this narrow meaning, the word also carried a much richer palette of associations. It encompassed commitment to communism, membership in an honor group, and pride in being entrusted with important party work. A cadre had a lifelong mission.

Erich Fromm identified a tension between two innate human imperatives, the longing for truth and the desire to submit to an authority. The first leads us to humanitarianism, the second to authoritarianism. This conflict is resolved when we subscribe to a religious or political belief system that locates both truth and authority in a single supreme being or entity.[16] To be a cadre sworn to uphold the party, the seat of authority and truth, was a worthy identity that could define an entire life.

Questions of identity and selfhood were central to Bolshevik morality. They were framed overtly in the workplace, in the press, and in literary works. The communist autobiography, a central part of the application for party membership, had to demonstrate a dedication to remaking oneself.[17] The socialist realist master plot featured a village lad forging a Bolshevik identity anchored in personal qualities of decisiveness, self-sacrifice, and incorruptible honesty. Books like Fyodor Gladkov's *Cement* (*Tsement*),

Fadeyev's *The Rout* (*Razgrom*), Dmitry Furmanov's *Chapayev*, Nikolai Ostrovsky's *How the Steel Was Tempered* (*Kak zakalialas stal*), Boris Polevoi's *The Story of a Real Man* (*Povest o nastoiashchem cheloveke*), and Konstantin Simonov's *The Living and the Dead* (*Zhivye i mertvye*) presented Bolshevism as a test of selfhood and invited readers to emulate their heroes and embark upon their own self-fashioning. The goal of the Soviet literary project was to inspire readers to decide who they wanted to be and create their own Bolshevik biographies. As Clark explains, the regime elevated literature as the only medium that could articulate a new Soviet identity by narrating biographies of self-transformation.[18]

As these books showed, a cadre's personal dedication to communism presupposed a high degree of individual agency. Yet Clark also notes the threat of "erasure of selfhood." This paradox led to what we might call the cadre conundrum, an erratic swiveling between agency and nonagency. The cadre's sworn duty to carry out party directives no matter what continually posed a potential threat to personal autonomy.[19] If it is hardly surprising that nonparty writers like Viktor Shklovsky, Boris Pilniak, and Marietta Shaginian were rebuffed in their advocacy of softening ideological censorship, it is more surprising that communist writer-officials like Fadeyev and Yermilov, who at times found themselves equally offended by literary policy, were similarly snubbed. Even their dutiful obedience elicited not approval from their superiors but scolding and humiliation.[20] Top ideology officials like Lev Mekhlis, Aleksandr Shcherbakov, and Dmitry Polikarpov liked to "instruct" their subordinates by belittling them, the better to make them know their place.

How did Writers' Union cadres resolve the conflict when they privately disagreed with policies they were sworn to implement? And what if such disagreements were not occasional but increasingly common? Posing these questions is controversial, with some scholars arguing that communists in the 1920s and 1930s did not experience a public/private divide. They cite personal diaries that testify to communists' intense work of self-purification, whose goal was to transcend and erase the self.[21] "Any notion of the private was [to be] rendered anachronistic," writes Jochen Hellbeck.[22] But if the goal was to bring private and public selves into alignment, the reality was different. Strenuous effort to achieve alignment shows that alignment was a wish, not a fact. Clark notes that some communists, like Koltsov, had "multiple identities," while others, like Sergei Tretyakov, whose hopes for an avant-garde, Russo-European "republic of letters" partly contradicted his duties representing Soviet literary policy abroad, "must have suffered from competing loyalties."[23] Yuri Slezkine tells of communists who experienced "a split consciousness striving for wholeness."[24] Whether the goal was unification of the private and communist selves, the actual erasure of the private self, or simply living with one's various identities, these communists recognized that, for better or worse, a private self did exist. Hellbeck acknowledges it, pointing to the Russian word *dvoedushie*—"doubled soul"—to describe a person whose public identity interferes with his private self.[25]

Slezkine, who has scrutinized many diaries and letters that reveal communists' intense work on the self to rid themselves of individualism, notes that true believers resolved their doubts "by 'realizing' that [these doubts] were part of an individualism (as opposed to collectivism) that had no place in Bolshevism."[26] Was it not these "realizations" that were the artificial construct, rather than the individualism and the doubts? Nikolai Bukharin, in a desperate letter to Stalin from his prison cell, "still did not understand, still distinguished between his private and public selves."[27]

Self-fashioning did not always entail discarding private feelings. The appeal of Bolshevik self-fashioning might even lie in its perceived compatibility with one's inborn predilections. Fadeyev, while embracing communism as a belief system and identifying as a cadre, was not attempting to change his fundamental inner being. His fictional characters have rich, deeply cherished inner lives. The noncommunist Gorky was a utopian and an ally, but he was not trying to reconstruct his own nature or eliminate his private feelings.

A shame culture has no interest in helping individuals harmonize their feelings or predispositions with public values. Prestige, reputation, and value do not derive from one's achievements but are determined by the honor group, which can confer them and take them away. An individual's worth is thus not innate but comes from his membership in the honor group. Without the group, the individual has no personal identity to fall back on; confiscation of one's party card meant losing one's entire self.[28] The shame culture preys upon the individual's fear of being cast out; its modus operandi is humiliation, and not even the most loyal communist is safe from it. Humiliation can come without warning at any moment, because the shame culture is inherently arbitrary.

Fadeyev discovered this when his 1946 novel *The Young Guard (Molodaia gvardiia)*, which won a Stalin Prize, was suddenly slammed a year later. He then spent three years rewriting it. He was eager—perhaps desperate—to show that he could learn from his mistakes. He was missing the point. The shame culture prizes its own prerogative to humiliate, and so it incessantly invents new "mistakes." Fadeyev was trying to cope with an oxymoron: a disgraced prizewinning novel. Again we can invoke Bourdieu. Existing in "two opposed universes" (aesthetics versus commercial value in nineteenth-century France; aesthetics versus ideology in the Soviet Union), the writer plays a "permanent double game" and himself becomes an oxymoron.[29]

Irina Paperno reminds us that the Soviet "new man" was thought of as an acting subject or agent.[30] Should we regard the work that communists performed on the self as active agency, as several scholars suggest, or was it a case of fashioning oneself into a master text, as Eric Naiman has argued?[31] The shame culture fosters a public/private divide and with it an erosion of agency. To cope with a disconnect between personal judgment and communist duty, a cadre needed to convince himself that his action was moral. Stalin provided exactly this sort of moral argument to his cadres when he was giving them unsavory instructions.

Some readers may object that I attribute too much control to Stalin and too little individual agency to his literary cadres. My point is that Stalin, whose personal supervision of literary policy is widely acknowledged,[32] purposely chose as Writers' Union leaders malleable men who would be susceptible to both his charisma and his logic; and he crafted administrative policies to constrain them. Some readers, similarly, may find that this study attributes greater individual agency to nonparty writers than to their communist counterparts. Any such impression may be due to the nature of the situations that this book examines, especially meetings of the Writers' Union's presidium and secretariat. These bodies included both party and nonparty writers; since party members were pledged to maintain party confidentiality, they could not always express themselves fully in front of their nonparty colleagues. There were times, too, when writer-officials were caught unaware by unexpected policy shifts and found themselves in the uncomfortable position of having to justify them (as happened with the disgracing of Dmitry Shostakovich, the campaign against formalism and naturalism, and the anticosmopolitan campaign). Yermilov's and Fadeyev's personal papers show their distress at such shifts, their urgent attempts to rationalize them, and their smarting at the low regard in which they were held by officials who thought it unnecessary to clue them in.

In the spring of 1956, three years after Stalin's death, the fifty-four-year-old Fadeyev received a visit from his close friend Yury Libedinsky and his wife, Lidiia. They wanted to share a neologism that Lidiia had overheard while out walking. "Ty—produkt!" (You are a product), a man had said to his companion. The Libedinskys explained to the puzzled Fadeyev that *produkt* referred to someone who had been shaped, or rather misshapen, by the long years of Stalin's personality cult. Fadeyev burst out laughing and then turned sober. All of us are to some extent "products," he offered, including the guy who made the remark.[33] The survivors of Stalinism were gaining the critical distance to see themselves as products of their culture.[34] Two days later, Fadeyev committed suicide. That act, and the note he left, are powerful evidence that the public/private divide did exist. Belonging comes at a price.

This study relies on the wealth of public and private documents that were inaccessible when John and Carol Garrard published *Inside the Soviet Writers' Union* in 1990.[35] I have used the archival records that subsequently became available to consider the Writers' Union leaders across the range of their official, semiofficial, casual, and private utterances. These come from minutes and transcripts of Writers' Union meetings (celebratory congresses and plenums, as well as closed meetings of the presidium and secretariat); the professional correspondence between Gorky and Aleksandr Shcherbakov; and personal letters, diaries, and notebooks of Fadeyev, Yermilov, Stavsky, and others.

My methods are those of the literary critic rather than those of the historian. Memoranda, speeches, debates and conversations with colleagues and friends, personal letters, private jottings, appeals for mercy, denunciations, solitary fretting—all of these were among the written and spoken genres of daily life. I have tested public and private utterances against one another, and sometimes a single document in Bakhtinian dialogue against itself. In Yermilov's private letters to Fadeyev, Fadeyev's memoranda to Stalin's Politburo successors, and Fadeyev's suicide note, hidden suppositions lurk unbidden, obscured even from the writer himself.

The intricate pas de deux between public avowal and private opinion danced its way between alignment, disparity, and conflict. Writers' Union leaders maneuvered through it with the same strategies and worries as other Soviet writers. While considerations were different for communist and noncommunist writers, we must exercise caution in thinking of writers as starkly divided into different camps. The communist hard-liner Vsevolod Vishnevsky served as Stavsky's hatchet man in 1937 and 1938 but made a monthly monetary contribution to help Osip Mandelshtam after the poet's return from exile in March 1937.[36] The moderate nonparty Nikolai Tikhonov appears to have shared a startling closeness with the secret police informer Pyotr Pavlenko.[37] The young poet and street brawler Pavel Vasilyev, a virulent opponent of Stalin's rule, shared an apartment with his brother-in-law Ivan Gronsky, who was Stalin's mouthpiece in the literary community. Vasilyev's association with a circle of writers who lampooned Stalin in private epigrams did not prevent him from sharing some of these confidences with Gronsky, who passed them on to the secret police. Gronsky arranged the arrest of Vasilyev's mentor, the poet Nikolai Kliuev, while protecting Vasilyev himself.[38]

With literary policy made by the party leadership and conveyed to the head of the Writers' Union as a fait accompli, Soviet writers had only their powers of persuasion. They put words to work not only in their fiction and poetry but also in their literary milieu—Bourdieu's force field—hoping to influence decisions ranging from censorship guidelines, to whether or not to stage a play or expel a writer, to the kinds of stories that should be considered "communist." This battle of persuasion was joined by the party leadership. Stalin augmented diktat and terror with arguments to allay the misgivings of his literary managers Gorky and Fadeyev. Mekhlis sensed how best to persuade Yermilov. Genrikh Yagoda used the power of suggestion to persuade the proletarian literary recruit Aleksandr Avdeyenko.

My task has been to determine the purposes and sincerity of each utterance. When were words earnest, when forced, when a pragmatic calculation? Heartfelt expression is usually easily distinguished from the formulaic language of the Stalinist terror, but on occasion they coincide. That, too, must be ferreted out.

This book is not about literature but about writers. It is in conversation with works by other scholars who have used diaries, letters, and memoirs to examine the intersection of personality and literary life in the Stalin years. They include Clark, Evgeny Dobrenko, Igal Halfin, Jochen Hellbeck, Thomas Lahusen, Leonid Maksimenkov, Eric Naiman, Paperno, Vitaly Shentalinsky, and Slezkine, all of whom have inspired me with their work.

Chapter 1 examines the prehistory of the Writers' Union. Fadeyev, Stavsky, and Yermilov, who held leading roles in the Writers' Union, had previously controlled important literary journals as leaders of the Russian Association of Proletarian Writers (RAPP). Their early dominance helps us understand their behavior in the power dynamics of the Writers' Union, where their public arrogance concealed a private sense of injury at their reduced autonomy. Their authority, more apparent than real, lay in their willingness to be used as the tools of a policy made without their participation.

Chapter 2 examines writers' hopes and expectations for their new union, and chapter 3 charts their attempts to find common ground with party authorities in the union's early years, when its titular leader, Gorky, was subordinate to the party ideologue Shcherbakov. The ensuing "intermezzo" takes up Yermilov's private letters to Fadeyev, which reveal the frenzied attempts of this official party critic to make sense of the counterintuitive public shaming of Shostakovich in 1936. Chapter 4 covers the Writers' Union under Stavsky during the terror surrounding the Old Bolshevik show trials. A second intermezzo investigates Yermilov's and Fadeyev's maneuvering to topple their rivals at the journal *Literary Critic (Literaturnyi kritik)*.

Chapters 5 and 6 examine the Writers' Union under Fadeyev, from 1939 through the war and the harassment campaigns that followed, when literary policy was affected by foreign policy and Politburo rivalries. The book concludes with a look at the shifting fault lines in the Writers' Union after Stalin's death.

This book is, then, about the day-to-day lived history of writers navigating a literary control system. We shall see the mechanisms that pressed writer-cadres into service as the enforcers of an ideologically driven literary policy. We shall see how Writers' Union members—from nonparty, old intelligentsia writers like Shklovsky, to the proletarian naïf Avdeyenko, to the working-class maverick Andrei Platonov, to the communist theorist Elena Usievich—interacted with the enforcers of literary policy. We shall bear witness to their individual responses to tyranny—the decisions they faced, the choices they made, and the political and personal effects of those choices.

"Mayakovsky's Choice"

AT THE HEIGHT of the Great Terror in 1937, the writer Sergei Budantsev remarked that every writer was now faced with "Mayakovsky's choice" (*VKI*, 349). Budantsev was alluding to the suicide seven years earlier of the communist avant-garde poet Vladimir Mayakovsky. Many writers blamed Mayakovsky's suicide on unbearable pressure to compromise his art, his politics, and his conscience.[1] For years he had resisted calls to join the preeminent communist writers' organization RAPP, whose prescription for a communist literary realism opposed his modernist, experimental sensibility. He founded his own group, the Left Front of Art (LEF). But the party leadership supported RAPP, and *Pravda* insisted that communist writers unite.[2] Literature was crucial to the battle for hearts and minds, and the success of the new society depended on communist writers' solidarity. Validated by the party, RAPP's leaders hammered away at Mayakovsky. He finally applied for RAPP membership in February 1930. Two months later he killed himself.

In the spring of 1956, when Nikita Khrushchev had begun to expose Stalin's crimes and granted amnesty to political prisoners, Aleksandr Fadeyev, the longtime general secretary of the Writers' Union, retired to his study ostensibly to take a nap, closed the door behind him, lay down on the sofa, and shot himself.[3] He left a note for his political family, the Communist Party Central Committee.

Fadeyev's literary career dated to the 1920s. He had taken active part in RAPP's hounding of Mayakovsky. Later, he dutifully followed party orders even when they brought him low, as when the party dissolved RAPP, shaming him and his colleagues. Even a career marked by staunch party discipline, however, failed to save him from Mayakovsky's choice. His suicide was perhaps the reverse of Mayakovsky's—not a distress cry from a writer at the peak of his powers but the breakdown of a compromised bureaucrat, drained of literary talent. What they shared, however, was the collision of aesthetics, power relations, and personal identity.

It was on the shards of RAPP that Stalin would build the Writers'

Union. He rejected a proletarian-led literature in favor of a more inclusive, big tent, but he continued to rely on trusted literary cadres who had until a moment before led RAPP. Three of them, Fadeyev, Stavsky, and Yermilov, play a major role in our story. Fadeyev and Yermilov became close friends through their association in RAPP and as young men saw their self-worth and value to the Communist Party reflected in their editorships at important periodicals. These sons of the intelligentsia joined the Communist Party as teenagers during the Civil War and proudly set out to play their part in an epic undertaking. Fadeyev's stories and novels chronicled the events being lived in Soviet history from the Civil War through the German invasion. Yermilov's critical studies of Gogol, Dostoevsky, and Chekhov hint at an unexpected connection between the Soviet hard-liner and the intellectual seekers who had been the conscience of tsarist Russia.

Fadeyev and Yermilov ultimately became their worst selves. At a time when denunciation could prompt arrest and death, they condemned their colleagues in confidential memos, from the bully pulpit atop the Writers' Union, and in the pages of its newspaper, *Literaturnaia gazeta* (*The Literary Gazette*). So vicious was Yermilov that no memoirist has had even a single good word to say on his behalf.[4] The most noteworthy mention of him occurs in an unexpected place—Mayakovsky's suicide note. In almost the last sentence he ever wrote, Mayakovsky invoked the bitter hostility between them. "Tell Yermilov . . . we should have fought it out."[5] Mayakovsky was alluding to one of his last public readings, at which he had festooned the hall with placards, including one mocking Yermilov. (Entering the hall before the event commenced, the incensed Yermilov had it removed.)[6] That Mayakovsky's last thoughts included the people who interfered with his creative process and smeared him confirms the powerful effect of the RAPP cadres on any writer they chose to browbeat.

RAPP's harassment politics under the self-important and widely hated Leopold Averbakh are well known. Well known, too, are the party's support for RAPP, especially in the period of "proletarianization" ushered in by Stalin's agricultural collectivization drive in 1928, and the party's liquidation of RAPP once collectivization had been largely achieved and Stalin turned from proletarianization to national Bolshevism.[7] The literary theories developed by the Onguardists, as the RAPP leadership was known, in their attempt to define a communist literature have received detailed treatment as well.

This chapter considers the Onguardists' attitudes toward power relations, self-image, and literary creativity as a context through which to understand their later roles in the Writers' Union. Averbakh's arrest in the Great Purge had coattails resulting in the arrests of other Onguardists, yet those closest to him, including Fadeyev, Yermilov, and also Stavsky, received important literary assignments instead of an executioner's bullet or a labor-camp sentence. Stalin put them to different uses according to their psychological proclivities. Each of them had their own particular brand of usefulness.

Fadeyev, Yermilov, and Averbakh, while appropriating the proletarian brand, came from merchant and intelligentsia families. Averbakh was born in Saratov, where his father owned a shipbuilding company. Fourteen years old at the time of the revolution, this nephew of Yakov Sverdlov began his party work in the Komsomol when it was established in 1918 as editor of its newspaper, *Youth Pravda* (*Yunosheskaia pravda*). He rose rapidly through the Komsomol ranks and soon joined the leadership of the youth division of the Comintern under Leon Trotsky. At nineteen, Averbakh published *Lenin and the Youth Movement* (*Lenin i iunosheskoe dvizhenie*), with Trotsky's introduction. Brother-in-law to Yagoda (who was married to Averbakh's sister Ida) and son-in-law to Lenin's comrade Vladimir Bonch-Bruyevich, Averbakh, like Yagoda, lived in a Kremlin apartment.[8] From every which way he was closely tied to the Bolshevik elite, and he took his connections as license to act with impunity. It is not hard to imagine that his golden-boy identity in the lap of the powerful helped draw Fadeyev, Yermilov, and the rest of his coterie to flock to him and form such a close-knit group.

Yermilov's father, whose class background was listed as "nobility" (*dvorianin*), was a professor and journalist, a friend of the symbolist poet Valery Briusov, and the author of books on Russian writers and artists who addressed aesthetics and spirituality in personal development—Nikolai Nekrasov, Vissarion Belinsky, the "pedagogical anthropologist" Konstantin Ushinsky, Aleksei Koltsov, and Mikhail Shchepkin. The senior Yermilov aroused enough suspicion among the tsarist police to be placed under secret supervision at various times. When he died in 1918, his son was just thirteen. Like his father, the son became a well-read lover of literature with a critical mind. At age fifteen he was made head of the Moscow Komsomol's press section and editor in chief of *Youth Pravda* when Averbakh moved on from that post. Upon Yermilov's graduation from Moscow State University's law department in 1924, the party sent him to the Urals to help run the Komsomol press there and to organize a regional branch of RAPP.[9] With the party's approval, RAPP brought him to Moscow in 1926 to serve as editor of its literary youth journal, *Young Guard* (*Molodaia gvardiia*), again taking over from Averbakh. He received graduate training at the Russian Association of Social Science Institutes and the Institute of Red Professors and became part of RAPP's inner circle.

Fadeyev grew up in the Russian Far Eastern town of Chuguyevka, about two hundred miles northeast of Vladivostok, in a family environment that primed him for revolution. His father, who abandoned the family when Fadeyev was seven, was a teacher and professional revolutionary. His mother, a medic, was a revolutionary at heart, well versed in the thinking of Nikolai Chernyshevsky and Marx. By Fadeyev's account, she was a lifelong activist, a person of deeply held convictions whose upbringing and moral beliefs emphasized the virtue of self-restraint. "Until the very end of her life she played an exceptional role in the spiritual life of all of us [her children]," Fadeyev recounted (*AFPD*, 327). Marxism, self-discipline, and an inner "spiritual" life were key elements of Fadeyev's upbringing, inseparable from the emotional bonds of his mother's love, teaching, and example. They became the pillars on which he thought to build his professional life.

Attending high school at the Vladivostok Commercial Institute, Fadeyev was a vocal advocate for the Bolsheviks. Seventeen years old in 1918, he dropped out just a few months shy of graduation to fight Aleksandr Kolchak's forces, joining a partisan unit as a political instructor and later fighting with the Red Army in the Baikal region.[10] In January 1921 he was made military commissar of the Eighth Rifle Brigade of the Third Amur Division.[11] As a delegate to the Tenth Party Congress that March, he took part in suppressing the Kronshtadt rebellion, which broke out during the congress, and sustained a serious wound. This was also the congress that declared party factionalism illegal. The considerable debate through 1925 over the issue of whether (and how much) democracy should be allowed within the party does not seem to have swayed Fadeyev. The self-restraint that he had cultivated from an early age likely made him exceptionally receptive to the concept of party discipline. He and others of his generation whose formative experiences were had in the Red Army understood party discipline as an extension of military discipline. In any case, there was no free will in the inexorable forward movement of history.[12] To remain outside the party was to oppose one's feeble individual will to the momentum of events.

Joining the Bolshevik party was synonymous, literally, with joining the battle, and the military mind-set did not end with the Civil War. Literature, whether or not on the theme of war, was sucked into the military mind-set. In a nation permanently at war with imagined saboteurs, the party regarded the reading and writing of literature as far more than a leisure pastime. Literature was the front line of the war for people's minds, and Fadeyev embraced the notion of writing in the service of the party cause.

By personality, upbringing, and experience, Fadeyev was perfectly suited to the demands of party membership. He was conscientious, self-disciplined, well educated, battle-tested, and in love with a cause. Articulate and conversant with Marx's writings, the young Fadeyev rose quickly. Assigned to party work in the North Caucasus in 1924, he sought a posting in which he could develop his writing talents. He joined RAPP and was sent to work in its Moscow headquarters. His gripping Civil War novella *The Rout*, published in 1927, gained him instant celebrity. It was a mainstay of the

Soviet school curriculum right up until the demise of the Soviet Union in 1991, influencing all three Soviet generations.

Fadeyev's later moral decline is all the more remarkable for having its roots in social idealism and personal bravery. One of his first stories, "Against the Current" ("Protiv techeniia"), takes for its title a common Bolshevik metaphor. Like many individual acts, it was also culturally symptomatic, and it speaks to Fadeyev's proud perception of himself. For the young Fadeyev, ideological conformity did not feel like ideological conformity—it coincided with his beliefs. What he was expected to write was the same as what he wanted to write.[13] But a disparity between the two grew steadily over time, until it became necessary to convince himself that he was still acting out of belief. Denis Kozlov has referred to the need to harmonize "two truths, evidential and ideological."[14] To the dutiful cadre on the verge of suicide three decades on, who had long ago begun to swim not against the current but with it in the murky zone where writers, their party supervisors, and the security forces rubbed shoulders, that early title must have come to seem a hideous irony.

RAPP dominated a literary scene marked by a panoply of colorful and often warring literary groups. Proletkult, Onguardists, Smithy, the All-Russian Society of Peasant Writers, Serapion Brothers, Imaginists, Inkhuk, Litfront, Opoiaz, LEF, Pereval, and the Pereverzev school jostled each other in a raucous literary jumble, often melding literary programs with class interests and disagreeing on whether or how to do so. These arguments were fed by frequent physical encounters, since the various writers' groups all had space in Moscow's Herzen House at 25 Tverskoi Boulevard. The party leaders regarded this fractious disorder as an impediment to a heuristic and inspirational literature of Bolshevik values. As early as 1922, they sought to move toward the creation of a universal writers' association.

This first attempt was prompted by Stalin's and Trotsky's worry that nonparty writers sympathetic to the Bolsheviks but poorly paid for their manuscripts and often treated disrespectfully by communist writers might yet turn against the regime. The Politburo in 1922 chose encouragement over fiat: it funded a new publishing house and journal for nonparty writers, in a strategy meant to cultivate them as allies, staffing it with editors who could draw them more firmly into a communist literary space (*VKI*, 36–38). Stalin and Trotsky envisioned a writers' guild growing out of the publishing house Circle (Krug) (*VKI*, 41). This friendly approach suggests Trotsky's influence, as does the choice of Aleksandr Voronsky to spearhead the journal, *Red Virgin Soil* (*Krasnaia nov*). Voronsky believed in nurturing literary talent and forming relationships with nonparty writers.[15] In him, they found a human connection to the Bolshevik regime and a reason to think they could make common cause with it. This was true both for nonparty writers whose sympathies lay with the regime, like Vsevolod Ivanov, Marietta Shaginian, and Nikolai Tikhonov, and for those who were more guarded, like Mikhail Zoshchenko and Boris Pilniak (*VKI*, 41).

In a modest sign of *Red Virgin Soil*'s success in attracting nonparty writers as allies, many of its contributors formed a new literary group, Pereval. Nothing, however, came of the hoped-for writers' guild. Fellow travelers and communist writers alike held fast to their preferred literary circles and resisted a big-tent association.[16] By the mid-1920s, with Trotsky in the opposition, his relatively benign approach to literary policy gradually gave way to Stalin's more heavy-handed one. Fellow-traveler literature still had a supporter in Bukharin, but a compromise Politburo resolution of June 18, 1925, made clear how much agency nonparty writers stood to lose as alliance partners. Although acknowledging a role for the fellow travelers, it designated RAPP "the future ideological directors of Soviet literature."[17] Unification of literature would be achieved by having RAPP's critics, led by Averbakh and Yermilov, corral writers into their dominion.

Averbakh publicly supported the party resolution, but many RAPP members were furious at the resolution's acknowledgment of any role for nonparty writers and split off from Averbakh's group.[18] Averbakh's allegiance gained him the dominant position. The Central Committee used the RAPP secretariat, which Averbakh headed, as its literary office, sending instructions and sometimes cadres to serve in its leadership.[19] Averbakh, Yermilov, and Fadeyev drafted literary policy papers together with Agitprop officials (*MMN*, 107).

Averbakh played both sides of the resolution. Under the aegis of its validation of nonparty writers, he spearheaded a new attempt to create a Federation of Soviet Writers to bring together party and nonparty writers, thereby demonstrating his obedience to the resolution (*MMN*, 34–37, 46). Under the aegis of the resolution's crowning the proletarian writers as literature's "future directors," he used RAPP's journals to berate and preach to those same nonparty writers, as well as his communist rivals in RAPP's left wing.

Averbakh's inner circle consisted of Aleksei Selivanovsky, Vladimir Kirshon, Fadeyev, Libedinsky, Yermilov, Vladimir Sutyrin, and Nikolai Shushkanov, the latter two being appointed to the RAPP secretariat by the Central Committee.[20] Self-described "literary workers" and "cadres of proletarian writers," they enjoyed thinking of themselves as the Central Committee's "literary cell," building communism and fighting for the purity of Marxist literature.[21] In 1925, Fadeyev was twenty-four, Averbakh twenty-two, and Yermilov twenty. Through the literary journals they respectively controlled, *October* (*Oktiabr*), *On Literary Guard* (*Na literaturnom postu*), and *Young Guard*, they pronounced verdicts and engaged in ad hominem attacks.[22]

They could arrange or block publication of particular works and authors. Libraries removed books by fellow travelers at RAPP's behest.[23] Averbakh's family connections to the party hierarchy and the secret police enhanced his value both to the Politburo and to the RAPP leadership. He made the perfect liaison between writers and the punitive organs.

The Politburo gave Averbakh's young Turks considerable leeway to make their own decisions. Most important, it allowed the Onguardists to fashion and promote their own literary program. In this they had complete creative independence. Possibly the Politburo found RAPP's traditionalist aesthetics in line with their own literary tastes, as well as a potential bridge to the noncommunist intelligentsia writers that the party wanted to attract.

Rival Marxist literary groups argued over three main issues. These were the significance of an author's class background, the relationship of communist literature to the classics, and the qualities a fictional hero should display. On all three counts, the Onguardists occupied the right wing of Marxist debate. They argued that an author did not have to be a proletarian in order to write proletarian literature; they advocated learning from classic Russian authors, especially Tolstoy; and they thought fictional characters should mirror the psychological complexities of real people, an approach they dubbed the "living man."[24]

This literary program went to the heart of the Onguardists' own identity. They were not themselves proletarians, and they had been brought up on the Russian classics, which taught them to appreciate psychological complexity. Probing the contradictions between individual subjectivity and Bolshevik objectivity, the living man theory resonated with the widespread practice of individual Bolsheviks' work on the self. In this sense it was a good match for Bolshevik culture. But under the pens of Fadeyev and Libedinsky, it displayed a humanistic sensibility imbibed from the classics and out of step with Bolshevik authoritarianism. Voronsky's review of *The Rout* shows why: "[Fadeyev's] heroes are intuitive; their reason, their conduct are subordinated to the subconscious principle within the person."[25] This characterization points directly to a humanistic bent acquired from the classics. In 1927 the personal psychology of Fadeyev's characters reflected his own confidence in the preexisting alignment of personal authenticity and political activity, so much so that the inner voice was a sure guide to correct political behavior.

Yuri Slezkine has argued persuasively that the literary classics, which endured as the favorite reading of the Old Bolsheviks and their children, ran counter to Bolshevik theory and transmitted the values that finally undid the revolution.[26] If in the mid-1930s, when the classics reentered the school curriculum, no one imagined such an outcome, the Onguardists' defense of the classics in the 1920s drew fierce opposition. The loudest came from the followers of Valeryan Pereverzev, who advocated unambiguous heroes and villains.[27] They believed that an author's class background determined his worldview, making it harmful to learn from the classics. On this basis, the censorship office under Pavel Lebedev-Poliansky banned the reissuing of Pushkin's works. The Onguardists showed a certain amount of courage, continuing to insist on "learning from the classics." When Voronsky's successor at *Red Virgin Soil*, the Pereverzevite Ivan Bespalov, rejected a story by Budantsev for its "psychologism," Yermilov wanted it for the Onguardist journal *October* (*TS*, 386–87).

Sensitive to their origins as nonproletarian converts rather than "natural" communists, the Onguardists declared open war on the Pereverzevites as a matter of self-protection. They defined "proletarian writer" as any writer who saw proletarian literature as an aesthetic program and who wrote in that manner. Concealed behind their vicious behavior toward anyone not part of their in-group lay an identity problem. They were sham proletarians leading an association of proletarian writers. Their opponents accused them of "bourgeois liberalism" and "petit-bourgeois subjectivism."[28] They shook off these labels, but they would always have the whiff of outsiders.

To compensate for the "rightism" of their literary program, the RAPP leadership sought to demonstrate their communist credentials by "unmasking" others as false communists or even opponents of the regime. They turned their journals into shaming mechanisms, taking aim at communist and noncommunist writers alike. Mikhail Prishvin summed up their message: "You've written a book, but you mustn't think it's good" (*SLNE*, 66). Belonging to the alpha group confirmed their identity as leading communist cadres and also gave them control over who could enter their society of elites.[29] They disparaged their communist opponents by calling them internal fellow travelers.[30] As for nonparty intelligentsia writers, the Onguardists attacked them ferociously (in spite of their shared love of the classics). An important stimulus for this behavior was their need to distance themselves from their own socioeconomic roots. The bourgeois labels that their opponents tried to stick on them they flung right back at others. Gorky (before Stalin began courting him) was a "bourgeois-democratic fellow traveler."[31] Mayakovsky (before he capitulated to RAPP) was a "bourgeois" intellectual trying to pass as a proletarian.[32]

Another reason for their merciless attacks on the old intelligentsia was surely the need to justify their undeserved power over writers whose literary achievement far outshone their own. To undercut Voronsky and Pereval, they accused Prishvin of "biologism" (he had researched the natural world for one of his stories). Audience members at a public reading given by the Leningrad writer Vera Inber asked her to describe the mistakes of writers whom they had heard were Trotskyists or "biologists."[33]

Nonparty writers, far from being assimilated into communist literature as the party wanted, were alienated by RAPP's harassment. They mistrusted the Federation of Soviet Writers and held fast to their own groups. To address this difficulty, the federation was restructured in 1927 to eliminate individual memberships in favor of organizational memberships. This compromise preserved writers' literary associations while at least theoretically attaching writers to a single organization. This revised structure was reflected in a slightly revised name, the Federation of Organizations of Soviet Writers (FOSP).[34] The simultaneous removal of Trotsky's adherent Voronsky from *Red Virgin Soil* suggests not only personal retribution but also that the intent behind FOSP was to bring more control from above into literature.

FOSP's creation meant that funds for several important literary enterprises were channeled through it rather than through RAPP. A writers' club was opened; the Federation (Federatsiia) publishing house was founded in place of the defunct Krug, again as a forum for nonparty writers; and a literary newspaper was founded as a FOSP publication, representing all writers. Like the earlier attempts to channel writers toward a common party goal, however, FOSP was a failure. It did not draw the fellow-traveler groups closer to communist aesthetics and simply became an additional locus of infighting. RAPP continued to control the major journals and dominate literary politics; and as Stalin turned his energies toward defeating the opposition and pushed domestic policy toward intensified class warfare, a new set of reasons arose for keeping RAPP in power. A proletarian hard core in literature would help him sell collectivization to the public. It did not matter that the 1925 Politburo resolution had contained a caveat, warning the Onguardists against high-handedness, and that the Onguardists had flagrantly violated that warning. They received redoubled support from the party in April 1928, and once Stalin defeated the Left Opposition, *Red Virgin Soil* came under the control of RAPP and turned into its own opposite.[35] A Central Committee resolution in December 1928 reaffirmed RAPP's supremacy and directed publishers to favor communist writers.[36]

As a literary match for the cultural revolution and the December 1929 resolution to eliminate the kulaks as a class, the Pereverzev school's class-based aesthetics would have made more sense than did the psychological complexities of the Onguardists' "living man." *Red Virgin Soil* had in fact initially been placed under a Pereverzevite upon Voronsky's dismissal. But Stalin could live with inconsistencies between literary theory and social policy as long as he had literary cadres eager to lead the charge against class "enemies."

As Stalin sought to destroy the Right Opposition, Averbakh mimicked *Pravda*'s coverage of the Shakhty and Prompartiia trials of technical specialists in 1928 and 1930, casting nonparty writers and critics as a Right Opposition in literature.[37] RAPP's journals defamed these writers as "reactionary," "counterrevolutionary," or "kulak," labels that could bring a death sentence. S. T. Grigoryev, labeled a "class enemy" by RAPP, lost his right to a ration packet. (Prishvin pleaded Grigoryev's case to Gorky—and a ration packet materialized.) One hand did not always know what the other was doing: Pilniak and Sergei Gorodetsky both received excellence awards from the party at the very moment when RAPP was shaming them in the pages of its journals (SLNE, 131, 187). Averbakh's activity transcended RAPP's journals. When a 1929 law stipulated the death penalty for defectors, the RAPP leadership happily furnished party agencies with a list of intellectuals whom it deemed likely to defect.[38] Many denunciations were addressed to Averbakh as the head of RAPP's secretariat; these he forwarded to Yagoda.[39]

The Onguardists' need to pigeonhole all writers as "us" or "them" affected even their attitude toward their natural allies. This was especially so with Mikhail Sholokhov, a member of the editorial board of October and ostensibly one of their own. The wild success of his The Quiet River Don (Tikhii Don) when its first installments appeared in early 1928 was a credit to RAPP, a demonstration of "proletarian" literary talent, and a compelling example of the living man approach. Unfortunately for Sholokhov, it also revealed the vulnerabilities of that approach. The novel's protagonist, Grigory, wavered and doubted, prompting Fyodor Gladkov to snipe that Sholokhov was good at describing rich peasants and was "not one of us."[40] As a teenager during the Civil War, Sholokhov had joined a Bolshevik food-requisitioning detachment, but it was well known that his father-in-law, an ataman, had opposed the Bolsheviks. One of RAPP's secretaries, Ivan Makaryev, told Stavsky that Sholokhov was unquestionably "one of us" but unschooled in party matters and susceptible to all manner of extraneous influences (MMN, 90).

Sholokhov's doubting protagonist posed a threat to the Onguardists. In the Bolshevik belief system, doubt was a stigmatizing hallmark of the intelligentsia to which they belonged. Communist belief meant leaving your doubts behind.[41] The Onguardists' opponents on the left, Litfront, mocked them for hailing The Quiet River Don as a proletarian novel and missing its kulak sympathies. It was a shining example of just how bad it was to learn from Tolstoy: readers were shown the inner life of the White Guards instead of being led to hate them.[42] Litfront had scratched a sore spot and the Onguardists' hand was forced: the theory of the living man did not include having doubts over whether to be a Bolshevik.

On becoming acting editor in chief of October in the summer of 1928, Fadeyev blocked publication of the next installment of The Quiet River Don, which showed Grigory participating in the 1919 Cossack uprising against the Bolsheviks.[43] Sholokhov sent Fadeyev a revised text in February 1929, but Fadeyev remained dissatisfied and responded sharply: Grigory had to be made a "Soviet person," or the novel was "buried."[44] Sholokhov got some of the offending chapters published elsewhere, but Fadeyev refused to relent.

Stalin took this opportunity to cast himself as a literary liberal. He warned the Agitprop official Aleksei Stetsky, who, like Fadeyev, complained about Grigory, against interfering in a writer's creative process. To Feliks Kon, the revolutionary and editor of the Red Army newspaper *Krasnaia zvezda* (*Red Star*), Stalin observed that *The Quiet River Don* contained errors and falsehoods, but "does that really mean the work of a famous writer should be removed from bookstores?"[45] Nonetheless, the block on further installments of *The Quiet River Don* lasted three more years. Stalin's indulgence was for show. While word of his liberalism fed the rumor mill, the banned books remained banned.

Well into the future, Fadeyev's attitude toward doubt and hesitation, like his relationship to Sholokhov, was marked by ambivalence and flux. In the fall of 1929, Fadeyev defended the Russian Jewish writer David Khait in print against an accusation of being a class enemy.[46] A mistake or hesitation, Fadeyev wrote, did not make someone a class enemy, and Marxist literary critics had to be able to tell the difference. A letter from Sholokhov to Fadeyev at around the same time indicates that Sholokhov, who deplored the abuse of the class-enemy label, wrote to Fadeyev on this matter as to someone of like mind. "As soon as you pick up a pen, it's 'Aren't you a White officer? And didn't an old woman write your fancy novel for you? And don't you give assistance to kulaks? And don't you believe in right deviationism?'" (*TS*, 397). In 1932, however, Fadeyev admitted that RAPP had tried to identify as many enemies as possible.[47]

FOSP, although descending into irrelevance, continued to exist, and its newspaper, *Literaturnaia gazeta*, began publication on April 22, 1929. Its first editor was Semyon Ivanovich Kanatchikov, a party bureaucrat with no literary profile. A former factory worker who had joined the communist underground in 1898 and sided with the Bolsheviks when the party split in 1903, he belonged to the United Opposition briefly in 1925–26 (for which he would be shot in 1940). In Kanatchikov's career assignments we can glimpse the Bolshevik conception of literature, higher education, and the press as a single infrastructure of educative and psychological engineering. He variously served as rector of two universities, chief of the State Journalism Institute, and interim editor of *Red Virgin Soil* after Voronsky's ouster. His stewardship of *Literaturnaia gazeta* in 1929 kept the paper from dominance by any one faction. The inaugural issue printed a mission statement suggesting a firm pressuring of writers into party service, but without RAPP's defamatory tactics. The fledgling newspaper vowed not to paper over the differences among FOSP's various constituent groups; any reassurance that might have been read into this promise was undone by the paper's accompanying vow to correct any "mistakes" by individual writers or literary groups.[48]

The Onguardists and their Litfront opponents set their sights on gaining control of the new paper, with Litfront attracting allies in the Communist Academy and the Pereverzev school, and Fadeyev complaining to Stalin that Kanatchikov was turning the newspaper into a tool for the Pereverzevites and the Smithy "to do battle with RAPP" (*TS*, 403). Under Kanatchikov, however, *Literaturnaia gazeta* did publish a wide range of opinion pieces, short prose, and poetry, including work by writers far from communism. The very first issue contained an open letter to Fadeyev from the formalist critic and LEF member Viktor Shklovsky. RAPP's journals would never have published such a letter, and the exchange that followed, playing out over the newspaper's first four issues, was a notable instance of a nonparty writer seizing an opportunity to call out RAPP's unwarranted arrogance. Shklovsky warned Fadeyev that his harassment of formalist and other critics in the pages of *On Literary Guard* would backfire:

> Being able to write an article creates an illusion of leadership . . . and hinders people from doing major work . . . I think you personally are making a mistake. Your novel *The Last of the Udegs* [*Poslednii iz udege*] will not come out . . . It shouldn't come out. In spite of *The Rout*'s partial success, it is derivative.

Fadeyev, cautioned Shklovsky, was trying to put new content into an old form (that of James Fenimore Cooper's *The Last of the Mohicans*) and was destined to fail. "In the name of your abilities," Shklovsky half chided, half implored, "don't cross the heavens in a chariot of extinguished stars."[49]

Fadeyev made a terse rejoinder in the following issue, observing tartly that he was too busy writing *The Last of the Udegs* to respond in detail; his views were readily available in print and Shklovsky should read them. The next issue carried another letter from Shklovsky reporting that he had followed Fadeyev's advice by reading back issues of *On Literary Guard* and found that "the bibliography [of harassment articles] can be considerably lengthened: the journal is packed with attacks on me, which for you evidently takes the place of literary theory." Shklovsky also exposed the journal's tactics in protecting the authors of its smear articles: "May I also inform you that [the journal's] copyediting is poor. For example, the review of my *Material and Style in L. Tolstoy's "War and Peace"* (no. 7, pp. 71–74) is signed by Y. Nikolaev, but in the body of the review on page 72, it says, 'My italics—Zh. E.' I have the impression that your staff cannot make up their minds to sign their work with their usual pseudonym" (*LG*, May 7, 1929). "Zh. E." was easily recognizable as Zh. Elsberg, the established pseudonym of Yakov Efimovich

Shapirshtein. Shklovsky's barb exposed the RAPP leadership as unscrupulous and cowardly: the copyediting oversight showed that they were hiding behind false names to conceal their own mudslinging.

Literaturnaia gazeta's next issue came to Fadeyev's aid with a cartoon depicting him as the Hindu god Vishnu in lotus position, triumphantly holding up a copy of *The Last of the Udegs* in each of his four arms. Ten demon-like, midget Shklovskys have latched on to his arms, legs, and neck, attacking him and the copies of *The Last of the Udegs* with pokers as Fadeyev-Vishnu remains serenely undisturbed (*LG*, May 13, 1929). In the end, however, Shklovsky's predictions came true. Fadeyev never completed *The Last of the Udegs*. It was not the only novel he would abandon.

Shklovsky used *Literaturnaia gazeta* to wrest back from RAPP his right to self-definition; his sortie against Fadeyev was equally about himself. "We, the formalists, and in particular the formalist Shklovsky, are for the revolution" (*LG*, May 13, 1929). This somewhat dubious *profession de foi* can certainly be taken as an exercise in self-defense. At the same time, it was genuine in its claim to deserve a place in Soviet society. This was not only about his past in Opoiaz. It was even more importantly about his future—his ability to remain relevant and to publish, an ever more crucial matter for nonparty writers and critics. It is what Eikhenbaum meant when he wrote that the question was no longer how to write but how to be a writer.[50] It is the agony of Kornei Chukovsky and Mikhail Slonimsky, friends desperate to find a way to self-identify as Soviet, discussing the problem of what could be written. Slonimsky confided to Chukovsky that he wrote for his desk drawer, while writing "horrid" things for publication. Through an improbably twisted reasoning, the two of them decided that the system would improve with time, and that the Soviet Union was unique in its ability to improve.[51]

This conversation shows that the problem of belonging was not simply a matter of getting published but one of doing so while remaining authentically oneself as an artist. Shklovsky's declaration of loyalty was shrewd: while other nonparty writers affirmed their desire to work with the Bolsheviks, Shklovsky cast himself as someone who had no need to seek common ground, because he fully belonged to the revolution.

Let us look now at three other nonparty writers whose public positions on the spectrum of loyalty and compromise differed from Shklovsky's. Boris Pilniak and Yevgeny Zamiatin took a position that was essentially "I want to be an ally, but if I am not accepted as one, I will publish abroad." Andrei Platonov tried to become an ally by working with party editors to make his work acceptable. These writers tried to win a place in Bolshevik literature on the understanding that they could be allies even if their inner thoughts and creative impulses might not always be in alignment with Bolshevik theory.

The publication of Pilniak's *Mahogany* (*Krasnoe derevo*) in Berlin and

Zamiatin's *We* (*My*) in Prague in the summer and fall of 1929 shook party officials, who resolved to put a stop to the smuggling of manuscripts across the border. RAPP called for the dissolution of the main fellow travelers' literary association, of which Pilniak was the elected president.[52] RAPP's public denunciation of him was composed by Fadeyev.[53] An episode two months later suggests that he felt quite at home with this assignment. He found himself sitting opposite Zamiatin in the packed dining hall of the Leningrad Writers' House; everyone else had avoided Zamiatin's table, until it was the only one left. At Fadeyev's approach, Zamiatin contemptuously advised him to find a safer place to sit. Fadeyev sat down and began a polemic: "If I'm not mistaken, you aren't really very embarrassed at sitting alone. Maybe you're even proud of it. You're convinced that a true artist always has to be in the minority against the majority, and against the state." In fact, Fadeyev continued, Zamiatin was in the majority—five-sixths of the world's population opposed the Soviet Union (*TS*, 401–2). Here we sense Fadeyev's relish in getting the better of an argument. We can also surmise his pride as the only one in the room who felt either safe enough (thanks to his powerful position) or courageous enough (thanks to his moral fiber) to sit with a political pariah.

The Onguardists took a different attitude toward another literary maverick, the proletarian Platonov, whose fiction was elusive and seeded with elements of satire, but whose class origins made him a desirable catch and who agreed to work with editors to make his work acceptable. Their inclination to publish him was met by Stalin's determination to punish him. Stalin reproached Fadeyev for including "Doubtful Makar" ("Usomnivshiisia Makar") in the September 1929 issue of *October*, calling it "ideologically double-voiced."[54] (The story had in fact been approved by Fadeyev's predecessor.)[55] Averbakh made amends for the error with a stinging critique of "Makar" that appeared not just in RAPP's journals but also in *Pravda*.[56] One of RAPP's accusations against Platonov was "podpilniachestvo" (being under Pilniak's thumb).[57]

It is tempting to imagine Averbakh and Yermilov in a gleeful competition to invent ever more vicious labels. Nonetheless, the "Makar" fiasco did not quell the Onguardists' interest in Platonov. They published another of his stories in 1930 without incident.[58] So when they published "For Future Use" ("Vprok") in 1931, neither they nor Platonov foresaw that it would spell his doom.

The tortuous path of this fateful story from inception to publication exposes the fault lines of the literary force field. Platonov visited the Central Black Earth Region in the spring of 1930, apparently with funding from a literary magazine seeking a story on the collective farm movement.[59] He wrote "For Future Use" only to have it turned down by three publishers. The feisty Bolshevik editor of *Novy mir* (*New World*), Viacheslav Polonsky, a firm advocate of literary quality who published many fellow travelers, warned Platonov against publishing it, finding it counterrevolutionary (*APVS*, 272). Polonsky was not rebuking Platonov so much as advising him. He spoke from experience: in 1926 he had published Pilniak's *The Tale of the Unextinguished Moon* (*Povest o nepogashennoi lune*), which was based on a rumor implicating Stalin in the death of Mikhail Frunze, commissar of military and naval affairs. The issue was yanked while in press, and Polonsky had to print an apology.[60] His was the soundest counsel that Platonov received. But Platonov had no crystal ball. He approached other publishers, asking for advice on making the story publishable. Most were highly critical of the story's elusive stance and lack of discernible socialist mind-set. One referee commented, "The author does not have his own attitude to events."[61]

Some editors, however, tried working with Platonov to make the story acceptable. This was a fairly common practice. Artists like Sergei Eisenstein and Shostakovich, who were seen as potential assets to the regime, were sometimes paired with reliable, orthodox writers like Pavlenko and Vishnevsky, who could guide the production of a film or an opera by providing a suitable screenplay or libretto.[62] The State Publishing House, Gosizdat, appointed a team that included Anatoly Lunacharsky's secretary, Ilya Sats, to help Platonov revise the manuscript. Ultimately, the working group's suggestions evoked Platonov's protest: "I am not against being educated, but in our country they educate us by cutting off our heads" (*SF*, 849). Platonov's aesthetics of ambiguity could not be made to fit into ideological prescriptions.

Eventually, Platonov wound up at *Red Virgin Soil*, which was now controlled by RAPP. Its editor, Bespalov, also found the story unacceptable but attributed its weak ideology to Pilniak's influence.[63] Platonov was a proletarian literary talent whom it was worth trying to reeducate. Besides, the story would make a good weapon in the battle against RAPP's latest rival. This was Pereval, the group that had formed around Voronsky's *Red Virgin Soil*. RAPP had once treated it as an ally, and Platonov himself had been associated with it. Pereval was now invoking the "Mozart principle" (*Mozartianstvo*) to affirm the importance of the individual personality (*lichnost*) in artistic creativity.[64] The Mozart principle was not incompatible with the living man theory, but it was a rightist position; by opposing it, Averbakh could position himself more advantageously to Pereval's left. (Averbakh schemed in this manner on other occasions as well, once proposing to the constructivist Kornely Zelinsky that he form a new constructivist youth group. When Zelinsky asked why, Averbakh showed his hand openly: any accusations of rightism would fall on the young constructivists rather than the Onguardists.) (*APVS*, 266). In a debate at the Communist Academy in April 1930, the Onguardists, joined by the Pereverzevites and some members of the Communist Academy, argued that history had outstripped Mozart and cited "For

Future Use" to support their view (*APVS*, 281–82). The debate concluded with Pereval's defeat.[65]

While "For Future Use" was inching through the publication process, literary politicking unfolded at a dizzying speed. No sooner had Pereval been discredited than a new novel by Libedinsky, *Birth of a Hero* (*Rozhdenie geroia*), gave Litfront an opportunity to force the rightist label back onto the Onguardists. At the peak of proletarianization, Libedinsky's living man hero with human flaws made an easy target.[66] When Litfront's ally Boris Olkhovy, a former deputy head of Agitprop, replaced Kanatchikov at *Literaturnaia gazeta* in May, Litfront had both *Literaturnaia gazeta* and *Pravda* in its corner.[67] Libedinsky's novel endured a ban that outlived everyone involved.

Even before Litfront's victory, the Onguardists were already weakened. Dissatisfied with Averbakh, the party leadership earlier that spring had reassigned him to Smolensk. A contentious meeting of the RAPP secretariat in July saw considerable objection to Averbakh, but the majority voted to request the Central Committee to bring him back to the RAPP central office.[68] Averbakh returned, and in short order succeeded in getting Litfront's leaders expelled from RAPP and Olkhovy replaced by a Communist Academy professor, Sergei Dinamov, who was more sympathetic to the Onguardists. Then he turned his attention to the Pereverzevites. The Pereverzev school had been hotly debated at the Communist Academy since 1929. The Onguardists, who had temporarily made common cause with several Pereverzevites who were allied with Litfront, now joined with anti-Pereverzev faculty at the academy.[69] In 1930, the Pereverzevites were discredited as "vulgar sociologists" who overemphasized class analysis. Litfront, too, was dissolved in November 1930. Its members signed statements in support of Onguard's program, and the Onguardist Selivanovsky took the helm of *Literaturnaia gazeta*.

By the time of the Prompartiia trial on November 25, 1930, the Onguardists were back in the driver's seat, bullying nonparty writers, whom they defined as specialists in "intelligentsia themes," into covering this trial of industrial engineers.[70] They dreamed up a new slogan—"not fellow traveler, but ally or enemy."[71] This fearsome shift in the idea of alliance apparently pleased the Central Committee, which two months later passed a resolution instructing *Pravda* to support the Onguardists more firmly (*MMN*, 128–29).

RAPP framed debate so as to force writers to choose between opposites. *On Literary Guard* published responses to a questionnaire that asked, "In your view, what is the difference between the former and the new type of writer?"[72] "Former" and "new" were the only two identities possible. Some respondents attempted to refocus the debate: the peasant poet Sergei Klychkov wrote that Soviet writers had failed to lay claim to a "restricted zone of ideas, feelings, and thoughts" and were losing the ability to not go along with the crowd.[73] The magazine printed Klychkov's response and appended a note about his "kulak mentality."[74] Presumably the Onguardists intended to harm Klychkov; in contrast, they spared Platonov by simply not publishing his response.[75]

It was at this point that "For Future Use" finally saw print. The better part of a year had elapsed since the Pereval debate, during which time Platonov's story underwent revision at *Red Virgin Soil*. In an absurdist scenario, the situation of two years earlier was repeated: immediately after Bespalov (who by now had recanted his Pereverzevism and paid obeisance to Averbakh) approved the story, Fadeyev was assigned to replace him and certified the completed issue for printing (*APVS*, 271). He had joined Bespalov in the Pereval debate, favoring "For Future Use" as an antidote to Pereval's "Mozartism." The story appeared in March 1931. Stalin read it, famously marking up the margins of the journal with his comments. "The slime. So that's what the directors of the collective farm movement are like, the collective farm cadres? The scoundrel" (*SF*, 816). That evening Fadeyev and Sutyrin were surprised in their homes by a Kremlin courier, who whisked them off to Stalin's office. The infuriated Stalin handed Fadeyev a piece of paper with his assessment:

> A story by our enemies' agent, written with the aim of derailing the collective farm movement and published by dimwit communists with the aim of demonstrating *their own* unsurpassed *blindness*.

> I. Stalin.

> P.S.: Both the author and the dimwits should be punished as a lesson to them "for future use" (*VKI*, 150; emphasis in original).

Stalin uses two tonalities in this note. Platonov and his story are described in a declarative, pedagogical tone, a form of "absolute language" that presents itself as uncontested truth. Stalin thus sets the stage for an "objective" press campaign against Platonov. When it comes to RAPP cadres, however, eager to "demonstrate . . . their blindness," Stalin switches to sarcasm, humiliating them with their failure to live up to their role as discerning Marxists. As literary cadres, they are sent off to implement the "objective" press campaign against Platonov while also receiving a private scolding designed to teach them a twin lesson in Marxist "objectivity" and in obedience born of fear and shame.

Fadeyev, while taking responsibility for the story, let Stalin know that Bespalov had been the one to approve it.[76] According to Sutyrin's memoirs, Stalin immediately summoned Bespalov. What happened next reveals much about the shaping of Fadeyev's self-image as a cadre. After berating the cowering Bespalov, Stalin turned to his personal secretary, Aleksandr Poskrebyshev, and said "contemptuously" (Sutyrin's word),

> "Take him out of here . . . So that's who is directing Soviet literature . . ." And turning to us: "Comrade Sutyrin and Comrade Fadeyev! Take this journal. My comments are written on it. Write an article for tomorrow's newspaper in which you expose the anti-Soviet meaning of the story and the person of its author. You may go." (APVS, 271)

The lesson was clear. Stalin, who made a habit of crossing out the word "comrade" before the names of people who had been arrested, deprived Bespalov of this honorific and implied an unspoken pejorative in its place. When Stalin then turned to Fadeyev and Sutyrin, the significance of his addressing them both as "comrade" surely was music to their ears.

Sutyrin's memoirs, written many years after the fact, place quotation marks around Stalin's words as he remembered them. Memory presumably supplied its own version of Stalin's actual words. But Sutyrin would have remembered the crux of Stalin's instructions: "exposing" the "anti-Soviet" nature of the story and its author. Fadeyev and Sutyrin spent the rest of the night at Sutyrin's writing their article. If Fadeyev was troubled by obeying Stalin's order to slander Platonov as a kulak agent at a time when Soviet law mandated the liquidation of the kulaks, he compensated for it by finding another way to preserve his communist honor. He insisted on being listed as the sole author, since the problem had been his own lack of vigilance (APVS, 271). Secreted in this decision to protect Sutyrin from the moral stain of authorship was a tacit recognition, although not necessarily a conscious one, that the article was a dirty deed.

Fadeyev and Sutyrin followed Stalin's language closely. Stalin had called Platonov "our enemies' agent"; Fadeyev and Sutyrin wrote that Platonov was a "kulak agent" and his story a "kulak sortie." The very title of the article, "About a Certain Kulak Chronicle" ("Ob odnoi kulatskoi khronike"), hammered home the kulak label, and some form of the word "kulak" occurred twenty-four times in this four-page article. "Class enemy" occurred seven times. The article ends with a close paraphrase of Stalin's P.S., minus the sarcasm: "And that is why we, the communists who work at *Red Virgin Soil* and who let a particular sally of the class enemy's agent slip by us, ought to be punished as a lesson, so that it can be learned for future use."[77]

Signing his name to Stalin's language, Fadeyev stamped himself with Stalin's imprint. The communist "brotherhood of the elect," as Halfin tells us, could not accommodate individual selves.[78] The sole exception was the charismatic leader whose self absorbs all other selves. At the receiving end of

Stalin's charisma and image as a stern but benevolent patriarch with a steady guiding hand was the starstruck follower whose adulation sucked away his own selfhood.[79]

Fadeyev's article defines enemies through the concepts of mask and doubt. "Tearing off the masks" was a slogan RAPP introduced for the 1928 cultural revolution.[80] The simpleton protagonist of "For Future Use," wrote Fadeyev, was no simpleton at all but only masked to appear "on the whole sympathetic [to communism] but just doubting, wavering . . . They implore us not to confuse their criticism of a particular defect . . . with their overall 'sympathetic' view."[81] This mask, said Fadeyev, "was calculated to fool trusting communists, infecting them with doubt, and Platonov himself wore it when he wrote his story at the behest of 'his class.'"

With this article, Fadeyev moved from a benign attitude toward doubt to an insistence that doubt was inadmissible. In a private story that he had written six years earlier to his bride-to-be, the writer Valeriia Gerasimova, Fadeyev's autobiographical narrator says, "I felt ashamed . . . because at that time I resembled a bourgeois type [*meshchanin*] familiar to you, who, while acknowledging that the GPU was indispensable, lost sleep and peace of mind when he was forced to work in that same GPU."[82] A conflict between authority and truth was in the making. The scene in Stalin's office decided it. Stalin's note did not refer to doubt.[83] But recurring doubts were a personal dilemma for Fadeyev. Reading Dante's *Inferno* in October 1934, Fadeyev was struck by the fate of those who did not take sides: "They're not even worthy of hell!" He read Dante in light of his own situation, in which he, too, was faced with taking sides in an archetypal war. Taking sides at all costs became for him the measure of integrity. He similarly disputed Goethe's point that rarely is a choice "either-or," writing in his notebook, "And yet, 'either-or' exists—without it there would be no truth. It's fair, though, that people try to slide in between, because choosing often means deprivation and suffering."[84] Now that an entire class of doubters was being liquidated, it was time for him to show he could choose. The same would be true when it was the intelligentsia's turn to be wiped out. His article on Platonov, essentially coauthored with Stalin, was not what he believed—so he had to find a way to believe it. He did not so much seek to align his subjective self with Bolshevik theory as to discover a logical argument that would allow him to accept the necessary conclusion as an objective fact.

There was an emotional side, too, that Fadeyev acknowledged and that may have made logical argument all the more important as a counterbalance. "I am afraid of two people," Fadeyev is reported to have said, "my mother and Stalin, I am afraid of them and I love them."[85] This could have been a self-protective assertion, but more likely it was a genuine expression of his feelings. An inward quaking at the thought of Stalin manages to be couched in the comforting corrective of loving parental oversight. Instead of "my mother and father," Fadeyev pairs "my mother and Stalin," acknowledging Stalin as the spiritual father who replaces the biological father who abandoned him. Fadeyev embraced his identity as a "son of the party," as if taking this phrase almost literally. The revolution was so closely tied to the moral imperative of social justice that when Fadeyev joined the Bolshevik party at age seventeen, it became the seat of his spiritual life. The moral imperative became synonymous with the party; the party became synonymous with his conscience.

Fadeyev and Yermilov climbed their career ladder on their public judgments of Sholokhov and Platonov. We shall see in later chapters that both sagas resumed a decade later, when Sholokhov completed *The Quiet River Don* and Platonov found a supportive environment among the staff of *Literary Critic*. Yermilov separated his personal dislike of Sholokhov from his high opinion of him as a writer.[86] Fadeyev, after half a dozen years of struggling unsuccessfully to complete *The Last of the Udegs*, looked to *The Quiet River Don* for the thing that eluded him: "Sholokhov implants in his Grigorys and Aksinias *his own* character and the Cossacks acknowledge it, Sholokhov's character, as their own character . . ."[87] Sholokhov managed to be a communist who maintained a unique personal identity. That it remained recognizable meant that he had not brought it into alignment with Bolshevik theory.

Polonsky was not the first editor to tell Platonov that his work was counterrevolutionary. FOSP's publishing house, Federation, had rejected his novel *Chevengur* on the same grounds in 1929. Platonov had then turned to Gorky, asking if he, too, found it counterrevolutionary. If Gorky liked the novel, Platonov asked that he "say that the author is right and that the novel is an honest attempt to portray the principle of communist society."[88]

Platonov's request both articulates his self-definition as an honest writer and prescribes a model of honesty for Gorky himself to follow. Gorky, who two years earlier had named Platonov as one of Russia's most interesting new writers, demurred. Replying to Platonov, he praised the novel as "extremely interesting" but avoided taking a stand:

I don't think it will get published. That is prevented by your anarchic cast of mind, which apparently is inherent to your "spirit" . . . your illumination of reality has a lyrical and satirical tint, and this, of course, is unacceptable to our censorship . . . For all your tenderness toward people in your works, they are painted with irony, and they come across to the reader less as revolutionaries than as "eccentrics" and "half-wits." I am not saying that this was done consciously, but it was done, at least that is how it comes across to the reader, that is, to me. Possibly I am mistaken.[89]

Gorky, of course, was not mistaken. *October* was just about to hit the newsstands with the "half-wit" Makar, drawing Stalin's ire. Gorky sidestepped the question of *Chevengur*'s literary merit. He later suggested a stage adaptation of it to the director of the Moscow Art Theater II, Ivan Bersenev, and advised Platonov to try writing plays, because his language, "coming from the lips of actors who know their profession, would sound splendid."[90]

Wary of Platonov's aesthetics, Gorky could not have been pleased when in July 1931 Platonov and Stalin both tried to draw him into the imbroglio over "For Future Use." Platonov appealed to him twice on this matter.

> The working class is my homeland . . . I am not saying this . . . to mask myself . . . To be rejected by your class while inwardly you are on its side is a much greater torment than acknowledging yourself to be alien to everything . . . I very much want you to believe me, to believe me in just one thing: I am not a class enemy . . . The press has stated many times that I am very cunning, that I have managed to deceive a number of simple, trusting people.[91]

Fadeyev's pen had disfigured Platonov's identity. Platonov wrote further to Gorky: "I myself now admit . . . that my story caused harm."[92] But to think he was hiding behind a mask was absurd, he wrote. Could twelve editors, most of whom had far more literary experience than the much younger Platonov, all have been deceived?[93] Platonov's plea shows the psychological effectiveness of "tearing off the masks" as a weapon of attack.

Platonov also wrote a penitent letter to Stalin—who then forwarded it to Gorky. Perhaps Stalin was, as one scholar believes, "entrusting Gorky with 'reforging'" Platonov, or perhaps he was setting a trap for Gorky.[94] Either way, Gorky was not about to embark on such a dangerous mission. The next time he was asked to evaluate one of Platonov's manuscripts (the play *High Tension* [*Vysokoe napriazhenie*]), he stated that he would limit himself to discussing its "literary, formal side."[95]

Two years later, Platonov tried again. Gorky, after all, was his last hope. Platonov requested a meeting to discuss "whether I can be a Soviet writer or whether this is objectively impossible."[96] But by now Platonov was a "kulak agent," and Gorky had spoken out publicly and vociferously against the "enemies" of collectivization. Platonov received no reply.

Gorky did reply to a 1934 letter from Platonov seeking his opinion of a short story, "Garbage Wind" ("Musornyi veter"):

> I have read your story, and—it stunned me. You write firmly and clearly, but that only serves to emphasize and expose—in this case—the unreality of the

story's content, and the content borders on gloomy ravings. I think this story of yours can hardly get published anywhere.

I regret that I cannot say anything different and continue to await from you a work more worthy of your talent.[97]

A year later, when the control mechanisms at work in the Writers' Union were already obvious, Gorky recommended against including Platonov in the anthology *Two Five-Year Plans* (*Dve piatiletki*) (*SF*, 816).

Stalin had begun persuading Gorky to forsake Sorrento and return home, at the very time when he was loosing RAPP on Soviet literature during the cultural revolution. No price could be put on Gorky's value to Stalin.[98] He had something of the aura of prophet and national conscience that had sanctified Pushkin, Dostoevsky, and Tolstoy; he had international stature; he could be claimed as a proletarian even as he linked the working class with the old intelligentsia. Stalin's triumph in drawing Gorky closer to him is the more noteworthy for occurring precisely when his government was committing mammoth atrocities in the countryside.

Stalin worked Gorky as he would later work his cadres, fully understanding how to turn the human psyche toward a passive acceptance of systematic atrocity (that the acceptance might take the form of denial does not change its fundamental nature). He sold them a comprehensive package designed to fulfill all their needs—material, emotional, psychological, and intellectual. It included desirable living conditions, public honor, and an important post, but there was much more than these material and political benefits. He was also selling cultural belonging, participation in a grand enterprise, and a sense of being a winner. Nor did he forget the most important element of all: a philosophical argument to assuage moral qualms and provide assurance that one was not trading ethics for self-interest. If all human thought arose from the material conditions in which the thinking was being done, then morality, too, like any other category of philosophical thought, arose from class interests. Stalin attached this conclusion to Marx's base-superstructure paradigm time and again, citing intensification of the class struggle and other developments to justify discarding the moral prohibition on murder. The kulaks had outlived their assigned time; as the economic base had changed, so had the needs and class interests of the proletariat. Mass murder was made more palatable by euphemisms like "liquidation" and "rapid tempos."

Where Lenin in 1921 had strong-armed Gorky into leaving the Soviet Union, Stalin washed away that insult, enticing him back home. He honored Gorky by naming a theater (the Moscow Art Theater II), a street (formerly Tverskaia), and an entire city (formerly Nizhny Novgorod) after him, explaining to cadres that these actions would flatter Gorky and bind him more firmly to the party.[99] Gorky hesitated. In Italy he had continual contact with both Soviet and émigré writers, whose visits provided society, literary stimulation, and a reliable ticker tape on which to follow the volatile political news from back home. The choice to return to the Soviet Union meant weighing a good against an evil. It was the rarest of opportunities to shape Russian literature, a political and aesthetic juncture that occurs not in every lifetime. Against that beguiling serendipity had to be weighed Stalin's utter disregard for human life. Even without the fear factor, Stalin's package was sorely tempting. But it was not quite enough.

Two elements in Gorky's intellectual makeup assisted his terrible rapprochement with Stalin's atrocities. These were his deep-seated utopianism and a disdain for the peasantry that had developed during his early years of wandering throughout Russia. His low regard for them helped him swallow the brutality of Stalin's collectivization drive. As Stalin was persuading his Politburo to approve "rapid tempos," Gorky assisted RAPP in persuading the public—and himself. In 1922 he had denounced the trial of the socialist revolutionaries; now he used his bully pulpit to support the kulak extermination and the Prompartiia trial. His 1930 newspaper article, "If the Enemy Does Not Give Up, He Will Be Destroyed" ("Esli vrag ne sdaetsia—ego unichtozhaiut"), was his personal equivalent of Fadeyev's article branding Platonov a kulak agent:

> Inside the country, the most cunning of enemies organize famine, kulaks terrorize collective-farm workers with murders, arson, and various vile acts—against us is everything that has outlived the time allotted to it by history, and this gives us the right to consider ourselves still in a state of Civil War. The natural conclusion that follows from this is: if the enemy does not give up, he will be destroyed.[100]

He was preparing himself for his return to the Soviet Union as Writer in Chief. The march of history is a force analogous to a supreme Consciousness that can confer a moral right, in this case to engage in massacre. Gorky's portrayal of historical progress unites his disregard for the peasant with his utopian eschatology. The cruel inhumanity of the one and the raw idealism of the other, seemingly so incongruous, were made compatible in the putatively scientific logic peddled by Stalin. Gorky allowed his cherished belief in human perfectibility to trump his mistrust of Stalin. He accepted lapses on the way to utopia—utopia would be worth the wait and the sacrifice. To reassure himself of his intellectual independence, he had only to recall his refusal to join the party.

Gorky's utopianism was influenced by V. V. Bervi-Flerovsky's 1869 book, *The Position of the Working Class in Russia (Polozhenie rabochego klassa v*

Rossii), which concludes with an image of the starry heavens as the sign of a future altruistic humanity.[101] A tribute to Lenin on the third anniversary of his death, published in *Pravda* over Gorky's signature, embellishes this vision with elements of the Eastern Orthodox liturgy:

> His superhuman will has not vanished; it remains incarnated in people on earth.
>
> The work which he inspired and began cannot be set aside, and it can hardly be interrupted, even temporarily. The world had waited for this person, the person had appeared, showed the way, and people will follow this path to the end with the bright image of the immortal leader before them.[102]

This description, published prominently by the official media arm of the atheist state, makes Lenin the new Christ—a long-awaited Appearance; an earthly incarnation; a ministry (or work) in "the world"; and the death of one man that makes it possible for all humanity to achieve a better world according to his will. In place of the Redeemer of mankind is the Redeemer of the proletariat. The vocabulary is imported from recurring liturgical motifs ("incarnate," "appeared," " immortal," "His will"), iconography ("image," "showing the way" [the name for a common type of icon of the Mother of God]), and various prayers ("people on earth," "bright"). The inadmissible "God" or "Lord" is easily replaced by "superhuman."

The image of the nation following Lenin's path to the bright ending hints at Gorky's interest in God building, which imagined the seat of moral authority not in a supernatural God but in the perfected society. This idea, which entered Russian thought through the work of Vladimir Soloviev, was condemned by Lenin but drew the enthusiasm of Bolsheviks like Aleksandr Bogdanov and Education Commissar Anatoly Lunacharsky. Whether authentically Gorky's or a fabrication, *Pravda*'s eulogy reveals the unarticulated substructure of the Bolshevik belief system. As Halfin has noted, communism took Orthodox eschatology and made lexical substitutions, such as "comrades" for "the faithful" and "classless society" for "paradise."[103] Cadres who had been brought up in the Orthodox faith could satisfy their need for a belief structure by simply switching the authority figure. This process could exist subconsciously without interfering with dialectical materialism's explicit rejection of an objective, "pure" truth unmoored from class interests. As monks and priests served as instruments of God, so cadres served as instruments of the party, the seat of justice, wisdom, and truth. We will encounter a personal variation of this replacement toward the end of our story, in Fadeyev's suicide note.

Stalin capitalized on Gorky's summer visits to the Soviet Union to stoke his desire to return for good, having him tour the construction sites that would build utopia, as well as a children's labor colony near Moscow and the Solovetsky labor camp on the White Sea. Gorky could have given the slip to his political police guides and learned the real story from prisoners, who were only too eager to tell him.[104] He preferred to imagine forced labor as tough love that would reforge the individual and benefit society. Gorky wrote to Stalin,

> Ever since the Party set the countryside so decisively on the track of collectivization, the social revolution has begun to assume a truly socialist character. This is an upheaval of almost geological proportions, and it is greater, immeasurably greater and more profound, than anything that has yet been done by the Party. A way of life which has existed for thousands of years, an order which has created people of singular monstrosity, people quite horrifying in their animal conservatism and proprietorial instinct—this order is being destroyed. There are some twenty million such people. The problem of re-educating them in the shortest possible time is an insanely difficult one. Yet it is being resolved in a practical way right now.[105]

No letter to Stalin can be taken as a true expression of its writer's real thoughts. But Gorky's letter contains some of his true beliefs and reflects a compromise with himself. The rhetoric of prisoner rehabilitation perfectly fitted his utopianism, with one camp newspaper declaring, "Every person temporarily deprived of freedom is not deprived of the opportunity to take part in the great construction of the USSR."[106] With atrocity redefined as benevolence, the end did not need to justify the means, because the means were above reproach. In this variation on cognitive dissonance, the rationale is masked as fact and carefully hidden from the rationalizer's conscious mind.[107] Gorky's vigorous defense of collectivization as reeducation was surely one of the ways in which he convinced himself to return home.

Like Averbakh, Gorky was tied to the secret police through myriad family relationships; but where Averbakh made use of these connections, Gorky was enmeshed. Nearly every member of his household was involved with the security organs in some way—his son Max, his daughter-in-law Timosha, his secretary Pyotr Kriuchkov, and his three wives, Ekaterina Peshkova, Mariia Andreyeva, and Mura Budberg. Yagoda worked through Budberg and Kriuchkov to persuade Gorky to return and, once Gorky was back, frequented Gorky's home, smitten with Timosha.[108] Gorky's adopted son, Zinovy (his relative by marriage), was also related to Yagoda and Sverdlov.[109] Kriuchkov fed Yagoda a running account of Gorky's doings and routinely withheld strategically selected mail.[110] Just how deeply Gorky was compromised was sensed by Prishvin in 1932, when he approached Gorky to help restore ration packets to the unfairly maligned Grigoryev. Gorky came through, but Prishvin said, "I did not feel convinced I had a friend I could go back to again" (*SLNE*, 67). Nikolai Kliuev, booted into exile by Gronsky in 1934, decided against appealing to Gorky, reasoning that Gorky could no longer be relied on, and that in any case Kriuchkov would make sure Gorky never saw his letter.[111]

In literature, Gorky shared the party's goal of recruiting proletarian writers but was distressed at its reliance on the factory literary circles, which encouraged workers to submit compositions, and then touted them as a budding proletarian literature. The circles themselves were overseen by RAPP, and the claim that RAPP's membership approached 5,000 was probably thanks to a large number of factory workers who were entered into RAPP's rolls after attending a literary circle.[112] The Writers' Union began its existence in 1934 with just 2,200 members, and in spite of steady growth thereafter, it did not approach 5,000 until the late 1950s.[113] The party funded two "mass" literature journals, *The Chisel* (*Rezets*) and *Growth* (*Rost*), to showcase these "literary shock workers." Both were published by RAPP, which used them to foment readers' hostility toward the nonparty literary intelligentsia. One satirical cartoon showed a literary circlist gazing up at a crowd of intelligentsia writers lounging on the summit of Mount Parnassus. One writer resembles Anna Akhmatova, and another holds a sign saying, NO MORE ROOM (*NLP*, no. 3 [1931]: 13).

Privately, however, the RAPP leaders admitted that the literary circles were a flop.[114] The journals turned out to be a case of putting the cart before the horse. The first issue of *The Chisel* appeared in 1926; three years later, the editorial board offered its contributors remedial training (eventually supported by a Central Committee resolution of August 19, 1931).[115] Those supervising the factory circles usually were teachers or staff members at cultural institutions who had no literary qualifications (*VKI*, 263). A grandly named Leningrad Workers' Evening Literary University was formed in the spring of 1931 to prepare leaders of the factory literary circles.[116]

There were woefully few consultants. In 1932, the state publishing house for fiction and literature had just twenty-three consultants for eleven thousand consultations covering twenty thousand pages.[117] Often the consultants were less literate than the people they were supposed to be training. In this context, their standard advice to semiliterate and grammatically shaky beginners—to read Boris Tomashevsky's *Theory of Literature* (*Teoriia literatury*), a densely written, academic text—was absurd.[118] After years of relentless attacks on Formalism, Tomashevsky's book, essentially a compendium of Russian Formalist thought, had somehow sneaked in through a back door as recommended reading. Many of the consultants probably had no idea what it was. Stavsky, for example, in the mid-1920s wrote little reminders to himself on the basics of good writing that sound like frayed remnants of Formalism: "Originality consists of uncovering and seeing in everyday objects what others do not notice but will always agree with."[119] RAPP's leaders, quipped Gorodetsky, were "really quite literate, when you consider the overall literacy level" (*SLNE*, 131).

Gorky detested the factory circles. From his Italian villa, he pushed his own vision of a proletarian writer equipped with an education that would wipe *The Chisel* and *Growth* from memory. Proletarians would take their first steps into literature through collective projects, carefully designed to give them a role suited to their abilities. Gorky devised three-way collaborations in which factory workers provided the material, historians shaped it, and professional writers worked it into a finished product.[120] These included *The History of the Civil War* (*Istoriia grazhdanskoi voiny*), *Our Achievements* (*Nashi dostizheniia*), *The History of Factories and Plants* (*Istoriia fabrik i zavodov*), and *People of the First and Second Five-Year Plans* (*Liudi pervoi i vtoroi piatiletki*). Gorky's projects, premised on cooperation across class backgrounds, reflected an egalitarian ideal diametrically opposed to RAPP's.

In part, Gorky saw these projects as a kind of schooling for proletarian writers.[121] New writers needed above all to study, and Gorky wanted a "teaching journal" aimed at them. It took form in 1930 as *Literary Study* (*Literaturnaia ucheba*), run jointly by Gorky and RAPP.[122] Gorky intended it as an "encyclopedia of literary mastery." Its articles introduced readers to classic Russian authors and notable Soviet writers, emphasizing their lives and work habits—Gorky's way of highlighting the importance of diligence. His warm welcome to proletarian literary recruits came with the expectation that they would pursue grammatical mastery and read the classics as models from which to learn. (His zeal to recruit stopped at the peasantry, whom he considered too lazy for sustained effort.)

Stalin's readiness to fund these projects may have given Gorky an inflated sense of his own influence. While needing Gorky's prestige, Stalin wanted to work through reliable cadres. Gorky was neither reliable nor a party member. The Onguardists, however, behaved with a troubling self-entitlement that increasingly overshadowed their obedience to party directives. Upon receiving redoubled party support in 1928, RAPP had begun holding congresses and plenums modeled on those of the Communist Party Central Committee, with Averbakh proclaiming literary policies in furtherance of the party's political positions.[123] In pompous speeches and resolutions, Averbakh styled himself a literary Stalin. When Stalin coined the term "general line" in reference to the first five-year plan, Averbakh started referring to his own decrees as the "general line in literature."[124] Averbakh was getting too big for his britches, but on the other hand he delivered: his plenums approved resolutions supporting the first five-year-plan, agricultural collectivization, "intensification of the class war," eliminating the kulaks as a class, and the Shakhty, Prompartiia, and Menshevik trials.

RAPP's defeat of Litfront turned out to contain the seeds of its own demise. The vanquished malcontents found a champion in Fyodor Panfyorov, and in spite of having been made to adopt the Onguardists' platform as the price for staying in RAPP, remained at odds with its leadership. The final year of RAPP's existence was marked by incessant infighting as Panfyorov gained the editorship of *October* and promoted his novel *Whetstones (Bruski)* as the exemplar of the dialectical materialist method, dethroning Fadeyev's *The Rout*.[125] As it happened, one of Panfyorov's group, Lev Ovalov, worked at *Young Communist Pravda (Komsomolskaia pravda)* and drew the Komsomol into the fight.[126] Its chief, Aleksandr Kosarev, derided the Onguardists as smug philistines who tried to make Bolsheviks into RAPPists instead of the other way around.[127] *Pravda* reaffirmed this criticism of RAPP the following month, November 1931, but Averbakh, instead of heeding this warning, had the RAPP leadership demand that the Central Committee secretaries order *Pravda* to cease its criticism.[128] This move, flying in the face of the communist codes of obedience and modesty, only confirmed Kosarev's characterization. The party ordered RAPP to convene an emergency plenum welcoming all communist writers into a friendlier RAPP.[129] RAPP was to abide by a revised mission: full equality for a wide array of communist writers; guidance and goodwill for nonparty writers. Stalin demanded three changes in literary policy. It must not be run by a clique; communist infighting had to cease; and nonparty writers must become fully Soviet.[130] At this stage, Stalin does not seem to have decided on liquidating RAPP.

The emergency plenum took place in January 1932. Averbakh's keynote speech paid lip service to respectful treatment of all writers but betrayed resistance to all three of Stalin's goals. After promising to welcome all RAPP constituencies, he reeled off a long list of individuals and groups that RAPP had proven wrong and "defeated," including Litfront.[131] The bulk of his speech was an aggressive reaffirmation of the Onguardists' literary theories.[132] He gave pride of place to RAPP's internal document on literary restructuring, rather than to the party resolution.[133] Averbakh was effectively asserting that control of literary policy would be in his hands, not the party's.

In tandem with the plenum, which was attended by communist writers, nonparty writers were summoned to an assembly of FOSP, where they learned that intensifying class struggle meant that they now had to choose sides. They were to write on communist themes. Literary critics would receive coaching from RAPP's critics. The largest of FOSP's constituencies, the VSP (Vserossiisky Soiuz Pisatelei, All-Russian Union of Writers), had the word "Soviet" added to its name and received a new mission statement: "to attract the fellow-traveler writer to the position of the proletariat" through a "radical and immediate restructuring of their worldview, and along with it of all creative methods."[134]

The restructuring of fellow-traveler literature, in other words, presumed a restructuring of the fellow-traveler psyche, whether through the self's erasure or its alignment with Bolshevism. Stalin's instructions to the Onguardists that they show greater comity to writers were meant to be observed selectively: at the FOSP gathering, the nonparty writers had to hear themselves compared to the most infamous buffoon in Russian literature: they were "political Mitrofanushki" who had yet to come of age.[135] One of many in attendance who bowed to pragmatism was Leonid Leonov: "When it comes to restructuring, a writer's first interest is himself: he has to live and work. The union of fellow travelers should think hard about this: hasn't it already arrived at the station?"[136] But there were holdouts. Ivan Yevdokimov, the author of a successful first novel, *The Bells* (*Kolokola*), said bluntly that proletarian literature was in no condition to lead and that the "RAPPists were always in the power of subject matter. They used it to hide their technical and technological helplessness."[137]

Following these meetings, in a divide-and-conquer strategy, the press began claiming that a "differentiation" was now starting to emerge within the ranks of the fellow travelers.[138] This was fearsome rhetoric, because if one prong of the divide constituted those who were close to the proletariat, the other prong could only be the opposite—class enemies or enemy agents. The rhetoric of class struggle was useful for intimidating nonparty writers, but Stalin was already contemplating his next policy zigzag. Averbakh's insubordination and Gorky's anticipated return entered a larger policy picture that was taking shape in the early months of 1932.

Tempted by Stalin's blandishments, Gorky still remained close to Bukharin and Lev Kamenev after their disgrace as oppositionists. Their unexpected return to public life may have influenced Gorky to return home, a propitious sign that he would have autonomy in running the Writers' Union. Kamenev's appointment as head of the Academia publishing house, on Gorky's urgent recommendation, must have been gratifying and a further cause for optimism. Plans to replace Stalin as general secretary might even succeed;[139] if they did not, he could still feel that Stalin would be receptive to other opinions. Stalin's shift away from proletarianization and cultural revolution toward the more moderate policy of national Bolshevism probably seemed another auspicious sign, as the new rhetoric of inclusion invited everyone, regardless of social class, to demonstrate their loyalty in return for the regime's acceptance.

Further evidence of reform appeared in the January 1932 issue of *October*. It contained the first new installment of *The Quiet River Don* in three years. The doubting Grigory Melekhov still had not been made a "Soviet person," yet *October* (under Panfyorov) published new chapters each month for the next eleven months. It has been plausibly argued that the completion of collectivization removed the novel's political sensitivity, allowing publication to resume.[140] Or perhaps the reappearance of Grigory, who was now seen taking part in the 1919 Cossack rebellion against the Red Army, was meant to signal that writers who had opposed Bolshevism during the Civil War could be forgiven if they renounced their mistaken beliefs.

The lifting of the ban was certainly on Stalin's instructions, but how and when he gave them is anything but straightforward. He had approved publication in a private meeting with Sholokhov and Gorky in July 1931, but as with his earlier letter to Kon, he did not inform others, and Fadeyev refused to budge.[141] Stalin timed the resumption of publication to emphasize the defeat of the Onguardists, including Fadeyev, exposing what was now portrayed as their misplaced arrogance in having blocked an important proletarian novel. Arrogance there may well have been, but Stalin himself in meeting with Sholokhov began by stating that part 3 would appeal to "émigré White Guards" and should not be published. Even assuming that this was merely his way of testing Sholokhov, it shows that Fadeyev's refusal to publish was exactly what would have been expected of him as an editor. Under Fadeyev's editorship, *October* in 1929–30 was either on the same page with Stalin or else (less likely) was making reasonable decisions (from the orthodox party viewpoint) in the absence of direct instructions.

No sooner had *The Quiet River Don* resumed publication than another work blocked by RAPP, Bulgakov's play *Days of the Turbins* (*Dni Turbinykh*), received a new staging, again with Stalin's "liberal" intervention. As Stalin prepared to unwind RAPP, he issued these literary amnesties to position himself as a friend of literature, blameless in RAPP's excesses. Yermilov, who had followed the party line in self-righteously characterizing Gorky as a bourgeois fellow traveler, now had to own up to the mistake—as his own. Meanwhile "the party," in the form of Stalin, the Politburo, and a handful of trusted officials like *Pravda*'s Mekhlis, preserved its image of infallibility and purity. The sacrificial cadres could potentially restore themselves to influential positions through purifying acts of "self-criticism," and time and again they hastened to do this. But as we shall see in later chapters, no amount of self-criticism could slake the shame culture's thirst for ever more of it.

On April 23, the Politburo disbanded all literary groups, RAPP included, and announced a new Writers' Union (*VKI*, 172–73). The stated reason was that nearly all the fellow travelers now supported the regime, and therefore they no longer needed proletarian guidance. The Writers' Union would now be the professional home of all writers regardless of party membership or class origin, provided that they "uphold the platform of Soviet power"—these words were italicized in the Politburo resolution. There was to be no literary career path outside the Writers' Union.

Averbakh, despite having been present at a Central Committee meeting where the draft resolution was circulated, and having voted to support it, went into denial.[142] He assured the RAPP secretariat that it would continue to hold the leading role.[143] He continued to argue RAPP's old positions in *On Literary Guard*, even reaffirming its now outdated slogan, "Ally or enemy."[144] And he delayed publishing the April 23 resolution, perhaps to buy time while seeking ways around it.

Behind the resolution's focus on nonparty writers was the problem of bitter factionalism among communist writers. A list provided to Stalin and Lazar Kaganovich does not bother to differentiate nonparty writers by literary group but divides communist writers into six categories (*ONI* 1:224). The Agitprop official Valery Kirpotin presented RAPP's secretaries with a statement admitting to cliquish behavior harmful to the party and ordered them to sign it. Incredulous and indignant, Fadeyev accused Kirpotin of exceeding his authority. Kirpotin's reply shocked him. The text had been approved by Kaganovich. Fadeyev wrote to Kaganovich:

> The text of this statement is gratuitously insulting to me, a party member of long standing who has served it in faith and truth at the most difficult moments of the revolution. By signing this text, I, along with a number of other comrades, am supposed to confess that no less than eight years of my mature party life have been spent not on the battle for socialism in the literary sector of this struggle, not on the battle against the class enemy for the party and its Central Committee, but on cliquishness and intrigues of some kind, which I—along with other comrades, who did battle with me shoulder to shoulder—am supposed to acknowledge publicly so as to be ridiculed by all the enemies of proletarian literature. (*VKI*, 176–77)

This was perhaps the first of many times when Fadeyev's feelings of self-worth would be wounded, and eventually eroded, by a pattern of disdainful treatment by party superiors acting for Stalin.

Averbakh, Kirshon, Bela Illesh, Makaryev, and Sholokhov also lodged protests with the Central Committee. Stalin convened a commission to look into the matter; the protesters quickly admitted error and withdrew their protests.[145] Averbakh, however, would not give up. He presented a counterproposal: to preserve an autonomous, proletarian entity (i.e., RAPP) within the larger tent of the Writers' Union, and to recognize RAPP's literary theory as foundational to Soviet literature.[146] RAPP's vaunted dramatists, Kirshon and Aleksandr Afinogenov, whose plays were mainstays of theater repertoires, joined with Averbakh, as did Illesh and Bruno Jasieński, whose novel *I Burn Paris* (*Palę Paryż*) had forced him to flee France. Fadeyev, Yermilov, and Stavsky demurred. Stalin dealt with the insurrection by again appointing a commission of Politburo and Agitprop officials—Kaganovich, Pavel Postyshev, Stetsky, Gronsky, and Stalin himself—to meet with the recalcitrants.[147] The meeting is reported to have lasted six or seven hours, bespeaking Stalin's determination to have a unified cohort of cadres to carry out party directives.[148]

One result of this meeting was the appointment of Gronsky to chair the Writers' Union's *orgkomitet* (organizing committee). When Gorky's name came up, Stalin reportedly said, "We didn't know that Gorky was striving to be the chair of the Writers' Union. Even if we had known, we wouldn't have appointed him. Are you sure that as chair of the Writers' Union he will uphold the party line? I am not so sure. Let Gronsky be the chair."[149] Stalin wanted Gorky as the public face of the Writers' Union, but he was wary of putting him in charge of its orgkomitet. The orgkomitet would report to Agitprop, and for this what was needed was not Gorky but someone who understood the Writers' Union's function as a holding pen.

Gorky's decision to return to the Soviet Union was a protracted process that gathered momentum throughout 1932 but was not finalized until mid-1933. The liquidation of RAPP was Stalin's trump card. Gorky now seemingly had a historic opportunity to put his stamp on a new nation's emerging literature and inspire its founding generation of writers. Quite possibly he thought he would be able to jockey with Stalin as he had with Lenin in the Civil War years, when he held his nose and supported the Bolsheviks in exchange for Lenin's agreement to literary projects that would employ those old intelligentsia writers who had remained in the country. Gorky had traded with Lenin for publishing opportunities, and it had been a painful compromise. Had he been looking out only for himself, he would have been a moral bankrupt in his own eyes. But his compromise provided a livelihood to a whole cohort of writers facing starvation. And his public denunciation of the government's brutal suppression of the Kronshtadt sailors (and his unsuccessful attempt to save the poet Nikolai Gumilev from execution alongside them) was the polar opposite of Fadeyev's proud participation in suppressing that uprising. Amid the doubt and perhaps remorse, Gorky had something to feel proud of. So now it perhaps seemed that there was another such opportunity. He had successfully interceded with Stalin for writers persecuted by RAPP—Zamiatin, Pilniak, the expelled communist Vladimir Zazubrin. Why could he not now again be the independent advocate, advising the dictator on literary matters? He was bursting with ideas and had reason to believe Stalin would fund them.

In 1921, Gorky, the voice of independence and moral authority, was poles apart from Fadeyev, the committed young communist in the vanguard of the revolution. A decade later, both in thrall to Stalin, they were not so far apart. Both needed to feel sure of their own integrity. Repeatedly, they sought ways of resolving their doubts about the leader; each time they did so, they were also resolving their doubts about themselves.

The move from cultural revolution to the more moderate policy of national Bolshevism and literary inclusiveness concealed the quiet passing of laws that would enable the next round of terror. Just one month before the inaugural gala meeting of the Writers' Union's orgkomitet in September 1932, hosted by Gorky at his new Moscow mansion, the minimum age for the death penalty was lowered to twelve.[150] Stalin's steady climb toward absolute power also showed in Martemyan Riutin's ten-year sentence for circulating among party cadres his famous letter against Stalin. (The Politburo did not approve the death penalty, as Stalin wanted—that had to wait until 1937.)[151] In the meantime, however, writers were overjoyed at the unexpected reversal of literary power politics, which went beyond the destruction of RAPP, affirming respect for all writers and promising belonging.

Chapter Two

The *Orgkomitet*: Resetting the Alliance, Retraining Cadres

WRITERS GREETED THE April 23 resolution with whoops of "Christ is risen!" "The 1861 manifesto!" and "An end to slavery!" Klychkov sounded the general relief: "Finally the swallow of art can fly where it wants."[1] The fellow-traveler label was discarded, and nonparty writers were validated as important contributors to Soviet literature. Never was the hope for a real alliance with the party greater than in the interval between the time of the announcement of the Writers' Union until its first congress two years later.

Furious at the surge of joy that greeted their downfall, Averbakh and his shrunken band of loyalists assured one another that their detractors were class enemies using literature as their hiding place.[2] It was not these supposed "enemies of proletarian literature," however, but Stalin himself who would humble them in front of their former victims.

An orgkomitet was named and charged with organizing the Writers' Union's first congress, as well as determining the composition of the union membership, composing a charter, and holding plenums to unite writers around the party line and "consolidate communist forces of the literary front."[3] This latter injunction hinted at the infighting within RAPP and was paired with calls to eliminate "cliquishness." The congress was repeatedly delayed; the orgkomitet was in existence for well over two years before the Writers' Union was officially launched.

Initially, the orgkomitet was chaired by Gronsky. Kirpotin (head of Agitprop's literature section) joined him on the secretariat. Gorky was named honorary president.[4] Fadeyev was in the first group of twenty-four people named to the orgkomitet and although not listed as such, appears to have acted as Gronsky's deputy.[5] Notably, Fadeyev was also named to the presidium.[6] The orgkomitet included writers representing the major literary groups—VSSP (Vserossiisky Soiuz Sovetskikh Pisatelei), RAPP, the proletarian and collective-farm writers' organization Rossiiskaia Organizatsiia

47

Proletarsko-Kolkhoznykh Pisatelei, the military writers' association LOKAF, and Pereval.[7]

Gronsky was the son of a revolutionary and was himself jailed for revolutionary activity under Nicholas II and the Provisional Government before serving for a year in the Cheka.[8] He studied history, economics, and philosophy at the Institute of Red Professors, whose mission was to produce the next generation of party theoreticians. Pedigreed as one of the country's experts in party doctrine, he became editor in chief of *Izvestiia*, a post that included frequent conversation with Stalin on the newspaper's hotline. Over time he learned to divine Stalin's thinking and gained sufficient confidence to put forth, without prior approval, his own interpretations of events in public forums.[9]

Gronsky was Stalin's conduit to the writers' community. Little though he had in common with writers, he tried to develop relationships, visiting and socializing with them. So much alcohol was consumed at these visits that a highly displeased Stalin heard them described as drinking bouts. Gronsky justified himself by citing enormous job-related stress, claiming that he answered the telephone a hundred to two hundred times a day to deal with writers, most of whom were quick to take offense and spent their time in squabbles and intrigues. "I have to make sense of all this, be in the know about all this scurrying around like mice, and manage to have things my own way without spoiling my relations with each one of these writers and artists but yet not yielding to them in anything" (*ONI* 1:255). Even accounting for Gronsky's self-interest in defending himself to Stalin, his description is not out of bounds. Infighting was rife; and among ideology officials responsible for the Writers' Union over the next two decades, Gronsky alone attempted to associate with writers.

The regime remained eager to increase the number of proletarian writers, and the Writers' Union did not immediately spell the end of the factory literary circles. In the six months preceding its dissolution, RAPP had given 150 consultations to young writers. In the six months following, the newly established orgkomitet of the Writers' Union took credit for increasing the number of factory literary circles and oversaw 472 consultations.[10] The Leningrad Evening Workers' Literary University had been absorbed by the orgkomitet in June 1932 and given the broader mission of preparing writers from the working class, but it continued to train leaders for the factory circles. Gorky, arriving in the Soviet Union at the moment of the April 1932 resolution, immediately got to work. In the pages of *Literary Study* and in conversation with Stalin, he argued for an academic education through a new Literary Institute. He met vigorous opposition from the orgkomitet's former RAPPists. This struggle was reflected at the first orgkomitet plenum, which heard Lev Subotsky's report on the recruitment of factory writers, and in *Literaturnaia gazeta* (under the Onguardists' Selivanovsky), which argued against creating a new institute.[11] But on September 16, 1932, Stalin granted Gorky's wish in the form of a Central Committee resolution, a present of sorts marking his fortieth year in literature.[12] Most students were expected to come from the working class and peasantry. Most important for Gorky, however, was that the path to Writers' Union membership would be through the Literary Institute.

Launched in November 1933, the institute's curriculum reflected Gorky's dogged advocacy and represented a sharp change in literary policy. It began as a two-year correspondence course and soon added an in-residence program, eventually offering five years of study as well as a two-year graduate program.[13] The RAPP model of the peripatetic Soviet writer visiting construction sites and collective farms was dwarfed by a heavy dose of reading and study at the writing desk. By early 1935, the circlist journal *The Chisel* was defunct, and *Growth* was absorbed by *Literary Study*.[14] Gorky could feel that he was winning the war for literary standards.

Admission to the Writers' Union required publications of sufficient quality and stated allegiance to the Soviet government (*PVSSP*, 663). By the time of the first congress in August 1934, the selection committee, headed by Pavel Yudin, had admitted 2,200 out of some 4,000 applicants.[15] Achieving a desirable demographic composition of the total membership, however, posed difficulties, since many applicants with the right social profile were novices. This problem was solved by creating a candidate member category, which covered about 1,000 of the 2,200 members. While Yudin insisted that the candidate members' "first works show[ed] that they had stepped solidly onto the path of literary study," they had "not yet achieved artistic mastery" or "independent artistic significance" (*PVSSP*, 664). Membership in many of the provincial branches consisted of 90 percent beginners.[16] Twenty percent of members belonged to the party (25 percent if we include Komsomol members).[17] About 70 percent lived in the Russian republic; the rest were from Ukraine, Belorussia, Georgia, Armenia, Azerbaijan, and Turkmenistan.[18]

The early Writers' Union invites comparison with Germany's Reich Culture Chamber, which oversaw culture policy under the National Socialist Party (NSDAP), which at this time was ensuring its own control over the arts. Both cases were marked by turf wars, so Hitler and Stalin were both concerned to set up effective control structures.[19] The Reich Culture Chamber oversaw individual chambers for theater, film, visual arts, music, literature, broadcasting, and the press, similar to Stalin's creative unions.[20] The individual chambers reported to the Reich Culture Chamber, which stood between them and the Propaganda Ministry.[21] The Propaganda Ministry was the analogue of Agitprop (not the less-important Soviet Ministry of

Enlightenment). Hitler, however, delegated power in a way that Stalin never did, intervening only when difficulties arose.[22] In Joseph Goebbels he had a propaganda minister who was a trusted party journalist and held a doctorate in literature, besides being the Berlin regional leader (Gauleiter). Goebbels appointed the presidents of the seven individual chambers, and each of those presidents was empowered to appoint an administrative council as well as impose penalties on members. Goebbels could veto their decisions, usually without Hitler's involvement.[23] By contrast, Stalin made frequent personnel changes in the Writers' Union's early years, sometimes using officials as counterweights to one another. Both regimes made use of nonparty eminences, like Gorky and Richard Strauss, to lend legitimacy to the control structure.

The creative unions and the culture chambers alike were the sole means to reach a public and earn a living in the arts. Admissions criteria were similar—ideological profile (political past in the Soviet Union, "racial extraction" in Germany), publications, income, and recommendations. The NSDAP's name for its cultural policy, Gleichschaltung, indicated a drive to "even out" culture by ensuring that every organization would be Nazi or Nazi affiliated, would have NSDAP members on its board, and would rid itself of Jews, communists, and others of suspect ideological leanings.[24] Whereas in Nazi Germany applicants had to declare their race, often triggering automatic rejection (although initially this did not always happen),[25] the Writers' Union accepted applicants who had once belonged to rival political parties if they asserted their loyalty to the Soviet regime. The information in their application, however, could be used against them at any time; membership rolls and applications were shared with the security organs and members were subject to surveillance. Applicants also needed supporting letters from members, who by virtue of providing such a letter were implicitly vouching for the applicant's ideological trustworthiness. Unlike the creative unions, the culture chambers, especially after the first few years, had to be self-financing, a result of political horse-trading in which Goebbels lost out.[26] The chambers had to rely solely on membership fees, hampering their mission. Literature's agitprop function, by contrast, was considered too important not to be fully funded by the state.

While the Soviet and German administrative structures were similar, their artistic priorities differed markedly (although both regimes rejected avant-garde and experimental art forms). The Soviet vision of the individual's ability to transform himself lent itself to literature, where heroic biographies could be narrated. The NSDAP's emphasis on the body—clean, strong, Aryan—prioritized art and cinema. During its short time in power, the NSDAP never managed to establish universal literary censorship. It resorted to an ex post facto "List of Harmful and Undesirable Literature."[27]

If the Writers' Union's raison d'être was to control writers, the org-komitet's mission was to convince writers of the union's value to them—essentially, to market the Writers' Union to writers. The mere issuance of the April resolution gained Stalin the provisional trust of some of RAPP's victims.[28] Stalin then gave the Writers' Union shiny packaging and a brand name in the form of Gorky. His permanent return to the Soviet Union after eleven years abroad, and his high-profile meetings with Stalin, presented as the partnership of two friends, fanned hopes for a friendlier literary climate. The ornate dining room at Gorky's Moscow residence became the venue for the orgkomitet's celebratory meetings, a marketing gambit aimed at writers no less than at Gorky himself. Gorky occupied the stunning art nouveau mansion built in 1903 by the industrialist Stepan Riabushinsky in Moscow's Belgorod quarter. The orgkomitet's grand first plenum from October 29 to November 3, 1932, was prefaced by two gatherings in the preceding days.[29] At the first of these, Stalin briefed key communist writers. Six days later, he met with a larger group of communist writers along with nonparty writers considered "close" to communism. This lavish banquet ushered in the era of writers as Soviet elites. With Stalin and other Politburo members in attendance, the event had the flavor of other such gatherings where party leaders mixed with celebrity writers, actors, singers, and ballerinas. Top officials cultivated these relationships to enhance their own prestige; Stalin, for his part, played to the hilt the role of sage whose political expertise made him a penetrating literary critic.

By the time of the plenum three days later, a sizable group of writers had had contact with Stalin himself. That personal contact validated them (while also delivering a message of outside control). The plenum, too, with five hundred delegates in attendance, was a remarkable first.[30] In the fifteen years since the revolution there had been nothing remotely like it. Writers of every ideological and aesthetic stripe, from the deposed Averbakh to the skeptic Klychkov to the symbolist Andrei Bely, were invited to take the floor. In the six-day plenum, ninety of them did just that. They included nonparty writers who stood for the separation of art and politics, like the former Serapion Brothers, and communist writers who had opposed RAPP. For nonparty writers, it was a historic moment, a chance to be heard and perhaps even influence literary life. The presence of delegates from the non-Russian republics, as well as a handful of foreign visitors, furthered the sense of inclusiveness.

Not invited were Akhmatova, Mikhail Bulgakov, and Osip Mandelshtam. Marginalized in the marketplace even while understood to be the masters of the age, they were Soviet versions of Bourdieu's "economically dominated but symbolically dominant" French writers.[31] Flaubert and Baudelaire, committed to pure art, had no choice but to forfeit an audience, because unless money and readers were eliminated, there would be another master besides one's art.[32] For Soviet writers, we can modify Bourdieu's description to read "ideologically dominated but aesthetically dominant." As Flaubert and Baudelaire could "triumph over the bourgeois" only by eliminating him as a potential customer, Soviet writers could be free of state ideology only by writing for the desk drawer. This was why Eikhenbaum invoked the artist's need for a "second profession" to provide a living.[33] Of the old intelligentsia masters, Boris Pasternak was the exception who figured in Writers' Union debates—both as a speaker in the heat of argument and as a writer in the public eye.

A savvy marketer understands that the products we buy reflect our self-image. The Writers' Union was a product that appeared far superior to the previous product, RAPP, and it was one in which a nonparty writer could imagine room for self-expression. At the plenum, writers debated whether critics were in a position to teach writers (yes, said Vsevolod Ivanov; no, said Abram Efros—the subtext was that the major critics to date had been Averbakh and Yermilov); whether writers' visits to construction sites resulted in valuable literary works (Pilniak said no, while Gorky, who did not speak, certainly favored these missions); and whether writers should adopt a collective or an individual ethos. But these debates, so important to writers' self-definition in that moment, in fact were irrelevant beyond the moment, because they were ultimately decided by ideological officials, usually with input from Stalin himself.

As RAPP was swept away, so was its living man theory, and a replacement was readied. "Socialist realism" dates to late May 1932, around the time of the orgkomitet's first meeting.[34] Gronsky's memoirs date it to a strategy session with Stalin to prepare for the meeting with Averbakh's insurrectionists. Although Gronsky does not say so, Stalin needed a replacement for RAPP's "dialectical materialism in literature." Gronsky suggested "proletarian realism" or "communist realism." Stalin modified that to "socialist realism." This account rings true: a reference to proletarians or communists would undercut his strategic welcome to nonparty writers. Gronsky's version is not inconsistent with what we know from other sources.[35]

To Gronsky and Stalin, no profound theoretical exploration of socialist realism was needed; they were looking for a marketing phrase that would send a simple message and have wide appeal. Censorship would take care of the rest. At the first plenum, Gronsky defined socialist realism as simply as possible—it meant writing truthfully about Soviet life. Writing "truthfully" did not preclude exaggeration if that helped make the message clear. Gorky, however, was keen on fleshing out a theory of socialist realism. He wanted a debate over what it should be, and the orgkomitet's first two plenums, in October 1932 and February 1933, spent much time trying to define it.

Gorky's aesthetics were a near-perfect match for Stalin's literary policy, as Evgeny Dobrenko has shown.[36] His endorsement of the inspirational lie was the antithesis of the Onguardists' theory of an artist who sees through externals to the inner truth, forswearing any illusions, inspiring or not. For Gorky, who had once praised Turgenev for "the good message he conveyed by describing only what was good,"[37] literature had the right, even the obligation, to complete and perfect reality. He envisioned a Soviet literature modeled on the transformative beings of Slavic animistic paganism and the magical folktale, imbibed by Russians from childhood.[38] New plotlines, linking the magical with the real, would inspire readers to transform themselves. Socialist realism for Gorky was more than a literary prescription. It was a belief—in a person's ability to transform himself.[39]

Gorky's need to believe in a utopian vision explains his grumbling to Stalin that the press spent more time covering the country's defects than its successes.[40] Stalin agreed. From now on, he told Gorky, literature would cover over Soviet failures: "You need have no doubt about that."[41] Whatever Gorky thought of this rejoinder, his rejection of the unheroic explains his admonition to Mikhail Zoshchenko for not always choosing his material "properly" and giving too much weight to atypical details.[42] The backward mentality that Zoshchenko satirized belonged to the past. Gorky had shown them in his own early stories and novels, but he was wary of letting the negative portrait continue into the Soviet present.

In its appeal to ideals, Gorky's version of socialist realism helped legitimize the Writers' Union. Russia's educated elite had historically seen itself as responsible for the masses' intellectual development, so the idea that the Soviet population should receive culture from a literary elite was well grounded.[43] For no small number of writers, it was a matter of conscience to write, as Gorky said, about high ideals and sacrifice for the collective. Where writers since Aleksandr Radishchev had been the nation's conscience in the face of authorized oppression, now many writers still understood their role to be one of conscience.

There was, however, another side to the question of conscience. For Gorky, as for many communist writers, this moment of renewed alliance with the party was based on the extravagant assumption that Soviet literature would be the first ever not to have to play the role of moral opposition. The corollary assumption was that writers, instead of themselves serving as the nation's conscience, would now place their moral authority in the service of a moral party. Writers with misgivings about censorship might swallow their doubts when they weighed them against a desire to create beneficial literary works. In this sense, Gorky's attitude was characteristic of innumerable other writers of lesser influence and significance.

Gorky himself enjoyed special treatment from the censorship when

Stalin was wooing him. He had felt censorship's sting at the hands of Lenin, when his newspaper *The New Life* (*Novaia zhizn*) was shut down and his play *The Workaholic Slovotekov* (*Rabotiaga Slovotekov*), a satirical critique of the government, was blocked.[44] Soon afterward, he left Russia at Lenin's insistence. By 1930, he bowed to pragmatism, rewriting the memoir of Lenin he had drafted six years earlier to eliminate praise of Trotsky and other things incompatible with the general line.[45] But Stalin's censorship allowed Gorky more than it did other writers. Stetsky, the head of Agitprop, permitted inclusion of two pieces by Nikolai Erdman and Vladimir Mass, "A Session on Laughter" ("Zasedanie o smekhe") and "The Law of Gravity" ("Zakon tiagoteniia"), in Gorky's almanac, *Year 16* (*God 16*), so as not to raise Gorky's suspicions on his return to Russia just as the volume was coming out.[46] Even as Stetsky stroked Gorky with this move, Fadeyev asserted his editorial authority against Gorky's, removing three stories by Isaac Babel from the almanac.[47] Gorky was experiencing censorship lite, accorded to him alone. The rest of the old intelligentsia would take the brunt of censorship.[48]

Socialist realism as defined by Gronsky and Gorky arguably matched the mass reader's stated preferences for optimism, a likable hero, and a vision of a happy future.[49] Urban workers wanted straightforward, unambiguous stories and plays that captured their experience of Soviet life, and theatergoers avoided stagings of Pushkin, Lermontov, Dostoevsky, and Tchaikovsky, as well as avant-garde productions by directors like Vsevolod Meyerhold or Yevgeny Vakhtangov.[50] Beyond this, however, the discussion of socialist realism was academic. Where RAPP had had at least tacit permission from the party to make its own literary policy, that prerogative was now conclusively taken away. Literary policy was not made in the Writers' Union. The orgkomitet was the enforcer of policy handed down from above, and this would be the model for the Writers' Union throughout its existence. The two major literary decisions of 1932–34 were made by Stalin in consultation with the Politburo or with Gronsky. These were the promulgation of socialist realism as the authoritative literary method and the decision (later reversed) to prioritize drama over the novel. A Politburo resolution of October 23, 1932, on theater, taken just before the orgkomitet's first plenum, showed that decision making took place elsewhere and that the plenum should be regarded as an impotent gabfest. The resolution mandated constant staging of the most ideologically desirable plays and established a five-man theater directorate that included no one with any expertise in theater or literature.[51] Stalin recognized that culture policy had to be guided by people's entertainment habits, and going out to a show was a popular pastime. He presented the resolution to the grand preplenum meeting as a fait accompli. Gronsky explained it at the plenum: "You," he told the assembly, "proceed from the supposition that we are a literate people, and if we take up a book, we read it to the end. But I proceed from the knowledge of the workers and peasants, from their opportunities and capabilities of reading a book cover to cover."

Gronsky then described a meeting with ten young writers, three of whom had never heard of Percy Bysshe Shelley.

> So what do you want? Do you think everyone reads the works of our writers from beginning to end? Don't flatter yourselves, comrades. But a play can be seen by a highly literate person as well as by an illiterate person. Both of them will understand the play . . . The theater is the most reliable, truest means of reeducating our class. (*SLNE*, 11)

The imposition of theory is the front line of censorship, and so it was with Gorky's exhortation to an inspirational socialist realism. At the plenum, Kirpotin unrolled a long and depressing list of prohibitions. Stop portraying the "dying, old individualist world" (Zarudin's *Thirty Nights in a Vineyard* [*Tridtsat nochei na vinogradnike*]). Avoid ahistoricity (Tynianov's portrayal of Peter the Great in *The Wax Figure* [*Voskovaia persona*]; Ilya Selvinsky's play *Pao-Pao*). Renounce allegory (Sergei Sergeyev-Tsensky's "Condemned to Die" ["Obrechennye na gibel]," "An Old Sledge Runner" ["Staryi poloz]," and "The Peacock" ["Pavlin"]) (*SLNE*, 29–30). Kirpotin said simply that allegory had little artistic worth, but presumably its Aesopian potential was a real issue.

Kirpotin praised a mix of works by communist and noncommunist writers as models to follow.[52] This attempt at inclusiveness drew an objection from Pilniak, who argued that literary models were really ideological prescriptions, and that following models meant forfeiting originality; what made Pushkin good was that he was not Lermontov (*SLNE*, 187). Vera Inber drew appreciative laughter when she expressed relief on hearing that artistry outweighed ideology, archly adding, "We didn't know that before" (*SLNE*, 156). Inber's relief was unfounded. When Lunacharsky wanted to give the keynote speech at the orgkomitet's second plenum, Stalin agreed, but on condition that Gronsky review and correct his draft. Gronsky, perhaps sensing in this a test, found an opportune moment to show the draft to Stalin, who disliked it and warned Gronsky not to let Lunacharsky praise "all manner of futurists."[53]

The discussions of socialist realism provoked a new wave of infighting among communist writers. The obvious loser was the Pereverzev school. With its view of class origin as the sole determinant of trustworthiness, it had to be discredited if the Writers' Union was declared open to all loyal Soviet writers regardless of class origin. But even as the Pereverzevites (and Litfront) were brought low, Kirpotin implicitly validated their critique of RAPP's living man theory, and he defined *Birth of a Hero* as "subjective idealism" and not socialist realist (*SLNE*, 29). Elena Usievich, one of the Onguardists' rivals now bidding for greater authority, was harsher, equating their "psychologism" with idealism and accusing them of citing Georgy Plekhanov, Bukharin, Abram Deborin, "and even Trotsky."[54] Fadeyev was faulted in the press for "Flaubertian objectivity" incompatible with party-mindedness (*partiinost*).[55]

The living man theory's emphasis on psychological and emotional complexity was denied a place in socialist realism. Yet the theory was more appropriate to the rhetoric of inclusion than to that of class struggle. That it prevailed during the cultural revolution and was discredited under national Bolshevism again shows that what mattered was less the theory than the personal qualities and usefulness of particular cadres.

The living man theory, with its emphasis on overcoming psychological survivals of the past, had reflected the Onguardists' own autobiography as middle-class sons who adopted a Bolshevik identity. Post-RAPP, a new chapter in that autobiography had to be written. Its overt topic was self-correction through self-criticism; its subtext was psychological subservience to Authority. Stalin's mantle of liberalism contained within its folds the humbling of the Onguardists, and he used the preplenum meeting with party writers for that purpose. Adopting the stance of a wise father sternly pointing out to his sons the mess they had made, he used the voice of reason to chastise them in front of their rivals.

> After all, what have you done? You promoted and sang the praises of your own, promoted them at times excessively and when they did not deserve it, you hushed up and persecuted writers who did not belong to your group, and in doing so you alienated them instead of attracting them to your organization and assisting their growth. What did you do, for example, with [the communist writer Georgy] Nikiforov? Why, you stripped him bare and smeared him with mud. Yes, yes, you smeared him with mud. And he is not a bad writer. And here you went and trampled him in the mud.
>
> Who needs this? The party doesn't need it . . . On the other hand, right next to you was an ever-expanding sea of nonparty writers, whom no one was guiding, whom no one was helping, who were homeless. And the party had put you in a position that obliged you not only to gather literary forces but also to guide the whole mass of writers. (*ONI* 1:225)

Stalin knew how to speak both in the voice of the party and in that of the nonparty intelligentsia he sought to win over. He elevated the nonparty writers RAPP had treated so mercilessly by comparing them with his earlier self:

> There was a time when I, too, was nonparty, did not know the rules of dialectical materialism, and did not understand many things. My senior comrades did

not rebuff me for this but taught me how to master the dialectical method. I also did not master it all at once. But you approached nonparty writers in these matters with impatience and an utter lack of skill. (*ONI* 1:231)

This analysis contained a heavy dose of disingenuity. Certainly in RAPP's final months Averbakh had led the Onguardists to flout party directives. But RAPP's harassment politics during the cultural revolution had mirrored the party's own. Stalin covered this over with a combination of four arguments. History had progressed beyond the stage when RAPP had been historically necessary; RAPP had impeded progress toward socialism by becoming "cliquish"; a variety of literary forms should flourish; "literary mastery" could be learned even from counterrevolutionary writers. The first point was a standard dialectical argument, which Stalin often invoked as if it retrojected incrimination. The second point was uncontestably true, but the party leadership already knew it when it issued and then reaffirmed its 1928 resolution buttressing RAPP. The third point was one of those vague statements that was invoked and revoked depending on the occasion; and to act on the fourth point would have been suicide.

Embedded in Stalin's reprimand of the Onguardists, however, was tacit reassurance that they remained the elite cadres whose political understanding and sophistication elevated them above even the best writers:

A segment of writers, like Pilniak, understood our resolution to mean that, hey, all the fetters have been removed and we have permission for everything. We know that this segment of writers does not understand everything that is happening in the country where socialism is being built; it is still difficult for them to understand this; they are turning toward the side of the working class slowly; but they are turning. The thing to do was to help them when it was time, and to patiently help them remake themselves. And you were impatient with them. (*ONI* 1:227)

Stalin was not getting rid of his cadres; he was retraining them. At the plenum a few days later, Gronsky explained that "to give the comrades the opportunity to correct their errors" and make their transition to a unified Soviet literature easier for them, Averbakh, Yermilov, and Makaryev would get seats on the orgkomitet (*SLNE*, 8).

RAPP's adversaries from the Communist Academy and Litfront, wanting to make sure the Onguardists would have no role in running the Writers' Union, devised their own slogans aimed at them: "Hands off the Writers' Union" and "Finish off the RAPP leadership."[56] But for Stalin, getting rid of RAPP did not mean that the RAPP leaders could no longer serve as leading cadres. In shifting to national Bolshevism and the "big tent" concept, Stalin fully intended still to rely on his cohort of literary cadres. The conditions, however, went beyond rededicating themselves to party-mindedness and adopting the new general line. They also had to repudiate their past behavior and affirm the party's right to reprimand or shame them. The myth of self-criticism was that it was an honored Bolshevik tradition, and that owning up to one's errors was a sign of Bolshevik maturity. The reality was that self-criticism was meant to erode the self. The party did its utmost to control not only what you wrote but also who you were.

Fadeyev, although spurning Averbakh's rebellion, waited as long as possible to break with him definitively.[57] He did it on the eve of the first plenum, staking out his position in a series of articles in *Literaturnaia gazeta* under the rubric *The Old and the New (Staroe i novoe)*.[58] Here and at the plenum, he parroted Stalin's arguments, much as he had imprinted himself with Stalin's language in branding Platonov a kulak agent. That experience surely resonated with him now, but this time his conscience could be at ease: he was not maligning anyone, except perhaps himself. And he was not even maligning himself. Victory in the class struggle meant RAPP's task was completed; life's new challenges would be met with new "organizational forms." Stalin's logic was a balm—it made his capitulation not an act of opportunism or fear but of principle, or at least a correct understanding of historical progress.

This historical-philosophical argument masked less-salubrious motivations for obeisance to Stalin. There was fear; there was the memory of his double gaffe in publishing Platonov. But he could plausibly deny the fear by finding other justifications for his choice. This was the trap of the dialectic. Stalin used it time and again to manipulate susceptible cadres.

The fallacy of such ex post facto judgment was pointed out at the first plenum by Marietta Shaginian, author of the popular novel and film *Mess-Mend*. She protested against book reviews that demanded the inclusion of shock workers in plots that predated the shock-worker movement (*SLNE*, 242). It was Stalin who modeled this tactic. Every shift in the party line created a new set of "mistakes" that were applied retroactively. Fadeyev nearly a decade later had learned to do the same, writing, "For Marxism-Leninism, what is 'the people's' [*narodny*] in a writer is whatever serves the interests of the laborers, whatever moves them forward" (*VKI*, 440). With this credo, Fadeyev attacked his opponents and set himself up to accept a shifting morality and retroactive blame.

Fadeyev's internalization of Stalin's argument points to a difference in the Soviet and Nazi approaches to propaganda. Goebbels thought propaganda should be inconspicuous. In his words, "the best propaganda is that which . . . works invisibly, penetrates the whole of life without the public having any knowledge of the propagandistic initiative."[59] Goebbels's view matched Hitler's belief, following Georges Sorel and Gustave Le Bon, that the primary motors of human behavior were to be found in irrationality.[60] Stalin, however, was not shy about promulgating explicit propaganda statements dressed up as logic. At the plenum, Fadeyev articulated a formula that would save him this time but in the long run would prove the undoing of his unified self. "If we [the Onguardists] claimed to lead proletarian literature forward, that is a very great claim. We were not up to the task. Life moves forward and was taking the next step, and in spite of our great claims, we did not take that step forward, so clearly sooner or later life would cast us aside" (*SLNE*, 125). Fadeyev's every "step forward" would be defined by Stalin, and each "step" would invalidate his previous actions.

The comfort of rational argument was in uneasy dialogue with Stalin's psychological maneuvers. Soon after the resolution dissolving RAPP, Yagoda invited Fadeyev to a gathering at his dacha. Fadeyev made excuses, but Yagoda insisted: Stalin would be there, too. Stalin walked up to Averbakh and Fadeyev: "Why are you two quarreling? Make up." Yagoda moved into place behind Averbakh; Stalin stood behind Fadeyev and repeated: "Make up." Averbakh extended his hand; Fadeyev had no choice but to take it. "Now," Stalin commanded, "kiss." Yagoda pushed Averbakh toward Fadeyev, and the two men kissed. That done, Stalin exclaimed, "You are a weak man, Fadeyev!"[61]

Behind Stalin's self-evident remark was its ironic corollary: while his cadres were trying to fashion themselves as fearless Bolsheviks, Stalin sometimes chose them for their weaknesses. The moment when Fadeyev obeyed Stalin's command to kiss Averbakh could well have been the moment when he made it onto the short list of candidates to head the Writers' Union. Fadeyev alone among the RAPP leaders publicly accepted RAPP's demise.[62] But choosing party duty, he still needed to feel that he was his own man and maintain his self-image as an independent fighting communist. Insisting on his right to his own opinion, he made a point of disagreeing with the new policy of allowing old intelligentsia writers who had written "counterrevolutionary" works to become Writers' Union members.[63] Already he had relinquished his independence; but several recent successes may have prevented him from fully realizing this. *The Rout* was reissued, and he received a contract for a new installment of *The Last of the Udegs*.

Fadeyev's, Yermilov's, and Libedinsky's plenum speeches offered self-criticism that Gronsky, in the plenum's concluding address, pronounced satisfactory (*SLNE*, 124–29, 165–69, 180–85). Yermilov, thumping himself on the chest for emphasis, repudiated the "ally or enemy" slogan and dutifully acknowledged RAPP's (not his own) sins (*SLNE*, 186). We criticized works for what they didn't contain, said Yermilov, but we should have criticized them only for what they did contain. He took issue, however, with Fadeyev, who had divided literary works into those that were "artistic" and those that were not: "We must break the habit of hanging labels on works, you have to prove what you are saying." This remark elicited applause (surely aimed at Yermilov's own practice of labeling without proving); however, it is noteworthy that Yermilov demonstrated his newfound objectivity by finding flaws in Fadeyev rather than in himself (*SLNE*, 180–85).

While Yermilov acknowledged cliquishness and managed a show of humility before the party, invoking it as his teacher and guide, he could not resist putting down his communist opponents.

> The logic of cliquishness sometimes prevented us from seeing the correct things that, along with many incorrect things, were written about us by our opponents in the war of cliques. I am talking about myself in particular—I give my promise to Comrade Usievich, since she has written about my literary works more than anyone else, right now . . . that I will reread her articles about my works and distinguish what is true from the very great amount that is untrue and cliquish, in what she said about my works. (*SLNE*, 184)

The Writers' Union herded writers into the fold, but it failed to stop infighting among cadres. For the next eight years, Usievich and Yermilov continued to wrestle each other for the mantle of chief literary critic. Usievich won the first round, gaining a spot the following June on the staff of the brand-new journal *Literary Critic*, edited by Yudin.

Acknowledging their errors and accepting the party as their confessor, Fadeyev and Yermilov accepted a new self-definition. A Bolshevik's self-assessment was necessarily the same as the party's assessment of him.[64] "Soviet practices of self," to use Aleksandr Etkind's phrase, reflected the shame culture's stated values at a given moment.[65] Maintaining their identity as honor-group members depended on accepting the party's judgment of them.[66] If they had accepted this axiom long ago, until now they had had to do so only in theory. Only now were they publicly demeaned by their own party. They hoped their display of communist humility and party discipline would earn them important posts in the new union, and it did. We next see Yermilov as the overworked editor of *Red Virgin Soil*; but in 1946, when an attack dog was required, he landed the top job at the literary gold standard, *Literaturnaia gazeta*. Fadeyev would eventually lead the Writers' Union. But as freely acting individuals, they were already crushed. The seat of conscience was now outside themselves.

Averbakh and Kirshon behaved differently. Kirshon counterbalanced his self-criticism with a challenge: "To help the orgkomitet in its continuing work, we will not refuse to criticize it" (*SLNE*, 197). Averbakh barely squeezed out a grudging acknowledgment of pluralism: Everyone at the plenum, he said, "even" Bely and Prishvin, stood "on the same side of the barricades" (116). He admitted fault for scolding nonparty writers but insisted that RAPP had had "no goals other than those dictated by party interests" (118). He then showed how imperfectly he had learned his lesson: "If [literary] criticism thinks a work is hostile, then it is obliged to say so without being afraid: if need be, one must strike this or that writer, just not with a club in one's hands" (122). After a bit of perfunctory self-criticism, he adopted the tone of a savant explaining the party resolution. His self-importance displeased Gronsky, who interrupted and tried to redirect him toward self-criticism: "Tell us, is the slogan, 'Write according to the method of dialectical materialism' right or wrong?" (120). When Mikhail Kozakov blamed Averbakh for branding Yury Tynianov and Konstantin Fedin class enemies, Averbakh shot back that Tynianov's "The Wax Figure" and Fedin's "Svaaker" were "reactionary" (122).

Gronsky's mission was to unite. As editor of *Novy mir*, he was publishing Mandelshtam, Pasternak, Babel, and other major literary talents whom Averbakh and Yermilov had tried to disgrace. Taking a leaf from Stalin's playbook, he delivered his opening speech in the tone of a parent admonishing squabbling siblings. But once the major addresses were over, the plenum had the flavor of a RAPP-bashing party. Notations of applause in the published transcript suggest that the delegates fell into two factions, with the RAPP contingent applauding one another and everyone else applauding speakers who took RAPP down.

Although Stalin's primary motive in shaming RAPP's leaders was to cut them down to size, their public shaming also made an effective marketing ploy to other writers, who got the satisfaction of seeing their tormenters brought low. They took the opportunity to answer half a dozen years of public insults and offer their own definition of the Onguardists (Prishvin called them barnacles on the ship of literature) (*SLNE*, 66).

At the plenum, nonparty writers took back control of their own self-definition. Their speeches can be read as nonparty alternatives to the genre of communist autobiography. In this, the plenum was a unique public moment. Gronsky signaled an openness to such redefinitions in his opening address. To an audience that certainly recalled Fadeyev's branding of Platonov as a "kulak agent," Gronsky offered reassurance. While warning that "we deal harshly with class enemies," Gronsky cautioned against calling someone a class enemy unless it was true and not a case of someone having made a mistake.[67] (It did not matter that Fadeyev's article had been outlined by Stalin. Fadeyev was the one holding the bag.) Acknowledging that the intelligentsia writers had "greater culture and knowledge than we do" and that "we must value that," Gronsky gave nonparty writers a positive building block for their autobiography (*SLNE*, 7).

They seized the opening. Their first step had to be disavowing the identities that RAPP had foisted on them, so they repeatedly insisted that they were not enemies (*SLNE*, 66, 135). They took issue with Gronsky's phrase "old writers," a commonly used term that referred as much to the political and ideological sympathies of writers as to the generation gap (*SLNE*, 66). They pleaded to be read and understood rather than prematurely labeled (*SLNE*, 135, 187).

Like most nonparty delegates, Pilniak avowed his Soviet credentials:

> I want to create and grow. I consider myself a writer of the revolution, a writer of my country and a person who is a citizen of his country, and a revolutionary, and a laborer at the bottom layer of Soviet revolutionary literature. I have shown this by my fifteen years of literary work. I have shown it by all my mistakes, which I made because I had a single stimulus: to be honest toward myself, to be honest toward the revolution, and I never forgot a very simple thing, comrades; namely, that my connection to the revolution is not accidental. I have traveled all over the entire northern hemisphere. I know what is done and how it is done all over the globe. I could have remained in any part of the world and done the same work as here. I did not do that, because my mind, my heart, and my knowledge tell me that the future of humanity, justice for humanity, exists only here at home. (*SLNE*, 187)

In hindsight, the big story of the plenum was not its indulgence toward nonparty writers—for this did not last—but the performance of RAPP's leaders. Stalin wanted to wrest public penance from each of them, establishing their subjugation to the party and the erasure of their own independent agency. Gronsky's concluding speech praised Fadeyev, Yermilov, and Libedinsky for renouncing cliquishness and expressed displeasure with Averbakh, Makaryev, and Kirshon, who had "left themselves room to maneuver" (*SLNE*, 257). When we consider the events of the plenum as a whole—the speeches of the Onguardists; Gronsky's public approval of Fadeyev and Yermilov; the decision to seat some of the Onguardists on the orgkomitet and Gronsky's admonition to those seeking the Onguardists' total disgrace; and when we further recall that for sixteen of the twenty-one remaining years of Stalin's life the Writers' Union was led by Stavsky or Fadeyev—the major purpose of the plenum becomes clear. Stalin was using it to redirect and redefine his literary cadres.

The plenum speakers who best articulated future literary policy turned out to be Averbakh, who was on the road to the Gulag, and Usievich, who would ultimately be vanquished by Yermilov. Usievich, declaring that literary critics (she had herself in mind) deserved to stand above writers and direct them, essentially described the future of literary criticism, which would continue to rely on shaming (*SLNE*, 147). Averbakh, quoting Marx, suggested replacing the idea of the "writer" with "a person who writes" (*SLNE*, 119)—that is to say, effacing individual subjectivity as the creative self moves into alignment with Bolshevik "objectivity." Averbakh's idea diminished the writer and modified the intelligentsia code of the writer as the nation's conscience. His speech prefigured Andrei Zhdanov's characterization of writers as "engineers of human souls" at the first congress two years later—the most famous example of Stalin's knack for hijacking and repurposing memorable phrases. In an age when industrial development went hand in hand with building a new society, engineering was a widespread metaphor. Yury Olesha, in a story published in *Izvestiia* in 1929, had imagined the writer as an "engineer of human material," and Sergei Tretyakov had envisioned "workers in the arts" as "psycho-engineers."[68] If Olesha's usage suggests the writer's power, and Tretyakov's belies a risky overexuberance, Stalin's reveals disregard for humanity. Obsolete conscience yielded to engineered consciousness.

Averbakh's declaration that art would be defined by the working class's preferences in fact became the presumptive standard for judging literature. The artist's individuality, which nonparty writers were celebrating at the plenum, was incompatible with party-minded art. The elite status conferred on writers was less a validation of creative individuality than of creative agitprop. Zhdanov's speech at the First Writers' Congress would answer Eikhenbaum-Bourdieu on "how to be a writer:" Two thousand members of the Writers' Union would all be at work shaping readers into party-minded citizens. It did not matter that Averbakh and Usievich offered the prescriptions that Stalin would actually use. Nor was the problem Averbakh's contempt toward writers; the scorn he heaped upon them was taken up by *Literaturnaia gazeta* after it passed to the control of the Writers' Union. The problem was his insubordination. He would have to be killed.

Alone among Soviet writers, Anna Akhmatova did not apply for Writers' Union membership.[69] For her and a small number of others who made their peace with outsider status, literary selfhood did not hinge so critically on belonging. One such literary outsider, however, did attend the plenum. This was the peasant writer and self-described "literary hermit and splinter" Klychkov. Delighted to finally be able to speak freely, he insisted on the writer's need to be solitary. He paid no lip service to the socialist future. He stated his views in terms antithetical to even the most liberal interpretation of the regime's requirements. "An artist by nature is the result of the strictest self-limitation . . . he is the product of limitation, the complete opposite of that bad universality bred by Averbakh and his colleagues" (*SLNE*, 159). No one applauded his speech. Several speakers repudiated it; Kirshon even implied that Klychkov should be shot.[70]

The month preceding the April 1932 resolution saw the arrests of a group of writers with one foot in RAPP and the other in a hidden literary counterculture. At their forefront was Nikolai Anov, a proletarian writer who had attracted the favorable notice of Gorky. A veteran of World War I and the Civil War on the Bolshevik side, Anov was bitterly critical of Stalin. By the late 1920s, he was fairly well known, having published three novels; one of them was banned after publication and its pages torn out of the journal where it had appeared. The main character of his novel *Dust* (*Pyl'*) is a White who becomes mentor to two youths. According to his interrogation record, Anov told his investigator that to get *Dust* published, he had the youths turn against their mentor and finally capture him, not, however, for his anticommunist beliefs—rather for incitement to murder. The title, according to the OGPU (political police) record, was an ironic reference to people whom the Soviet regime regarded as dust to be swept away (*RT*, 88).

Exiled from Leningrad to Novosibirsk in 1924, Anov remained there following his three-year term, forming Pamir, a group of Siberian writers opposed to collectivization (Anov himself was an ethnic Russian from Kazakhstan). Its other members were Ivan Ababkov, Ivan Yeroshin, Sergei Markov, Leonid Martynov, and Nikolai Feoktistov. In 1929 the group disbanded under pressure from Averbakh, Fadeyev, and Stavsky, who presumably did not realize the extent of Pamir's discontent but found the group "reactionary." Anov was nonetheless put in charge of RAPP's Novosibirsk office. Like most of the Pamir writers, Anov moved to Moscow later that year, where he got work as an editor at *Red Virgin Soil*. They soon regrouped as the Siberian Brigade, joined by Pavel Vasilyev, Yevgeny Zabelin, Lev Chernomortsev, and a few others.

Vasilyev's 1932 interrogation record states that Anov had mockingly referred to Stalin's rules for journals, posted on the wall of the editorial office of *Red Virgin Soil*, as the Six Commandments brought to the people by the new Moses. At Anov's suggestion, Vasilyev put the "commandments" into rhymed hexameter. Anov also hatched a plan to publish bogus "translations" from the Soviet national literatures in *Red Virgin Soil* (*RT*, 76–77). Whether or not these statements are true, the Six Commandments story recalls Stalin's famous remark to his son that "the people need a God" and lays bare (as Shklovsky might have said) Stalin's device.

Anov, Markov, Martynov and Zabelin were sentenced to three years' exile in June 1932. Just then, Riutin was circulating his famous letter against Stalin; his arrest on September 23 came five months to the day after the April 23 resolution on literature. Vasilyev and Chernomortsev were also arrested, but quickly freed. Vasilyev continued to be an object of suspicion. Gorky was scandalized by his public fistfights and, in the months before the First Writers' Congress, decried his "hooliganism" as just one short step away from fascism. Vasilyev apologized to Gorky in print and forswore hooliganism. Gorky accepted the apology but continued to sound the alarm of fascism, connecting it to personal behavior and to the work of the peasant poets who had grouped around Sergei Esenin, including Vasilyev, Kliuev, and Klychkov.

Gorky's phrase was pressed into service a year later in an open letter from twenty writers, declaring that Vasilyev had "long since crossed over from hooliganism to fascism" (he had gotten into a fistfight with Jack Althausen in the House of Writers' dining room).[71] Vasilyev was sentenced to a year and a half in a labor camp. From there he wrote to Gorky, asking for his help in commuting his sentence to exile so that he could write.[72]

Vasilyev obtained leniency thanks to the intervention of his brother-in-law Gronsky. But Gronsky's own biography was soon to be rewritten. Stalin removed him from the orgkomitet in July 1933. Gronsky's risky protection of Vasilyev became toxic once Vasilyev's secret epigram against Stalin came to light;[73] and if, as some believe, Gronsky revealed Stalin's behind-the-scenes authorship of socialist realism, Stalin may have had an added reason to be displeased. In any case, this demotion was Gronsky's first step toward the Gulag.

The orgkomitet chairmanship now belonged to Gorky. Gorky instead of Gronsky seemed a sign that the promise of the first orgkomitet plenum was being fulfilled, and with the oppositionists restored to political life, 1933 was a good year for writers to overcome lingering doubts. Grigory Zinovyev and Kamenev had returned from exile in May. The rise of Hitler and fascism injected new energy into Bolshevism; discontents seemed minor compared with this new threat. Zinovyev and Kamenev called for oppositionists to close ranks behind Stalin. Nonparty intellectuals, too, found it easier to choose Stalin as the lesser of two evils, especially given his magnanimity toward his opponents.

To counterbalance Gorky on the orgkomitet, Stalin added Yudin and Stavsky, both of whom Gorky despised.[74] Having hemmed him in, Stalin could make good use of Gorky in his new role. The energetic Gorky bombarded writers with excursions so that they could "study life." Organized trips to factories, construction sites, collective farms, and the non-Russian republics had already been occurring during the first five-year plan under RAPP's sponsorship. Still, Gorky's belief in the rehabilitative properties of labor camps prompted his first undertaking—sending writers to the White Sea–Baltic Canal. Certainly Gorky, at some level, realized the abuses that were taking place. Benedikt Sarnov has argued that Gorky's understanding of Stalin is clear from the unique linguistic register he adopted when writing to Stalin, one that had nothing in common with his other writing.[75] This is not in dispute. The point is that he was in possession of an argument that could salve his conscience.

Prodded by Gorky, about one hundred twenty writers visited the canal. This excursion was yet another marketing campaign, this time less to writers than to the reading public. Most of the writers may have understood that they were being shown a Potemkin village, but they contributed to a volume of thirty-six "inspirational" stories lauding the canal's twin successes in socialist construction and human rehabilitation. It was published in a print run of about one hundred fourteen thousand copies, and the canal built by worn-out, undernourished prisoners bashing pickaxes into the permafrost assumed its place in the Gorky-inspired pantheon of Soviet milestones, a sequel to *Our Achievements* and his other collective marketing projects.[76]

The White Sea Canal volume was a variation on Gorky's favored collaborations among writers, historians, and proletarians. This time, writers' collaborators were prisoners along with the OGPU camp commandant, Semyon Firin, who coedited the volume with Gorky and Averbakh.[77] The traveling writers' "brigade" received copious food and drink in which to drown their distress.[78] They spent nearly all their time on the ship that took them through the canal, getting little opportunity to talk to prisoners, most of whom were gone now that the canal was completed.[79] Still, some writers, like Dmitry Mirsky, who, having returned to the Soviet Union from Britain the year before, found himself roped into this unsavory excursion, and the nonparty Valentin Katayev, asked pointed questions of Firin. How had it been possible to construct the canal so cheaply? Wasn't it because of free labor? Why was the project kept secret for two years? Why were there no cemeteries?[80]

A countergenre showing the dark side of the canal also began to take shape. Prishvin, who, out of an abiding interest in the Russian north, asked to join the writers' brigade but was refused, made the trip on his own two years later. Only two small excerpts from the novel he wrote, *The Tsar's Road (Osudareva doroga)*, were published. The rest of it had to wait until 1957. Nikolai Kliuev's narrative poem *Ruin (Razrukha)* was confiscated by the security police on his arrest in February 1934.

Another who asked to be included in the White Sea trip was Platonov. In spite of the reassuring language at the orgkomitet plenum, Fadeyev's branding of him as a kulak agent had acquired a permanence, and Platonov remained unable to recover his literary career, even though Fadeyev himself now referred to "For Future Use" in far milder terms (it "distorted the collective-farm movement" and its jocular tone was inadmissible for a subject so important).[81] Platonov saw the canal trip as a ticket to literary acceptance and wrote to Gorky asking to join it.[82] Meanwhile he submitted his play *High Tension* for publication in the almanac *Year 16*. The referees were Gorky, Yermilov, and Fadeyev. Gorky and Yermilov recommended publication. Fadeyev had reservations but thought the play merited reworking

(*APVS*, 316). Despite multiple revisions, however, the play did not appear. Nor was Platonov permitted to join the canal trip. It seems reasonable to conclude that Stalin had no intention of letting Platonov back into literature.

While the maverick proletarian Platonov was refused, space was made for the young railway worker and novice writer Avdeyenko, who had little education or critical aptitude. By class and education, he stood apart from ·most of his traveling companions. A miner's son, Avdeyenko had grown up a *besprizornik* (homeless orphan) in the Donbass. As a young man during the first five-year plan, he worked as a miner in the Donbass and then took part in the building of Magnitogorsk, in the mines and as an assistant train engineer. He burst onto the literary scene at the age of twenty-five in 1933 with his novel *I Love* (*Ia liubliu*), based on his years as a *bezprizornik* and his discovery of Bolshevism. Gorky was in raptures. Avdeyenko embodied the dream of creating a cadre of proletarian writers.

Mirsky's and Katayev's probing questions to Firin were a kind of schooling for this intellectually underequipped former *bezprizornik*. He found he had troubling questions of his own. One of the prisoners they encountered was the futurist poet and popular lyricist Sergei Alymov. Why had Alymov been sentenced to a labor camp? The question went unanswered.[83]

Including Avdeyenko in a brigade with Mirsky and Katayev had been a mistake; so two years later a similar visit was arranged for him, this time to the Moscow-Volga Canal, and without any skeptical traveling companions.

The first link in the chain bringing Avdeyenko to the Moscow-Volga Canal was Mekhlis, head of Agitprop's press section and editor in chief of *Pravda*. Mekhlis approached Avdeyenko with exciting news—he had arranged for Avdeyenko to visit the canal. Avdeyenko balked; Mekhlis impressed upon him that it was unthinkable to refuse such an honor. Stalin and the Central Committee considered this canal the centerpiece of the second five-year plan and a battle for people's souls. Avdeyenko countered by citing his "umbilical" ties to the Urals and his commitments in Magnitogorsk. "But who's asking you to leave the Urals? It's just a leave of absence. I'll call Kabakov right now." Mekhlis made a quick phone call and dispatched Avdeyenko to see Yagoda.[84]

Yagoda, the second link in the chain, worked Avdeyenko further, musing that if the prisoners knew Avdeyenko was a writer, they might not be frank with him. Perhaps Avdeyenko might have pondered why this should be so. But Yagoda did not give him time to pause over any puzzling thoughts. He proposed that Avdeyenko win the prisoners' trust by "work[ing] there like everyone else. We'll give you a new identity, illegally." Frozen with fear, Avdeyenko imagined himself disguised as a prisoner. Yagoda's next words flooded him with relief. "We'll make you a chekist—two diamonds."[85] In the space of five seconds, Avdeyenko lurched from panic to joy. A mythology had grown up around the image of the fighting chekist as the tough guardian of communist purity. Even had Avdeyenko not been susceptible to that image, the specter of being a prisoner would have driven him to embrace the identity of a chekist.

In essence, Yagoda dangled three identities before Avdeyenko: writer, prisoner, and chekist. Yagoda went through them one by one. It was a sequence designed to co-opt Avdeyenko, even to make him glad to be a chekist. Two diamonds was impressive, a rank of ten in a scale whose top rank was thirteen.

At the canal site, a prisoner told Avdeyenko that most of them had been arrested for nothing more than "wanting to eat God's bread." Disturbed, Avdeyenko turned to Firin—the third link in the chain that "worked" Avdeyenko. Firin reproached Avdeyenko for his naiveté. The prisoners were kulaks and man-eaters (*liudoedy*); we treat them all the same, and our attitude is always that their sentences are correct; they can shorten their terms by hard work; and now let's go have dinner.

After dinner, Firin brought in his wife and daughter for a little party with music, so that Avdeyenko could enjoy a dance with the ladies. Even amid the gaiety, however, Avdeyenko could not completely free himself of the day's impressions, and he turned to Firin with a question: Whose idea was it to build canals with prisoners in need of rehabilitation? Comrade Stalin's, came the answer. Avdeyenko stopped asking questions.[86] He retreated into the cold comfort of assuring himself of his own safety—after all, he had committed no crime. In his memoirs, he writes that believing you would remain untouched was a defense mechanism, without which one could not face living. "And this was not a deal with my conscience—my conscience was clear." Yet a few lines later he writes, "I condemn my earlier self."[87]

Avdeyenko's experience points to a feature of the Bolshevik social model that we have already seen with Fadeyev. The group leader is responsible for assuring the well-being of the group and its individual members, who are considered to be immature. The members idealize the leader as having god-like powers[88] and accord more importance to the group's shared assumptions or values than to their own observations. Yagoda, Mekhlis, and Firin all treated Avdeyenko as a fledgling to be shepherded. We shall see that Mekhlis treated even Fadeyev and Yermilov as if they were stuck in a kind of intellectual pubescence, incapable of mastering Bolshevik logic. It was Stalin, of course, who modeled this tactic, as with his famous later comment to his Politburo that "you are blind like young kittens."[89]

In the language of social identity theory, three potential in-groups were dangled before Avdeyenko. In-group and out-group were unstable referents, counterparts of the linguistic shifters "we," "they," "here," and "there," whose meaning changes with the speaker's location. Being among the prisoners must have brought home to Avdeyenko that at any moment he could be forced to trade his in-group for that of the *zeks*. How could Avdeyenko ensure remaining in the in-group Firin had defined as "we"? For Gorky, "they" were in rehab and would rejoin "us" as productive members of society (a psychointellectual stance that enabled him to accept the camps). With Avdeyenko, Firin did not even bother to make the rehabilitation argument. He was giving Avdeyenko a lesson in brass tacks career choices. Like Yagoda, Firin planted the fear and then immediately diverted attention from it. The fear was more effective as a whispered undercurrent of the subconscious.

Avdeyenko was worked over three times by Stalin's top cadres. Mekhlis appealed to his ideological commitment, obligations, and gratitude for authorities' high opinion of him. Yagoda bestowed honor and power, but only after first seeding him with fear. Firin showed him a possible future. Thus Mekhlis appealed to Avdeyenko the writer; Yagoda to Avdeyenko the potential chekist; and Firin to Avdeyenko the potential *zek*. Avdeyenko was ill equipped to fathom that the prestigious image of the chekist depended on defining an underclass of subhumans. He formed his self-concept through the career opportunities being offered him and through reading about Soviet achievements in the press. The White Sea Canal was part of the semiotic system that fed his own construction of self. Once launched as a proletarian writer, he had his literary trajectory programmed through visits to "rehabilitative" construction projects. His rise was meteoric—delegate to the First Writers' Congress, published author of books and film scripts, featured speaker at official triumphal gatherings, special correspondent for *Pravda*. Each time he traveled as a *Pravda* correspondent, he received a beautiful new uniform that made him proud, or he was given a car.[90]

The identity swap that Mekhlis, Yagoda, and Stalin laid bare to Avdeyenko too often became a reality. When Mandelshtam returned to Moscow in 1937 after three years in exile, one of the Writers' Union secretaries, Abolhassan Lakhuti, tried to help him by arranging a visit to the White Sea Canal, by now established as a dependable way for suspect writers to prove their fidelity. Before he could make the trip, Mandelshtam became a forced laborer himself.

Gorky had long been trying to gain writers decent housing so that they could have a place to write. For this, he fought almost as hard as he did to set a rigorous educational standard for Writers' Union membership. At the very moment when Gorky took over the orgkomitet, a resolution was passed to build a writers' settlement in the lovely Peredelkino woods outside Moscow. There is evidence that Gorky opposed a separate settlement for literary superstars,[91] but Stalin could point to it in a show of the Politburo's support for writers. The dachas were owned by Litfond, a fund established by the Politburo at this time to help needy writers financially.

The Peredelkino resolution unleashed a mad dash for the gravy train by seemingly everyone who had any hope of hopping on. Writers scrambled to get their names put on the list of the lucky few slated for a dacha. (Leonid Leonov even contrived to subvert the prohibition on private property and buy his dacha for himself.)[92] The dachas and Litfond grants quickly divided writers into the "haves" and "have-nots," as Gorky put it. The lucky ones received paid vacations to the Black Sea, while more deserving writers battled poverty; Gorky cited the case of one writer who could not go swimming all summer because he could not afford a bathing suit (*SL*, 202).

Indeed, the results of the dacha initiative were painfully at odds with Gorky's vision. This level of privilege bred an unwarranted sense of entitlement. One writer reportedly threatened to burn down her dacha because the windows weren't where she had wanted them.[93] Eighty percent of letters to Stalin regarding the culture sector were from writers, mainly "whining, demands to have their genius recognized, pleas for prizes, [large] print runs, and editions of their complete collected works" (*ONI* 1:215).

Gorky himself lived luxuriously at party expense, as he had in Sorrento. Stalin took the precaution of buying Gorky's docility and insisted on providing him with three residences. When rumors reached Gorky in Italy that "a palace or some church or other" was being readied for him in Moscow, he urgently instructed Kriuchkov to refuse any such thing: "My residing in a palace or cathedral will make a justifiably repugnant impression on people who, while working devilishly hard, live in a miserable cowshed. This will be bad not only for me personally. For this reason I implore you: do not settle the question of my taking up residence in a palace before I arrive."[94] Gorky's instructions went unheeded. It was a sore point to feel he had been bought. A dinner guest once raised a toast "to the master of the house"; Gorky's expression became almost malignant as he retorted, "The master of this house is the Moscow soviet!"[95]

The elite lifestyle and entitlement mentality were most embodied by Aleksei Tolstoy, the hugely popular novelist whose books were also favorites of Stalin's. Tolstoy lived next door to Gorky in the Riabushinsky mansion's carriage house, turning it into an opulent lair with sumptuous furnishings. While in emigration from 1918 to 1923, Tolstoy had made many anti-Bolshevik comments that could have been a death warrant. Even in the 1930s he felt safe enough, while traveling in Europe, to refer sarcastically in private to Stalin as "the father of the peoples" and "our Joseph," and to express irritation at constantly having to adjust his writing to reflect the shifting party line. This gifted opportunist happily wrote to order in exchange for living the good life, even as he held in contempt the literary "acrobatics" of Sholok-hov, Fadeyev, and Ehrenburg.[96] His play *Ivan the Terrible* (*Ivan Grozny*) fol-lowed Stalin's instructions to show the tyrant's historical role as progressive, thereby providing subtextual justification for Stalin's terror. His 1937 novella *Bread* (*Khleb*) eulogized Stalin.

In a famous episode, Tolstoy made an insulting remark about Mandel-shtam's wife, Nadezhda, to which Mandelshtam replied by slapping him in the face. The enraged Tolstoy cried out, "I can destroy you!" Tolstoy was confident of his power. He belonged; the literary genius Mandelshtam did not. Perhaps coincidentally, Mandelshtam actually was arrested six weeks later. Three months afterward, Tolstoy mocked Mandelshtam's poetry from the tribune at the Writers' Union's first congress (*PVSSP*, 416).

The seven hundred thousand rubles that the government allotted for the dachas were insufficient, and the dachas were not completed on time, as construction workers profited from selling the building materials illegally or taking them for their own use. The construction chief, when questioned, attributed the increased costs to writers' continuous demands for extras, and he explained the delay by an insufficient number of building crews. No builders were ever charged with crimes.[97]

Many Moscow writers who did not receive a dacha benefited from the building boom in 1930s Moscow. A new apartment house on Nashchokin Street and another on Lavrushinsky Lane were inhabited exclusively by Writers' Union members and their families. The luxurious Lavrushinsky building contained apartments with three, four, and five rooms. Writers who were left out of these buildings moved into at least somewhat better quar-ters vacated by their luckier colleagues. When Fyodor Gladkov moved into a four-room apartment on Lavrushinsky, his previous five-room apartment in a less-desirable building was divided up and given to three writers.[98]

Housing writers together in dedicated buildings made surveillance and arrests easier to carry out; at the same time, it made it easy for writers to socialize, sometimes in undesirable ways. Like-minded writers could easily congregate in one another's homes and hold informal readings of their work in progress, a situation that party ideologues saw as a version of self-formed literary clubs, the very thing that the Writers' Union was meant to replace. Beyond this, writers who might not ordinarily come together could find themselves sharing vodka and zakuski at a neighbor's. In a continuing loop, all this frequent contact served as a pipeline to the security police.[99] Many conversations between writers and friends they trusted were reported to the NKVD.[100] The security services had always recruited writers as secret in-formants (*seksoty*); having the informants live among the target group must have increased the flow of information that the NKVD received.

Thus Stalin found ways to implement Gorky's ideas while also using them for control and co-option. Moscow writers' whereabouts were always known to the NKVD. From Moscow apartment to Peredelkino dacha to sanatorium for a working vacation—the NKVD followed them as if on a GPS. The coveted apartments were ready for occupancy in time for the Great Purge. In 1939, when the Writers' Union leadership recommended thirty-one writers to receive awards, most were approved, but contingency plans were in place. The NKVD had files on every single one of them with compromising material (*PT*, 15–16). The obverse of privilege was arrest.

On occasion, a savvy writer could turn this fraught situation to temporary advantage. A story goes that Isaac Babel (himself a *seksot*), when asked to intercede on behalf of an arrested friend, paid a visit to Gorky, choosing a time when Yagoda was likely to be there paying attentions to Gorky's daughter-in-law. Babel correctly calculated that Yagoda would want to impress Timosha with his power and magnanimity in saving a victim (*VKI*, 317). No one, however, was there to save Babel when he was arrested in 1940. His protectors had already been wiped out. Vishnevsky moved into his dacha.[101]

The thirty-one-year-old poet Ivan Pribludny agreed under pressure to serve as a *seksot* but never submitted any reports.[102] This lapse brought about his own arrest. Pribludny explained to his interrogator that had he carried out his *seksot* work he would have felt responsible for the arrests of his acquaintances. He added that he believed the OGPU exaggerated the political significance of people's words and actions and that he would not do such work to improve his own material circumstances (*RT*, 235–36). Pribludny was shot.

Gorky and Tolstoy, with whom party leaders enjoyed socializing over lavish dinners, received dachas away from Peredelkino.[103] Gorky had two—one outside Moscow in Gorki and another in the Crimea. The Crimean dacha had to serve him as a Soviet Capri; after he returned in 1933, Stalin denied all his requests to travel abroad. Party leaders cultivated other writers as well. Pilniak was friendly with Yagoda.[104] Boris Gorbatov was married to the movie star Tatiana Okunevskaia, who received attentions from Defense Commissar Kliment Voroshilov. Hobnobbing with the leaders was potentially life-threatening. Okunevskaia's arrest was likely payback for rebuffing the NKVD's Viktor Abakumov.[105] Fadeyev ran into trouble when Yagoda, who covertly sided with Averbakh in his bid to preserve RAPP, brought Fadeyev to his dacha and threatened him in the billiard room. Sensing imminent arrest, Fadeyev declared his party loyalty in his stentorian voice, hoping to be heard in other parts of the house, and made a hasty exit. Reportedly he then slipped a letter into the Kremlin sentry booth—possibly a denunciation that later figured in the arrests of Yagoda and Averbakh.[106]

At the opening of the much-awaited First Writers' Congress, on August 17, 1934, Gorky sat enthroned on the dais, appearing as the benevolent presiding literary authority. By the time this public moment of glory arrived, however, his influence was already spent. Signs of his weakness were visible in the Seventeenth Party Congress, held earlier that year, in his son Max's death in May, and in Sergei Kirov's assassination on December 1. Shortly before the party congress, Gorky had challenged *Pravda*'s praise for Panfyorov's collective-farm novel *Whetstones*, dubbing it "junk literature" (*literaturny brak*).[107] Gorky presumably did not know that *Pravda* under Mekhlis had been turned into Stalin's mouthpiece.[108] Stalin then taunted Gorky by giving Panfyorov the honor of being the sole writer to speak at the Seventeenth Congress. Gorky countered with another article against junk literature, spotlighting Vishnevsky.[109] Gorky did not yet see that he was destined to lose this fight. *Pravda*'s Mekhlis and Agitprop's Stetsky were acting with Stalin's approval and not merely on their own judgment. In May, as the selection committee began admitting writers into the new union, Max was found dead in the grass after an all-night drinking bout with Yudin.[110] This incident seems to have reflected a new assignment for Yudin, who had just been removed as organizer of the writers' congress. (The Central Committee *orgbiuro* [organizational bureau], upset with the many delays, put Zhdanov in charge.)[111] That summer the security apparatus was expanded as the OGPU was subsumed into a new commissariat, the NKVD (*ONI* 1: 249, 252). Kirov's murder, if done at Stalin's order, was his answer to the Seventeenth Congress, at which a significant number of delegates secretly voted against Stalin, hoping to replace him with Kirov (the vote count was falsified, and 90 percent of the delegates were eventually executed).[112] In any case, the law of December 1, 1934, which decreed immediate execution for crimes against the state, undid any hopes for free expression that might have lingered after the writers' congress in August.[113]

In the run-up to the First Writers' Congress, however, there were also signs that suggested Gorky's dominance. The countervailing influence of Gronsky, already reduced when he left the orgkomitet, was all but wiped out when he lost the editorship of *Izvestiia*. His replacement was Gorky's darling Bukharin, in what seemed a spectacular comeback.[114] Bukharin printed Pasternak's translations of Georgian poetry and Ehrenburg became the paper's Paris correspondent.[115] More good news came when Bukharin was named to deliver the keynote speech on poetry at the congress.

Bukharin at the helm of *Izvestiia* was confirmation for Gorky that Stalin was reasonable.[116] Bukharin as one of the congress's keynote speakers appeared to mean that Gorky had placed his stamp on literary policy. Another major speaker was to be Nikolai Tikhonov, who earlier had belonged to the Serapion Brotherhood with its calls for a literature free of politics. So widely were these signs interpreted to mean a moderate Writers' Union under Gorky's stewardship that Yudin worried that the Writers' Union might be dominated by nonparty views.[117] But like the publicity heaped upon the congress, these speaking assignments were for marketing purposes only.

The congress was a two-week extravaganza aimed at both writers and the public, demonstrating a bond between them. The speechmaking was periodically interrupted by grand entrances of delegations of workers, collective farmers, military units, and youth groups brought from around the country to affirm the writers and offer themselves as subject matter for stories, novels, poems, and plays. In contrast to the first plenum, the keynote speakers were not back-office ideological workers like Gronsky and Kirpotin but household names—Bukharin, Karl Radek, and Zhdanov.

Six hundred of the Writers' Union's twenty-two hundred members were selected as delegates. Their class origins and party membership did not reflect the overall composition of the membership. Communists, who accounted for 20 to 25 percent of members, outnumbered nonparty delegates by a factor of one and a half to one.[118] Seventy percent of delegates were of working-class or peasant background; and while there are no published figures on social origins for the entire union, in the Moscow branch only one-fifth of members were of worker or peasant origin, with more than half from the *sluzhashchie* (office workers) (*PVSSP*, 663, 700). Two-thirds of delegates were forty years old or younger, reflecting a tilt toward younger, more communist-leaning writers. The delegates also included forty foreign writers, including, most notably, André Malraux. Delegate selection helped ensure that the congress would convey unity even while permitting free expression; floor speeches were predominantly loyalist.

As the congress offered up the image of the Soviet writer as a valued professional, the potential alternative identity of prisoner, so suggestively revealed by Yagoda to Avdeyenko, rippled throughout the hall: each delegate received a hot off the presses copy of the Gorky-induced volume on the White Sea Canal.[119] The delegates knew colleagues who had been exiled—Mandelshtam, Erdman, Mass, Kliuev, Anov, Markov, Martynov, Vasilyev, and Zabelin—but this mild form of punishment was reassuring; Mandelshtam was in the very decent provincial city of Voronezh. Stalin calculated shrewdly in deciding when to "isolate but preserve" versus when to eliminate. He wanted writers to support the new union; the time to do away with Mandelshtam had not yet arrived.

Kliuev, exiled to Kolpashev and too poor to buy food, appealed for help in a letter to the delegates, which his brother handed to Nikolai Aseyev.[120] He had been charged with counterrevolutionary activity and homosexuality based on Gronsky's reading of his poems. He apparently hoped that someone would raise his case at the congress; no one was brave or foolhardy enough to do so.[121]

The congress's twenty-six sessions were each presided over by a different writer, making it appear that writers controlled their union. Zhdanov had warned communist writers against expressions of factionalism (*VKI*, 231), and Pasternak's chairing a session seemingly accorded value to literary mastery and confirmed the equal treatment of all writers. Writers debated one another from the floor. Vsevolod Ivanov and Lidiia Seifullina followed Gorky's lead and argued for collective literary works; Ehrenburg and Olesha argued for individuality.[122] Afinogenov, a proponent of the living man, argued for showing inner conflict.[123] Olesha, in a candid speech that stood out in a way that it would not have at the plenum, announced that he would never be able to learn how to write about being a worker (*PVSSP*, 235–36). This admission turned out to be an epitaph; although he averted arrest, he perished as a writer.

In contrast to the orgkomitet first plenum, some writers were wary of expressing their true views.[124] Their speeches mix sincerity, pragmatism, and falsehood, and it is not easy to sort out which is which. It was Avdeyenko, who more than anyone else owed his writer's identity to the party, who was most able to project his writer's "I" into the new literary environment. As a *besprizornik*, he had lived "like a beast—I could have cut someone's throat, committed the most dreadful crime" (*PVSSP*, 243). In jail, he wrote a letter for a cellmate, which he now thought of as his first literary work. In the intervals between sessions, Avdeyenko tried to get into conversation with the professional writers who were now his colleagues. He told them of a knife that got sharper with each use (another of Gorky's enthusiasms). To his surprise, none of them had heard of it. To his greater surprise, no one was sufficiently interested to ask anything more about it. They did not share his excitement over the young pioneers bursting into the hall as if spontaneously. He could not understand why so many writers, when he asked them about their work, gave mechanical responses (*PVSSP*, 243). As Avdeyenko had not seen through Yagoda and Firin, so he could not see the staged nature of the delegations' visits to the congress, nor the variegated literary talent that Zhdanov was bent on leveling out, or the ultimate goal of a country full of engineered readers with knowable, obedient minds. In the various intrusions of citizen-worker delegations, the writers could see the embodiment of Zhdanov's instructions. Here were some of the people whose souls they were to engineer.

Gorky is said to have made his presiding over the congress conditional on giving Bukharin a major role.[125] Stalin assented, arranging for Bukharin to be monitored by Zhdanov and Kaganovich, who were overseeing the congress (Stalin himself spent those two weeks at his Crimean dacha). The keynote addresses, although allowed to show a range of opinion, were vetted in advance,[126] and care was taken that independent opinion was outweighed by more authoritative messaging. Zhdanov's opening-day speech on writers' responsibilities overshadowed the other major addresses (on poetry, prose, drama, literary criticism, and the wider sphere of literature in the non-Russian republics and worldwide). The poetry address was given by Bukharin. His role at the congress has been discussed elsewhere;[127] here we shall examine it as an illustration of the cycle of individual expression and public shaming.

His address, on the tenth day, turned out to be the congress's major event, provoking a storm of opposition and support. This well read Bolshevik argued forcefully for literary mastery and upended the official literary hierarchy, especially the proletarian poets Demyan Bedny, Aleksandr Bezymensky, and Aleksandr Zharov, who had failed to "set themselves the goal of technical mastery." He praised nonparty poets, including Selvinsky, Tikhonov, and especially Pasternak. He tried to undo the equivalence between literary mastery and ideological deficiency, by distinguishing the "formal," which was inherent to literature, from the "formalist," whose unconcern with ideas made it superficial.[128]

Bukharin graciously attributed the tumultuous applause that followed his speech as a tribute to the party, not himself.[129] He was not allowed to get away with this. Zhdanov and Kaganovich wanted a forceful response to Bukharin's address; Stetsky, Yudin, and Mekhlis arranged it. They made sure the floor debate that followed Bukharin's speech would be led off by the proletarian poets, starting with Aleksei Surkov, who had recently joined Mekhlis's staff at *Pravda* (*PVSSP*, 512–15). In the middle of his remarks, Surkov was passed a note, on which Yudin had written down the points he should make (*MMN*, 348–49). Bukharin's assessment of Pasternak and Selvinsky, said Surkov, proved that he cared nothing for proletarian poetry or class analysis of literature. Surkov was ostensibly speaking for himself as a poet, but he was also a proxy for authority, and his attack on Bukharin implicitly questioned the latter's Bolshevik fidelity.

Surkov played his role well. He had been on the RAPP secretariat, although not in Averbakh's inner circle. He was now building a literary career anchored by administrative posts. He returns to our story in chapter 6, in a power struggle with Fadeyev at the pivotal moment of Stalin's death. His rebuttal of Bukharin was followed by similar pronouncements from Bedny, Bezymensky, Zharov, and the futurist Semyon Kirsanov, who accused Bukharin of "manufactur[ing] balconies for the enormous building of our contemporary life."[130]

Bukharin's response is worth quoting, at least in part, because he would be made to retract it on the congress's final day. He mocked Bedny for claiming to speak as one of a "united front of like-minded" poets who opposed him:

The composition of this front is extremely diverse: it includes Demyan Bedny, who in essence is far from being either enraptured by, or even just an admirer of, Mayakovsky [*laughter, applause*]; it includes Mayakovsky's "poor re-lations," who wrap themselves in his name without understanding his essence [*laughter, applause*]; it includes Comrade Surkov, who spoke about Paster-nak's "enormous talent," and it includes that same Demyan Bedny, according to whom Pasternak is a "most likable individual" and a "grasshopper of Soviet poetry" who is incomprehensible to everyone [*laughter, applause*] . . . So the "unity" among the opponents consists in only one thing—the unity of an un-principled bloc: the party of those who feel offended [*applause*]. (*PVSSP*, 573)

He then pointed out Surkov's misrepresentations:

Comrade Surkov accuses me . . . of placing Pasternak and Selvinsky on the "peaks of Soviet poetry" . . . Therefore (a tacit conclusion): Bukharin is "liq-uidating" proletarian poetry while placing nonproletarian poetry on a pedes-tal. Let us explain this. We have already seen how I am "liquidating" proletar-ian poetry. We have seen that I am liquidating *arrogance* in poetry. And now about "peaks." In a work of poetry . . . form and content are united, but this unity is *contradictory*. Therefore, the "content" can be good and the form can be bad, and vice versa. And so: unquestionably the proletarian poets pene-trate much more deeply and intimately into the essence of the epoch, the struggle, the construction, the heroism of our time. But in no way does this mean that *by virtue of that* they stand, when it comes to *mastery*, above, say, Pushkin.

With his next words, however, Bukharin wound up in a defensive posture:

It is not true that I place *all* the proletarian poets beneath Selvinsky and Ti-khonov in mastery. For example I analyzed Demyan Bedny as being among the country's five strongest poet masters. I place Pasternak, for example, very highly, but in doing so I give an extensive critique of him. Surkov has said of Pasternak here that he has an *"enormous talent."* So on this point there is no argument. Surkov says it is necessary to talk of another vision of the world. Very true. But I spoke *very* sharply about that. I said that at root Pasternak has an incorrect assessment of poetry, that he doesn't feel the epoch, that he is one of the least relevant to our time, that he lives in a narrow circle of ego-centric survivals, and so forth. (*PVSSP*, 574–75; emphasis in original)

His phrasing was that of someone who is cornered: "But I did say that," and "Everyone saw that I defended a wide range of art [and not just lyric poetry]," "My address contained a whole chapter on socialist realism."

Perhaps unwisely, he invoked Stalin in support of mastery: "Where does the slogan 'Study!' come from, that Stalin speaks of so loudly?" (*PVSSP*, 576). And he noted that the party had approved his speech, so there couldn't be anything wrong in it. This claim galled Zhdanov and Kaganovich, who resented Bukharin's making it sound as though his personal opinions reflected official party views. They made Bukharin write a retraction that was read out to the congress on its final day (*MMN*, 364).

> I really did allow myself excessively sharp formulations and sallies against certain comrade poets, in connection with a series of incorrect accusations about me . . . If anyone understood me to mean that my assessments of individual authors as poets were being put forth by me as mandatory directives, this is a clear misunderstanding . . . In no way was I trying, nor am I trying, to undermine the authority or to discredit my opponents as poets. (*PVSSP*, 671)

The conclusion could only be that Bukharin's formal address carried no more authority than remarks from the floor by Avdeyenko, Olesha, or anyone else. That this indignity occurred after Bukharin's return to prominence sent a message: power did not derive from internal authority. It was conferred from outside and subject to revocation. Worse was what the takedown of Bukharin's address meant for the writer-party alliance. Its credibility, which rested on support first from Trotsky and then Bukharin, was now zero.

Bukharin's apology was read to the assembly in his absence by the chair of the congress's closing session. It was Fadeyev (*PVSSP*, 671). Being selected to chair the final proceedings reflects a certain authority; yet reading Bukharin's apology aloud must have reminded him of his own attempt to muster dignity amid humiliation two years before. Stalin had read Bukharin's address in advance of the congress. It did not need to be censored if it could simply be undermined. When the congress was over, he expressed his satisfaction with how it had all turned out (*MMN*, 342).

Gorky, having stamped the congress with his imprimatur, seems to have spent most of it in distress. Two weeks before it opened, he was dismayed to see that a proposed slate of 101 writers for the Writers' Union's board included writers he considered intellectually "decrepit," like Aleksandr Serafimovich, Vladimir Bakhmetyev, and Fyodor Gladkov. Gorky urged Stalin to remove their names, as well as those of Vishnevsky, Libedinsky, and Mikhail Chumandrin (*MMN*, 293–94). (The only ones removed were Chumandrin and Libedinsky, who was placed on the auditing commission.) This letter, in which Gorky confided that he believed Yudin and Mekhlis to be part of a group bent on gaining control of the Writers' Union, shows Gorky's cluelessness. At the congress, he continued to lobby frantically behind the scenes, complaining to Zhdanov that the communist writers were unfit for leading roles, recommending others in their stead, and repeatedly asking not to serve as board chair (*MMN*, 364). In the hubbub over Bukharin's address, he threw his weight behind artistic mastery one more time, in a final desperate bid to make it the sine qua non of the Writers' Union, writing in a memo to the Central Committee that the congress had "almost unanimously" asserted the need to raise literary quality (*VKI*, 231). Fadeyev, Yermilov, Stavsky, and Panfyorov he described as unqualified intriguers

> who do not know how or do not wish to study, but who have grown accustomed to playing the roles of administrators and strive to secure for themselves leading posts . . . However, Comrade Zhdanov has informed me that these people will be given places on the board . . . I personally know these people as very skilled and experienced in the "creativity" of various intrigues, but I absolutely do not sense communists in them and do not believe in their sincerity.[131]

Gorky stated categorically that he refused to work with them, again requesting not to serve as board chair.

Gorky was barking up the wrong tree. Stalin was done indulging him. Including Bukharin as a speaker at the congress had been his final concession to Gorky. And as soon as Fadeyev had read Bukharin's retraction to the delegates, they approved the slate of board members en bloc by a unanimous show of hands (*PVSSP*, 671–74). Not only would the "intriguers" be in the Writers' Union; they would lead it.

The Gorky-Shcherbakov Team Model:
Seeking Common Ground

WITH THE WRITERS' Union officially launched, writers made several good-faith attempts to harmonize their creative interests with party goals. For the next year and a half, they did this repeatedly in presidium meetings, and also more publicly at the Writers' Union's second and third plenums. In this chapter we shall see that writers of various persuasions expressed dismay at the mediocre literary crop and suggested solutions to party officials in the spirit of compromise. This included nonparty old intelligentsia writers like Pilniak and Shklovsky, the so-called left wing of nonparty writers like Ivanov, Tikhonov, and Shaginian, and communist cadres like Vishnevsky, Surkov, and Yermilov. Understanding that party-mindedness was nonnegotiable, these writers tried to widen its meaning.

Gorky's successes in the orgkomitet period seemingly had provided a foundation to build upon. He had won Stalin's agreement for all the major pieces of his vision. He got the multivolume collaborations among writers, scholars, and workers (and in some cases, as we have seen, agents of the OGPU). He got writers better housing. He got the teaching journal *Literary Study*. Most important, he got the Literary Institute, a decisive victory over RAPP and *Pravda* in the war over literary qualifications.

For Stalin, however, the point of state-supported literature was a literature-supported state, and for this he needed a reliable ideological cadre and not Maxim Gorky to lead the union. What is surprising is the last-minute scramble to find someone. The orgkomitet had been at work for more than two years, yet three days before the congress's conclusion, the matter of who would lead the union was still unattended to. Only on August 29, three days before the congress ended, did Zhdanov and Kaganovich present Stalin with a list of five potential cadres for this post. None were writers. The one finally chosen was Aleksandr Shcherbakov, deputy head of the Central Committee's Department of Leading Party Organs (Otdel rukovodiashchikh partiinykh organov) (*ONI* 2: 257; *MMN*, 364–65). Shcherbakov was not a reader and had no literary interests. The son of a factory worker, he had entered the workforce at age ten and joined the Communist Party at age seventeen in 1918. His first party assignment, like Yermilov's, was as a teenager heading provincial and republic Komsomol offices, but he made a more brilliant career than did Yermilov—social origin, personality, and luck all played their part. He attended the Sverdlov Communist Institute, which he did not complete, and the Institute of Red Professors. In one of many examples of inbreeding among the party elite, his sister married Zhdanov.

On August 31, Kaganovich and Zhdanov informed a flabbergasted Shcherbakov that he was being tapped to lead the Writers' Union. Shcherbakov tried to get out of what was to him an utterly unappealing assignment. Zhdanov would not take no for an answer. He informed Shcherbakov that his start date was in forty-eight hours, and Stetsky whisked him off to the congress, which was in its penultimate day, for his first taste of his new job. Shcherbakov stayed for half an hour and recorded his reaction in his diary: "It was nauseating" (*ONI* 2: 266).

Hard on the heels of Bukharin's humiliation, Gorky now experienced one of his own. Zhdanov and Shcherbakov showed up at his door to break the news that Shcherbakov was now in charge. Gorky immediately wrote to the Central Committee requesting to be released from serving as chairman of the board, citing the presence on it of Panfyorov, Yermilov, Fadeyev, and Stavsky. The Central Committee named him chairman of the board anyway, turning him into Shcherbakov's junior partner.[1] Gorky's post was now purely ceremonial, and in the worst possible way, as a mascot for policies he disagreed with. Shcherbakov's diary conveys Gorky's unhappiness with this turn of affairs. "He stepped down. We convinced him" (*ONI* 2:267).

Gorky had written to Stalin asking to be relieved of his duties as chair (*predsedatel*) a month earlier, with a different scenario in mind. Citing ill health and the need to spend time on his own writing, he wrote, "I do not know how to be a chairman, and even less am I capable of finding my way through the Jesuitical machinations of group politicking. I will be much more useful as a literary worker" (*MMN*, 294–95). He recommended other people, hoping that this post would go to Kamenev.[2] Now, however, the dark horse Shcherbakov gave an entirely different meaning to Gorky's stepping aside. He was to have no say in how the Writers' Union would be led.

Stalin had gifted Gorky a fifteen-month lease on the orgkomitet, with Yudin beneath him but no single official as his superior or equal. Those fifteen months were the anomaly in the history of the Writers' Union under Stalin. Stalin from now on would choose as union head either an ideology official like Gronsky or Shcherbakov, or a rabid but gullible enemy hunter like Stavsky, or a writer who was a tested cadre with an exploitable weakness, like Fadeyev. Gorky had his own weaknesses that Stalin exploited, but the possibility that an enraged Gorky might explode could never be ruled out.

Unlike the trade unions, which were situated within the government sector, the Writers' Union (and the other creative unions that followed) belonged to the more ideologically minded party sector. Stalin made the Writers' Union's chief directly accountable to Agitprop. Tellingly, just four months after the congress, Agitprop, or the Department of Culture and Propaganda as it was then known, was reorganized. It was replaced by four new departments, one of them devoted almost exclusively to literature, to provide stricter oversight. Despite its innocuous new name, Department of Culture and Enlightenment (Otdel kulturno-prosvetitelnoi raboty), its controls were stricter than in the government sector's Commissariat of Culture and Enlightenment (Narkompros). Agitprop itself reported to the Central Committee's five-man secretariat.

The head of the Writers' Union reported to Agitprop; moreover, he and his deputies could hold concomitant appointments in Agitprop or in other offices devoted to ideological oversight. As Stetsky, Kirpotin, and Gronsky had been orgkomitet secretaries while also holding top posts in Agitprop or in the press, Shcherbakov was both first secretary of the Writers' Union and chief of the new Agitprop.[3] His power derived from Agitprop, not the Writers' Union. Fadeyev, who in the late 1940s headed the Writers' Union with the august title of general secretary but did not hold a simultaneous appointment in Agitprop, was limited in his authority, as we shall see. The same held true for branch offices of the Writers' Union in the periphery. When Mandelshtam was exiled to Voronezh in 1934, he announced his presence at the local branch of the Writers' Union and requested permission to participate in it; Yudin sent a letter of support for Mandelshtam not to the local Writers' Union branch but to the Voronezh Agitprop office.[4] Similarly, if the Writers' Union central office in Moscow wanted to replace a local secretary, it needed permission from the local *obkom* (regional party committee) or *kraikom* (district party committee).[5]

As Writers' Union first secretary, Shcherbakov reported to his immediate superior at Agitprop, who, conveniently, was himself. As the designated narrators of the Soviet experience, writers had to be more carefully monitored than other creative artists. An artist, musician, or architect who wanted to travel abroad needed approval from Viacheslav Molotov; a writer needed approval from Stalin.[6]

Ensuring tighter controls through such dual appointments was also practiced in Nazi Germany, where the Theater Chamber and the Propaganda Ministry's Theater Department were at one point headed by the same person, Rainer Schlösser, who used his power to eliminate independent theater agencies.[7] Hans Hinkel served in the SS and headed the Reich Culture Chamber, the Reich Propaganda leadership, and the Reich Association of Jewish Culture Leagues, all at the same time.[8] By 1941, all Hinkel's deputies were long-standing members of the NSDAP, and most were members of the SS, with no artistic credentials.[9]

Stalin wedged the Writers' Union securely between Agitprop and the security services. Whenever the secret police opened a dossier on a writer, the Writers' Union forwarded his entire file, including his membership application, referee reports on his manuscripts, and various questionnaires.[10] The union thus served as a delivery system for the political police. As in other organizations, the head of the union's party cell was charged with recruiting informants to report on conversations among writers.[11]

Gorky's voluminous correspondence with writers was a boon to the security police.[12] Kriuchkov decided whether letters to Gorky would go to him or the security organs.[13] Writers mingled knowingly and unknowingly with chekists. It was not uncommon for them to have a family member in the security apparatus—a sibling, a spouse, an in-law. Fadeyev's sister-in-law by his first marriage, Marianna Gerasimova, worked in the security services; when Fadeyev later divorced and remarried, he and his new family moved into an apartment building for NKVD employees.[14]

The Writers' Union statutes defined the union as a voluntary organization with a structure modeled on that of the Communist Party.[15] As in the party, nominally the supreme governing organ was the congress, which elected a board to act as interim authority between congresses; the board, in turn, was to hold plenums "no less than three times a year" (*PVSSP*, 717). Plenums were charged with electing the presidium or secretariat. No term limits were specified for these two bodies; the implication was that they would be elected (or reelected) at each plenum, although this never happened. The presidium was to coordinate the work of the board and committees. The secretariat, which, as in the Communist Party, was the real seat of power, directed the union's day-to-day affairs and had the authority to expel members. Grounds for expulsion were "deprivation of civic voting rights," "a contradiction between a member's activity and the interests of Soviet society," anti-Soviet activity, prolonged cessation of literary activity, failure to pay dues, or "at the desire of the member" (*PVSSP*, 717) The statutes also specified an auditing commission to be elected by the congress and whose members were not to be on the board. The first congress "elected" a board of 101 members en bloc by acclamation, and the first plenum elected a presidium of thirty-seven members and a secretariat of five members (*PVSSP*, 711).

This central administrative structure was mirrored at the level of the union republics, autonomous republics, regions (*oblasti*), and territories (*krai*). Each branch had its own board and was to hold its own congress at three-year intervals (*PVSSP*, 714). New members were admitted by the board of their union republic. The decisions of the all-union governing bodies applied also to the branches in the periphery, but in practice the branch secretaries were left to their own devices with little or no oversight. In 1937 the Kuibyshev writers complained that they had no contact with the central office of the Writers' Union, which evinced no interest in knowing who they were or what they were writing. No Writers' Union official from Moscow had ever visited Kuibyshev, even though the 101-member board included writers from the various regions precisely in order to assure contact between the regions and the center. The mistaken listing of an Orenburg writer as being in Kuibyshev suggests an indifference toward writers outside Moscow, Leningrad, and perhaps Kiev (*MMN*, 690).

As with other organizations, each branch held meetings of its party group. This "communist fraction," as it was called, was led by a *partbiuro* (party bureau); the central *partbiuro* had about nine members and directed the party group, which held both open and closed meetings. These meetings seem not to have influenced union affairs except when the Writers' Union secretary wanted to cite the party group's judgment to justify an expulsion. Party-group meetings therefore played a larger role during the Great Purge.

Shcherbakov ignored the charter. The board never met; the plenums convened in its name were organized by the presidium or secretariat. Between these two latter bodies, there was in practice no clear division of labor. The amount of planning needed for plenums made it unrealistic to hold them three times a year, so they were held once a year, although the charter was never amended.

Shcherbakov, as first secretary, should have run the secretariat, and Gorky as *predsedatel* should have convened the presidium. Gorky, however, never attended any meetings; Shcherbakov ran the presidium and conducted the union's business through it and not the secretariat.[16] The presidium took over the board's function of admitting new members and the secretariat's function of expelling them. The second congress, which should have been held in 1937, was not held until after Stalin's death, in 1954. In violation of the statutes, in 1946 a new secretariat was elected by the presidium rather than the board.[17]

The congress delegates thought their union was headed by Gorky. Shcherbakov's name did not come up until the day after it ended. The board that had been approved on the congress's final day convened on the next day for the first plenum, where they were presented with a slate of candidates for the secretariat and presidium. This was the sole plenum to be held out of the public eye. It affirmed the five secretaries as Shcherbakov, Stavsky, Ivanov (representing nonparty writers), Ivan Kulik (representing Ukraine), and Lakhuti (representing the non-Russian nationalities; he was an Iranian poet who had emigrated to the Soviet Union in 1922) (*PVSSP*, 715; *VKI*, 238). The only reliable cadre in the group was Stavsky, but that was enough. In any case, Shcherbakov and his successors called upon trusted writers in the presidium or board, like Pavlenko and Vishnevsky, to assist them in sensitive tasks.

Gorky, who though diminished was nonetheless supposed to preside over the plenum, tried to get out of attending it. Zhdanov informed Stalin that "we had to press him rather strongly" (*MMN*, 363). The plenum selected Gorky chairman of the board, while Zhdanov ignored his urgent requests to put Kamenev on the secretariat. Writers regarded Shcherbakov as an ignoramus. The NKVD learned from its *seksoty* that one called him "dull-witted and rather rude," while another remarked wryly that he made Yudin look like a "first-class intellectual."[18] The establishment of the Writers' Union in a country where for a century and a half writers from Radishchev to Leo Tolstoy had served as the moral counterweight to the autocrat was a triumph for Stalin, who now showed Gorky how little he mattered by ceasing his visits.[19]

It is likely that it was Gorky's own preference to avoid the presidium meetings he was supposed to chair, but the effect was to marginalize him. After each meeting, Shcherbakov would write to him summarizing it and soliciting his opinion on manuscripts, plans for anthologies and public addresses, and how best to work with young writers.[20] Gorky's disagreements with Shcherbakov were sealed within the privacy of their letters, so their impact was contained in a way that would have been impossible had he expressed them in the presidium. The lionizing of favored writers, the launching of harassment campaigns like the one against formalism and naturalism in 1936, the persecution of politically unreliable writers, and the parameters of literary discussion—all of these occurred without Gorky's public participation.[21] Despite his influence on what Evgeny Dobrenko has called the aesthetic consciousness of an entire generation of writers,[22] his impact on literary *policy* was reduced by his preference to conduct business privately rather than more visibly in the presidium.

How soon did Gorky and other writers grasp his figurehead status? The celebrity and honor accorded to Gorky, and Shcherbakov's solicitations of Gorky's literary judgments, made it easy to see him as the authority. Even Khrushchev in his memoirs stated that he heard that Shcherbakov served as an assistant for ideological affairs to Gorky, who ran the union's operations.

Gorky may well have seen himself as the "literary half" of the Writers' Union leadership in partnership with Shcherbakov's "administrative half." Since Gorky read all the many unsolicited manuscripts sent to him by writers, from hopeful novices to established literati, writers, too, saw him as a key figure, not realizing that this work was entirely outside the Writers' Union. While Gorky provided Shcherbakov advice on manuscripts, Shcherbakov in turn had already asked Stalin for another kind of advice—on how to deal with Gorky. Stalin advised him to concede only on small points (*ONI* 2: 269). Gorky tried to dissuade Shcherbakov from pressuring writers to produce more, urging him to emphasize quality over quantity; but Shcherbakov was following orders from above.[23]

Gorky, who had been unhappy with Gronsky and Yudin, had no choice but to hope Shcherbakov would be an improvement. He sounded genuinely pleased with Shcherbakov's critique of a manuscript by Avdeyenko, whom the party was nurturing. "I read your letter to Avdeyenko, dear comrade, with a feeling of deep satisfaction . . . You wrote a businesslike, convincing review with a fine, authentically literary tone. This gives me great hope that in your person our young literature will find a firm, sensible, concerned leader."[24]

The presidium held its first meetings in the fall of 1934. Gorky's absence was not the only irregularity. The official list of thirty-seven members only partly matches the record of actual participants. At least twelve writers not on the list attended its meetings in the first year, and many writers who were on the list never attended. Besides Shcherbakov, the most frequent contributors to discussion were Agitprop's Kirpotin, Stavsky, Vishnevsky, and Pilniak, whose presence alongside his quondam persecutors, Kirshon, Selivanovsky, and Stavsky, seemed to make good on the Writers' Union's welcome to nonparty writers. Another participant was Shklovsky, who is not listed as a presidium or even a board member (*PVSSP*, 712–15); he was presumably a late addition.

The first meeting turned into a battleground over the union's mission. Shcherbakov distributed a proposal, symptomatic of what Stephen Kotkin has described as " the organization of the work process as a series of campaigns,"[25] for all writers to attend streams of meetings with officials, journalists, and workers to learn about achievements in science and industry. Party and nonparty writers alike erupted in protest. Surkov and Tretyakov complained that writers would be spending all their time in meetings instead of at their writing desks. Since Shcherbakov had not distributed the proposal in advance, Kirshon suggested that everyone be given a chance to read it, to which Shcherbakov replied, "That will take too long."[26] At this point, Pilniak asked Shcherbakov to clarify the presidium's responsibilities.

SHCHERBAKOV: Cost estimates.

PILNIAK: That's money. That's not what I'm talking about.

SHCHERBAKOV: There is a proposal to delegate final revisions to the plan to comrades Bespalov, Shaginian, Kirshon, Surkov, and Vishnevsky. And that's enough. The exchange of opinion will be taken into account.[27]

At another meeting, devoted to reviewing the work of *Red Virgin Soil*, now edited by Yermilov, Shklovsky and Pilniak explained to Shcherbakov that *Red Virgin Soil* had grown too boring to attract readers, a problem that could be solved if editors would nurture writers. Shklovsky brought up Platonov:

> I did not like the fact that Yermilov made no mention of [Platonov's] "Takyr." When Shcherbakov read me excerpts from it and said it was bad, I did not believe it. It was good. It might not have been true, but it was good. There's no feeling that an editor prizes a writer, that the editor tries to help the writer write well. Platonov is one of the best writers of our time; there should have been a meeting to talk about his book, but instead people talk privately and wait until a writer is amnestied and it is possible to speak with him.[28]

This episode abounds in ironies. Yermilov had consistently recommended Platonov for publication but did not want to call attention to that fact. "Takyr" was Platonov's first published story since Fadeyev's "kulak agent" article, and its publication in *Red Virgin Soil* reinstated Platonov in literature and enabled him to gain Writers' Union membership.[29] It is further ironic that Yermilov, chastised by Stalin two years earlier for failing to nurture the fellow travelers, was now (1) entrusted with an editorial post that ostensibly required nurturing and (2) admonished by a nonparty writer making an argument very much like Stalin's. For Stalin, "nurturing" had an underside of fear and co-option, which was why he continued to make use of Yermilov for the same tasks at which he had supposedly failed.

No one else spoke up in support of Shklovsky and Pilniak, and Shcherbakov handled this exchange of opinion by simply not responding to any of it. He offered Yermilov the concluding word. Pilniak broke in, proposing that the discussion be continued at the next meeting. Shcherbakov, after initially appearing to agree, then turned to Yermilov for the final word, and the matter ended there.

"Takyr" did not suit party leaders. Mekhlis published a derogatory notice about Platonov in *Pravda*, and Shcherbakov warned menacingly that Platonov would suffer unless he wrote a story with clear political meaning "this instant" (*SF*, 857). Yermilov and Pavlenko, who was editor of the almanac *Year 19* (*God 19*), immediately refused Platonov's submissions. These rebuffs provoked an indignant response from the head of *Pravda*'s literature and art department, Subotsky, who declared that the notice had in no way been intended to hound Platonov out of literature, and that he would telephone Yermilov and Pavlenko to tell them so.[30] Quite possibly Mekhlis concealed his agenda from Subotsky.

This meeting illustrates just how far Yermilov had fallen. Not three years earlier he would have scoffed at the thought that he might sit in the same room with Shklovsky and Pilniak discussing literary matters on a more or less equal footing with them.[31] Yermilov had been left out of the Writers' Union's governing bodies even as Fadeyev and Stavsky were included. In some ways, the outcome of this presidium meeting was the same as it would have been under RAPP—Platonov's case was ignored and Yermilov had the last word. But Yermilov was now dependent on Shcherbakov, whom he disliked, and whose power highlighted his own reduced status.

As for nonparty writers, their relationship to the Writers' Union was established by Shcherbakov's unresponsiveness to the entreaties of Shklovsky and Pilniak. The Gorky-Shcherbakov tandem embodied the dual approach that Stalin used in other contexts, moderating harsh policies in one area while ratcheting them up in others. In 1930, "Dizzy with Success" ("Golovokruzhenie ot uspekhov") signaled a relaxation in violence toward the peasants even as the Prompartiia trial was in preparation; in 1936 a democratic constitution was publicized with fanfare just when the oppositionists were arrested.[32] When writers like Shklovsky and Pilniak tested the Writers Union's promise to reach out to nonparty writers, Shcherbakov displayed the harsh underside of the rhetoric of inclusion. Gorky, had he been present, would have had to either move into a confrontation with Shcherbakov by backing them up or else compromise his symbolic authority by going along with Shcherbakov. But Gorky was blissfully unaware.

Both communist and noncommunist writers lamented that the union was uninvolved with writers and failed to arrange readings of their work in progress, yet sponsoring events devoid of literary interest (*VKI*, 258). The same was true in the regional branches. Tikhonov, the "left wing" nonparty writer who was titular head of the Leningrad branch, complained of being ignored both by Shcherbakov and by his own branch secretary, Anatoly Gorelov (formerly a Litfront member and editor of *The Chisel*). Other Leningrad writers put it more bluntly: Gorelov treated the branch as his personal domain.[33]

Unable to arrange readings through the Writers' Union, writers gathered informally at one another's homes. We have seen that this practice irked culture officials, who saw it as circumventing the Writers' Union.[34] At one such gathering in November 1935, Ehrenburg spoke out for artistic freedom and was interrupted by an artist, Fyodor (?) Bogorodsky, who disagreed and was hounded out of the apartment (*VKI*, 273). Also picking a fight with the Writers' Union was the *Chisel* group that had been promoted in RAPP's journal of that name. They insisted that they "belonged" to the journal and not to the Writers' Union. Stavsky, describing this situation with the hyperbole and outrage that would win him the top spot in the Writers' Union during the Great Terror, claimed that *The Chisel* had been infiltrated by "three criminal shysters" and turned itself into a small, second-class Writers' Union. *The Chisel*, already opposed by Gorky as a literary fraud, was quickly dissolved.[35]

Five months after the first congress, Shcherbakov wrote to Gorky,

> The time has come to check the work of a series of writers—how they are fulfilling the promises they made at the writers' congress. This review could take the form of a session of the presidium that you would direct, at which the writers would report on their work.[36]

Shcherbakov included a list of seventeen writers to be checked. Gorky replied that such a meeting would antagonize writers, who would regard it as limiting their creativity and degrading their status to that of civil servants. Diplomatically, he suggested that the same kind of review would occur through two of his own forthcoming articles on the demands of the epoch on literature and on writers. Shcherbakov desisted.

Having won the point, Gorky had to submit to an indignity from another quarter. *Pravda*, which opposed Academia Press's intention to reissue Dostoevsky's *The Possessed* (*Besy*), cited Gorky's objection, made twenty years earlier, to adapting the book for the stage, implying that he also opposed reprinting the novel.[37] Gorky was losing control of his own advocacy. Angrily, he made clear his view that publication should go forward. He made the pragmatic arguments: yes, the novel painted revolutionaries in a bad light, but it was necessary to know one's enemy; and book banning increased the desire for forbidden fruit.

Mekhlis was only too happy to publish Gorky's response, which *Pravda* then countered by citing the need to ward off saboteurs. Where would it all end—with the publication of every hostile author right on up to Zinovyev and Kamenev?[38] It is quite possible that Mekhlis unwound this scheme on his own; subsequent rumor among writers was that Stalin approved his action after the fact.[39] Mekhlis commissioned another article against Gorky as well. A year earlier, Gorky had denigrated Panfyorov, and Stalin had ensured that Gorky came out the loser. Now Mekhlis gave Panfyorov the last word. Gorky had repudiated class background as an automatic ideological litmus test, pointing out that many dedicated revolutionaries came from the bourgeoisie and that the nineteenth-century revolutionary democrats Chernyshevsky and Nikolai Dobroliubov were born to priests.[40] Panfyorov lashed out at Gorky for praising Zazubrin's *Gory* (*Mountains*), which "slanderously . . . [describes] a war that the party supposedly declared on the peasants."[41] This time, Mekhlis refused to publish Gorky's response.[42] *Pravda* was staging a public display of Gorky's vanishing authority.

Gorky also found himself again faced with the slapdash literary recruitment techniques that he had fought so hard to end under RAPP. They were reincarnated in Shcherbakov, who was devising an accelerated track to the literary profession. He proposed a ten-week course for provincial writers applying for union membership. They would come to Moscow for lectures, meetings with writers, and visits to museums and theaters. Gorky objected strenuously:

> What can they learn in two and a half months? . . . there is no doubt whatsoever that courses such as these will be a means of increasing the number of untalented and semiliterate people who are "involved" with literature. There are already so many of them that I think it absolutely necessary to review the list of Writers' Union members and relieve the union of superfluous and harmful ballast.[43]

Shcherbakov dropped the idea, but nothing came of Gorky's desire to purge the membership lists.[44] After Gorky's death the practice of offering quickie "courses" was revived.

The issue of unqualified members plagued the Writers' Union throughout its existence. To increase the number of working-class writers, the Leningrad Evening Workers' Literary University continued to scan the "literary page" of factory newspapers for promising recruits.[45] It graduated a class of twenty-six students in 1934.[46] In March 1935, it enrolled one hundred ten students, comprising 50 percent working class, 34 percent *sluzhashchie*, 9 percent students, 4 percent military, and 3 percent "other."[47] Nonetheless, in 1936 Surkov lamented to Shcherbakov that the working class had yet to produce a single writer of note;[48] and more than a decade later, the head of the Writers' Union admissions committee, Leonid Sobolev, noted that the committee had had to stand firm in rejecting the application of a recruit "fresh from the lathe," who had applied seven times.[49]

Novice writers' shaky grammar and style became still more of an issue once the novel was declared the preferred genre of heroic biography and epic achievement. Writers lacking the skills to write lengthy narratives wrote them anyway. Panfyorov's *Whetstones*, panned by Gorky as "junk literature," was hailed as an encyclopedia of village life and proclaimed a Soviet classic, but even his supporters were put off by its turgid prose and overloaded plot. Serafimovich bemoaned its "colorlessness"; Yermilov privately conceded its inferiority.[50] The lackluster literature spewed forth by Gosizdat appalled him: "God, god! And this is all presented to the Soviet reader in complete seriousness."[51] Yermilov's cry is striking in that it could easily be mistaken for that of an old intelligentsia writer like Eikhenbaum. Yet this was RAPP's legacy, and he seems not to have recognized his own role in it.

Gorky was a one-man bridge between literary mastery and proletarian recruitment. Alone among writers and party officials he believed in both, and that they were not incompatible—that through reading and study, an Avdeyenko could become a worthy writer. Gorky tried mightily to separate the question of mastery from ideological credentialing. Ever since RAPP, ideology and artistry had been literature's odd couple. Mastery was associated with old intelligentsia writers who had remained nonparty, exemplified by Pasternak, Akhmatova, and Mandelshtam, while communist literature more often came from the pens of younger authors of humbler background and education. This socioeconomic divide caused mastery and ideology to be seen as antipodes. Nonparty writers had reopened the question after April 1932, declaring the mastery-ideology split a false inequality. They were vindicated by the Bukharin-Gorky position that mastery was for party members, too. Many communist writers, however, found the equation of literary mastery with suspect ideology to their liking and were intent on turning it into a syllogism: insistence on mastery is a screen for ideological unreliability; x favors mastery, therefore x is ideologically unreliable.

Gorky's high hopes notwithstanding, the price of recruiting workers into literature turned out to be too high. Gorky could understand writing to further party aims, he could talk himself into accepting limited censorship in the interests of party goals, but he was aghast when faced with a community of "writers" who lacked writing skills and saw "being a writer" as a career opportunity. Avdeyenko, upon whom he had lavished his attention, praise, and hopes, finally provoked his angry reproach: "You are not studying."[52] Averbakh's prediction that the accomplished writer would be supplanted by the ordinary "person who writes" was coming true.

While the planned economy had no use for capitalist notions of supply and demand, when it came to literature, party leaders made an argument that could be described as ideological supply and demand. Writers were expected to produce continuously as if to avert ideological starvation. The concept of "tempos," although Writers' Union officials did not use that word, carried over from the social and economic spheres into the cultural. The director of the Bolshoi Theater, Mikhail Arkadyev, did use it, writing to Stalin, "The work on these plays is proceeding at full tempo and is nearly complete. We will then have, instead of the usual one play every two years, four plays in one year."[53]

In the twelve months after the first congress, however, writers produced few manuscripts. According to Gorky's estimate, out of the now approximately three thousand members of the Writers' Union, only about three dozen had published a book in the past year. In the fall of 1935, Shcherbakov, probably after reading reports from *seksoty*, wrote to Gorky,

Our enemies are speaking of a "crisis." "They've put the squeeze on writers; how can anyone write under those conditions." Or: "They're forcing writers into a collective farm, they're killing literature."[54]

Even "our own writers," Shcherbakov continued, were beginning to have doubts.

Unwilling to accept that the decline in submissions could be the result of overbearing pressure to conform, Shcherbakov suggested that writers were taking longer over their manuscripts to meet the higher literary standards called for by some at the congress.[55] (Shcherbakov himself never called for higher literary standards.) Perhaps to preempt any suspicion of poor job performance on his own part, he published a notice in *Pravda* listing forthcoming titles by Afinogenov, Aleksandr Kron, Andrei (?) Semyonov, Boris Levin, Selvinsky, Yury Yanovsky, Aleksei Faiko, Vsevolod Lebedev, Sergei Mstislavsky, Pavlenko, and Lev Nikulin. To Gorky, too, he offset the rumors of a literary crisis by praising various works, assuring him that Pavlenko's "The Great War" ("Bolshaia voina") was "a significant literary event," that Leonov's *The Road to Ocean* (*Doroga na okean*) was better than Gorky allowed, that Avdeyenko's *Fate* (*Sudba*) would appeal to readers, and that V. N. (?) Orlov's *The Last Appearance* (*Poslednee yavlenie*) was "fresh and original."

For the first time in their yearlong professional relationship, Gorky unleashed the full force of his anger on him:

> I am very much embarrassed and grieved by your optimistic assessments of our current literature. I would not undertake to protest against them if these assessments were confined to your letters to me. But you are publishing them far and wide, exciting hopes and expectations among the Soviet public that can hardly be realized. My skepticism is based on my reading of those manuscripts to which you particularly call attention as specimens of great significance. You have not read the works of which you speak.

Gorky gave a scathing assessment of Pavlenko's *The Fate of War* (*Sudba voiny*) and asked,

> What is the party's role in writers' social and revolutionary upbringing? What is your personal role? When you were appointed secretary of the Writers' Union, you said, "I will learn." It is not evident that you have learned anything. Under your leadership literature has remained just as homeless as it was under the senseless, fogged-up bureaucrat Yudin. Yudin unsuccessfully attempted to create a RAPP-type clique. You, it would seem, have the desire to reconcile everyone with everyone else and create within the union "peace

on earth, good will toward men." But we need something quite different, because we need to show conflicts, expose narrow-minded materialism, and mobilize literature as a force that will elevate the masses.[56]

No answer to this letter exists, and the next extant letter in their correspondence is dated more than three months later. But each man turned to the Central Committee secretaries. Cut off from Stalin, Gorky wrote to Andrei Andreyev, the secretary who oversaw Agitprop, complaining that Shcherbakov "conducts a 'policy of reconciliation,' praises everyone, gives gentle 'fatherly' instructions. For him literature is secondary" (*SL*, 203). Trying to salvage the pieces of his vision that were rapidly disintegrating, he proposed reorganizing the secretariat. He also urged raising the level of literary criticism via an ongoing critics' seminar.

While Gorky approached Andreyev, Shcherbakov wrote to Stalin, expressing incredulity at public denunciations of literary works as "junk" and "dung." He further described a Writers' Union party-group meeting, at which someone mentioned that the novelist and former director of the Rumiantsev Museum, Anatoly Vinogradov, had attempted suicide; Yermilov, on hearing this, scandalized even the unfeeling and churlish Shcherbakov by remarking, "His kind can poison themselves; I'm not sorry for them."[57] But beyond this, Shcherbakov's letter to Stalin shows that he had absorbed Gorky's complaints:

> If eight to ten months ago we were disturbed about why there were no new literary works, now we cannot help but be alarmed by why there are no genuinely good works worthy of these great times. (*SL*, 206)

Shcherbakov soon advanced to become second secretary of the Leningrad *obkom* and *gorkom* (city party committee), serving as chief deputy to Zhdanov, who had succeeded the dead Kirov as Leningrad party secretary.[58] He then quickly became first secretary of Irkutsk and then Donetsk, both important *obkomy*. In 1938 he was transferred back to Moscow, now with much greater experience and status, succeeding Kaganovich as head of the Moscow *obkom* and *gorkom*. This rapid rise through the party ranks ultimately cycled him back to an even more powerful position as caretaker of ideology and literature. By mid-1941 he was a Central Committee secretary, and it was to him that Agitprop officials reported. He reenters our story in chapter 5.

In literary policy, Stalin often would make a general statement, as when coining the term "socialist realism" in 1932, leaving writers to fill in the blanks with new characters and plots. Could a model hero have character flaws? Could he make errors in judgment? What about showing conflicts between a hero's personal desire and his pursuit of socialist goals? If such portrayals were admissible, how prominently could they figure? There were no clear answers to such questions. Answers emerged after the fact, and sometimes inconclusively, in the form of press reviews; and even then, the answers were frequently in flux. In the wake of a pronouncement like "socialist realism," writers had to guess. Sometimes they interpreted it too loosely to gain approval, but eventually, as more and more new works received official praise, a body of literature accumulated that gave fuller definition to the original proclamation. Operating in this fashion, Stalin essentially denied the creative intelligentsia the ability to formulate theory, downgrading their role to one of merely filling in a template. Nonetheless, in the Writers' Union's first two years, writers tried to influence literary policy at their plenums, hoping that party officials would meet them halfway.

Beginning with the second plenum, held March 2–7, 1935, these assemblies addressed a particular theme. Plenums, which usually lasted five or six days, opened with a keynote speech setting ideological parameters, followed by two formal addresses from prominent writers. After this, delegates could sign up for a chance to speak (*VP*, 354). Plenums thus had the dual function of briefing writers on the party's expectations while also allowing them to express themselves. In spite of the pressure to conform in such a public venue—the plenums were widely reported in the press—a significant minority of speakers used their speeches to exchange views with their colleagues or to try to define areas of productive collaboration with the authorities.

The second plenum's theme was literary criticism (*VP*, 515–17). This reflected criticism's importance—critics often spoke for the party and had authority over writers. Since this authority was greatly resented, the theme of literary criticism was also a contentious one as seventy-five delegates took the floor to speak. The keynote speaker was Bespalov, who had survived the withering scene in Stalin's office over "For Future Use" to preside over Gosizdat's fiction department (again showing Stalin's reliance on duly reformed literary cadres). The two formal addresses were given by Afinogenov and Shaginian, signaling a desire to maintain a RAPP-like communist core while validating nonparty writers. Afinogenov, who had joined Averbakh's rebellion after RAPP's dissolution, was a prodigal son returning to the fold. Shaginian was the kind of writer that the Writers' Union was appealing to when it cast its net wide. She had a seat on its board, and in 1935 she applied for party membership.[59] Gorky, however, cautioned Shcherbakov about entrusting her with a major address:

There is a danger that Shaginian, a gifted person but extremely "subjective" and . . . always successfully emphasizing her originality—the unique character of her thoughts, feelings, and organization of her impressions—there is the danger that she will not be able to give a sufficiently complete and clear evaluation of nonparty criticism.[60]

Gorky was right to suspect that Shaginian's originality would cross party orthodoxy. This was immediately evident from her title, "What Writers Expect from Literary Criticism" ("Chego zhdet pisatel ot kritiki") a reversal of the press practices that put critics in the position of "expecting" something from writers. Shaginian faulted critics for measuring works against preconceived categories instead of reading them to discover what they held. She mocked critics' tortuous attempts to hedge their bets by using both positive and negative evaluations to offset one another, offering a tongue-in-cheek parody of press reviews:

> [Ehrenburg's] *The Second Day* [*Den vtoroi*] is a novel about the five-year plan, with a theme of restructuring the old and the growth of the new person, who represents a new, positive stage in Ehrenburg's development, although this novel is also still devoid of party consciousness. Its verbal fabric is studded with irreproachable epithets; Ehrenburg struggles in this novel with his old devices and doesn't vanquish them, although he outlines something qualitatively new. This qualitatively new thing turns out to be an imitation of biblical style, sustained well in the work of the American missionary [*sic*] Pearl Buck but sustained poorly in the work of Ehrenburg.[61]

One wonders how this section of Shaginian's report escaped wholesale deletion. It is likely that the parody flew over the head of Shcherbakov, whose job it was to approve the official reports in advance.

But Shaginian's satire was also meant constructively. She sought common ground for party authorities, critics, and writers. Writers' aesthetic concerns and the party's ideological agenda could be brought together, she proposed, through an axiom of literary thought: each generation interprets great works of art in its own way. This formulation acknowledged the party's interest in interpreting works for its own purposes; it acknowledged the legitimacy of multiple interpretations of the same work; and implicitly, it preserved writers' prerogative to write as they wished. Her solution was sympathetic both to writers and to an ideologically driven regime. It held literary critics responsible for examining influences and interactions, while granting them a party-minded interpretation. But the idea that works could be interpreted variously posed a danger to party authority. The stewards of culture needed there to be a single correct interpretation.

Shaginian's report resonated among the assembly. It is startling to find Yermilov of all people, as if taking his cue from her report, ridiculing absurd book reviews, quoting one that described Gladkov's *Cement* as "a bad novel but a useful and even epoch-making one" (*VP*, 182). Yermilov, who was passed over for the role of featured speaker, used his diminished status to express his real opinions, although he took care to stripe them with party orthodoxies. His literary prescriptions remained those he had held in RAPP, and just as they had then been the "right wing" of communist literary prescription, now they sounded positively lenient. As he had taken a risk in publishing Platonov's "Takyr," he took risks at the plenum. He insisted that family plots could express Bolshevik social life, a position starkly at variance with the emphasis on heroism and grand undertakings that accompanied the official shift from drama to the novel.[62] So, too, was his encouragement to writers "whose theme [was] the *intelligent*" not to feel that they had to discard their hero but rather to show that hero in a new way (*VP*, 181). He went out on a limb in praising Olesha for having done exactly that in *A Strict Youth* (*Strogy iunosha*), defining his work as loyalist.

On the tension between ideology and literary excellence, Yermilov stammered out to the whole plenum a thought that he expressed privately to Fadeyev: "We—this must be said forthrightly—have to some extent lowered our aesthetic criteria . . . if we do not raise our aesthetic requirements, then we will not be able to cope with a single one of our tasks" (*VP*, 182–83).

He did not say everything on his mind—for example, that Soviet literary journals were inferior to émigré journals, a situation that made him feel ashamed.[63] And he inoculated his liberalism by criticizing liberalism in others: the critic Dmitry Gorbov's "rotten liberalism" led to "slavish homage to the supposed 'artistry' of works that are hostile to us . . . This slavishness always characterized Menshevik, Trotskyist criticism" (*VP*, 183). With this maneuver Yermilov undid his own attempts at syncretism. Having wriggled out of the conundrum "literary mastery = ideological indifference," he wound up with a variation of it: liberalism = mistakenly attributing artistry to hostile works. The implication was that hostile works could not be masterful, a proposition that Yermilov was prepared to tolerate if the definition of hostile works excluded Platonov's and Olesha's. But in that case he would have to accept its corollary—literary mediocrity that was "socially useful." He boxed himself into a lame conclusion: if a poor literary work nonetheless deserved a readership, then the critic's job was to explain why, while still pointing out its literary deficiencies. This proposition, which he was offering in all seriousness, was exactly the same one he (like Shaginian) had mocked at the beginning of his speech.

Fadeyev had been flummoxed by the same conundrum two years earlier at the first orgkomitet plenum. He stated firmly that literary quality must be raised and pointed to his own early story "High Water" ("Razliv") as a work that he had decided not to reissue because it was artistically weak. But he explained that he went ahead with publication after colleagues pointed out that it could be useful to unsophisticated readers (*SLNE*, 127).

The Central Committee secretaries had no interest in entertaining writers' attempts to reconcile aesthetics and ideology. There was a certain logic to this inflexibility. Leaders in every branch of socially organized activity, including literature, had to be communists. To privilege mastery, or even to count it on an equal footing with ideology, would mean forgoing the image of communists as the literary vanguard. The only way to protect the rules of the relationship between communist and nonparty writers was to downgrade mastery. So the question that was formulated as mastery versus ideology was really mastery versus cadres. And this was a vicious circle. Without a party-backed commitment to mastery, the cadres would never achieve it, assuring continued resentment of their orchestrated literary leadership.

Stalin indirectly addressed the interplay between aesthetics and ideology that December, when he pronounced Mayakovsky the "best and most talented poet of the Soviet era."[64] Mayakovsky united aesthetics and ideology, thereby allowing an equals sign between mastery and ideology. His canonization was the perfect opportunity for marking out common ground. Stalin, however, paired his elevation of Mayakovsky with a new literary watchword—accessibility. He was refashioning Mayakovsky as a poet whose poems were immediately clear to the mass reader. The experimental part of his oeuvre was poetica non grata.

Little of this was immediately evident. Many writers, party and nonparty alike, understood the elevation of Mayakovsky as an endorsement of "left" art: if the best poet was Mayakovsky, then the best theater director must be Vsevolod Meyerhold, the best film director Sergei Eisenstein, the best photographer Aleksandr Rodchenko, and the best composer Shostakovich.[65] This impression was corrected in due course, when *Pravda* disgraced Shostakovich, the Writers' Union held its third plenum, and a campaign was unleashed against formalism and naturalism.

Pravda's attack on Shostakovich on January 28, 1936, shocked many writers. Olesha expressed a widespread view: "I don't understand the two contradictory acts: the adulation of Mayakovsky and the humiliation of Shostakovich. Shostakovich is Mayakovsky in music."[66] His offending opera, *Lady Macbeth of Mtsensk* (*Ledi Makbet Mtsenskogo uezda*), had been playing for months to a packed house, receiving rave notices from *Pravda* itself; it had even been performed for the delegates to the Seventeenth Party Congress.[67] "They praised and praised him," marveled the writer Grigory Sannikov, "and now, all of a sudden, bang on the head!" (*VKI*, 291). Avant-garde art was about to be rejected as "formalist." Shostakovich was advised by the head of the newly formed Arts Committee, Pyotr Kerzhentsev, to do fieldwork in the countryside and incorporate the "one hundred best songs" into his music.[68]

Given Stalin's Mayakovsky declaration, the theme of the Writers' Union's third plenum, held February 10–16, 1936, could only be poetry. The keynote speech, "On the Poetry Cadres" ("O kadrakh poezii"), fell to Stavsky, who demonstrated the slanted reading of Mayakovsky by the poem he chose to read aloud, "Kulak."[69] The major address was given by Surkov, who had played his part so well at the first congress. Gorky was absent, nursing his health at his Crimean dacha. Barely a year and a half after the congress, its two most influential advocates for literary quality were absent. The plenum did, however, mark one last success for Gorky. The literary circlists were cast out. In a startling policy shift, Stavsky, who had praised the circlists at the first congress, now mocked their verses, reading them aloud to laughter from the hall.[70]

The plenum saw heated debate over whether it was legitimate to read Mayakovsky selectively, whether Pasternak "belonged" to Soviet poetry, and who had the authority to judge poetry and according to what criteria. Bukharin had obediently assured the first congress that his assessments of poets were purely personal and that any "official canonization" of individual writers would be improper (*PVSSP*, 671). Now Stalin's decision to canonize Mayakovsky became party dogma.

Aseyev, who had been close to Mayakovsky, argued passionately against reading Mayakovsky selectively. This argument, while antithetical to Stalin's intention, did not on the face of it contest his public proclamation on Mayakovsky, and Aseyev had been allowed to express his view in *Pravda*. His insistence on reading Mayakovsky in his entirety would have been acceptable to some communist writers, on the grounds that the "individualist" Mayakovsky was a manifestation of contradictions that were quite common and should be shown. But this position was on communism's right wing, the same argument that the Onguardists had advanced with their living man. Aseyev was challenged by Althausen, who argued for omitting individualist and petit-bourgeois poems that Mayakovsky eventually "outgrew." This prescription fits the practice of erasing the subjective self by bringing it into alignment with the "objective" party position. Similarly, the call for accessibility, while it may be understood as ensuring a clear message for an unsophisticated reader, may also be rooted in a fear of the reader as interpreter—as an autonomously judging self.

Althausen turned the issue of selective reading into a moral judgment, complaining, RAPP-style, of writers who liked Mayakovsky only when he expressed

the gloomy, crumpled consciousness of a solitary, barbarized, déclassé person of the prerevolutionary period. These are mainly people for whom the Mayakovsky of 'A Cloud in Trousers' ['Oblako v shtanakh'] is dearer than the Mayakovsky of 'That's Good!' ['Khorosho!'], for whom the Mayakovsky of 'The Yellow Shirt' ['Zheltaia kofta'], the Mayakovsky who hit his fists against schoolroom desks, who was a mammoth destroying literary canons—decadents, symbolists, acmeists, mystics, naturalists, aesthetes—is dearer than the Mayakovsky who built the poetry of socialism, for whom Mayakovsky the petit-bourgeois rebel, the individualist, is dearer than Mayakovsky the revolutionary, the member of the great proletarian collective.[71]

Althausen's argument was not new, but it prefigured a new view of oppositionism that would underlie the coming purges. Just as for Althausen poetic tastes defined loyalty and were grounds for enmity and moral condemnation, so oppositionism, which earlier had been viewed as an intellectual position that could be corrected through an understanding of one's error, was coming to be seen as a permanent character trait.[72]

Stalin's action on Mayakovsky elicited an equal and opposite reaction, with many plenum delegates choosing to discuss Pasternak. More than any other writer, he symbolized to his contemporaries the tangled relationship between aesthetics, ideology, and loyalty. Communists disagreed over whether Pasternak "belonged" to Soviet literature. Bezymensky, describing Pasternak's poetry with the common trope of a stuffy room, admonished Pasternak for not stepping into the wider Soviet world. "You have more to learn from Mayakovsky . . . than does any beginning poet."[73] But Evgeniia Mustangova expressed awe in the presence of a great poet, whom she would not presume to teach.[74] A former member of Litfront and admirer of Voronsky, Mustangova declared Pasternak more influential than any other Soviet poet, prompting Bezymensky to upbraid her for giving Pasternak assurances rather than guidance.[75] Mirsky, pointing out that the International Congress of Writers in Defense of Culture against Fascism had recognized Pasternak as the foremost Soviet poet, declared, "And, Comrade Bezymensky, Pasternak's poetry now plays a greater role in the propagandizing of Soviet culture . . . than Bezymensky's poetry," at which those seated on the dais cried out, "That is still debatable," and "That is unquestionably not true," triggering hubbub among the delegates.[76]

As in previous forums, writers continued to propose solutions for a meaningful alliance with the party leadership. Party-mindedness, they said, need not exclude literary creativity; literature's mission to portray the building of socialism need not exclude interior life; aesthetics and ideology could be partners. Behind these postulates lay the unspoken questions of who got to identify promising new talents. Surkov criticized Mirsky for his positive evaluation of the young poet Pyotr Semynin. Mirsky countered that Surkov had quoted no verses to support his low opinion of Semynin's work and lamented the failure to nurture: "The only people who can be mature masters are the generals of poetry, and young poets must be demeaned until they attain the rank of general." Mirsky praised the young Margarita Aliger in a way that brings to mind Yermilov's defense of family themes as Bolshevik. Her verse, said Mirsky, was "remarkable . . . for its profound intimate lyricism and . . . for its political depth, and for the feeling that her intimate existence is inseparable from the existence of the whole."[77] Prudently quoting a poem of Aliger's invoking Stalin, Mirsky also mused half-jokingly that the result of his praise might be a harassment campaign against Aliger.[78] This drew laughter; with the first of the Old Bolshevik show trials six months away, writers could still share a moment of uneasy levity.

Bezymensky insisted that literary nurturing be left to communists and showed how it should be done. "With all the heartfelt forthrightness of Bolsheviks we showed [Selvinsky] his failures, shortcomings, or diseases. That was the duty of genuine Bolshevik friendship. This kind of friendship commands us to help any comrade to check his weapon so that it can better strike the enemy, for this comrade is necessary and dear to us." [turning to Selvinsky]: "Well, then, Ilya, do you still feel you have no one with whom to exchange a word in your luxurious language? Can you really not be understood if the communists of the Writers' Union, after gathering for the purpose of hearing your poem read aloud, have asserted your literary success with a full measure of joy?"[79] Bezymensky went through a list of nonparty poets, instructing each one on how to improve (and creating a reservoir of resentment). Of Semyon Utkin, he said, "The dream of standing over the country with a glass of wine in a suit of foreign cut prevails upon the consciousness of Iosif [*sic*] Utkin." At this, someone called out, "Stop him, he mustn't talk like that. I am not a fan of Utkin's, but you can't talk like that."[80]

The adulation of the deceased, airbrushed Mayakovsky, the disgracing of the living, pathbreaking Shostakovich, and the invocation of "accessibility" to justify these judgments were part of Stalin's windup to the Great Terror. Having increased literary controls in the party bureaucracy a year earlier, Stalin in January 1936 made a parallel change in the government bureaucracy, ensuring closer scrutiny of the arts by removing them from Narkompros's department of leisure and recreation (where literature was on a par with schools and playgrounds) and placing them under the newly created All-Union Arts Committee (Vsesoiuzny komitet po delam iskusstv pri SNK SSSR).[81] It was through this government sector arts committee that the terror was launched in literature. Its chief, Kerzhentsev, belonged to the radical wing of party critics, who equated a bad work with an author who was a bad person.[82] This was the attitude Stalin needed for the terror.

It has been suggested that it was Kerzhentsev who took Stalin to hear Shostakovich's opera *Lady MacBeth* on the hunch that he would not like it, and that when Stalin demonstratively walked out, Kerzhentsev proposed the infamous campaign against formalism and naturalism.[83] Like Gronsky and Mekhlis, Kerzhentsev could guess Stalin's intent. Although his official portfolio comprised only the arts, his impact on literature during the Great Terror surpassed that of Stavsky, who took charge of the Writers' Union that August.[84] *Pravda*'s bombshell article against Shostakovich, "Muddle Instead of Music" ("Sumbur vmesto muzyki"), was the opening shot.[85] For the next four months, *Pravda* ran articles on the twin diseases of formalism and naturalism every few days.

Four weeks into the *Pravda* campaign, the Writers' Union experienced its first public scandal. Shaginian, who had been courted with high-profile speeches and a dacha, declared her withdrawal from the Writers' Union. Shcherbakov swiftly dispatched Pavlenko, whose loyalty and co-option by the NKVD cast him in the role of an unofficial deputy, on a mission to get Shaginian to reverse herself. Shaginian stood firm. She told Pavlenko that she disagreed with the *Pravda* articles and had had misgivings about the Writers' Union from the start. Shcherbakov then summoned Shaginian to a secretariat meeting. Shaginian dodged this invitation, telephoning Shcherbakov shortly before the session to say she had written to the Central Committee fully explaining herself and that she had nothing more to add. Shcherbakov held the meeting without her. The secretariat (it is unclear who was present) characterized her action as "anti-Soviet" and resolved to "come down hard" on her as an example to others.[86] The party group prepared a resolution accusing Shaginian of anti-Soviet conduct; Shcherbakov held it in reserve while he made one more attempt to pressure Shaginian, summoning her to a meeting of the somewhat less tightly controlled presidium. Shaginian meanwhile had approached the commissar of heavy industry, Sergo Ordzhonikidze, asking to be attached to his commissariat for a research trip to Baku for a novel about Soviet oil production (*SL*, 211–12). This attempt to find sponsorship outside the Writers' Union was rebuffed, and she had to attend Shcherbakov's meeting.

Shcherbakov began by misrepresenting Shaginian's declaration, saying that it slandered the Writers' Union as a harmful organization that should be dissolved, described writers as less valued than milkmaids, and criticized the Writers' Union for not offering material assistance.

SHAGINIAN: What does material assistance have to do with it, when did I say anything about material circumstances?
SHCHERBAKOV: You did in your letter to Molotov.
SHAGINIAN: In the first place a letter to Molotov is not for you to read, and in the second place I did not speak about material conditions.
SHCHERBAKOV: All right, we won't talk about the material side here.[87]

Shaginian then explained that she had in fact said something quite different—that the union provided its members with *too much* material assistance. This remark becomes comprehensible once we understand that the root of Shaginian's discontent was the confluence of three Writers' Union policies: censorship, dismissive treatment by literary officials, and the lavish privileges intended to co-opt writers into accepting the first two. Ideological controls and material benefits, seemingly so at odds, had been joined. The "too much" that the Writers' Union gave its members was the quid pro quo for their obedience as commercial producers.[88]

Shcherbakov avoided addressing Shaginian's main point: that writers were becoming the intellectual counterpart of manual laborers, doing a routine job lacking creativity. This is why he cast the comparison with milkmaids, which Shaginian had in fact made, as a matter of material possession and prestige. On that score, Shcherbakov could prove that Shaginian was wrong: writers had every bit as much opportunity for material assistance and prestige as any milkmaid. Shaginian herself, Shcherbakov observed, had received a dacha. But this was exactly the problem: although the material benefits that the Writers' Union was offering were precisely those Shaginian needed most—she shared her Moscow apartment with her mentally ill sister—she rejected them out of a sense that she was being bought. In her letter of withdrawal, she renounced her claim to the dacha that was being built for her.[89]

The problem was not just that writers could be bought with dachas, food allotments, vacations, trips abroad, awards, and celebrity. It was that buying off writers was the Writers' Union's founding assumption. Shaginian exposed the interdependency between ideology and economics. Communism, having exposed the debilitating effects of capitalist free markets, replaced literature's commercial value with a high-minded ideology only to have financial gain creep back in through the back door. The party was paying writers to distribute its ideology.

This is not to say that Shaginian could not have made her peace with some kind of exchange. Serving a literary bureaucracy dedicated to communist ideals held some appeal, especially when compared with a free-market literature that catered to mob tastes. Whether one felt compromised depended on an array of interchanges and relationships. Shaginian had applied for party membership and been denied; the creative suggestions she had offered in her second plenum speech were ignored. (Vishnevsky reproved her for expecting her proposals to be acted upon: "That is arrogance.") Instead of feeling respected, she felt insulted.

Am I so sure that I deserve to be accepted, am I sure that I will be accepted? When I protested that my application had languished for two years I was protesting the fact that no one from the party organization took any interest in the application, in the condition of the comrade who submitted this application; no one spoke with this comrade or summoned her for an appointment.[90]

Now Shcherbakov introduced the resolution accusing Shaginian of anti-Soviet conduct. Shaginian recanted.

I know that the Soviet Union and the party have enemies, I know that these enemies can make unscrupulous use of my action . . . I am in complete agreement with Comrade Shcherbakov that I did not follow Soviet methods of struggle and today, comrades, I take back my declaration withdrawing from the [Writers'] Union.[91]

But she reaffirmed her criticisms: her actions had been dictated by the "impossibility of continuing to do further work under the conditions that have arisen in our union."[92] "What we are doing," she told the presidium, "is not part of the traditional activity of a writer."[93]

The communists present, Pavlenko, Nikolai Pogodin, Kirshon, Vishnevsky, Stavsky, Semyon Reizin, and Subotsky, unanimously condemned Shaginian's act.

Pilniak tried to defuse the issue: "Let's accept her retraction and go home. And let's have another meeting to discuss the shortcomings she sees in the Writers' Union."[94] That last suggestion was ignored, but Shcherbakov amended his resolution, and Shaginian escaped being labeled "anti-Soviet."[95]

Only now did Shcherbakov inform Gorky of Shaginian's declaration. "I think you will approve of the secretariat's handling of this matter."[96] No reply from Gorky exists, but he did write to Stalin alluding to the matter and connecting it to the *Pravda* campaign.

The criticism [of Shostakovich] is not convincing. Why is this a "muddle"? Where and how is this "muddle" expressed? The critics should provide a technical evaluation of Shostakovich's music. Instead of this, all the *Pravda* articles provided was the opportunity for a pack of mediocrities and hacks to persecute Shostakovich in every possible way.[97]

The Shaginian episode shows that the provision in the statutes permitting writers to leave the union was part of a now abandoned marketing strategy. As the second five-year plan, whose launch in 1933 had been a victory for moderates, now gave way to a resurgence of the radicals, the Writers' Union's welcoming rhetoric was replaced by calls for "profound self-criticism" and a Stakhanovite ("shockworker") movement in literature.[98] Streams of meetings were held so that writers could admit to formalist and naturalist errors. The accounting that Shcherbakov had wanted a year earlier but scotched in deference to Gorky was now happening as a shaming exercise.

In a month of meetings, nearly one hundred Moscow and Leningrad writers were made to speak.[99] To judge from the press coverage, only nineteen Leningrad speakers, well under half, denounced formalism and naturalism, and only three engaged in the severe self-criticism that *Pravda* demanded. In Moscow, twenty-five speakers fell in line behind *Pravda*, with another ten attempting to balance party policy and artistic independence. Most speakers chose self-defense over self-criticism and further ignored *Pravda*'s calls to expose their colleagues for formalism and naturalism.[100] They made the same arguments as at the first congress and the plenums, but no longer in the spirit of willing cooperation. They met *Pravda*'s indignation with their own.

Pasternak got the discussions off to a contentious start. "Don't howl," he told the party's literary critics, "and if you do howl, don't howl in unison, howl in different ways."[101] He was made to disavow his remarks; but *Literaturnaia gazeta* reported tartly that he continued to express "naive ideas."[102] A sizable minority followed Pasternak's lead, including Kirsanov and Afinogenov in Moscow, and the nonparty Kozakov, Fedin, and branch head Tikhonov in Leningrad. *Literaturnaia gazeta* expressed disapproval with the general tenor of the discussions.[103] The literary scholar Aleksandr Leites and the Yiddish-language poet Perets Markish "failed to satisfy the audience"; Panteleimon Romanov spoke about various topics "without saying anything about them."[104]

The Leningrad writers also reiterated Shaginian's point at the second plenum—that writers, not critics, were the experts. No one, said Fedin, can give a writer rules for how to write. Channeling Eikhenbaum's "How Gogol's 'Overcoat' Is Made" ("Kak sdelana 'shinel' Gogolia"), he noted that one could describe "how a work is made" but not how to make a work. Zoshchenko, quoting unjust criticism of Vladimir Lidin, described the situation as a "dangerous" one in which critics had license to damage the reputations of fine writers.

Eikhenbaum, Zoshchenko, Fedin, Nikolai Nikitin, and Kozakov eloquently defended the aesthetics that had been disparaged as formalism and naturalism.[105] Nikitin: the kind of naturalism associated with Émile Zola and other French writers was to be valued. Zoshchenko: the problem was not overemphasis on form but too few works that exhibited good form. Fedin (whose novel *The Abduction of Europe* [*Pokhishchenie Evropy*] had been panned): "It takes courage for a writer to admit his mistakes . . . but it takes greater courage not to admit his mistakes—that is, mistakes that he does not find in his work." These three also challenged accessibility, cautioning that insistence on simplicity would lead to simplistic literature and noting that Mayakovsky's original readers had found his poetry incomprehensible.

The terse press coverage of other writers' remarks suggests a rebellion. Daniil Kharms spoke "rather abstractly . . . on children's literature"; Yevgeny Shvarts "evaded the question of formalism even when asked."[106] The paper expressed disapproval of Vladimir Lifshits and the young writers Pozdyshev and Druts and kept silent on Chukovsky and Nikolai Oleinikov.[107]

Concluding the proceedings in his official capacity as Leningrad branch head, Tikhonov spoke more moderately, seeking common-sense principles that writers and officials could agree on. He voiced the same desire for nurturing that Pilniak and Shklovsky had expressed to Shcherbakov. The "lack of a friendly atmosphere," said Tikhonov, hindered writers' development.[108] This former Serapion was no longer asking for artistic freedom but simply for amicable treatment from party editors like Yermilov, Gronsky, Vishnevsky, Panfyorov, and Bespalov.[109]

What, then, were the principles that writers articulated between April 1932 and April 1936, in hopes of finding common ground? (1) Editors should cultivate relationships with writers with whom they have common literary interests. (2) In reading manuscripts, editors should assess a writer's strengths in order to help develop them. (3) Showing society's imperfections should not be considered disloyalty. (4) Optimism about the future should not preclude showing the full spectrum of human emotions. (5) There is no predetermined, correct form for a literary work. (6) Many classics would fail the test of accessibility, which should not be a literary requirement.

Attempts at common-sense agreement played out in other venues as well. The staff of *Our Achievements* agreed on the need for distinctive writers' groupings, each of which could be attached to a particular magazine. They resolved to put their proposals in a public declaration and to send Gorky a transcript of their meeting.[110] The staffing of literary journals with loyal or co-opted cadres ensured that none of these would be pursued. Editors' main concern was surviving their magazine's annual review, where what mattered was their ideological, not their literary, judgment. In any case, they were often less qualified than the writers they were supposed to mentor. Yermilov could not "help" Platonov develop his talent.

Gorky, following the newspaper reports from his Crimean dacha, failed the writers who found the courage to speak out publicly against *Pravda*. He is said to have expressed his disagreement with the *Pravda* articles to Malraux, who was visiting him there. His only public statement came in a painfully hedged article that appeared as the discussions were taking place.[111] He kept to generalities and avoiding naming names, but in denouncing formalism and naturalism he did the job Stalin had hired him for: he lent his prestige to the campaign.

Gorky's death in June, whether or not at Stalin's order, could not have come at a more convenient time, with the first trial of the Old Bolsheviks planned for September. In the next two years, Stalin would decimate the ranks of the old intelligentsia writers, doing away with Pilniak, Mandelshtam, Babel, and many others. Natural deaths would aid the process. The shrunken rank that was allowed to remain would be ignored and eventually anathematized. The alliance was over.

For many writers, Gorky had been the only one who encouraged them, took the time to read their manuscripts, and gave valuable criticism. He left a threefold legacy: his literary advice and teachings to myriad individual writers; the Literary Institute; and improved living and working conditions. The first was incorruptible and lay outside the actual structure of the Writers' Union. The other two were perverted by Stalin. The invaluable education provided by the institute was smirched by its own engineering of literary souls. Gorky's motives were to provide writers with the education and living conditions necessary to produce fine literature. Stalin's motives were co-option and surveillance. Stalin put into place the building blocks of Gorky's vision, corrupting and redirecting them to suit his own needs. Future Writers' Union leaders would have the power to bestow material rewards, and the duty to promote mediocrity.

A Personal Psychology of Terror

AMONG THOSE CAUGHT off guard by *Pravda*'s disgracing of Shostakovich was Yermilov. His editorship of *Red Virgin Soil* required him to understand the party line, and yet he could not make sense of it. He had received no directives. The turnabout appeared illogical, even capricious, but such a conclusion was inadmissible. In the six weeks after "Muddle instead of Music," Yermilov confided his agitation to Fadeyev in seven letters totaling ninety-seven pages. In this intermezzo, we shall hear Yermilov's voice through these letters, which bespeak desperation to make sense of party policy, and humiliation at reaffirming obedience to the very party by whose leaders he felt abused. The cadre who publicly berated the nonparty intelligentsia and his communist rivals privately expresses outrage less at them than at the party itself. Through these letters we can observe the self-perpetuating mechanism of state-sponsored terror. Perplexity sparks fear; the cadre struggles to understand what the party wants of him so that he can give it and thus inoculate himself from disfavor. Since party-line shifts were frequently signaled through a denunciation in *Pravda*, the cadre took denunciation as the model for demonstrating his own fealty. In this way, the mass copycat actions of individuals ensured that state terror would be self-renewing.

The party's failure to brief Yermilov was no oversight. It was a deliberate put-down—a message that he was not important enough to be briefed. Even if the turnabout was not arbitrary, its purpose was intentionally hidden. The unpredictability of the party zigzag made it the perfect test. With each twist, the party intentionally initiated rupture with its cadres as a way of demanding ever stronger demonstrations of their loyalty. The cadre had to repeatedly "realign" his subjective self with what he convinced himself was the party's objective wisdom. Yermilov was a power seeker rather than a true believer, but the personal response to terror was in many ways the same. As Jochen Hellbeck has observed, all communists' identity depended on the conversion narrative, which needed to be "reaffirmed time and again."[1] The only predictable thing is the constant shifting between stability and rupture, comfort and crisis. Accepting the party pronouncement, intended to solve the problem, never does. However many objectionable propositions the cadre accepts, there is always another and another. Each time he accepts a new pronouncement, he acknowledges the judge of right and wrong to be not his "subjective" conscience but the ruling authority. But though he makes this sacrifice, it fails to win him validation. On the contrary, the party regards him with indifference or mistrust.

Yuri Slezkine writes that during the terror communist believers distinguished between "good people" and "bad people."[2] "Good people" put themselves at risk rather than abandon a nephew or niece whose parents had been arrested; "bad people" protected themselves at all costs. Yermilov was a consummate writer of denunciations even before the Great Purge, and, as we shall see, he wrote them not only for self-protection but also in hopes of self-advancement—as a performative act of self-credentialing before the party, meant to demonstrate his vigilance.

Yermilov was assigned to *Red Virgin Soil* around the time of the April 1932 resolution, when, hard upon the dethroning of Averbakh and the liquidation of RAPP, most major literary journals were nonetheless kept under the control of former RAPP cadres.[3] Their authority was greatly reduced, however, by Stalin's decision to install high-ranking party officials as their overseers. Shcherbakov (and before him Gronsky) was a reminder to Yermilov, no less than to Gorky, of his own diminished status. When Yermilov tells Fadeyev that he has "always fought actively for the party line" (even, he could have added, when he disagreed with it), we hear his disappointed expectation that the party should have rewarded him with a top-level editorship such as that of *Literaturnaia gazeta* (*SL*, 221). That job went to Subotsky. Relegated to *Red Virgin Soil*, Yermilov did the work of soliciting and reading manuscripts and composing each issue but was not even dignified with the title of editor. He was listed simply as a member of the editorial board.[4]

His literary proclivities—learning from the classics, admiration of Leo Tolstoy, arguing for including family themes in Bolshevik literature, and a whispered support for artistry—had always placed him on communist literature's right wing and his remarks at the second plenum sounded positively indulgent. *Red Virgin Soil* brought the public-private divide into his editorial work. He published the novice writer Vsevolod Lebedev's *Childhood* (*Detstvo*), an exploration of a child's private life, while turning away weaker but safer work by Avdeyenko.[5] He was incredulous at claims by communist critics, like Bespalov's declaration that the first writer to use nature as an active force rather than a simple backdrop was Gorky:

My god! What about the oak that Andrei Bolkonsky rides past, and the landscapes of Pushkin, Lermontov, Turgenev, the Petersburg scenery of Dostoevsky—in fact the whole of world art! Gorky himself would have whipped Bespalov like a schoolboy for this kind of "discovery"![6]

In *Red Virgin Soil* he panned a middle school textbook for "sociological analysis" (the derogatory quotes are his) of literature that omitted to define terms like "artistry" and "image" (*obraz*).[7] He asserted that textbook authors lacked aesthetic upbringing and love of literature, and the result was a worthless textbook.[8] Yermilov wanted children to see that what made the classics great was literariness, although he did not use this word and would never have admitted to any commonality with the Formalists. He complained that the textbook devoted two pages to Avdeyenko's *I Love*, while *Cement, The Rout, The Quiet River Don*, and works by Aleksei Tolstoy and Prishvin received no mention. (Squeezing in Prishvin among these certified notables reveals Yermilov's true tastes.) This article, published during the antiformalism campaign that grew out of the Shostakovich denunciation, reveals deeply held literary views at odds with party policy.

Like the old intelligentsia writers whom he made it his business to hate, Yermilov found himself wondering why his career depended on people with a fifth-grade education.[9] He saw other critics as his competition and held them in contempt as unworthy rivals.

In its criticism section, *Znamia* [*The Banner*] cultivates the genre of frolicking schoolboyism. All these Lev Levins and [Anatoly] Tarasenkovs were boys who wrote honest and boring articles. Then they decided—or someone told them—that criticism should be *interesting*. At that point they just stopped working and began to blather away in the belief that they were writing "essays." You will be surprised that I am taking all this seriously, that I even waste time thinking about this. But spite takes over, Sasha, the most painful spite that makes you start to throw up morally and intellectually at the mere thought of the Writers' Union, of our literary criticism, of our magazines and all that. Honest to god, it's a union of overgrown schoolchildren who for whatever reason intrigue against one another. (Yermilov to Fadeyev, Dec. 4, 1936, l. 39; emphasis in original)

Unmentioned is his own greedy participation in the intrigues "for whatever reason." There is every reason, however, to accept the sincerity of his judgments of literature, literary criticism, and journals. The divide between his private assessments and public stances is there for us to see.

Before we take up Yermilov's reaction to the Shostakovich affair, let us consider his actions over the preceding year or so, during the hysteria that followed Kirov's assassination. Amid warnings of a conspiracy against the state, the law of December 1, 1934, mandated immediate sentencing upon arrest. Kamenev, Zinovyev and more than six hundred of their associates were arrested,[10] as were Kremlin staff accused of conspiring to assassinate Stalin. Loyalty checks resulted in the confiscation of a quarter million party cards, producing further arrests.[11] Kulaks, bourgeois families, and former landowners were resettled in remote eastern regions. In this atmosphere, Yermilov reaffirmed his commitment to the party:

> Since Kirov's murder, the thought of leaving the USSR for an extended period has lost its appeal for me. I saw that I could be useful here. I must remain here—in short, it immediately became clear how impossible it is to drop all this, and how fundamentally and vitally I am bound to the concerns of our art, that this is my *calling*, and what would I be thinking if I were to leave my post?[12]

Whatever had caused Yermilov to consider living abroad, and whatever the sincerity of his change of heart, it is clear that he understood that in this crisis atmosphere he must prove his "usefulness" to the party. He spent the winter of 1934–35 trying to attract the attention of the party secretaries:

> I wrote a series of detailed, extensive informational reports [*dokladnye zapiski*] to the Central Committee, the three main ones (major efforts!) being (1) about the politics at Glavlit [the censorchip office], (2) about writers' political moods . . . sent to Stetsky, Mekhlis, and Shcherbakov—Mekhlis forwarded it to Andreyev, [NKVD head Nikolai] Yezhov, and Gorky, noting that it was "very interesting," (3) about *Literaturnaia gazeta*. I'm awaiting the resonance from this last report—somehow Shcherbakov isn't hurrying to bring it to the party cell.[13]

Yermilov's "informational reports"—denunciations—were the kind of thing routinely sought by the security police, but he wanted a different audience. Any appointment to a position of literary power would come not from the NKVD but from the party secretaries. He repeatedly tried to convince them that *Literaturnaia gazeta* was in the wrong hands. The "resonance" he was hoping for was surely its editorship.

He tried to leverage *Red Virgin Soil* to mount a challenge to Shcherbakov. The magazine's most prized feature was the installment publication of *The Last of the Udegs*. Shcherbakov, however, had criticized it, repeatedly suggesting that Fadeyev's slow progress was due to his heavy drinking. This political subtext reflected dueling reviews of the novel. Six years earlier, it will be recalled, Shklovsky had predicted its failure. Mirsky had subsequently panned part 2, coming under fire but winning the support of Gorky, who told Stalin that Mirsky was "absolutely correct" and defended him in

Pravda.[14] Gorky declared that everyone knew Fadeyev's novel was bad, and why couldn't a British communist say so? When part 3 appeared, Usievich wrote a favorable review, but Mekhlis refused to publish it.[15] Yermilov used *Red Virgin Soil* in the second half of 1935 to battle the anti-Fadeyev forces. He took on Shcherbakov indirectly, by denouncing the head of the Writers' Union's party cell, Dmitry Marchenko.[16]

He describes to Fadeyev the presidium meeting that we saw in the previous chapter, which heard his report on *Red Virgin Soil*. Such annual reviews were not uncommon, but Yermilov interpreted this summons as a hostile move by Shcherbakov.[17] His report was followed by a response from *Literaturnaia gazeta*'s Selivanovsky, who was now one of Yermilov's rivals. During Selivanovsky's remarks, Yermilov strategically seated himself behind a stack of newspapers (a year's worth of *Literaturnaia gazeta* and *Red Virgin Soil* had been brought to the meeting). Screened by the newspapers, he wrote out a denunciation of *Literaturnaia gazeta*, addressing it to Andreyev and Yezhov, with a copy to Stetsky. He wrote a second denunciation to the Writers' Union party group. All of this he described gleefully to Fadeyev. "[I wrote] about the paper's *lack of principle*, about a series of very serious political and theoretical errors and distortions."[18]

He invokes principle and "serious political and theoretical errors" to mask his own participation in the culture of intrigue (which so disgusted him when practiced by others). Far from hiding his denunciations as secret, shameful acts, he shares them with Fadeyev. Stanley Milgram's conclusion regarding the potential of ordinary people to become monsters is applicable here: when people obey an authority's commands, even to torture or kill, they do not abandon their sense of morality. They instead find a new moral yardstick. Morality is equated with diligently fulfilling the expectations of authority.[19]

Publication of literary magazines in the three months after Kirov's assassination was delayed as Glavlit combed through every name in every page and reviewed each magazine's entire content, sometimes taking five or six days to decide on a single line of text. Names of the arrested were removed and new covers had to be made.[20]

It was April 1935 when Yermilov marked large sections for excision in a poem by Selvinsky, a frequent contributor to *Red Virgin Soil*. Instead of simply showing Selvinsky the damage and asking if he would agree to the cuts, Yermilov decided to "test Selvinsky's reaction," as he put it to Fadeyev, and added a nasty twist. "If you want," he told Selvinsky, "we'll publish it, but with harsh criticism."[21] Selvinsky withdrew his manuscript and took it to the State Literary Publishing House (Goslitizdat), which published it with the offending passages intact.

Yermilov reacted with outrage and spleen. "I thought for a long time about what to do," he told Fadeyev. He decided to submit a review of Selvinsky's book to *Pravda*.[22] "I wrote it pondering and chewing over every line, I wrote with subtlety, with hints and contemptuous courtesy, giving Selvinsky's mastery its due."[23] He calculated that a tone of professional restraint would be more effective than the indignant screeching that had become *Pravda*'s hallmark under Mekhlis. With his review, Yermilov hoped to punish Selvinsky, show himself to be vigilant, and increase his own authority. He was by no means certain that Mekhlis would publish his review, but he was unprepared for what actually happened.

> [My review] appeared with a different title, without my subtleties, and with the addition of a phrase I did not write: "It's not as though Selvinsky is such a great master." . . . I thought this was vulgar and diminished the significance of the blow to Selvinsky.[24]

Mekhlis got Yermilov to accept being treated dishonestly and disrespectfully:

> I sought out Mekhlis—he immediately elevated [the matter] to great political importance—we are on the eve of an international skirmish, we can't allow anyone to wriggle this way and that, this is Selvinsky's first warning, "You have done a magnificent, very important thing."[25]

Mekhlis's game of dirty tricks disguised as communist rectitude should have been familiar to Yermilov. By implying that party leaders could foresee outcomes that had never occurred to Yermilov, Mekhlis cut him down to size. By adding a few flattering words, he persuaded Yermilov to accept the slight.

Yermilov was impressed with Mekhlis's directness and ideological argument, but he still thought that strategically it was best to acknowledge Selvinsky's mastery. He proposed devising a gentler phrase to characterize Selvinsky's artistry. Mekhlis dismissed this idea:

> You will excuse me. I want you to learn consistency in delivering a Bolshevik blow. At one time we criticized you in *Pravda* for displaying liberalism—but now I think you should be given a chance.[26]

In a psychological maneuver not unlike his treatment of Avdeyenko, Mekhlis dished out flattery with an implicit threat embedded deep within. The result: Yermilov relinquished his last remnant of independent thought on the Selvinsky matter—the issue of granting his poetic talent.

But a note of uncertainty creeps into his letter to Fadeyev: "[Mekhlis] thought I had diminished the significance of my article by half—maybe so—he's not familiar with the literary milieu, and considerations that are important to us could seem trivial to him. What do you think?"[27]

Had Yermilov's article appeared as he had written it, he would have regained some of the public authority he had had in RAPP. The message instead was that he lacked the sophistication to divine or construct the party position. Slavoj Žižek's description of the internal Other applies here:

> The subject is confronted with some substantial Truth, a secret from which he is excluded, which evades him *ad infinitum*—the inaccessible heart of the Law beyond the infinite series of doors . . . his external position *vis-à-vis* the Other (the fact that he experiences himself as excluded from the secret of the Other) is internal to the Other itself . . . precisely as excluded from the Other, we are already part of its game.[28]

Also in 1935, Yermilov had to give his opinion of Dmitry Maznin, a literary critic who had been part of Averbakh's group in RAPP and with whom Yermilov continued to work at *Red Virgin Soil*. Following Kirov's assassination, Maznin was expelled from the party for double-dealing (*dvurushnichestvo*).[29] As part of that process, Yermilov voted to expel him from the Goslitizdat party group. But a few months later, in June 1935, the Party Control Commission recommended reinstatement, and Yermilov was again asked for his opinion.

Yermilov wrote in favor of reinstatement, citing the investigation that had cleared Maznin. In October, however, there was a new investigation, and Maznin was arrested for "insufficient vigilance against Zinovyevism." Yermilov panicked: his support for reinstatement could now be used as evidence of insufficient vigilance or even sabotage. He sent the Writers' Union party group a lengthy self-defense, emphasizing that he had based his recommendation on the Party Control Commission's conclusions (*SL*, 217–22).

Shcherbakov replied drily that Yermilov had had "no right" to be guided by those findings, since two months later Maznin had met with "some swine or other,"[30] and prior to the second expulsion Maznin had been checked "from every angle" by the *raikom* (district party committee). But, Yermilov wailed to Fadeyev, it was unthinkable that the Party Control Commission also had not checked Maznin "from every angle."

> I am even surprised that a comrade as highly qualified as Shcherbakov could put forth such an argument. Just think about it: how many appeals from Trotskyists and Zinovyevites did the Party Control Commission reject? And if in *June 1935* the Party Control Commission reinstates Maznin, one among hundreds or maybe thousands, isn't it clear that it considered *everything* that there was to consider? (Yermilov to Fadeyev, Apr. 21, 1936, l. 27; emphasis in original)

Besides, Yermilov went on, if Maznin's contacts were a threat to national security, why would the party even bother soliciting party members' opinions on whether he should be reinstated?

Was the party capricious in expelling, reinstating, and re-expelling Maznin? Or was it laying a trap? Each assessment forced Yermilov to make a recommendation that could turn treasonous with the next assessment.

> Was I really supposed to follow the example of those pathetic, contemptible mediocrities who are afraid to "leave a paper trail," who don't refuse to give information over the phone where there won't be any witnesses but fight tooth and nail against providing written confirmation of their words? Nothing was easier than to behave like that. But I would have felt like a *coward*— and before whom? Before my party! I would have been *concealing* my opinion from the party on a matter that the party had *asked* me about! How can people like that become fighters against enemies? These are people who are afraid of their party and fill the ranks of traitors and deserters.[31]

Were we to come across this excerpt without knowing its author or context, we would imagine its writer to be a true believer. Yet it does not matter whether this passage reflects the credo of the Bolshevik ideal self or if it is an imitation by an unprincipled cynic. The psychological response is the same. The cadre has tried to follow the party's judgment, but the party prevents him from doing so. It has offered two contradictory judgments and withholds the final resolution.

The cadre has no way to protect himself. But still he must try. Yermilov explained to the Writers' Union party cell that he believed Maznin was trustworthy based on his own and his colleagues' judgment, but that

> after the murder of Comrade Kirov, naturally I could not help asking myself whether [Maznin's trustworthy demeanor] was just the skillful mask of a double-dealer. Therefore I not only didn't speak out at the meeting of the Goslitizdat party group . . . against expelling Maznin from the party, but I even made a point of emphasizing that never having been in close or personally friendly relations with him, I of course could not vouch for his not being a double-dealer. (*SL*, 220)

To atone for his error, he promises greater vigilance. A matter of survival, this promise also reflects an important aspect of party culture—the recognition of certain party elders as, in Halfin's words, "hermeneuts of the soul" who can see through a person's exterior to his inner essence.[32]

> *The comrades know my ability to expose the enemy's wiliness, the various forms it assumes to extend its influence, the various ways in which it deceives the party.* And if for the first time in my life I did not sense in Maznin a person who succeeded in deceiving the party and its highest control body, then

to me that means first of all that the rotten Zinovyevite swine, the accursed band of murderers, will find in my person an even more heavily armed and vigilant enemy. (*SL*, 221; emphasis added)

Here we see Yermilov's self-credentialing as he tries to claim the special status of hermeneut, citing his numerous denunciations as proof.

But he is no hermeneut. He sent Fadeyev a copy of his recommendation for Maznin's reinstatement, asking him whether he found anything wrong in it. Yet without even waiting for that verdict, he resolves the dilemma in the very next sentence by reaffirming his devotion to the party: "But if I had it to do over, I'd still do it the same way, because otherwise I'd hate myself for cowardice—hiding my opinion from the party. And besides, what other opinion of Maznin could I have had, given the Party Control Commission's decision?"[33]

Shortly before the Shostakovich affair, Yermilov had planned an article for *Red Virgin Soil* blasting its competition—*Literary Critic, Novy mir, October, Molodaia gvardiia, Zvezda (The Star)*, and even *International Literature (Internatsionalnaia literatura)*. *Znamia* was the only journal he exempted. That he even thought of these journals as his competition is revealing: he wanted to regain the ascendancy he had had in RAPP. He assigned the article to Isai Lezhnev, providing him with "all the material for it" and then personally approving "every single word."[34] To give the article more weight, he got Fadeyev and fourteen other party writers to sign an accompanying letter of support. He submitted the issue to the censorship office on January 27, 1936, the day before "Muddle Instead of Music" appeared. While he was awaiting permission for the issue to go to press, he opened *Pravda* and could not believe his eyes. Staring back at him from the page was Lezhnev's article. (Mekhlis had filched it from the page proofs of *Red Virgin Soil*.) There was an important revision, too: the list of errant journals now included *Red Virgin Soil*.[35]

His scheme had boomeranged. In a rage, he wrote to Fadeyev. "So much for the integrity of your beloved Mekhlis, for whom I have lost all respect!"[36] Yermilov explained the episode as payback—he had heard gossip about Lezhnev and relayed it to a press official, Bogovoi. Yermilov justifies himself to Fadeyev using the standard formula for denunciations: "I considered it my party duty to inform him of this."[37]

Humiliated and apprehensive, Yermilov procured a medical recommendation to be relieved of his editorial duties. Shcherbakov countered that there was no one who could replace him. Yermilov turned to Fadeyev:

Write to Yudin [deputy head of the press section and editor in chief of *Literary Critic*] immediately, and for once in his life let that spineless seatwarmer show some (a) persistence (b) comradely relations toward me, and arrange my speedy removal from *Red Virgin Soil*. Make him see that I can't work there one more day under these conditions. Have him put me on the editorial board of *Literary Critic*. I gave all my time and strength to *Red Virgin Soil* and because of that I didn't do any of my own writing—and in return they've used Lezhnev's article not only to piss all over me but also to shit all over me and cover my head with vomit. (Yermilov to Fadeyev, Jan. 31, 1936, l. 100–101)

Four days later, however, damage control seemed the better part of valor, and he wrote again:

In my last letter I was all heated up because I had just read Lezhnev's article . . . I allowed myself some unacceptable expressions about Mekhlis and I regret them. You understand that I feel this inside. However unjustifiably cruelly he behaved toward me, I still can't not respect him—if only for the simple reason that he is the editor of *Pravda*. Looking closely at myself, I very soon found in myself true respect for L. Z. [Mekhlis] . . . All this is *inside*, deep and serious, so that there is no more need to talk about it.[38]

Mekhlis was not done with Yermilov, however. Shortly afterward, *Pravda* slammed Lebedev's novella *Childhood*, which had appeared in *Red Virgin Soil*.[39] Yermilov defended himself to Mekhlis, pointing out that *Pravda*'s review ignored the novella's content. In reply, Mekhlis ran a second review. It characterized Lebedev's story and Yermilov's decision to publish it as left deviationism.[40]

Faced with this dangerous charge, Yermilov worried: did it represent the party view, or only Mekhlis's personal opinion? When Kirpotin in 1932 warned against the "subjective idealism" of Libedinsky's *Birth of a Hero*, he cited a letter from Lenin to Gorky. Mekhlis felt no need to cite a higher authority.

Meanwhile, Yermilov struggled to make sense of the attack on Shostakovich. Bowing to Mekhlis's authority did not resolve the intellectual problem of reconciling the attacks on Shostakovich and other "left" artists with the elevation of Mayakovsky. He wrote to Fadeyev,

Someone has to explain this to those who work in the arts, and make it systematic, and explain that it's not a matter of chance . . . everyone perceives it as chance—I'm not talking about people like Olesha or Shklovsky, who has unrolled all his cynical tendencies, but about socially and psychologically healthier people![41]

A week later, he was still puzzling through it:

Meyerhold and Shostakovich were constantly being exalted, not long ago in a piece on *The Queen of Spades* [*Pikovaia dama*], *Pravda* proclaimed Meyerhold a genius (literally!), while Shostakovich's opera *Lady Macbeth of Mtsensk*, again in *Pravda*, just three months ago was proclaimed practically the best work in all of Soviet art. And now this same *Pravda* speaks of *Meyerholdism* as one would of a starkly negative phenomenon, and has struck both of them—Meyerhold and Shostakovich—so hard that they have both been knocked off their rails and, rumor has it, have gone off and gotten themselves dead drunk. With no preparation of any kind, without any transitioning or mitigation![42]

Unlike Aleksei Tolstoy, who wrote what "they" wanted in exchange for a luxurious lifestyle, accepting whatever curve balls the party threw, Yermilov wanted the party to be logical. That was exactly what the party would never do. His perplexity verges on distress; his reaction belies one writer's supposition that "RAPPites of all stripes are rubbing their hands with glee [at Shostakovich's disgrace] now that freedom has come to an end for writers and artists" (*VKI*, 292).

The party's refusal to offer a logical explanation of its line forced the cadre to do it himself:

The general direction of the attack is absolutely correct, and if nuances had been observed . . . it would have been a great joy . . . The two articles on Shostakovich (of which the second—"An Off-Key Ballet" ["Baletnaia falsh"] (Feb. 6)—is an excellent article, are written or inspired by comrades whose names mean a great deal to us—whose names mean *everything* . . . so . . . it was important to employ what I am calling nuance. The articles produced the impression of an earthquake![43]

The "excellent" article was rumored to have been instigated by Stalin. Again we sense the lingering unease; even as Yermilov insists that the articles are "mainly correct," he is still upset, because "writers at this point are seriously disoriented, they do not sense the *line* in the arts . . . many talented artists feel that whatever happens is a matter of chance."[44]

Having declared that it is not a matter of chance, he reveals in his next letter that he indeed regards it as chance:

Meyerhold, too, has his revolutionary side (his early shows in the first years of the revolution—*The D. E. Trust* [Trest D. E.], *Mystery-Bouffe* [Misteriia-buff], *The Magnanimous Cuckold* [Velikolepny rogonosets], *Roar, China!* [Rychi, Kitai!] etc.), but even so he's been removed *in his entirety*. And it's true, there really is no system here, only complete chaos of chance and patronage, and it's as if they're telling us, '"You think up a system for it, because that's what you're there for!"'[45]

Yermilov has slipped into his real voice. He recognizes the "chaos of chance and patronage." In it he also reads insult: to Shostakovich, Meyerhold, to himself, and to all cadres charged with explaining the new line to their staff and readers.

Indignation notwithstanding, he accepted the task. He groped his way to an awkward defense of *Pravda*'s position.

> Somewhere in all this there is an objective line. The masses have matured and are on the road to art . . . the masses are becoming Stakhanovites, cultured; tomorrow the whole people will be creative. In this context it's necessary to strike a blow against both the big and little Shostakoviches and Meyerholds to clear the way for the people in art![46]

A contrived justification was better than none at all. A true believer would have done the same—sought whatever justification possible to uphold his faith in the party.

With each unexplained policy shift, the party betrays its adherents. The adherent must make the cognitive dissonance go away; he must, in Žižek's phrase, "reestablish the broken network of communication."[47] He redefines the betrayals so that they are no longer betrayals and renews his vows of obedience. But the justifications are never sufficient to keep the questions and the feeling of insult from bubbling back up.

The end result is a crisis of selfhood. For the true believer it is either obliteration of the self or a betrayal of faith. For Yermilov, it was self-hatred.

> I hate myself for exuding a dubious aroma of such pitiful failures! For writing these long letters, and because all of you out there in Sukhum are, as you write, "rooting for me!" Just look at me—what a pathetic martyr for art! Another figure of our Stakhanovite times![48]

Hearing that his comrades are "rooting" for him has brought Yermilov to a moment of self-awareness, in which he sees himself through the eyes of others. This shift in perspective shows him that he is "inferior to what [he] believed, assumed, or hoped to be."[49] In a culture that encouraged self-transformation through taking control of one's own biography, Yermilov's perception of the pitiful figure he cuts makes him despise himself.[50] He could hardly be further from the model of the resolute Bolshevik commissar exemplified by Mekhlis, a true hermeneut of the soul.

Having built his biography on a zeal for denunciation, Yermilov wound up isolated:

Besides you and Yury [Libedinsky], I have no one I can talk to about literary-political matters. I . . . have been in a literary environment where I have no friends or colleagues to socialize with, but where there are many people hostile to me. What a lot of them I've had to offend and disappoint! (and in most cases for cause) . . . the party group secretary himself [Marchenko] takes offense at me—for cause, for his own serious political error—but he takes offense! I am like the coachman Iona in Chekhov's story: "To whom can I tell my anguish?"[51]

"In most cases." He implicitly admits that sometimes he has done so out of malice.

Mediocre submissions to *Red Virgin Soil* were another cause for anxiety. How could he demonstrate satisfactory performance? When Fadeyev missed a deadline for a new installment of *The Last of the Udegs*, Yermilov implored him to send something, somehow: if the next issue appeared without it, "it would be a catastrophe in today's conditions."[52] Seven months before the Zinovyev-Kamenev trial, Yermilov already felt how dangerous it was to be an editor. Each issue was a compendium of potential incriminating evidence. Were even a single one of his contributors arrested, he could be next. When two of his authors, Viktor Orlov and Mikhail Svetlov, came under a cloud, *Pravda* attacked the magazine. Terror begets more terror: *Pravda*'s criticisms prompted Shcherbakov to investigate *Red Virgin Soil* in April 1936.[53] Yermilov wrote to Fadeyev,

If *Pravda* had taken *Red Virgin Soil* to task for cause—for Viktor Orlov (who by the way is now being out and out called a *counterrevolutionary* writer!), and, say, for Svetlov (although the way they liquidated Svetlov was, of course, *completely impermissible*—even monstrous—but that's another question)—then it still would have been possible to live with it. If Lezhnev's article had retained its original formulation about *Red Virgin Soil* and *Znamia* being the best journals, then it would absolutely have been possible to live with that, even with a grilling [*prorabotka*] over Orlov and Svetlov. But *Pravda* doesn't take into consideration that when you're editing a magazine, especially one that's at the center of attention (in Czech the word for "attention" is *pozornost*, "shame"—"the center of shame"!), in some conditions, since the editor is engaged in a struggle, something may arise for which it really is necessary to scold him, and therefore scolding him *for nothing is completely out of the question*![54]

The party has once again forced him into crisis. He responds with the prescribed method of proving his loyalty and vigilance—denunciation. Yermilov looked for a suitable victim—someone vulnerable, but also someone whose exposure as an enemy would be an event. Afinogenov had just registered a vigorous protest against the shuttering of the Moscow Art Theater II, a casualty of the Shostakovich affair.[55] The theater's closing had been by Politburo decree, and Yermilov saw his opening (*VKI*, 297). In an "informational memo," he painted Afinogenov's protest as a crime—using his posts in the theater and the press to defy a party resolution.[56] Afinogenov, Yermilov wrote, was discrediting Soviet literary criticism with claims that it was unprincipled. We recall that Yermilov himself had decried this lack of principle, privately to Fadeyev and even publicly at the second plenum. Yermilov also got in a swipe at the Writers' Union party group (Marchenko again) for failing to discipline Afinogenov. Self-protection, self-advancement, envy, and spite all fed one another.

Yermilov addressed his denunciation to Shcherbakov and Mekhlis, the very officials at whose hands he himself had been shamed. To remove the shame from himself, he demonstrated to them his proficiency in shaming others. He did not omit to send a copy to Shcherbakov's boss, Andreyev. Andreyev had it printed in *Young Communist Pravda* and *Soviet Art* (*Sovetskoe iskusstvo*), so that at the formalism-naturalism discussions Shcherbakov was forced to bring up Afinogenov's defiance of the Politburo resolution. Yermilov crowed to Fadeyev, "Both Shcherbakov and Stavsky speak out against the thick journals in the language of my memos and the one you wrote. *Novy mir* [Gronsky] has been routed."[57] "All my calculations on the Afinogenov question have turned out to be correct: *Young Communist Pravda* and *Soviet Art* both supported me—both of them ran editorials quoting my letter to the party group almost in its entirety."[58] To complete the victory, Yermilov was invited by Mekhlis to contribute to *Pravda*.[59]

At this moment of triumph, Yermilov assured Fadeyev that any Soviet citizen who held to his principles would be vindicated regardless of whether he had connections and patrons. Yermilov washed his hands of any responsibility for Afinogenov's fate: "Everyone sees that [Kirshon's and Afinogenov's] downfall . . . is not *accidental*, but is the result of their whole life."[60] This assurance was a manifestation of what Milgram would later call the "systemic devaluation of the victim" by a perpetrator who convinces himself that the victim deserves what he gets.[61] One can only wonder whether Yermilov recalled this episode on hearing of Fadeyev's suicide twenty years later.

In a shame culture triumph is ephemeral. The following year, Yermilov's fear of arrest reached fever pitch. He tried desperately to be rid of his "post" at *Red Virgin Soil*: "Sasha, I'm simply *imploring* you to arrange this matter speedily. Understand that I no longer have the right to make any mistakes."[62]

Not until August 5, 1938, did he leave *Red Virgin Soil*—Stalin removed him for publishing Shaginian's novel *Ticket to History* (*Bilet po istorii*) (perhaps because of its references to Lenin's non-Russian ancestry). In any case, the terror was ending—perhaps his particular talents were no longer needed. He was put in dry dock at the Gorky Institute of World Literature.[63]

Describing the psychological conflict experienced by someone whose prestige requires him to write what he doesn't believe, Fromm writes, "The more he wants to protect himself from recognizing his true motivation, the more ardently he must believe in [his rationalizations]."[64] Yermilov experienced the same anxious self-examination as did his victim Afinogenov and judged himself by the same standard of self-alignment with communist "objectivity." Two months after the Zinovyev and Kamenev trial, Yermilov wrote to Fadeyev, in a tone that suggests he was convincing himself, that the "shaking out" of the Trotskyists, who "dirtied the air" and had no claim to accompany the nation further into socialism, was a consistent and lawful development (zakonomernost).[65]

And what about Afinogenov? In 1937 he was expelled from the party. His close ties to Averbakh, who was arrested in April of that year, could have clinched his expulsion even without Yermilov's interference, as could his marriage to an American. Yermilov's March 1936 denunciation may or may not have had a role. Hellbeck has shown that Afinogenov's expulsion from the party shattered his self-image and prompted him to embark on a self-purification campaign to make himself worthy of the party's trust, attempting "to align his 'subjective' self with 'objective' reality."[66] He purified himself by rationalizing Stalin's purges as the only route to the communist paradise.

Reinstated in the party a year later as the terror wound down, Afinogenov could take comfort from a Central Committee resolution blaming unjust expulsions such as his own on false denunciations by enemies.[67] Yet the conclusions he drew require scrutiny. He decided that the party had been right to test his loyalty even though he was innocent—otherwise he would never have worked to purify himself. And he persisted in believing that some of his colleagues had deserved to be "dragged to the NKVD"—they had "had the audacity to waste so much paper" on fiction that was "insipid," "cold," and "vile."[68] These conclusions were necessary because the party's mistake in crediting the false denunciations raised troubling possibilities. Either the party had erred, in which case it was fallible; or the party was infallible, in which case the expulsions were not a mistake, and the Central Committee's explanation was a cover-up for intentional arrests of dedicated communists. The believer will do anything to avoid such a conclusion. Once again, he constructs justifications for the party, in whose betrayal he cannot bear to believe.

There was no good answer to the question of how to be a cadre. Cynics and true believers alike had to justify to themselves every party transgression. This led them toward an ever deeper dvoedushie, one that increasingly called to mind that favored term of the terror press, *dvurushnik* (double-dealer). In suggesting a self behind the public self, this term struck at the heart of the cadre's dilemma. The "double-dealing" that provoked *Pravda*'s sanctimonious outrage—the concealment of unsanctioned acts behind an appealing mask—was, when it existed at all, merely the flip side of the doubled soul that grew in the party's loyal cadres. The divided self knew that it, too, was a masked double-dealer.

Vladimir Stavsky and the Language Codes of Terror

WITH GORKY SAFELY dead and Shcherbakov having moved on to new career horizons, Stalin was looking for a cadre to lead the Writers' Union through the next political shift. He was now strong enough to kill off his political opposition, and in the midst of preparations for the Zinovyev-Kamenev trial, he was looking ahead to the trials that would finish off Radek, Aleksei Rykov, and Bukharin.

The show trials served multiple purposes. In addition to condemning Old Bolshevik colleagues who might have acted as a brake on Stalin, they served as enormous nets for catching millions of citizens who could be linked to the defendants; and the public nature of the proceedings, covered prominently in the press over a period of eighteen months, created a new layer of culture complete with its own set of suppositions, and a vocabulary to express it. Allegations and putative evidence of widespread enemy activity fanned patriotism while stoking fear, and deepened the culture of us and them. Lexical formulas like "double-dealers" and "enemies of the people" became cultural signposts as people encountered them in the press, repeated them in conversations, and eventually internalized them.

The next Writers' Union leader was to spearhead the mass physical destruction of undesirable writers. Within three weeks of Gorky's death in June 1936, Stalin informed the Writers' Union party group that the Writers' Union needed radical change, and that party leaders were taking up the question of who should lead it (*MMN*, 521). Shcherbakov's departure reduced the number of Writers' Union secretaries to four—Stavsky, Lakhuti, Ivanov, and Kulik. Kulik operated from Kiev as head of the Ukrainian branch and was never considered a potential first secretary; he was arrested the following year. The Persian émigré poet Lakhuti and the nonparty Ivanov were also not viable candidates to run the union.

Without moving to fill the vacancies, the Politburo simply let the day-to-day operation of the union devolve onto Stavsky.[1] He was never named first secretary, and indeed he brought neither literary stature nor political savvy to the job. The author of four slim volumes of wooden fiction filled with stereotypes of collectivization and sabotage, he was widely derided as a writer, even by his RAPP colleagues.[2] He lacked Gronsky's mental acuity to surmise Stalin's goals; he lacked Shcherbakov's dispassionate disregard for writers' protests and exhortations. His main qualification was his zeal. In 1932 he had seen class enemies in those who welcomed RAPP's demise;[3] that mentality would be useful now.

Stavsky's two years at the helm of the Writers' Union coincided almost exactly with Kerzhentsev's at the Arts Committee and Yezhov's at the NKVD.[4] Arts policy was influenced not by Stavsky but by Kerzhentsev, who had the ability to propose legislation to the Politburo and eclipsed even Agitprop, which, like the Writers' Union, operated without a formal head after Shcherbakov's reassignment.[5] Andreyev, the secretary who oversaw Agitprop, also had a lesser role than Kerzhentsev.[6]

By birth a member of the working underclass, by temperament a hothead and a moralist, Stavsky had been formed by his political education and field experience into a rabid enemy hater. For the time being, Stalin needed a destroyer and not a builder, and Stavsky fit the bill. A remark Stalin is said to have made about Mekhlis applied to Stavsky as well: "You mean you want to put Mekhlis on a project that involves building things up? If you're demolishing things, smashing, destroying—he's good for that."[7] Stavsky's naiveté and underdeveloped critical mind meant that Stalin could not rely on him to intuit his intentions or theorize party policy as he did with Mekhlis, but he had Kerzhentsev for that. What Stavsky could be relied on for was to unmask hidden "enemies" with abandon. His susceptibility to the power of suggestion turned him into exactly the kind of fanatic that Stalin needed during the Great Purge, so when Stalin gave two speeches on March 20 and April 1, 1937, on the need to unmask enemies in the party,[8] Stavsky could be counted on to get busy.

Like Shcherbakov, Stavsky was one of those fortunate members of the working class who found their way into the apparat.[9] He was born Vladimir Petrovich Kirpichnikov in the provincial capital of Penza in 1900. His father, a pipe fitter who was either disabled or otherwise not viable, died when Stavsky was four. The boy and his mother, a tailor, lived in poverty; she died when he was about fourteen. With only a fifth-grade education, the teenager supported himself by hammering metal in a smithy and finding jobs in pipe and paper factories, where he encountered the activists who infiltrated the factories to spread Bolshevism among the workers. When the Bolsheviks swept through Penza in the fall of 1917, the seventeen-year-old joined their ranks.[10] His Civil War experiences in the Red Army proved decisive in forming his outlook and self-image. He fought in a "village pacification" unit, killing peasants who resisted the brutalities of War Communism. Later he was assigned to a special unit (*osoby otdel*) of the Cheka on the eastern front. The Bolsheviks gave him a sense of belonging, a cause to fight for, and perhaps most important, the ability to succeed—he was made a military commissar and decorated for his intelligence work.

Stavsky's initiation into Bolshevism, which gave his life meaning and respect, was thus defined by class enmity, the dispossession and murder of the peasantry, and the secret police techniques of targeting individuals and compiling incriminating dossiers, and it was these behaviors that provided him with the résumé as well as the habits of thought that would guide his career. He belonged to the subset of the urban proletariat that Lenin sought to incite against "kulak hoarders," the better-off peasants who were blamed for bread shortages during the Civil War.[11] Inflamed against the kulaks, Stavsky during his stint in the countryside would have seen just how tenuous the party's hold there was.[12] A decade later, when the government sent legions of urban workers to the countryside to subdue peasants resisting collectivization, it found in Stavsky a cadre experienced in such work.[13] When Stalin traveled across the country in 1928 intent on establishing squads to extract grain from the peasants at gunpoint,[14] Stavsky was made plenipotentiary for grain requisitioning in the agriculturally rich Kuban region.[15] He had full authority to conduct operations according to his interpretation of central party directives and without regard for orders from local officials.[16] He prefigured the 25,000ers whom Stalin sent into the countryside in early 1930.[17]

Stavsky's service as a plenipotentiary occurred at a time of growing contempt for the law. Law codes were regarded as bourgeois institutions designed to regulate private property and irrelevant to the Soviet Union, which was expected soon to become a classless state. Procurator General Nikolai Krylenko and Yevgeny Pashukanis, the foremost authority on legal thought, advocated simplified legal processes as a transition to the expected withering away of the law.[18] Pashukanis therefore rejected the careful distinctions and finely drawn laws of the law code in favor of a simplified legal transfer culture. Robert Sharlet has pointed out that Pashukanis's preference for "simplicity" and "flexibility," while never resulting in changes to the law code, was influential in the law school curriculum and in the eyes of society.[19] Dekulakization and the February 1930 decree that allowed plenipotentiaries to disregard the law were examples. Once having withered away, the law would give way to communist morality and revolutionary consciousness.[20] Stavsky likely never thought about the meaning of a legal transfer culture, but his understanding of law and legality would have come from these ideas.

By the time Stavsky took charge of the Writers' Union in August 1936, the Pashukanis school had been discredited and a normative legal culture was being rebuilt under the authority of Andrei Vyshinsky (the draft constitution of June 1936, for example, promised elections by secret ballot and an end to discrimination based on social origins).[21] Nevertheless, key elements of the Pashukanis model remained. These included an emphasis on confession over objective evidence, the goal of eliminating the kulaks as a class, and employing terror in disregard of the law.[22] In a conflict with rule of law (*zakonnost*), party objectives prevailed.[23]

Stavsky's formative experiences, then, came during periods of the greatest radicalism in government policy and developed in him a siege mentality. With dekulakization as his training ground, he developed an obsession with kulaks and other "enemies." He appears to have genuinely believed in the threats of industrial and agricultural sabotage. In the context of internal party debates over economic and social policy in the first half of the 1930s, Stavsky was a radical in the mold of Yezhov, who advocated expulsions and purges over education and indoctrination, and who brought his own entourage of "enthusiasts" into the NKVD.[24] Stavsky's *mentalité* may best be understood through Lynne Viola's characterization of 1930s Soviet culture as "based on a mixture of traditional Russian radical fanaticism and voluntarism, a siege-like paranoid mentality, and the force of unleashing years of pent-up class rage and retribution."[25]

His broken-childhood upbringing, extreme poverty, and his fifth-grade education turned the regime's leaders and spokesmen into his tutors and made him receptive to state-created formulas; in this he recalls Avdeyenko. Exterminating the kulaks was an act of social purification necessary to achieve communism; destroying the "old exploiter society" was the highest moral good and a cause for communist pride.[26]

In his diary he recorded melodramatic reports of saboteurs caught in the nick of time by a party official.[27] Against this background he charts his literary future in words that sound like a caricature of communist self-fashioning: "My heart beats with the sensation of struggle. Yes, struggle!"[28] He models his imagined literary career on military glory: "What fighting pages I will write!"[29] He seeks to purify himself by losing weight and cutting back on his drinking: "It's amazing: I found the strength to rid myself of alcohol and nicotine—I just put my mind to it and broke the habit, just like that, but this time it's not working. But it will. I'll start today."[30]

This informer whose job was to send writers to their deaths saw himself as a principled and ethical communist.[31] If he heard of dishonest or corrupt communists, he reacted with apparently unfeigned indignation. One such incident concerned an official who routinely used his government car for intimate encounters with his female staff. His wife, not to be outdone, got a driver's license herself and used the car for her own trysts. Their chauffeur, wisecracking that "it wasn't a car but a whorehouse on wheels," wondered at how this official of working-class origin had come to resemble "a pig at the trough," and Stavsky shared his amazement.[32]

He also recorded his disgust upon learning, some three years too late, of the widespread theft of state property during the construction of the Peredelkino dachas. A friend who had worked as a driver admitted to Stavsky that he had pocketed a quick two thousand rubles hauling sand, brick, and other materials for an official bent on building a luxurious dacha. Stavsky asked his friend if he was not ashamed.

"Why should I be?" [rejoined his friend.] "Everyone was grabbing whatever he could!"

"And Leshkevich?" [asked Stavsky.] "Did he build his dacha honestly?"

"Oh, come on. Of course he took stuff for himself. Lumber over here, bricks over there, no charge for transporting them. He made the rules, and he built himself a good one!"

Stavsky added his own comment in his diary: "What blind fools the secretaries of the Writers' Union were—Shcherbakov, Stavsky, and the others."[33]

Stavsky's ability to be outraged at theft, graft, and adultery and yet participate in the extermination of his countrymen without a second thought again reflects his party upbringing. Even as the party was carrying out its extermination policy, the Party Control Commission kept watch on members' personal conduct, investigating charges of drunken behavior, corruption, and "moral dissoluteness."[34] Discussing the party's perceived need "to maintain the highest standards of ideological and ethical purity" (routinely attained through membership purges), David L. Hoffman writes, "Throughout the 1930s officials were repeatedly instructed to use coercion and violence, so the fact that the Party reprimanded them for rudeness seems odd. Yet it was precisely the emphasis on propriety and decorum that helped legitimate . . . extreme coercive acts."[35]

The career path that led Stavsky to literature began after the Civil War, when he was sent to Rostov-on-Don as a political instructor and workers' correspondent covering grain collection for the local newspaper. Drawing on his war experiences and the social prejudices he had internalized, he wrote sketches and short stories about battlefield heroism, grain requisitioning, and sabotage. He had a conversational writing style that was clear, direct, and forceful, streaked with sarcasm and righteous indignation. These qualities matched the party's expectations of worker correspondents, who were supposed to "instill the newspapers with a new, fresh, and even 'succulent' language, based on the colloquial speech of the factory and the farm . . . [they] wrote 'simply,' 'clearly,' and 'precisely,' making no effort to embellish or engage in abstraction. Their style may have been a little rough around the edges, but it was direct and to the point."[36] He was drawn to anecdotes of self-sacrifice, which he recorded in his diary:

> And the heroes we have! A wounded soldier gets an order: Report to sick bay. He answers: "I cannot!"
> "But you've been given a battle order!"
> He stands up [illegible word] and enunciates each word: "As a citizen of the USSR I cannot leave the field of battle! I feel well. I serve the revolution." There it is—a ready-made story. I will write a story about this soldier.[37]

In his quest to become a writer, Stavsky followed the vision of self-transformation through industry and persistence. Selected to take the "Red Lenin" courses, he related the experience to Fadeyev in glowing terms, quoting Heraclitus and describing his intellectual growth after reading three thousand pages on Leninism and political economy: "I was an illiterate fool."[38] As to what Stavsky internalized from his reading, Moshe Lewin's observation comes to mind: "Speedy and half-baked mass education may tend to make people more vulnerable to propaganda and indoctrination."[39]

Although Stavsky's first book, a collection of Civil War sketches titled *They Made It Through* (*Proshli*), was published in 1924, his notebook jottings over the next eleven years reveal the extent to which he was still learning the elements of expository writing. "A writer worthy of the name does not repeat words." "Wherever possible, shorten your sentence. The most forceful sentence is the shortest."[40] He was among the cohort of novice writers who were given Tomashevsky's *Theory of Literature* as a technical handbook a few years before the Russian Formalists became objects of official opprobrium. In 1924 Stavsky copied down the lesson he was learning from the Formalists—that "the particular feature of art always remains its aesthetic, artistic side."[41]

In seven years in Rostov, Stavsky rose to become the editor of a newspaper and a literary magazine, secretary of RAPP's regional branch, and director of the press section of the North Caucasus *kraikom* (area party committee).[42] He gained the latter two posts after they were vacated by Fadeyev upon his transfer to Moscow in 1926. Fadeyev arranged Stavsky's transfer to Moscow two years later.[43]

His diary shows his hopes to develop into a bona fide literary talent. He lists plans for stories and exclaims, "The main thing in my life is to write, write, write!"[44] But when he ventured beyond newspaper reportage, he was hampered by an insufficient literary imagination and a facile view of characters as good or evil. In his 1931 novella *A Running Start* (*Razbeg*), which describes resistance to collectivization in the Kuban region, a parade of characters are predefined as "good" or "bad" according to their class, and words like *kulak* or *snokhach* serve as a shorthand substitute for a literary or dramatic portrait. Stavsky's works have neither the inner conflict that enlivens socialist realist heroes like Fyodor Gladkov's Gleb Chumalov, nor the suspense of Fadeyev's *The Rout*, nor even the heavy-handed symbolism of Libedinsky's *Birth of a Hero*. Stavsky's fiction reads as a numbing exercise in cliché. His writing was widely denigrated in private conversations even among his own cohort. Averbakh described it as "low-mediocre"; Boris Levin was moved to exclaim, "My God, what wretchedness!" (*MMN*, 124, 140). Gorky made it known to Shcherbakov that he found Stavsky's fiction appalling. Formulaic phrases like "what a large Bolshevik heart!" and "in a word, a Bolshevik," thought Gorky, showed Stavsky's "fundamental indifference."[45] More likely they were ineptitude's crutch.

Stavsky himself suspected as much and dreaded the thought.

It is not a question of content! The point is that [Zazubrin] has his own voice! I hear his voice very strongly! And, and I know that I, too, must have my own voice. Do I have it yet? I can't say for sure. And what a [illegible word] if I don't have one, and everything I've written is just part of the mass of dull and mediocre reading matter . . . Whose works should I study, and how? And now I see that so far I haven't studied anyone's works, I haven't studied at all. Fadeyev has Tolstoy, that's clear. And so? I reject Tolstoy—he's not it!

The appeal of Jack London? But what's there to say, when the task at hand is not studying in order to imitate but studying to go beyond! And one's own creation! Clear! To the point! Not done before! It's a competition without which there is no literary creation![46]

These uneasy ruminations underscored Stavsky's officially secure but emotionally uncomfortable place in literary life—somewhere above the literary circlists whom he was given the task of ridiculing at the third plenum but well short of any literary respectability behind the press's accolades.

The Formalist teachings from which Stavsky tried to learn were daily overwhelmed by counterexample in *Pravda*. Automatized language, identified by Shklovsky as the thing the writer must at all costs avoid, was for *Pravda* the very thing to strive for. Boris Groys has suggested that the automatization of Soviet slogans was the ultimate measure of propaganda's success: when thought has been automatized, the subconscious has successfully been manipulated. What Groys describes as "shaping the subconscious without revealing the mechanisms of the process" was particularly effective with poorly educated enthusiasts like Stavsky and Avdeyenko.[47] The regime's ideological language was utilitarian and relied on oppositions that oversimplify.[48]

Stavsky's first task as head of the Writers' Union was to open a "front" against Trotskyist "enemies" inside the Writers' Union with a series of front-page editorials in *Literaturnaia gazeta*. These articles of autumn 1936 accused writers by name and demanded a hunt to unmask "enemies"; at the same time, they were liberally seeded with the words "honor" (*chest*) and "honorable" (*chestny*).[49] These words were frequently associated with the security police; the more rabid the hunt for "enemies," the more frequently honor and purity were invoked. The fanfare surrounding the drafting of the Stalin constitution at this time allowed a perception of the party's benevolence even amid mass arrests. An unsigned article of September 1936, probably by Stavsky, praised the constitution as a reflection of the Soviet Union's "moral and ethical norms."[50]

Although the only remaining secretary besides Stavsky was Ivanov, Stavsky held meetings of an "expanded secretariat" with some fifteen or twenty people in attendance, continuing Shcherbakov's practices.[51] Shcherbakov's goal had been maximum conformity; Stavsky's was maximum accusations.[52] Others in attendance tried to restrain him. On one occasion, the Writers' Union's Azerbaijan office alleged Aseyev, Kirsanov, and Svetlov had taken advance payment for Russian translations of Azeri poetry, which they never completed. Stavsky brought the matter to the secretariat and proposed publishing a complaint against the three in *Literaturnaia gazeta*. This course of action, the likely outcome of which would be the poets' arrest, was strongly resisted by several of those present:

V[ALENTIN] KATAYEV: That's not the right way. We must summon the writers in question. We must hear their explanation.

STAVSKY: How come any commissar can publish a letter with an inquiry but a writer cannot. Here we have gotten used to deciding matters privately. Let them answer for themselves.

V. IVANOV: I think that it can be an inquiry from them, from the Azerbaijan union, but not from us. If they were given sloppy translations, we haven't read them to judge how far that is true.

STAVSKY: That is weak, comrades. At any workers' meeting there would be a storm over this.[53]

Katayev pointed out that Aseyev had submitted a partial translation that most likely justified his advance payment. The children's poet Agniia Barto suggested verifying the facts and then perhaps publishing a letter naming only those who had really done something wrong. Fedin agreed: "I think that the path the comrades suggest is the more correct one—talk [to the translators] first and then beat the drum. We could scare off a writer and ruin things instead of helping him."[54]

At this point it emerged that midway through the project Svetlov had lost several of the ponies (literal translations into Russian) that the Russian poets, who did not know Azeri, relied on for their verse translations. The Azerbaijan branch scrambled to find people who could do a hasty translation in order to meet the publishing deadline, after which part of the money originally allotted for the book's publication was spent on lavish banquets.[55] Now Stavsky gave in. But he berated the others for their "timidity":

STAVSKY: . . . there has been a colossal amount of swindling—I've been swindled as a worker of the Writers' Union, the whole organization's been swindled, the people [narod] have been swindled. If we think bringing peoples together is a matter of great significance, then what else can we call this kind of attitude to the matter, if not swindling . . . Since people do not want to publish [a complaint against the poets], I won't insist, but to me this shows the need for large-scale education among us all on the question of criticism and self-criticism. There is no other way I can explain the speeches of those comrades who argued against the publication of this letter from a whole organization on a matter in which they have a vital interest . . . Any issue of *Pravda*, from the first page to the last, even in the local news section, raises the issue of criticism. There is criticism of the police and so on, but we don't want to print our own.

IVANOV: We can print one, it just has to be based on evidence.

STAVSKY: A fact is still a fact. When I proposed publishing the gist of the matter the comrades said no, don't publish. In no way does that agree with the general line that one finds throughout the country . . . it is insulting to have comrades who don't consider it an obligation when they give promises and don't keep them. If this were a minor poet we were talking about, there would be no argument. I must say straight out, we are completely at the mercy of big names in poetry and prose. Since it's a major writer, keep quiet, don't disturb him. One can't even ask him a question.[56]

Stavsky's tirade has the ring of genuine belief. Here as in his diary, we hear a conviction in stark contrast to official language, including that of his own editorials. A few examples of the formulaic utterances taken from transcripts of similar meetings at this time and from newspaper pieces should suffice to show the difference between formula and Stavsky's real feeling in his words quoted above.

[Libedinsky under pressure at a meeting of the Writers' Union presidium:] The disgust and hatred for the villains sitting in the dock cannot be put into words. They are the scum of humanity—that is clear.[57]

[Pilniak defending himself in the Writers' Union presidium against accusations that would lead to his arrest and death:] I know only one thing, that the intelligentsia is going forward with the proletariat, with the peasantry, which is the construction of socialist society.[58]

[Stavsky in a front-page editorial for *Literaturnaia gazeta*:] Waves of the people's rage, hatred, and loathing for the heinous fascist murderers, demands by millions of working people from all nations are sealed within the wise sentence of the proletarian court.[59]

The exchange between Stavsky and the others at the secretariat meeting was completely different from the exchanges under Shcherbakov's tenure. Then, too, writers had defended beleaguered colleagues, but without success.[60] Stavsky had neither the authority nor the commanding personality to override the sentiment in the room. Precisely because he was speaking from the heart and in the heat of the moment, Katayev, Fedin, and Ivanov were able to seize upon their human connection to him and restrain him. His unmediated emotionalism burst through even in a letter to Stalin defending himself against his critics and ending with, "Comrade Stalin, I cannot stand it anymore! Help" (*MMN*, 127).

Stavsky did not suffer from the internal divisions that plagued Yermilov. There is a near-perfect coincidence between the personal attitudes he expresses when speaking from the heart and his public stance in *Literaturnaia gazeta*. His example shows that linguistic contrivance such as we find in official Stalinist formulas does not always denote hypocrisy or calculated self-protection. The paradoxical coupling of formulaic utterance and heartfelt emotion occurred in other variations as well. No writer was ever more in earnest than when hoping to save themselves from arrest, and yet at this moment many of them looked to prepackaged language to demonstrate their credibility. The way to show their worthiness was to employ prefabricated, overused, and sullied formulas in defense of what they most cherished, their lives and reputations. Let us add one more example, this one from *Literaturnaia gazeta* during the Piatakov-Radek trial in January 1937:

> To betray the working class, you have to be a scoundrel [*podlets*]. Therefore for every traitor there exists a fateful, irrevocable fate. Paraphrasing a well-known idea, we might say: socialism and villainy [*zlodeistvo*] are two incompatible things.

The author goes on to ask, "Can they really be called people in even the most elementary sense?" (*APVS*, 349–50).

Were it not for the intellectualizing reflection and uncommon locutions like "paraphrasing," we might guess that the author was Stavsky. The intellectualism that glances through might suggest Yermilov. In fact the author of this article is Platonov. Formula homogenizes identity, concealing even the most original mind.

Upon the conclusion of the Piatakov-Radek trial, the Hall of Columns, where it had been held, became the space for the Writers' Union's fourth plenum, devoted to Pushkin's centennial and held February 22–26, 1937.[61] At the same time, a jubilee plenum of the Central Committee celebrated the twentieth anniversary of the revolution. These events were part of a carefully timed alternation of fear and festivity, sending threatening messages followed by a welcome diversion.[62] We have seen this strategy at work on the individual level, when Firin let drop an implicit threat in conversation with Avdeyenko and then brought in his wife and daughter for music and dancing.

A plenum devoted to Pushkin was good news. The father of Russian literature had been on the do-not-publish list throughout the 1920s, a member of the landowning class to be "booted out of literature." This view of Pushkin faded as Stalin formulated a policy of national Bolshevism to succeed the cultural revolution. Pushkin was turned into a Soviet symbol, a political progressive whose vision of the future was realized by the Bolsheviks. As the Writers' Union was open to writers of any class background, the root of Pushkin's art would no longer be his class but instead his progressivism.[63] A Politburo resolution of July 1934 mandated the memorializing and popularizing of Pushkin, who had "perished by the bullet of a foreign adventurer doing the will of the landowning aristocracy."[64] A new cliché claimed the poet for the Soviet state: Pushkin was a fighter against tyranny; a friend of the Decembrists whose dream for the future had been fulfilled by the revolution; the first Russian writer to consider literature a socially engaged, national cause; a writer who was accessible.[65] Pushkin had a new biography.

The transformed Pushkin was presented to the mass reader in a 1936 book by Kirpotin, which provided a way to imagine Pushkin and a vocabulary for speaking about him in terms of Soviet achievements.[66] This book, written by an Agitprop official on behalf of a party firmly opposed to the idea that a text could be variously interpreted, inadvertently served as a primer in how to read for hidden meaning. In linking Pushkin to the revolution, Kirpotin winds up teaching his mass reader how to read for analogy. He points out, for example, that "To Licinius" ("Litsiniiu"), addressed to a Roman dictator, was really aimed at tsarist Russia. Here and in other poems, Kirpotin provides excerpts to show how a text can generate multiple meanings.[67] That these readings-by-analogy fed the Stalinist view does not undo their potential as a subversive lesson to the mass reader in allegorical and Aesopian interpretation.

The plenums had become an annual opportunity for writers to address one another in a way that was both public and personal. At the first of these gatherings in October 1932, writers had spoken with extraordinary candor, and many writers still held out hope for productive relations at the February 1935 plenum, when Shaginian offered her prescription for bridging the differences between writers and the party. As we have seen, the following year all of that had changed as the third plenum was held amid *Pravda*'s disgracing of Shostakovich and demands for self-criticism.

The Pushkin plenum might have been expected to be a continuation of this discouraging trajectory, especially after the show trials. The opening addresses by Stavsky and Andrei Bubnov, the commissar of education and culture, connected Pushkin to Soviet justice and imagined his approval of the trials.[68] Many of the nearly two hundred delegates followed Stavsky's lead, referring to Bukharin, Radek, and other "traitors" in their own speeches.[69] But conformity was only one of three literary postures that we find among delegates to this plenum. A second posture was to boycott the plenum and stay home. This risky option was chosen by several high-profile party and nonparty writers: Aseyev, Bedny, Bezymensky, Kirsanov, Vladimir Lugovskoi, Pasternak, Selvinsky, Svetlov, Utkin, and Zharov. The ten of them constituted 5 percent of the delegates. A third literary posture was adopted by the three writers who accepted invitations to deliver keynote speeches. They used Aesopian language to speak to their colleagues over the heads of Stavsky and other overseers (although perhaps not Kirpotin).

Coded language may seem unlikely, even out of the question, in an official plenum speech. Article 58, section 10 of the law code made critical statements cause for a charge of anti-Soviet agitation.[70] Section 12 criminalized anyone who heard someone else make a criticism and failed to report it. Even apart from these considerations, it may be hard to imagine that all three speakers would settle on the same strategy. We should keep in mind, however, that in February 1937 most arrests of writers had not yet occurred, and also that, in the quest for answers on how to behave under political repression, Russian writers in the 1930s sought models of behavior among the pantheon of writers who had endured persecution under the tsars. In particular the reign of Nicholas I, with its mistrust and surveillance of the intelligentsia, presented an analogy to the 1930s; and descriptions of the 1830s were widely understood among writers and intellectuals as commentary on the present. In official discourse, Pushkin was opposed to the autocrat and therefore was "with us." This characterization made it easy to play on the question of which autocrat was meant, Nicholas I or Stalin, and who exactly was meant by "us." Pushkin could serve as a symbol of resistance not only to Nicholas I but also to Stalin.

Tikhonov gave the formal address on Pushkin's poetry, Tynianov on Pushkin's prose, and the party theater critic and scholar Iogann Altman on Pushkin's drama. All three cited Pushkin to critique Soviet literary policy, to deplore hack literature, and to argue against the selective interpretation of a writer's oeuvre. It is clear from the archival record that Tikhonov's audience understood his remarks as double-voiced, as when he quoted lines from Pushkin that could also describe the false Soviet poets of the 1930s:

> O you who, feeling valor,
> Seize a pen and soil a sheet of paper—
> Hastening to give your labors to the printed page,
> Stop a moment—find out what fills your soul—
> Unmediated inspiration or only unbridled crawling forth,
> And do you itch to write at every trifle,
> Or do you just need money to pay your debts?

> O vy, kotorye voschuvstvovav otvagu
> Khvataete pero, maraete bumagu—
> Tisneniu predavat trudy svoi spesha,
> Postoite napered—uznaite, chem dusha
> U vas ispolnena—priamym li vdokhnovenem
> I cheshetsia u vas ruka po pustiakam.
> Il vam ne veriat v dolg, i dengi nuzhny vam?

Tikhonov was interrupted here by applause;[71] when it subsided, he completed the passage: "Shouldn't you rather, in submissive hope, / Take a civil or a military post?" ("Ne luchshel vam s nadezhdoiu smirennoi / Zaniatsia sluzhboiu grazhdanskoi il voennoi?").

This final couplet elicited another round of applause. Those present would also have recalled other lines from this poem, "A Severe Judge of French Rhymesters" ("Frantsuzskikh rifmachei surovyi sudiia") even though Tikhonov did not read them:

> The liars of today merit the liars of yesterday—
> And their chatter disturbs me much too much.
> Must I really hold my peace and listen? Oh grief! . . .
> No, I'll tell them off once and for all.

> Noveishie vrali vralei starinnykh stoiat—
> I slishkom uzh menia ikh bredni bespokoiat.
> Uzheli vse molchat, da slushat? O beda! . .
> Net, vse im vyskazhu odnazhdy zavsegda.

Stavsky, who vetted the reports, was hardly the man to perceive double-voicedness. One loyalist who surely did notice was Surkov, who told the assembly, "I didn't like Tikhonov's address. He didn't relate Pushkin to issues that are important for us today."[72]

A large portion of Tikhonov's speech was excised in which he identified several Soviet poets influenced by Pushkin, including Nikolai Zabolotsky, Boris Kornilov, and the absentees Pasternak and Aseyev, to whom he devoted a substantial portion of his address.[73]

"Aseyev is a restless poet," Tikhonov had planned to say. "He knows that poetry is a dangerous craft, because it needs to be approached with the same intelligence as explosives, or else it will blow the person who treats it carelessly to bits."[74]

Tynianov gave his address an unimpeachable frame, noting that Pushkin sided with the disenfranchised and the "new man" and quoting a passage from *The Moor of Peter the Great* (*Arap Petra Velikogo*) that, like many Soviet works, described laborers through the metaphor of a machine: "To Ibrahim, Russia seemed a gigantic workshop . . . where nothing but machines were in motion, where every worker occupied his place in the established order, busy with his own task . . ." Tynianov then offered his own comment on this passage: "This excerpt . . . sounds like an excerpt from our own [Soviet-era] prose . . . [T]he new man . . . fights alongside Peter for reform and . . . masters a new, high culture."[75] Within this frame, however, Tynianov embedded a critique of socialist realist aesthetics, arguing that Pushkin gave readers ample interpretive freedom to fill in the missing details of characters like Silvio and the stationmaster in *The Tales of Belkin* (*Povesti pokoinogo Ivana Petrovicha Belkina*) and that Pushkin's stories amounted to one half of a narrative, in dialogue with the reader, who supplies the other half. His crowning example was "Kirdzhali," which ends by asking readers their opinion.[76] The implication was that Pushkin's invitation to active reading was the opposite of a "correct" interpretation of an "accessible" text.[77] Tynianov also pointed out Pushkin's criticism of monotony (*odnoobraznost*) and reminded his audience that Pushkin had battled the prevailing literary tastes and fought back when critics attacked his work.[78]

Like Tynianov, Altman suggested that socialist realism should learn from Pushkin, who "shows us that the comic, the tragic, the lyric, and the intimate can all be mixed without detriment."[79] Altman's characterization of Pushkin's main themes as freedom, dignity, the "conflict between [an individual's] personal will and the needs of the state," and the spread of personal immorality under tyrannical regimes, could be read as double-voiced or not.[80] He observed that under more benevolent circumstances, characters like Germann, Aleko, and Onegin would not have been so villainous. As for Salieri, after "a tortuous struggle within himself . . . He remains alive, but morally he has perished."[81] Altman offered a provocative quotation from "The Mermaid" ("Rusalka"): "I loved him so much . . . or is he a beast?"[82]

These double-voiced speeches could offer a counterinterpretation of "Pushkin for our time" because they could also be understood as referring simply to tsarist oppression. Inber was more direct. Relaying a librarian's remark that Soviet poets were in trouble because readers were asking only for Pushkin, Inber drew laughter when she remarked that the real problem would come if, after reading Pushkin, people read Soviet poets.[83]

The Aesopian language of the keynote speeches was flanked on one side by party-line speeches and on the other by a blistering protest from Selvinsky, who, like Pasternak, came under fire for his absence and showed up on the final day. Both of them explained that they had stayed away because of harsh criticism, or, in Selvinsky's words, "being spat upon, covered with garbage, and kicked into the dirt."[84] Raging that literary critics had misrepresented him by excerpting "four lines out of a thousand," Selvinsky added, "Let someone better than me say that I'm a bad writer. Then I'll take the criticism seriously."[85] Writers should not be criticized for departing from a model. Look at Stalin's biography, he continued, and you'll see that he continues Lenin's cause by pushing away from him—something that is normal and necessary.[86] This statement, which might have seemed to clinch his argument, could have caused great trouble for Selvinsky had the press turned it into a claim that Selvinsky was separating Lenin from Stalin. That did not happen. Selvinsky sat down to applause from his colleagues.[87]

The five days of tributes to Pushkin were bookended by Stalin's crushing of the opposition. The Piatakov-Radek trial had been the plenum's preface; Bukharin's arrest came on the day after it ended. Writers had lost their most highly placed protector and they were next.

The epicenter of literary arrests was the taking of Averbakh on April 4. The press had been building up to it for six months to create attention and hysteria. *Literary Critic*, whose chief editor, Yudin, took the lead with Stavsky in publicly denouncing writers, had attacked Averbakh as a Trotskyist associated with the disgraced party official Beso Lominadze.[88] The tight bonds to the Bolshevik elite that had once elevated Averbakh now served as his strangulation rope. His closeness to Yagoda, who had been arrested a week earlier, was invoked time and again. The cudgel of Trotskyism he had once used against Litfront was now used on him.[89] The scenario of out-group *zeks* that Yagoda had once revealed to Avdeyenko had rebounded onto the security chief and his brother-in-law. "Ally or enemy" received a new twist. The ally was turned inside out to reveal the enemy.

More than any other single arrest among writers, Averbakh's, when it finally came, pulled in large numbers of party writers declared guilty by association. They included many who had been prominent in RAPP, including Elsberg, Kirshon, Jasienski, Makaryev, Maznin, Selivanovsky, and others. Their Litfront opponents were arrested, too, among them Bespalov, Mikhail

Maizel, and Mustangova. Accused communists were typically brought before their workplace party cell to be judged by their comrades, and sometimes also before the Party Control Commission. In theory, this was an opportunity to defend themselves. Averbakh appears to have been arrested without such proceedings. Kirshon and Jasienski, however, were brought before two party groups within the Writers' Union.

Kirshon, whose plays had been on the Politburo's "master list" of October 1932 and were popular with the public, endured no fewer than five *prorabotki*, or "grillings." In early April, a Moscow city meeting subjected Kirshon to harsh questioning led by Yudin. Then came a series of meetings inside the Writers' Union—first the board's *partkom* (party committee) and then a joint meeting in May of the *partkom* and the larger *partgruppa* (party group) of the entire Writers' Union. Defending himself before his honor group, he tried honesty as the best policy. He admitted to agreeing with RAPP's slogans and helping to spread them. After RAPP's dissolution, he had helped Averbakh "in everything." As editor of *Growth*, he had accused the Writers' Union orgkomitet of cliquishness. Following the communist honor code, he did not seek to make excuses or minimize his offense but took responsibility: "I am greatly guilty" (*MMN*, 665–67).

Averbakh had been defined as the archenemy, the accusations against Kirshon emanated from authoritative sources like Yudin, and the honor group was honor bound to obey its leaders. It concluded that Kirshon was the "leader of a Trotskyite counterrevolutionary group in literature" (*MMN*, 660). His expulsion from the *partkom* and the *partgruppa* precipitated further meetings that augured expulsion from the entire Writers' Union and, as Kirshon must have realized, arrest. In desperation he turned to Stalin:

> Forgive me for writing to you so much, but I do it out of despair at being completely alone. Comrade Stalin, I am thirty-four years old. Do you truly believe that as a person I am through? There is still a lot I can do for the party and the motherland. Comrade Stalin, my own [*rodnoi*], help me (*MMN*, 684).

Instead of help, Kirshon got a long and tormenting wait. It took until August for Stavsky, Surkov, and a Central Committee staffer to formalize a memo proposing Kirshon's expulsion from the Writers' Union, and the presidium voted only on September 1.[90]

Even now, brave writers took the risk of standing up for their accused colleagues. When Stavsky brought a motion to expel Kirshon and Afinogenov from the Writers' Union, Seifullina, Afinogenov's neighbor in the writers' apartment building on Lavrushinsky Lane, tried to save him by disassociating him from Kirshon.

SEIFULLINA: Make separate motions for Afinogenov and Kirshon . . .

STAVSKY: We have exposed Kirshon and Afinogenov as associates of Averbakh, an enemy of the people. We have exposed them and expelled them from the party. We expelled them as the closest aides of the traitor Averbakh, who organized their own harmful parallel center in literature and fought against the Central Committee resolution . . .

[*Stavsky continues at length, reading from a text denouncing Yagoda.*]

SEIFULLINA: Hold separate votes on Afinogenov and Kirshon.

STAVSKY: I can't separate them. There can be discussion about which of them is more talented, which of them less talented. I am introducing a proposal to expel them both.[91]

Taking Seifullina's side was the playwright Nikolai Pogodin, who around this time received the honor of having his new play, *Man with a Gun* (*Chelovek s ruzhyom*), selected for production during the twentieth-anniversary celebration of the revolution.[92] No one else joined them. Afinogenov, married to an American, was rumored in party circles to be a spy, making Seifullina's defense of him doubly dangerous.[93] Seifullina spoke again:

It is no secret that [the recently arrested writer] Pravdukhin was my husband for nineteen years; it is no secret that his arrest is hard for me to bear . . . Not once did I suggest that he remain in the [Writers'] Union, because I want to be fair. He hasn't made a contribution. If he is right, he will be vindicated; if he is a writer, he will write. I know that he is not a spy . . . I propose dividing the motion on Kirshon and Afinogenov. I have always considered Kirshon untalented . . . If I were summoned to the NKVD, I would tell them he should be expelled from the [Writers'] Union. I have factual information that he bribed actors to perform in his play . . .

Afinogenov is another matter . . . Politically he is not compromised, because the NKVD hasn't fixed upon him. I propose to exclude Afinogenov and expel him from the [Writers'] Union conditionally until the next review.[94]

In the end, Stavsky did introduce separate motions on Afinogenov and Kirshon, and he also put to a vote Seifullina's motion to make Afinogenov's expulsion conditional, to be reviewed after one year. The vote to expel Kirshon was unanimous. Afinogenov, too, was expelled, with Seifullina and Pogodin casting the sole opposing votes.[95]

Since expulsion was often the precursor to arrest, those in the room must have been shaken when Stavsky read a list of writers whom he accused of being "enemies of the people" and introduced a motion to expel them en bloc.[96] But Afinogenov, and Libedinsky, too, evaded arrest and were eventually reinstated in the party. Perhaps Fadeyev intervened for Libedinsky. But Fadeyev is reliably reported to have called Afinogenov "a bourgeois remnant," a *poshliak* (boor), and a "person who has nothing in common with the party" (*MMN*, 656). And years later, Fadeyev told a colleague, "Kirshon has my bullet in him, too."

The invulnerability of Stavsky, Fadeyev, and Yermilov to even a stray dart in the hysteria over *averbakhovshchina* suggests that they were protected by Stalin himself. An article in *Literaturnaia gazeta*, referring to the harm done by "Averbakh's group" passed in silence over Fadeyev, Stavsky, and Yermilov, and an article by Yudin a few days later mentioned as Averbakh's associates only Jasienski, Kirshon, and Afinogenov.[97] Part of Yudin's evidence against Kirshon at the Moscow meeting in April was that he had allegedly tried to influence Gorky against Fadeyev, Vishnevsky, and others (*MMN*, 684). Vishnevsky (who was also likely protected by Stalin), in denouncing Jasienski for having spent fourteen years at Averbakh's side, also said nothing about Fadeyev, Yermilov, or Libedinsky (*MMN*, 658). As if by some universal understanding, no one raised their names in the party group, either. Perhaps Fadeyev momentarily felt a rising fear when Kirshon stated that upon RAPP's dissolution he "received a telegram from Averbakh and Fadeyev," but this passed without comment, and Kirshon then made sure to point out that Fadeyev had accepted the party resolution and that Yermilov immediately sided with him. The party group meetings were a venue for all kinds of denunciations, but Fadeyev was off limits.[98] The twenty-five-year-old communist writer Aleksandr Gladkov, writing in his diary, noted the oddity:

And Fadeyev, on whose account they want Mirsky's head, keeps to the side. Both he and Yermilov were extremely close friends with Averbakh, but somehow this doesn't touch them. Or maybe they've already "justified" themselves somewhere? (*MMN*, 656)

Fadeyev explained it as a simple matter: upon RAPP's dissolution, he had severed relations with Averbakh; he had immediately accepted the party's decision; he had publicly confessed his errors and dedicated himself to the Writers' Union. "Everyone knows that I broke with Averbakh on that matter and that when I learned of Averbakh's arrest, I wrote an extensive declaration to the NKVD."[99] Fadeyev's defense of himself seems an admission that he wrote a denunciation. By itself, this would not have been enough to assure his protection. What gained Fadeyev immunity was surely the character flaw that could be exploited through appeals to communist obedience and that Stalin, as we saw in chapter 2, reportedly had voiced ("You are a weak man, Fadeyev!"). Stalin was now his patron.[100]

One who did denounce Fadeyev was the peasant writer Aleksandr Tarasov, whose novel *The Orthodox Ones* (*Ortodoksy*) Fadeyev had called a Trotskyist book in 1931. Fadeyev glibly flipped the accusation back on the accuser: "It follows that he is trying to cover his tracks." The *partkom* forwarded Tarasov's denunciation in a bundle with three others, which came from nonwriters who had known Fadeyev in the Far East. He wrote a detailed response, which appears to have ended the matter. Forcefully, but in the dispassionate language of objectivity, Fadeyev wrote that two of the denunciations had "a party character; that is, they want to find the truth," but that the other two, including Tarasov's, were "slanderous and suspect" (*AFPD*, 68).

While party writers fell prey to *averbakhovshchina*, nonparty writers were swept into the net of *voronshchina*. Arrested in 1935 and again on February 1, 1937, Voronsky was the excuse to incriminate them, especially those who had belonged to Pereval. Fadeyev's political armor was evident here as well, as nonparty writers like Mirsky and Pilniak came under fire for earlier belittling his books. Mirsky now tried to distance himself from his 1934 article on *The Last of the Udegs*, which had elicited Yudin's indignant complaint to Stalin, Kaganovich, and Zhdanov that an "ex-White" dared attempt to "drum . . . Fadeyev out of . . . literature."[101] Vishnevsky, too, had been awaiting an opportunity to "put [Mirsky] in his place."[102] Gorky had once risen to Mirsky's defense.[103] Now there was no Gorky to defend Mirsky, no Bukharin to protect Mandelshtam, and no Yezhov to shield Babel. The patronage relationships that had given writers some protection were destroyed by the terror. Mirsky, whose associates Jasienski and Grigory Korabelnikov were now labeled enemies, wrote a repentant letter to Stavsky explaining that they had led him astray.[104] Pilniak tried to save himself by claiming that *The Tale of the Unextinguished Moon* had been suggested by Voronsky and Radek (*MMN*, 652). Mirsky and Pilniak used a moral code in which it was acceptable, if defending oneself against unfounded accusations, to denounce innocent people who had already been arrested. But the tactic also did not generally work.

Every layer of society formed part of the terror web. The Politburo set arrest quotas; the NKVD fulfilled them; the chief at every workplace countersigned employees' arrest warrants in compliance with a secret Politburo resolution of 1937.[105] The Central Committee mandated "simplified interrogation procedures"; interrogators followed those orders; torture victims would finally sign. Individuals wrote denunciations out of envy, vengeance, self-protection, or a desire for career advancement or a better apartment; these could spark an arrest, help define criminal charges, or assist in an interrogation. The Writers' Union party group appears to have given less weight to denunciations that were anonymous.[106] But the need to respond even to anonymous accusations bred further denunciations in a self-perpetuating cycle.

Communists who saw their colleagues cast out of the honor group and arrested fought to avoid this fate. They had, or thought they had, two weapons: documenting their loyalty and demonstrating vigilance by composing denunciations. A signed denunciation, even when an act of vengeance, could simultaneously be proffered as a performative act of party loyalty, as in the case of Yermilov.

Beyond protecting himself from arrest, the writer of a denunciation must also protect himself from his conscience by convincing himself that what he is doing is not reprehensible. He constructs for himself a logical argument that his denunciation—not all denunciations, but the particular one he is writing—is a moral good. In this sense, the denunciation could serve an even more important purpose than self-credentialing before the party. The denunciation could serve its writer subconsciously as its own moral opposite—an act of self-credentialing before oneself. We saw something similar in chapter 1 in the "package" Stalin offered Gorky (and selected communist cadres), in which trading one's principles for an elite lifestyle was balanced, or even masked, by a moral argument that kept at bay any rumblings of conscience. These arguments varied with the times and a person's own psychological needs. In 1931, kulaks and industrial saboteurs were presented as mortal threats to the country's existence. Five years later, the Old Bolshevik trials delivered the message that anyone at all might turn out to be an enemy. As Katerina Clark has shown, through the show trials ordinary people could internalize the mentality needed to justify denouncing a colleague or neighbor.[107] We see this mentality in the diary of Olga Berggolts, where she describes the arrest of her friends, including Mustangova:

> Am I "walking on corpses"? No, I am doing what the party commands. My conscience is basically clear. And the tiny, ftealike pangs probably come from intellectualism [*intelligentshchiny*]. Out of "humanity" you feel sorry for Levka Tsyrlin, Zhenka Mustangova, and Maizel, but you understand that there's no other way. Because it's true that neither Zhenka nor Maizel acted as they should have—they didn't disassociate themselves, they didn't curse [Mustangova's husband, Georgy] Gorbachev, and when I think that I was with that scum on November 31 [*sic*] 1934 in Svir, on the same stage, in the same train compartment, and on December 1, when Kirov was killed, and that he probably knew what was being planned in Leningrad—I become hateful to myself.[108]

This variant of self-hatred is a psychological defense mechanism that allows Berggolts to see the act of betraying her friends as redemption for a moral lapse. It goes like this: I was careless or blind enough to associate with Gorbachev; I hate myself for that; I did what I could to make amends by denouncing my friend who is married to him. Berggolts, instead of hating herself for betraying her friends, manufactures self-hatred *in advance of* betraying them so as to have a need to redeem herself. The betrayal is redefined as an act of redemption. This is completely unlike Yermilov's self-hatred, born of the realization that he cuts a pathetic figure (as we saw in the first intermezzo).

With oppositionism now treated as an indelible character trait, communists could find morality in denunciation. A glance at one's prized party card offered a slogan for quick reassurance: "The party is the mind, conscience, and honor of the Soviet epoch." As with the God of Fromm's authoritarian religions or Žižek's Big Other, all authenticity has been sucked out of the individual and handed over to outside authority.

A classic example of denunciation as vengeance is Pavlenko's assessment of Mandelshtam's poetry, which Stavsky solicited and then forwarded to the NKVD. This literary-evaluation-as-denunciation thus embeds within it a double dose of a misplaced vengeance born of envy. Pavlenko wrote that Mandelshtam was "not a poet but a versifier," that his poems were "cold and dead," and that his language "smell[ed] of Pasternak."[109] In the inverted force field of Soviet literary reputations, Pavlenko, a frequent conduit between the Writers' Union administration and the NKVD, had the standing to pass judgment on Russian literature's geniuses. He had won accolades for his recent novel *In the East* (*Na Vostoke*), mythologizing the Soviet military in Manchuria (and ending with a workers' revolution in Japan), and he would go on to win four Stalin Prizes. He had been present (hidden behind a door) at one of Mandelshtam's interrogations in the Lubianka four years earlier.[110] (The NKVD had a dossier on Pavlenko, too, in case of need. But he was useful enough to be protected by Stalin himself.)

With Mandelshtam and others, Stavsky behaved with a duplicity that he would not have defined as "double-dealing," even though he would sometimes meet with a writer ostensibly to offer assistance, only to follow up with a denunciation to Mekhlis, Matvei Shkiriatov (of the Party Control Commission), Yezhov, or Stalin. "Double-dealing" referred exclusively to anti-Soviet actions, not to acts undertaken for the party and the greater good. As bad timing had it, Mandelshtam's three-year exile in Voronezh came to an end in the spring of 1937. On returning to Moscow, he sought assistance from Stavsky. Stavsky did not receive him. He was offended by the deference accorded Mandelshtam among writers. Not only nonparty writers like Chukovsky, Valentin Katayev, Yevgeny Petrov, Tynianov, and Zoshchenko, but Surkov and Vishnevsky, too, aided Mandelshtam with money and by arranging informal readings for him.[111] Fadeyev was among those who gathered to hear him read his poetry.[112]

When Mandelshtam made a second attempt to meet with him, Stavsky turned the matter over to Lakhuti. This is a telling detail. Stavsky disliked Lakhuti and generally bypassed him in favor of unofficial deputies not on the secretariat, like Vishnevsky, Pavlenko, or Fadeyev.[113] Having Lakhuti meet with Mandelshtam was a feint: while Lakhuti arranged the predictable trip to the White Sea Canal so that Mandelshtam could begin to reestablish himself with a laudatory poem, Stavsky was making other arrangements with the NKVD.[114] Lakhuti also arranged a public reading for Mandelshtam, which Stavsky appears to have canceled without informing Mandelshtam, who showed up and was told that no such event had been scheduled.[115]

It has been suggested that Mandelshtam may have interpreted Stavsky's refusal to meet with him as embarrassment at being unable to help.[116] Finally, in early 1938, Stavsky received Mandelshtam and made an unexpected offer—two months' stay at a sanatorium in Samatikha.[117] The Writers' Union had several sanatoriums, but Samatikha was not one of them. Fadeyev, on hearing from Nadezhda the name of the sanatorium, showed signs of distress, apparently realizing that the poet was being delivered to the NKVD.[118]

The Mandelshtams received their vouchers for Samatikha on March 2, the opening day of the trial of the "rightists and Trotskyists," including Mandelshtam's protector, Bukharin.[119] On March 16, the day after Bukharin was executed, Stavsky denounced Mandelshtam in a memo to Yezhov, appending Pavlenko's denunciation and complaining of Mandelshtam's unofficial reputation as the country's premier poet. He ended with the words, "Once again I ask you to help decide this question of Osip Mandelshtam."[120] It is hard to avoid concluding that Stavsky waited for the moment when he could set a foolproof trap for Mandelshtam.

The NKVD did not date-stamp Stavsky's memo until a month after he had written it. Yezhov presumably took the matter to Stalin, and only when the decision had been made did he record receipt of the memo, signifying the opening of a case.[121] Mandelshtam was arrested a few weeks later at Samatikha.

Nadezhda Mandelshtam relates that only later did it dawn on her what Stavsky's role had been, and this reminds us that in their personal contact with Stavsky, some writers saw a reasonable human being who might be a naive enthusiast but not a habitual denouncer. Selvinsky reportedly thought well of Stavsky until noticing that any time a writer came to Stavsky with a complaint about censorship or with a confession of errors, Stavsky denounced him to the NKVD or the Politburo.[122]

Stavsky played a more ambiguous role with Sholokhov, with whom he had far more in common than with Mandelshtam. As very young men during the Civil War, both had served in Red Army grain-requisitioning brigades. Afterward, they both pursued literary careers in Rostov *oblast* in the

North Caucasus, Sholokhov in his native village of Veshenskaia and Stavsky in Rostov. Both became prominent in RAPP. Both of them, too, witnessed the starvation in the North Caucasus during collectivization. The same violent confrontations that energized Stavsky to liquidate enemies prompted Sholokhov to expend great time and effort interceding with Stalin on behalf of the starving peasants.[123] Their responses to the purges were also diametrically opposed. In 1937, amid a wave of arrests of *obkom* and *raikom* secretaries, Sholokhov, who served on the Veshenskaia *raikom*, spent months trying to obtain the release of his arrested colleagues.[124] Instead of being held in a local prison, they were transported to Moscow, an unusual move suggesting the personal involvement of Yezhov, who may have been seeking damaging testimony against Sholokhov.[125]

Sholokhov had multiple vulnerabilities. He had failed to produce the long-awaited final installment of *The Quiet River Don*. He was associated with his arrested *raikom* colleagues. His father-in-law was a former ataman who had sided against the Bolsheviks in the Civil War. He had written lengthy letters to Stalin detailing the famine in the North Caucasus in 1931–33 and urgently demanding aid.[126] In June 1937 he tried unsuccessfully to get an audience with Stalin to plead his case. The following month he declined an invitation to join the Soviet delegation to Madrid for the Second International Anti-Fascist Conference, an unthinkable refusal that was meant to protest his friends' arrest.[127]

Later that summer, Stavsky traveled to the North Caucasus and paid a visit to Sholokhov, quite possibly at Stalin's behest.[128] Like Gorky (and unlike Mandelshtam), Sholokhov was considered a valuable writer whom the party did not want to "lose"—a communist who was prey to doubts and in need of reassurance. Sholokhov appears to have welcomed his old comrade. He confided that he could not bring himself to make Grigory Melekhov, the hero of *The Quiet River Don*, turn Bolshevik. He further confided that he did not believe that his good friend Pyotr Lugovoi, who was among the arrested *raikom* members, was guilty. Eager to persuade Stavsky of Lugovoi's innocence, Sholokhov brought out a letter he had received from another *raikom* member, Pyotr Krasiukov, written from exile. Sholokhov had concealed this illegally sent letter,[129] but he trusted Stavsky enough to show it to him.

Stavsky advised Sholokhov to leave Veshenskaia, which in his opinion was crawling with "bad influences," and get his mind off his troubles by immersing himself in *The Quiet River Don*. Didn't Sholokhov see that delaying the novel's completion only played into the hands of the country's enemies? This appears to have been the point at which Sholokhov grasped Stavsky's shortcomings as a confidant. Stavsky told Stalin that he "grew pale and was at a loss for words."[130]

It is difficult to gauge Stavsky's intent from his letter to Stalin, but what is clear is that the *raikom* officials' arrests were proof enough to Stavsky of their guilt; that Stavsky could not abide Sholokhov's wife's family, which, he told Stalin, "radiated counterrevolution";[131] and that Stavsky thought Sholokhov susceptible to anti-Soviet influences. "It is evident that enemies active in the district have been hiding behind Sholokhov, have appealed to his pride (the *raikom* bureau has met at Sholokhov's place more than once), and even now are trying to use him as their intercessor and protector." Stavsky alleged that Sholokhov had stopped doing socially useful party work in favor of going hunting or spending time at home. Stavsky concluded, "Sholokhov admitted and promised to correct his errors, both with regard to Krasiukov's letter [which he agreed to turn over to the local authorities] and with regard to his social and party work . . . But the main thing is that his shifting back and forth, his isolation (which is his own fault), and his doubts raise serious apprehensions, and it is of this that I am informing you."[132] Stalin replied, "Try to have Sholokhov come to Moscow for a couple of days. You can say it was my idea. I am not against speaking with him."[133]

Sholokhov met with Stalin on September 25 and November 4. His colleagues were released and reinstated in the party and their *raikom* posts.[134] Sholokhov did not rest with that. In another meeting with Stalin and in a thirty-page letter to him of February 16, 1938, Sholokhov exposed the NKVD's recruiting of false witnesses to fabricate testimony and gave detailed descriptions of the torture of *raikom* officials.

[Krasiukov's] first interrogation lasted four days. In ninety-six hours he was fed twice. During this time he didn't sleep for a single minute. [several sentences omitted] He was thrown into a punishment cell—a stone container two meters long and half a meter wide, damp and unheated, completely dark. He slept on the bare floor. He was in the punishment cell for twenty-two days. And again . . . they dragged him into the interrogation room and interrogated him for three or four days at a time . . . [five pages omitted] Comrade Stalin! Investigative methods in which the detainee is given into the hands of the investigator without supervision is deeply flawed. These methods lead and will inevitably lead to errors . . . This shameful system of torture must be ended . . . Incessant questioning for five to ten days at a time must not be allowed. That kind of interrogation method sullies the glorious name of the NKVD and makes it impossible to discover the truth.[135]

Sholokhov demanded the release of eleven prisoners who had been arrested because of their association with the now exonerated *raikom* members, release of prisoners whose arrests were based on false testimony under torture, and punishment for the agents who had cooked up the plot against the *raikom* members and then tried to get them to provide false testimony against him. He objected to the defense of the NKVD made by the Rostov *obkom*, which was now claiming that the arrests of the innocent *raikom* officials came about through slanderous reports from Trotskyists and Whites.[136]

Stalin had the Party Control Commission's Shkiriatov and NKVD agent Vladimir (?) Tsesarsky investigate the prisoners claimed innocent by Sholokhov. In May they reported to Stalin upholding most of the arrests and claiming there had been no torture.[137] On October 23, Stalin, already preparing Yezhov's end, brought Yezhov and Sholokhov together at a meeting where Sholokhov confronted Yezhov over the case being built against him. A week later Stalin brought them back for another meeting, this time with the North Caucasus NKVD agents as well. The agents insisted that they had been told their instructions came from Yezhov; Yezhov denied any knowledge of the matter.[138] The timing was auspicious for Sholokhov and disastrous for Yezhov. It was probably this meeting that Stalin is said to have concluded with the remark that the famous writer Sholokhov must have good conditions in which to work. The brunt of the terror was over anyway, and Yezhov was arrested two months later.

The outcome of course could have been much less benign for Sholokhov; and there has been plenty of speculation as to Stalin's thinking: he was winding down the terror of the Great Purge; raising Sholokhov up was a means of bringing Yezhov down; he played the magnanimity card; he needed Sholokhov as the new doyen of Soviet literature after Gorky's death.[139] There is surely some truth in all these scenarios, but the greatest weight has to be given to Stalin's perception of Sholokhov's future usefulness. Stalin wanted Sholokhov to finish *The Quiet River Don* and write other banner works through which the world would know Soviet literature.[140]

Yezhov's strategy of using personnel reviews to raise the arrest rate reached the Writers' Union in September 1937.[141] Stavsky informed the "expanded secretariat" that he was reviewing the personnel files of all Writers' Union members to identify anyone whose admission application contained references from now discredited individuals. He stifled a protest from the floor:

> STAVSKY: A review of paperwork might seem trivial, but it turns out that one person was recommended by [Sergo] Amaglobeli [a theater critic associated with Zinovyev], Pikel also got involved with great enthusiasm and then so did Litovsky, whose situation is extremely complicated. It is necessary to look into all this.

At this point someone apparently tried to interrupt; the transcript continues with Stavsky saying, "I am purposely not stopping. We have now formed a group. Or another document, Kamenev gave a recommendation."[142]

Stavsky took his cue to root out enemies. He composed a frenzy of denunciations to Shkiriatov and Mekhlis, now head of Agitprop's press section. His targets included Yudin, Mark Rozental, Igor Sats, and Usievich of *Literary Critic*, and others, including Inber, Panfyorov, Zelinsky, and the Agitprop official and *Izvestiia* editor Boris Tal (*SL*, 237–44). In November 1937, he dispatched his deputies on inspection tours of the Writers' Union republic branches. Previously, neither he nor Shcherbakov had made even the slightest attempts to stay in touch with the branch offices. Vishnevsky, whom Stavsky assigned to report on military writers' organizations (*SL*, 263, n.1), understood that his job was to unmask enemies. He unmasked as Trotskyites three editors who had rejected his own work (and with whom he had also worked on an editorial board)—Reizin, Mikhail Landa (the editor of *Krasnaia zvezda* and *Znamia*), and Leonid Degtiarev (the editor of the army-navy journal issued by LOKAF). Vishnevsky's nine-page report began, "To Vladimir Stavsky. Greetings! I have undertaken work of importance to the Soviet Writers' Union and probably the NKVD."[143] It concluded, "From what I have set forth it is clear that the traitors and betrayers Landa and Reizin, who were linked to [the now arrested] Subotsky, took a definite hostile literary and political line."[144] Vishnevsky sent a copy of his denunciation to the military administration. Reizin and Landa were arrested.[145] Stavsky must have been grateful for Vishnevsky's work. It might help him avert the fate of Sergei Ingulov, the head of Glavlit, who was arrested for insufficient vigilance.[146]

Stavsky called upon the Kiev-based writer Valery Tarsis to inspect the Writers' Union's Ukrainian branch. Its chief, Kulik, had been arrested in July. Rather than assume, as Vishnevsky did, that he was to produce a list of enemies, Tarsis behaved like a professional. He visited Writers' Union officials and members in Kiev, Kharkov, Odessa, and Dnepropetrovsk, and was horrified. Kulik's replacement, Ivan Le, was hostile toward the entire membership. Le was the son of a landless peasant with a biography similar to Stavsky's—he had entered the labor force as a child, fought for the Red Army in the Civil War, received a degree from a workers' faculty, and launched a successful career as a writer. Tarsis reported to Stavsky that widespread arrests, besides cutting membership by one-third, had all the writers living in fear of one another and paying daily visits to their Writers' Union office in hopes of heading off any plots that might be brewing against them. Although the Kiev office had supervisory responsibilities over the branch offices in the smaller cities, Le and the other secretaries never bothered to be in touch with these branches and had no idea whom to contact when the head of the Donbass office was arrested. In Odessa, the entire staff had been arrested, and the office was being run by inexperienced younger folk in need of instructions and guidance that never came.[147] The six writers who made up the tiny Dnepropetrovsk branch were "busy with endless meetings, accuse one another of every mortal sin, get worked up into a frenzy confessing their errors, even nonexistent ones, and do no writing. The organization is in need of significant assistance, but Kiev does nothing" (SL, 247). The Ukrainian branch was a mirror of the Moscow organization under Stavsky, and Le's behavior duplicated Stavsky's own. The chaos described by Tarsis was universal. Gorelov, the arrogant second secretary of the Leningrad branch, had been arrested in March 1937, and his replacement, Emmanuil Tsilshtein, was arrested in October.[148]

Some six hundred writers were arrested between 1936 and 1938. Absent exact figures for those years, we can estimate this as 25 to 30 percent of the Writers' Union membership.[149] Writers were typically accused under article 58, which covered espionage, sabotage, treason, wrecking, and other crimes against the state. Pilniak, Babel, Kliuev, and Klychkov were shot, as were the less well-known Pribludny and Zazubrin. Communist cadres who were shot included Averbakh, Bespalov, Maznin, Selivanovsky, Voronsky, Ivan Katayev, and Mustangova. Vasilyev, Mirsky, and Mandelshtam perished in labor camps. If we estimate 600 arrests out of 2,400 members, 1,800 remained. The arrested old intelligentsia writers were replaced by new, younger, and more Sovietized members.

Agitprop officials were distressed by Stavsky's vindictiveness and tried to alert the secretaries (Stalin, Andreyev, Yezhov, Kaganovich, and Zhdanov) to the dysfunctionality in the Writers' Union. As early as May 3, 1937, eight months after Stavsky assumed the leading role, Agitprop's top two officials, A. I. Angarov and E. M. Tamarkin, urgently recommended replacing him (LF, 23–25). Stalin, Zhdanov, and Andreyev had already received numerous complaints.[150]

Fadeyev wrote to Andreyev in March 1937 that Stavsky was mistrustful and suspicious.[151] According to Subotsky's replacement at Literaturnaia gazeta, Olga Voitinskaia, Stavsky had attempted to retaliate against his critics by having an assistant compose a scurrilous article with quotations so distorted that publication was out of the question (LF, 29). Surkov, confirming a widespread complaint that the Writers' Union never discussed literary works, told Shcherbakov that Stavsky dished out medals to aspiring worker writers without helping them improve their manuscripts.[152] Stavsky lacked the competence to undertake this role even had he wanted to.

Angarov and Tamarkin wrote that Stavsky showed contempt for lesser-known writers, never read any new literary works, and relied instead—as we have seen—on the opinions of putatively authoritative critics. They blamed the poor quality of young writers' work on Stavsky's inattentiveness to them. They also blamed Stavsky for alienating important writers, including Pasternak, Pilniak, and Aseyev, as well as lesser figures whose work collectively was important for Soviet literature. They noted with alarm that all cooperation between party and nonparty writers had ceased. Their recommendations: restore the secretariat to its full cohort of five members by adding Vishnevsky and Yudin, who should take over Stavsky's role as first secretary. Apparently believing that Stalin and the other secretaries needed to be better informed, they also proposed having a group of writers brief them on the situation (*LF*, 24–25).

With the trial of Rightists and Trotskyists (Bukharin, Rykov, Yagoda, and others) still months away, however, Stavsky's role was not yet done. No changes were made to the Writers' Union secretariat. It was Agitprop that underwent changes. Angarov was executed. So were his next two successors, F. I. Shablovsky and Konstantin Yukov.[153] Tamarkin was removed, to elude arrest for nine more years. Shablovsky wrote about Stavsky with approval (possibly drawing a lesson from Angarov's fate) and requested Andreyev's permission to have the vacancies in the presidium and secretariat filled at the Writers' Union's fifth plenum, with candidates selected by Stavsky. This recommendation was not acted upon (*LF*, 26–27). Even as the vacancies went unfilled, the *oblast* and *raikom* branches of the Writers' Union were slated for restructuring, their presidiums and secretariats to be replaced by an "institute of plenipotentiaries" responsible to the board (*MMN*, 691).

Stavsky was too incompetent, uninterested, or consumed by hysteria to manage this reconfiguration.[154] An old Litfront antagonist, P. D. Rozhkov, had drawn up fifteen charges against him, claiming that under pretence of unmasking enemies, Stavsky was actually protecting them and covering up his own missteps (*SL*, 234). Stavsky struck back with an eight-page counter-denunciation, dragging in a dozen other "enemies," including some he had denounced earlier: Sergei Beliaev, Gronsky, Inber, Yudin, Rozental, Sats, Selvinsky, Usievich, and Zelinsky (*SL*, 237–43). An investigation committee exonerated Stavsky and he remained in charge of the Writers' Union for another eight months. In a manifestation of the schizophrenic atmosphere of intertwined fear and celebration, Stavsky's frantic efforts to protect himself were followed by his election in September to the newly created Supreme Soviet.[155] Elections to this body always included a small number of writers. At its first election in 1937, these were Stavsky, Aleksandr Korneichuk, Aleksei Tolstoy, and Sholokhov. The first three were reliably loyalist. Sholokhov was perhaps being co-opted on the heels of the *raikom* affair.

The drawing down of the terror was signaled on January 18, 1938, in a Central Committee resolution blaming opportunistic party officials looking to prove their vigilance by going after innocent communists.[156] Kerzhentsev was removed as head of the Arts Committee.[157] Mekhlis, whose talent for "tearing things down" was no longer needed, was removed as head of Agitprop's press section.

Mekhlis's replacement at the press section, A. E. Nikitin, did not share

Shablovsky's complaisance toward Stavsky. On February 28, two days before the trial of Rightists and Trotskyists began, Nikitin wrote to the Central Committee secretaries, asserting that the Writers' Union served people "on the periphery of literature" and engaged in endless meetings to the neglect of literature and writers, who had no time to write.[158] "Real writers face a dilemma: they must either 'work' at the union—that is, attend meetings—or write" (SL, 269). Here was a stunning slip of the pen: an admission from a top culture official that the Writers' Union contained writers who were not "real." "Real writers," a commonplace phrase in private conversations among writers, crept into Nikitin's assessment, presumably without his noticing that his private value system had leaked into his official correspondence. Nikitin's memo was acted on two weeks after the trial ended and a month after he sent it. Finally the time was right to remove Stavsky, and this explains an open letter in *Pravda* signed by Fadeyev, Tolstoy, Valentin Katayev, and Anna Karavayeva decrying interminable, time-wasting meetings and endless waits endured by writers wanting to see him.[159] Zhdanov and Andreyev continued to receive written complaints about Stavsky (LF, 27–33). Once the trial was over, they held three meetings with the Writers' Union presidium and another twenty or so party and nonparty writers.[160] Andreyev wrote to Stalin,

> It is apparent that there has been premeditated sabotage, causing disorganization in the writers' community. In all this Stavsky comes out looking very bad, and his behavior toward writers has been frankly suspicious and provocative. It is obvious that he was closely connected to Kirshon, Jasieński, and other saboteurs.
>
> In the Writers' Union everything has been done to create divisions between party and nonparty writers, uphold divisions and feuds along the lines of old writers' groups, keep writers away from union business, and at the same time many idlers feed on the union and its administration.
>
> In practice Stavsky replaced the presidium and the secretariat of the Writers' Union with himself and by his behavior created a great deal of dissatisfaction on the part of writers toward the union. (SL, 276)

Andreyev recommended a Central Committee resolution addressing operational problems in the Writers' Union. Of note, too, is that his mention of Stavsky's closeness to Kirshon and Jasieński amounts to a recommendation for his arrest.

On April 21, two weeks after the third meeting, Pilniak was shot. (It may or may not have mattered that in 1933 Stavsky had called for Pilniak to be unmasked for writing that 80 percent of writers did not belong in the Writers' Union and disparaging Fadeyev and Libedinsky.) (MMN, 226) On

June 1, the USSR Procuracy issued a directive "to quash all unfounded prosecutions that [had] been started" and to "cease this practice in the future."[161] When the Politburo finally drafted a resolution on the Writers' Union in August, it did not mention Stavsky by name, but he was relieved of his duties (*LF*, 35–38).

Nikitin broke the news to Stavsky and saw him to the door with words of encouragement: "You made such a brilliant debut. Your books were a resounding success. No one cares about the Writers' Union, but everyone wonders why Stavsky isn't doing any writing. Why is he silent? Doesn't he have anything to write about?"[162] But Stavsky, who had gotten on well with Mekhlis, was disconsolate and blamed Nikitin, who he suspected had a plan "to do me in—me, a Stalinist, a Bolshevik."[163]

Stavsky continued as editor of *Novy mir*, where he succeeded the arrested Gronsky, until the outbreak of war. At the Writers' Union, a group of five (*piaterka*) was appointed to act as a de facto secretariat, replacing the original one from 1934. It consisted of Pavlenko, Karavayeva, and Gerasimova, Valentin Katayev, and Leonid Sobolev (*AFPD*, 9). For the moment, no first secretary was named.

Stalin protected his most valuable literary cadres, Stavsky, Yermilov, and Fadeyev, from being swept into the vortex of *averbakhovshchina*. Each was useful in his own way. The next time Stalin needed a hotheaded enthusiast, he could call upon Stavsky. If he needed a critical mind with a mean streak, he had Yermilov. What Stalin needed just now was a moderate personality who by temperament and literary reputation could begin rebuilding a bridge to traumatized writers and whose fealty had been demonstrated time and again. Fadeyev.

Vulgar Sociologism and the Dual Self

IN MARCH 1934, having decided on a policy of national Bolshevism, Stalin summoned to the Kremlin a dozen historians from the Academy of Sciences and charged them with writing new secondary-school history textbooks.[1] The new textbooks presented outstanding figures of the tsarist era as landowner-progressives who advanced the cause of revolution, and were ready in time for the 1937 Pushkin celebrations. It has been argued that the jubilee itself was aimed at revamping the school literature curriculum to emphasize the classics; a textbook competition for sixth- through eighth-grade literature planned for the spring of 1936 coincided with the jubilee preparations.[2]

The new textbooks and Stalin's comments about them in *Pravda* and *Izvestiia* seemingly resolved the vehement disputes among party critics over whether there could be value in literary works by bourgeois or landowner authors.[3] We recall that when Pereverzev and his followers had used the tools of class analysis to discredit the literary classics, the Onguardists derided them as "vulgar sociologists." This vicious attack was partly self-protection: Averbakh, Fadeyev, and Yermilov were redefining themselves as proletarian writers, a project that was incompatible with Pereverzev's premise. The outcome was defeat for both sides. Just as the big-tent Writers' Union meant disqualifying the Pereverzevites' strictly class-based analysis, so equally did it mean removing the Onguardists from their judgeship. Their injunction to learn from the classics, however, survived in Stalin's call for the new textbooks three years later.

It seems against all expectation, then, that in the late 1930s Yermilov and Fadeyev would revive class analysis. Switching sides, they took a position at odds with their literary sensibilities in a bid to bring down a rival group. They used as their weapon the remnants of Bolshevik squeamishness over the class background of Russia's literary pantheon.

The Onguardists' charge of vulgar sociologism against Pereverzev had been consistent with their own emphasis on learning from the classics and depicting the inner psychological battle through which an individual ultimately could remake himself. We have seen that their literary prescriptions evoked bitter opposition and the Onguardists were uncomfortably positioned on proletarian literature's "right wing." The psychological exposés that characterized their fiction, revealing the class enemy within each individual, were what Usievich had in mind in 1932 when she zeroed in on the Onguardists' literary portrayals of the battle between an individual's psychology and his adopted ideology: this showed, she claimed, that for them the cultural revolution was purely psychological.[4] That insight must have stung.

Yermilov and Usievich vied in rebranding the battle for power as a battle for purity. RAPP's demise benefited Usievich's group, which enjoyed increased influence at the newly created *Literary Critic*, which effectively replaced the discontinued *On Literary Guard*. The new journal's staff were a close-knit group of "international communists" or "Westernizers," whose interest in European and world literature distinguished them from the Onguardists.[5] They included Usievich, Georg Lukács, Vladimir Aleksandrov, Vladimir Grib, Vladimir Kemenov, Fyodor Levin, Mikhail Lifshits, Rozental, Yakov Rykachev, and Sats. Yudin as chief editor ensured political reliability. The early issues argued against RAPP's literary method, and the journal's mission statement likely made the deposed Onguardists feel they had been hijacked: "the creation of a socialist, and the assimilation of classical aesthetics" and "conceptualizing Soviet literature as the new world literature." Its call to "elevat[e] the philosophical-aesthetic level of criticism" and "forg[e] together critics who were divided by cliquish struggles" was a clear slap at Averbakh and Yermilov.[6] In the mid-1930s, these "internationalists" appeared poised to take over the mantle of literary leadership. RAPP's death had been followed by a turn toward leftist European writers as the unseen hand of the Soviet government organized the International Congress in Defense of Culture, in France and Spain in 1935 and 1937.[7] Yermilov's sense of grievance in 1935, as we saw in the preceding intermezzo, played out on this background. The outbreak of the Spanish Civil War and the enthusiastic participation in it by Soviet writers and intellectuals also contributed to the ascendancy of Usievich's and Lukács's group.[8] The new importance accorded to leftist European literature resulted in the establishment in December 1935 of a Foreign Commission within the Writers' Union, which took over this portfolio from the Comintern.[9]

Literary Critic cited the new textbooks to claim authority for its own theories and as a reminder to avoid vulgar sociologism. *Pravda* signaled approval,[10] emboldening these critics to promote their theories with well-chosen citations from Lenin. They dove into the thorny question of what Gorky had called junk literature, pointing to the prefabricated feel of Soviet literary works and daring to assert that political correctness had precipitated literary decline. To revitalize literature they proposed greater creative freedom, arguing disingenuously that since Soviet writers favored communism—this was, after all, the prerequisite for joining the Writers' Union—whatever they wrote would be ideologically sound. As if to demonstrate this proposition, the journal in the summer of 1936 began featuring Platonov.[11]

Platonov was still trying to shake off his pariah status. At Yermilov's invitation, he had contributed a story, "Immortality" ("Bessmertie"), to an anthology featuring the heroism of railway workers (APVS, 327). It was greeted as a sign that he was developing into a loyal Soviet writer (APVS, 328). Even Stavsky praised it.[12] Yermilov then arranged Platonov's travel to Medvezhya Gora for an interview with a railway switchman who had prevented a disaster by hurling his body against a runaway railway car, slowing its momentum and crushing his hand (APVS, 329). The story Platonov wrote, "Among Animals and Plants" ("Sredi zhivotnykh i rastenii"), contained a twist on this heroic theme: the switchman's father suggests staging an accident as a way to receive a medal of heroism that came with a monetary prize and consumer goods.[13] Despite this potential for raised eyebrows, Gronsky wanted the story for Novy mir and Vasily Ilyenkov, the referee at October, also favored publishing it (APVS, 329).

Not everyone shared this benign attitude, and the manuscript wound up in the Writers' Union, which, although not in the chain of agencies that led to publication, could get involved in disputes and make nonbinding recommendations. The prose section met to discuss Platonov's story in July 1936, shortly after Gorky's death. Stavsky, though not having received word that he was in charge of the Writers' Union, was running its daily business; perhaps it was he who arranged for two representatives from the Commissariat of Roads and Railways to attend.

Platonov, who was also present, excised the offending scene in advance of the meeting and made the train's derailment an accident. Those at the meeting found this problematic, and they found a host of related problems: (1) the lives of the hero, his family, and his village were completely lacking in joy, satisfaction, or meaningful activity; (2) the hero, while longing to be part of the new life that he had heard described on the radio, remained stuck in a remote, backward village; (3) his act of heroism came about as the result of a chance occurrence that might just as easily never have happened; (4) the story offered no solution to the problem it posed: the hero, despite receiving a medal for his heroism, appeared to feel neither pride nor happiness, and his meaningless, unhappy life continued unchanged; (5) in places the author seemed to be making fun of his hero; (6) Platonov's literary world was one of unrelieved suffering. The railway officials thought the story misrepresented railway work and would demoralize railway workers and repel job seekers (MMN, 511).

The meeting's tone was civil. Platonov was severely criticized, but on the eve of the first show trial no one used words like "enemy," "kulak," or "counterrevolutionary."[14] Four people defended him. *Literary Critic*'s Rykachev asked, "Why does irony have to be aimed only at the class enemy; why can't it be aimed at you or me?" Shklovsky argued that Platonov had taken steps toward communism and should be encouraged.[15]

Yermilov was not at this meeting. Until now he had supported Platonov, helping him climb back to political respectability with "Takyr'" and "Immortality." He probably would have agreed secretly with Rykachev about the use of irony. Many of *Literary Critic*'s positions were similar to those once advanced by the Onguardists. Even some that did not, like the appreciation of European literature and need to raise the quality of Soviet literature, match Yermilov's and Fadeyev's private beliefs. Usievich argued publicly that literature by leftist European writers outperformed Soviet literature both in literary quality and in promoting revolution, something that Fadeyev and Yermilov would not do. We have already seen that between themselves Fadeyev and Yermilov bemoaned the quality of literature and acknowledged that it was being sacrificed to ideology. Their personal assessment of Soviet literature was nearly identical to Usievich's, but they proved their vigilance on the backs of writers and critics whom they disliked, who were convenient or obvious targets, or who posed a threat to their influence. By contrast, Usievich, Lukács, and Lifshits were much more consistent in their literary theory, even when it did not match the party line.[16]

The one substantial disagreement between the rival groups was in their attitudes toward psychological realism and portraying characters' inner life, which were roundly rejected by Lukács and Usievich.[17] An article by Platonov in *Literary Critic*, however, was strikingly in tune with the Onguardists' living man. Platonov pointed out Gorky's belief in the need to eradicate enemy influences in oneself (*SF*, 821). The Onguardists, too, had insisted that even exemplary communists had to uproot their undesirable traits. Fadeyev, reading a new translation of Hegel's aesthetics that the internationalists published in 1935, found that it vindicated the Onguardists' own theory. He reported to Libedinsky that he was "struck by how close you and I came to the truth" (*FP* 1973, 143).

Intellectually and aesthetically, Yermilov and Fadeyev should have been the natural allies of the *Literary Critic* group. The power struggle made them the bitterest of foes. A notebook entry of Fadeyev's from April 1938 reads,

> Yesterday I was at a meeting of *Literary Critic*. A waste of time. With Yudin's departure their wretchedness has become clear. An absence of love for literature, first and foremost . . . people full of citations and small-minded self-importance. They are ignorant of the Russian language. Spiteful and petty pedants.[18]

It is not clear which came first, the negative assessment or the animosity. In any case, Yermilov plotted their demise. He awaited a favorable opportunity. It came in January 1939 with Fadeyev's appointment to lead the Writers' Union. In March, Fadeyev held a meeting with graduate students at the Institute of Philosophy and Literature, where Lukács and Lifshits taught. Perhaps he found a convenient excuse in Stalin's announcement that month that Agitprop's press and propaganda sections would be merged—a sign of stricter requirements for literature (*PT*, 16).

Fadeyev opened the meeting by voicing skepticism about the need for a journal devoted exclusively to criticism (*SF*, 818). Lukács and Lifshits, however, were well loved by their students, who offered measured responses but without exception supported the journal's continued publication.[19] If Fadeyev and Yermilov had hoped to use student opinion to make a case against *Literary Critic*, they miscalculated.

Yermilov's next opportunity came five months later. Lukács had just published *Toward a History of Realism* (*K istorii realizma*), containing anti-fascist statements that became an instant tinderbox with the surprise signing in August of the Molotov-Ribbentrop pact (*SF*, 819). Yermilov published attacks on *Literary Critic* and Platonov in *Literaturnaia gazeta* and the Central Committee journal *Bolshevik*.[20] A follow-up denunciation to Zhdanov produced results: Platonov's book *Reflections of a Reader* (*Razmyshleniia chitatelia*), which had already been typeset, never saw the light of day (*APVS*, 428; *SF*, 817). It was a collection of the articles he had published in *Literary Critic*, so the book's demise reflected badly on the magazine as well. Usievich had arranged its publication at Sovetsky pisatel, where she was an editor; the volume editor was Lifshits (*APVS*, 425; *VKI*, 443). Yermilov described them to Zhdanov as an unsavory trio: "*Literary Critic* increasingly risks becoming a center of politically harmful moods among writers and critics." He pointed out the frequency with which it featured Platonov, "the author of 'For Future Use'" (*APVS*, 428). Yermilov did not mention that until recently he himself had been helping Platonov get published.

To bring down their antagonists, Yermilov and Fadeyev, even in the face of the new textbooks, revived old arguments (that had been made by their opponents) favoring class analysis of literature. Pereverzev had insisted on the class basis of all literature. In accusing him of vulgar sociologism, his attackers made the point that under party leadership, people could remake themselves. But now Fadeyev blasted *Literary Critic* for going too far in cautioning against vulgar sociologism—for interpreting it to mean that art had no class basis. He did this in February 1940 in a lengthy denunciation/report to the Central Committee secretaries, cosigned by Kirpotin (*VKI*, 439–44). This move would seem not to have been without risk. Once the textbook decision had been made, the banner of class analysis was abandoned by most activists. The notable exception was Bukharin, who had raised it at the First Writers' Congress and been answered by Stalin in the form of the Pushkin celebrations, which culminated with Bukharin's arrest. Pereverzev was arrested in 1938.

Fadeyev and Kirpotin characterized *Literary Critic*'s concept of nationality (*narodnost*) as ahistorical and non-Marxist. They professed outrage at the "antiparty" argument that politically motivated literature was artistically inferior and recommended "condemning" the group's ideas in *Pravda*. Having argued in 1930 against his leftist opponent Pereverzev, Fadeyev now wielded Pereverzev's own argument to battle his rightist rivals at *Literary Critic*. (Stalin had modeled this tactic, making temporary alliances to bring down his opponents on the left and then the right.) Prevailing over *Literary Critic* required adopting a position similar to Pereverzev's, even in the face of Pereverzev's disgrace and a Writers' Union that accepted loyal writers of any class background. Pereverzev had fallen victim to accusations of applying class analysis too broadly and overlooking the value of some writings by landed or bourgeois authors. Fadeyev now looked to the opposite pole to find fault with *Literary Critic*. Lukács was downright suspect:

> G. Lukács is a person with a very disorderly biography; early in his career he was an unabashed bourgeois idealist who later joined the Hungarian Communist Party, a left-winger of whom Lenin wrote in 1920, 'G. L.'s article is very leftist and very bad. The Marxism in it is mere words' and so forth. (*VKI*, 439)

As to Platonov, they repeated Yermilov's reminder that this was, of course, the author of "For Future Use," who moreover had sullied the purity of Gorky's name. Stalin underlined that part of the report (*SF*, 821).

Did Yermilov turn against Platonov out of pique that he had gone over to his rivals at *Literary Critic*, or did he simply calculate that the way to defeat his rivals was through Platonov? He weaponized *Red Virgin Soil* with a long review article signed by Abram Gurvich. There is every reason to believe that Yermilov supplied his reviewer with the main arguments, a tactic he had made use of before, as we saw in the previous intermezzo. The article employs the artful counterargument that is Yermilov's hallmark: if Platonov had finally managed to create selfless characters, their quest for immortality showed that their selflessness derived not from socialism but from religion (*APVS*, 393).

Earlier we considered the description of Lenin that *Pravda* had published over Gorky's signature, recognizable to any Orthodox parishioner as a version of Christ; and Stalin himself privately defended his own use of dictatorial power on the grounds that "the people need a god." That hidden religious topos underlying a mythologized party was a recurrent and even essential feature of Soviet culture, and Platonov made use of it in "Immortality." But an unspoken condition was that it be concealed. By exposing it in Platonov's story, Yermilov was able to turn it against him.

Yermilov and Fadeyev now painted Platonov as anti-Soviet with arguments that they would have been happy to refute under other circumstances. Platonov had argued that Pushkin's genius answered a deficiency in Russian culture; Fadeyev and Yermilov called this slander of Russia. Platonov had argued that after Pushkin, Russian literature had nowhere to go but down; Fadeyev and Yermilov called this a lack of patriotism. They further claimed that Platonov was defaming Gorky. Yermilov, who in RAPP had dismissed Gorky as a "bourgeois democratic fellow traveler" (and had been made to apologize) now cynically played the Gorky card, professing outrage at Platonov's disrespect for Gorky. It did not matter that Platonov's commentary on Gorky was fully compatible with Yermilov's own living-man theory as an Onguardist, which rejected pure psychologies of virtue or villainy.

Fadeyev and Kirpotin's memo was just one salvo in a barrage. Soon after, they asked the Central Committee secretaries for permission to fully expose the *Literary Critic* group. A separate missive from Yermilov supplied the secretaries with further criticisms of Lukács (*SF*, 822).

The secretaries instructed Agitprop's Georgy Aleksandrov to investigate the overall situation in literary criticism.[21] They did not, however, specifically mention *Literary Critic*. Aleksandrov uncovered a grand total of one instance of an "egregious political mistake," and it was not made by *Literary Critic*.[22] The secretaries then instructed Aleksandrov to "make recommendations for improving literary criticism." Aleksandrov took the hint, noting in his follow-up report that *Literary Critic* was guilty of avoiding important issues in criticism. But he also alluded to the infighting between *Literary Critic* and *Literaturnaia gazeta* (naming Kirpotin, Yermilov, and Altman), explaining, "For a long time now these groups have been engaged in smear campaigns and empty debates only peripherally related to literature (*SF*, 823)."

Aleksandrov's patron was Zhdanov's rival Georgy Malenkov, so he may have resisted giving Zhdanov what he wanted, but nonetheless the response of the Central Committee *orgbiuro* was to close down *Literary Critic*.[23] At the same time, the *orgbiuro* appears to have taken seriously Aleksandrov's mention of infighting, because it also abolished the critics' section of the Writers' Union and decreed that no journals would be devoted solely to literary criticism.[24] Criticism would be folded into literary journals, which were to include a section dedicated to it. Responsibility for recommending books to the public was entrusted to institutions such as the Marx, Engels, and Lenin Institute, the Gorky Literary Institute, the Academy of Sciences, and Narkompros (*VKI*, 464). Reviews and lists of recommended books were to appear in general-interest periodicals. All of this was intended to forestall *gruppirovka* (cliquishness). It was an echo of the 1932 disbanding of RAPP and other literary groups. Back then, Stalin had opted to stick with Fadeyev and Yermilov; eight years on he was still arbitrating the fallout from their scheming.

When the dust cleared, the only critic left standing was Yermilov. The infighting among communist literary critics was again resolved in favor of Stalin's longtime, trusted cadres. By that measure, Yermilov's intriguing had paid off. There was a price to be paid for this victory. It would be exacted in professional alienation and ruined friendship. Yermilov's actions were the moral equivalent of Platonov's railwayman, who accepted permanent bodily injury in exchange for a role in the new society. Eric Naiman's reading of Platonov's story, which he interprets as a comment on Soviet subjectivity, can be applied to Yermilov as well: "Self-mutilation is seen as the admission ticket to the new utopia."[25]

General Secretary Fadeyev

"WHAT A POET we have destroyed!"[1] Fadeyev's inebri-
ated cry over drinks with friends, lamenting Mandelshtam's second arrest
in May 1938, contains echoes of his overlapping selves. Who does he mean
by "we"? "We" the Soviet people? "We" the Communist Party, which he was
duty bound to obey? Or is this the royal "we" serving to mask the responsibility of his "I"? Fadeyev's cry is neither a confession of shame nor a move to
repair a rupture caused by wrongdoing. It is instead the splitting of a single,
whole ego into two distinct and incompatible selves. The self of origin momentarily wrenches free and becomes an outside observer, horrified at its
unscrupulous doppelgänger. This is not to say that Fadeyev had anything
to do with Mandelshtam's case. But his exclamation sounds an acknowledgment of his complicity as an honor-bound member of the honor group. Soon
he would be drawn more fully into many cases as head of the Writers' Union,
where one of his duties would be to sign warrants for the arrests of colleagues and friends.[2] By the time Fadeyev assumed his new responsibilities,
Mandelshtam, shipped to a camp in the Soviet Far East, was dead.

Fadeyev meanwhile received a Peredelkino dacha. Doing penance for
RAPP, he had not been among the lucky twenty-eight who were the first to
move in back in 1936.[3] He had had to prove his reliability and then wait for
a dacha to become vacant. That vacancies occurred through an occupant's
arrest was well understood. According to one account, when Leonid Leonov
complained to Stalin that he was not on the list to receive a dacha, Stalin
mused out loud in front of the entire company that the dachas of Kamenev
and Zinovyev were both free, so Leonov could have one of those (*MMN*,
156). Fadeyev knew that he owed his dream house to the arrest of Zazubrin.

Fadeyev was named first secretary of the Writers' Union in January
1939 (*VKI*, 424). The preface to his newfound prestige was the disappear-
ance of some six hundred writers. There were major talents like Kliuev,
Klychkov, Boris Kushner, Mandelshtam, Mirsky, Yury Oksman, Pilniak, and
Vasilyev. There were former RAPP comrades like Averbakh, Bespalov, and
Kirshon. There were friends who had fought alongside him against the

Whites, like Grigory Bilimenko and Pyotr Nerezov.[4] Perhaps he was thinking of these things when, after a few months in the top job at the Writers' Union, he sat frowning and downing vodka with other guests at Meyerhold's dacha.[5] It was May 22, 1939; Fadeyev was with his new wife, the actress Angelina Osipovna Stepanova; the other guests were Ivanov, Aleksei Tolstoy and his wife, and the artist Pyotr Konchalovsky. Babel had been arrested the week before. Fadeyev would hardly have been at this gathering had he known that the NKVD was preparing his host's arrest. They came for Meyerhold the next month.

With Fadeyev as with Gorky, Stalin laid on the honors at the precise moment when his cadre's troubled conscience was most in need of salve. Fadeyev not only became head of the Writers' Union but also was elected to the Central Committee, an honor accorded to a handful of writers.

Fadeyev embodied what Moshe Lewin has referred to as the counter-trend to the terror—the effort to foster "a set of classical measures of social conservatism," including "discipline, patriotism, conformism, authority, and orderly careerism."[6] His friends described him as bold but with a firm commitment to strict party discipline that caused him to sacrifice many of his positions in deference to the party line.[7] If a party member sometimes disagreed with a party decision, was there not a nobility in sacrificing one's personal views for the party? He must have thought back to his principled position in siding with the Bolsheviks before 1917. If it was a principled position then, was it not still a principled position now? The attempt to maintain principled independence while also submitting to party discipline posed a giant conundrum. Duty and virtue, unfortunately, were qualities that, as the Stalin era deepened, would more and more resemble lack of principle and spinelessness.

Where Shcherbakov and Gorky had once embodied two faces of the Writers' Union—the humanitarian and the authoritarian—now Fadeyev carried them both, uncomfortably, within himself. He is said to have been a close friend of Nikolai Shivarov, the NKVD agent who interrogated Mandelshtam, among others.[8] Fadeyev convinced himself to accept illogical and toxic changes in the party line by invoking a favorite piece of Marxist logic: as history progresses, we gain an ever clearer vantage point from which to make our judgments. In 1935, when Libedinsky was working on a "corrected" version of his 1925 play *Commissars* (*Kommissary*), Fadeyev expressed his eagerness to read the new version: "Certain issues concerning the revolution really were posed and solved incorrectly [in Libedinsky's original play] if you look at it from the vantage point of today's historical towers" (*FP* 1973, 142). He suggested adding a scene about Stakhanovites, observing, "Many things are being written now about Stakhanovites. They will be wretched and flat, but they will answer the prime requirement of seeing this enormous movement embodied in images" (*FP* 1973, 148). If Fadeyev's public denunciation of Platonov as a kulak agent was the first seed of his suicide, here was one more. In his suicide note, he would blame the party for destroying Soviet literature. Yet for twenty years he allowed himself to make the very argument that would destroy it—a literary project of mythologizing the Soviet Union at the cost of artistic merit. The problem was not the mythologizing. It was that the vehicle for mythologization was literature.

Those close to him saw the problem in the making. Gerasimova, still close to Fadeyev after the breakup of their marriage, warned him not to be tempted by the offer of a prominent post in the Writers' Union: it would mean sacrificing the time he needed to complete *The Last of the Udegs* (*FP* 1973, 142). She nearly convinced him. "If I'm to do that," he wrote to Libedinsky, "then it's better to switch to party (or other) work, so as to either return to literature with renewed strength or else become a party worker— otherwise, there is indefiniteness, vegetation, emptiness." Fadeyev added that despite his wrecked marriage, he could still look boldly ahead into the country's social and literary future and felt strong enough to do battle to the end. Worried that his friend had perhaps never recovered from RAPP's demise, he offered encouragement: "I urge you, too, to [move forward]—this is what will determine our value and usefulness in life" (*FP* 1973, 142).

Writing to Pavlenko a month after the Zinovyev-Kamenev trial, Fadeyev recalled the noble cause he had fought for during the Civil War:

I was absolutely unafraid of anything—until my first battle . . . Even before my first battle I began my military biography, and began it splendidly—I was held up as an example. But my first battle made a horrifying impression on me. Only my pride could keep me from showing that I was simply frightened to death. And there began a long period of "having the shakes," as they say in the telegraph office, until through force of habit (or, in our métier, professional development), and mainly through force of acquired wisdom, I suppose, and constant effort of will, a new attitude arose to myself, to death, and to revolution—and in truth, only then did I begin to do anything useful.

Fadeyev confided to Pavlenko that he was experiencing similar difficulties in writing *The Last of the Udegs*. Again he felt the need to achieve a further stage of growth:

I am getting nearer to a very great and important *clarity*, but something is still acting as a brake, frightening [me], holding [me] back, and just when you break free toward what seems to be a genuine peak, suddenly you feel you have lost the ability to speak. So what in fact is frightening and holding [me] back?

163

He tries to answer this crucial question by defining the difference between Soviet writers and their European and American counterparts:

> It's much harder [compared with European and American literature] to show how we, *as we are*, discovered a new truth about interpersonal relations (precisely we ourselves), new ties to one another, models of life for humankind. And I'm convinced that we can and must write about this as we experienced and understood it ourselves, because we are the *true sons* [*syny*] *of our time* . . . Sholokhov implants in his Grigorys and Aksinias *his own* character and the Cossacks acknowledge it, Sholokhov's character, as their own character . . . I am absolutely convinced that for both you and me . . . it's not just a matter of *knowledge* of life—after all, we've seen and know an awful lot!— but the whole thing lies in the authentic, true expression of *our own* thoughts and feelings from the most exalted to the basest—and *here* we have not yet attained "fearlessness," *here* something frightens us and holds us back.[9]

His life experience is extraordinary, but he dares not express his conclusions truthfully. He hints at this and then abruptly pulls back. The exalted metaphorical form *syny*, "sons of our time," is one way in which Fadeyev preserves his self-image and self-esteem in the face of the unnamed thing that is "holding him back" from expressing himself fully and achieving his literary potential. He includes Pavlenko, and apparently other writers as well, in the circle of those who are being held back (again he prefers the shared responsibility of "we" rather than the spotlight of "me"). We hear his wistful envy of Sholokhov for having managed not to be held back. Fadeyev wonders what the thing is that acts as a brake. Surely he knew, and either did not want to face it or could do no more than hint at it in a letter. He could hardly write, we had something noble, but it has been destroyed. But perhaps he did not fully formulate this thought to himself, suppressing it as it arose.

He confided that what he most wanted to express in his fiction was "bitterness" (*gorech*). "However, at present somehow one's whole being wants to convey the joyful side of life, and that of course is what is causing me difficulties with *Udegs*." More than that, there is no "culture of the writer's labor and of that 'intent attention to a thing that allows one to see it from a new, unexpected side' (L. Tolstoy's words about Maupassant). Maybe it will still come." He fretted over another stumbling block, too: disregarding the work of others so as to advance what is one's own.[10]

All Fadeyev's concerns in this letter—the urge to express bitterness, to find a new viewpoint, to pursue one's own truth and not accepted truth— were taboo. The disclaimer he appends to his defense of bitterness—"*at present* one's whole being wants to convey the joyful side of life" (emphasis added)—is an uneasy glance over his shoulder at literary prescriptions, censorship, press attacks, and looming above them all Stalin's declaration that "life had become more joyful."

Sholokhov, whose *The Quiet River Don* Fadeyev once blocked and of whom he now writes as an admired Other, did not worry about life having become more joyful. After months pursuing the release of his friends on the *raikom*, he finally concluded the saga of his doubter Grigory in 1940, showing him at the end of the novel overwhelmed by grief and with no emotional anchor to help him cope. It was not a moment to criticize Sholokhov; critics were on their own to explain this ending in their reviews. Yermilov wrote that the reader's pain at Grigory's fate was simultaneously gladness for those who "fear none of the old world's poisons."[11]

That Fadeyev still clung to some shreds of perceived autonomy as late as June 1936 we can surmise, in part, from an exchange at a small gathering of elite party writers who were being reprimanded by Mekhlis for failing to submit pieces to *Pravda*. Like everyone else, Fadeyev wanted to guard his time for his own writing; perhaps he was also trying to avoid penning the kind of harassing articles that Mekhlis courted. With a touch of arrogance, he observed that he had no financial need to contribute to *Pravda* because he received handsome royalties from *The Rout*, which was regularly reprinted several times a year. This remark shows that Fadeyev did not see himself as taking orders from Mekhlis, nor, apparently, did he think of Mekhlis as Stalin's mouthpiece. Mekhlis immediately put Fadeyev in his place. "*The Rout* must continue to be reprinted, but do you have to be paid for it?"[12]

Some months later, during the Piatakov-Radek show trial, Fadeyev cosigned a letter demanding the death penalty for the defendants. He also wrote his own letters to *Pravda* and *Literaturnaia gazeta* revisiting the question of doubt.[13] He had once looked on doubts with leniency; he had had them himself. Then came "For Future Use," and he had to remake his philosophy on doubt. He now reaffirmed the conclusion he had adopted then: any doubts, he wrote in *Literaturnaia gazeta*, should be scrutinized with a view to unmasking enemies.[14]

His personal notebooks strongly suggest that he believed in the defendants' guilt. He took fifty-six pages of personal notes on the trial of Piatakov and Radek, seemingly riveted by it. Interspersing quotations and descriptions of the proceedings with his own indignant commentary, Fadeyev sounds outraged, and with apparent disgust writes down Radek's words—"I knew I was betraying the state."[15] By contrast, his personal notes in 1949 during the campaign against cosmopolitanism sound mechanical, like tutored prompts for his public speeches.

Replacing Stavsky with the more moderate Fadeyev was part of Stalin's winding down of the Great Terror. A Politburo resolution of January 25, 1939 appointed Fadeyev to the top job and named a new presidium of fifteen members (flouting the Writers' Union charter, which stipulated that the presidium be chosen by the board).[16] Eight of them were on a list of "compromised" writers who had active files in the NKVD,[17] of whom three—Fedin, Valentin Katayev, and Pavlenko—were Fadeyev's closest advisers. Two others, Tikhonov and Surkov, would in future be chosen to lead the Writers' Union. Their appointments were not due to oversight or sloppiness. Fear of *kompromat* (questionable prior associations) made for an obedient official.

Under Fadeyev, a subcommittee of seven initially decided what business to bring before the full presidium. Besides Fadeyev, this included Stavsky's right-hand men Pavlenko and Vishnevsky, but also Fedin, Valentin Katayev, and Sobolev, plus Agitprop's Kirpotin.[18] Fadeyev turned most often to Fedin and Katayev, two highly respected writers with commonsense views, and both nonparty. Compromised though he was, and in spite of the dangerous left flank he had in Yermilov, Fadeyev began his tenure by trying to restore a creative agenda to the Writers' Union and assist individual writers with publication. He was the first Writers' Union head to share writers' feeling that useless meetings cut into their creative work.[19] He addressed a long-standing grievance—never had the Writers' Union bothered to arrange readings of work in progress. A delighted Aseyev was the first in a series of writers whom Fadeyev invited to share his work with colleagues.[20]

On Fadeyev's recommendation, the Writers' Union came to include a special section for children's literature (Komissiia po detskoi literatury) (*MMN*, 880). Fadeyev also tried to cut through the literary controls that drove writers to frustration. A manuscript submitted to a literary magazine typically passed through the magazine's editorial board, Agitprop, and the censorship office. Plays, in addition to going through these channels, also had to be approved by the Arts Committee. The Writers' Union, the Central Committee secretaries, *obkom* and *gorkom* secretaries could also get involved. Each reprinting of a novel entailed a completely new censorship review.[21] Censorship thus operated, as Denis Kozlov has pointed out, at three levels, that of author (self-censorship), editorial offices, and state bodies.[22] With so many stages where manuscripts could get "stuck," writers uniformly felt aggrieved at being treated "like little children."[23] The NKVD's *seksoty* reported a variety of complaints: they had to write as if "taking directions from a traffic cop" while "thirsting" for freedom of the press (Pasternak); they were forced to relinquish subtlety (Fedin); the Writers' Union was not for "real writers" (Aseyev); the result of twenty-five years of Bolshevism was starvation (Fyodor Gladkov) (*VKI*, 494–99).

Although the Writers' Union had no formal role in approving manuscripts for publication, Fadeyev worked to push through deserving manuscripts that were languishing in bureaucratic limbo.[24] He argued with officials who rejected manuscripts or demanded too many changes and excisions. He read manuscripts, and assigned other union officials to read manuscripts that writers sent him, forwarding those he liked to a journal (at which point it would pass through the journal's referee process). If he liked a manuscript that had been rejected for political deficiencies, he assigned someone like Libedinsky to help the author revise it. He involved himself in the ambitious efforts to publish the ninety-volume edition of Tolstoy and Arkady Dolinin's ten-volume edition of Dostoevsky, keeping after reluctant publishing houses (Khudozhestvennaia Literatura balked at publishing the fourth volume of Dostoevsky's letters, citing the "restricted thematic plan" for 1940).[25] These monumental scholarly editions were worth fighting for, because they had a hope of being published. The same was not true for brilliant works still being produced by the handful of literary masters who had eluded arrest. Fadeyev is reported to have read *The Master and Margarita* while Bulgakov was alive and to have been upset that there was no chance of publishing it.[26] He appears to have supported Akhmatova's collection *From Six Books* (*Iz shesti knig*)—published in May 1940, after a seventeen-year ban on all her work—for a Stalin Prize. Agitprop's Aleksandrov and Polikarpov did not object, but Zhdanov was incredulous that the book had been published, and Andreyev insisted on banning it (although by the time bookstores received this instruction, the book had sold out) (*PT*, 49).

Intervening with censors on writers' behalf, Fadeyev yet professed belief in censorship as necessary to ensure the mass reader's proper upbringing. This was a tricky balancing act: despite *Pravda*'s mantra that "Soviet literature [was] the most advanced in the world," behind the scenes officials expressed distress at literary mediocrity. Various reasons were given except for the actual ones, which were censorship, blackballing, and the loss of good writers through imprisonment, emigration, and execution. Fadeyev told Andreyev that the problem was the need to fill up the pages of too many literary magazines, all offering the same diet. Just as *Red Virgin Soil* had begun as a forum for fellow travelers and later became a party organ, once the congeries of literary associations had been swept away, other journals that previously had reflected differing literary philosophies—*Literary Contemporary* (*Literaturnyi sovremennik*), *Young Guard, Novy mir, October, Znamia*, and *Zvezda*—now all competed for the same manuscripts. Demand exceeded supply, opening up a market for substandard literature to fill up all those pages. "Eight journals?" Fadeyev wrote to Andreyev (it is hard to imagine him expressing himself in this tone to Stalin).[27] But Fadeyev avoided posing the more basic question. Why were eight previously distinctive journals now all alike? The answer was clear. So were the consequences. Graduate students were choosing to specialize in prerevolutionary rather than Soviet literature. Even the school-age children of the Bolshevik intelligentsia, who were imbibing patriotism from parents, teachers, and Soviet rituals, were unmoved by Soviet literature. Voracious readers, they were devouring the classics.[28]

Another factor in literary quality was the social engineering of the Writers' Union, which had been greatly aided by the Great Purge. The destruction of literature was analogous to the destruction of agriculture—the best writers were treated as literary kulaks and destroyed. The 25 percent of members arrested from 1936 through 1938 were disproportionately critical and independently minded. The rolls were replenished by new admissions, younger and more fully acculturated to Soviet mores and who therefore could be expected to be more compliant. Writers' privileged status and access to housing, goods, and services reshaped the literary profession by attracting people who chose literature as a lucrative career rather than as a calling.

Since membership statistics were published only in conjunction with the congresses, and since twenty years elapsed between the first and second congresses, we must estimate the number and nationality of members in those years, using guesswork plus the few figures to be found in archives. No member directories appear to have been circulated before 1959, perhaps because of continual arrests and expulsions. Directories would have served as reminders of those who had been erased.

The 1934 initial membership of 2,200 had risen to 2,760 by 1946. Thus the Writers' Union managed to grow in spite of the purges and war losses. The 600 writers lost to the Great Purge shrank the Writers' Union to 1,600 members, even without accounting for natural deaths. This ground had to be made up by new admissions. An average of 85 new acceptances per year from 1935 to 1941 would have kept the membership steady through the outbreak of war. In fact, wartime admissions statistics allow us to deduce that the number at the outbreak of war had surged to 2,850.[29] Some applicants were likely fast-tracked with an eye to regaining lost ground. Konstantin Simonov, for example, published his first poems and was admitted to the Writers' Union in 1936, when he was just twenty-one and still a student at the Literary Institute. Fully 800 members belonged to the Moscow branch in 1941.[30] This reflected demographics as well as Moscow's desirability; many writers who had the opportunity to relocate to the capital did so.

It was no secret that the Writers' Union harbored within it a literary underclass. Those charged with vetting manuscripts and assisting young writers were often at a loss, and Fadeyev, too, found himself correcting their grammar.[31] When an Evenk poet maintained that his Russian translator had brazenly changed his "meaning, rhythm, rhyme, and form," Fadeyev contacted the translator, who could barely contain herself: "It's hard to imagine a poet complaining about poetic 'distortions' in this doggerel. The poem has four stanzas. Here is one of them:

> In the distant tundra and in the pine grove
> The kolkhozy live a bright life.
> Everywhere Stalin's word can be heard,
> Inspiring us to song and labor."

The translator enclosed a printed page from *Literaturnyi sovremennik* containing another poem by the same author. It was titled "I Will Become a Commander" ("Ia stanu komandirom") and ended with the couplet "Goodbye, mother! / Your son will return home a commander." "This one is better," she wrote. "It has folk rhythm."[32]

Fadeyev tried through Litfond to assist impoverished writers who had suffered from ideological retribution. At a closed meeting of the presidium in November 1939, Fadeyev introduced a resolution to give financial assistance and an apartment to Akhmatova, who lived with her ex-husband, his current family, and his mentally unbalanced first wife.[33] Suspecting that Akhmatova had no furniture of her own, he intended to have a Litfond official visit her in the new apartment, so as to tactfully take note of what furniture she needed. When the Leningrad *gorsovet* (city council) failed to provide an apartment, Fadeyev turned to Vyshinsky at the Council of Ministers, emphasizing that younger poets continued to learn from her work, and that the discrepancy between her poetic achievement and her material condition made a bad impression on these young writers. Vyshinsky supported the request (*PT*, 48), but Akhmatova never did receive an apartment. The presidium was reduced to passing a resolution "to consider it wrong" that Litfond assistance did not prioritize a writer's "creative significance."[34]

Fadeyev also tried to arrange financial assistance for Ilya Ilf, the widows of Aleksandr Blok and Bulgakov, and even Yermilov's archenemy Elena Usievich.[35] When the Writers' Union publishing house, Sovetsky pisatel, insisted that Nikolai Nikandrov return an advance he had received for a manuscript he never produced, the Writers' Union tried repeatedly to have the debt cancelled, explaining that Nikandrov lived in extreme poverty and had been traumatized when a court officer showed up at his apartment to confiscate his belongings as payment for the debt. The officer, who determined that Nikandrov did not even have any property worthy of being seized, was so shocked at his poverty that he was ready to give him money out of his own pocket.[36]

While Fadeyev was trying to make the Writers' Union a useful resource for writers, Stalin was undermining him by arranging stricter oversight of literature. Barely two months after Fadeyev took over the Writers' Union, the Eighteenth Party Congress in March 1939 heard Stalin's proposal to consolidate oversight of the press (including literary journals), and a Central Committee resolution of August 20 upgraded Agitprop from a department (*otdel*) to an administration (*upravlenie*). The entity that had been created in 1935, the Otdel kulturno-prosvetitelnoi raboty (Department of Culture and Enlightenment, known as Kultpros), was replaced with the Upravlenie Propagandy i Agitatsii TsK (Propaganda and Agitation Administration).

The new Agitprop contained five separate sections: (1) party propaganda, (2) Marxist-Leninist cadre training, (3) the press, (4) agitation, and (5) institutions of cultural enlightenment. Literature fell under the press section, which had oversight of all newspapers and magazines, approved editorial staff appointments, and monitored editors' publishing decisions.[37] All literary journals received new editorial boards and a "responsible editor" (*otvetstvenny redaktor*). Initially, the new Agitprop was headed by Zhdanov, but in September 1940 Aleksandrov, the head of the propaganda section, was promoted to become head of Agitprop. He reported to Zhdanov, but as we noted in the previous intermezzo, his patron was Malenkov, head of the Central Committee's personnel department (*PT*, 24). Also that month, a fiction office was created within the press section to assure closer supervision of literature. Its four-member staff was headed by A. M. Yegolin, a literary scholar and Writers' Union member (*PT*, 53, 77). Yegolin's patron was Zhdanov. It was only a matter of time before writers became caught in the rivalry between Zhdanov and Malenkov.

Stalin used the restructured Agitprop together with the Politburo to unleash a new literary campaign that began in August 1940 and lasted through the autumn. It was built upon Stalin's personal demand for harsh portrayals of enemies. The inaugural victim was Avdeyenko, the proletarian literary darling whom the party had lifted to fame and showered with luxury items, including an American-made Buick. Avdeyenko, now on the staff of *Pravda*, was bewildered when it denounced a new movie with his screenplay, *The Law of Life* (*Zakon zhizni*). Upon inquiry, he was told that the article was partly written by Stalin.[38]

Avdeyenko's account of his *prorabotka*, or "grilling," before the Central Committee sheds light on the general procedures of a *prorabotka* as well as its function in traumatizing the victim. By the appointed day, the victim had had plenty of time to work himself into a frenzy. Avdeyenko, who lived in the Donbass, received an urgent summons from the Central Committee and traveled to Moscow, only to be told that Zhdanov was too busy to see him; he should await further word. The urgent summons was followed by nearly three weeks of silence. When news finally came, it was that the meeting was being held that very day. He was ushered to a seat that, he noticed, bore a plaque with the name Mekhlis. This detail resonated in myriad unpleasant ways: Mekhlis, Avdeyenko's former boss at *Pravda*; Mekhlis who spoke for the party at all times; Mekhlis, who had forced him squirming into the Moscow-Volga Canal trip. What Mekhlis, Yagoda, and Firin had shown him six years before—that he could wake up one day to find his identity switched from writer to *zek*—might now actually be happening.

Zhdanov, Malenkov, and Andreyev were on the podium, but Stalin was absent. Other Central Committee members, including Fadeyev, sat at rows of desks. Valentin Katayev and Aseyev were there as Writers' Union representatives. Zhdanov opened the proceedings with an hourlong speech bubbling with outrage. As he spoke his concluding words, a voice interrupted him. Stalin was now revealed to be in the room, having been shielded from view by an enormous column.[39] He spoke at length, deriding Avdeyenko as a bourgeois "junk peddler" (*barakholshchik*).

With that insult, Avdeyenko suddenly saw himself—so he thought—through Stalin's eyes. Here was Stalin, wearing a shapeless gray tunic and baggy trousers tucked into his boots, while Avdeyenko, who had dressed in his best clothes for this all-important meeting, had on suede shoes, a starched shirt, a nice tie, and a well-made suit jacket that he had bought while on assignment for *Pravda* in Chernovtsy, which Zhdanov and Stalin had just made a point of deriding as a "bourgeois city."

Two observations come to mind. First, desirable consumer goods, like American cars and quality clothing, lavished on writers as a sign of approval and privilege, could at any moment become material evidence of bourgeois enmity. Second, even with the benefit of hindsight in the age of perestroika, Avdeyenko misconstrued the *prorabotka* moment as one of seeing himself through Stalin's eyes. The octogenarian memoirist still failed to understand that what Stalin saw was not an Avdeyenko who had acquired bourgeois tastes but a usable cadre whom he had set up to be shamed when the time was right. Avdeyenko remained Stalin's mental captive to the end of his days, continuing to think exactly what Stalin had set him up to think.

A *prorabotka* was meant to defame the entire person rather than address a particular error. Committing an error made you a vile person. Stalin reinforced this notion with the false claim that Avdeyenko had been admitted to the party on the recommendation of two people subsequently unmasked as enemies (*PT*, 27).

Even after Avdeyenko realized that the defendants at the Moscow show trials, which he had attended by invitation, were innocent, and that the *Pravda* he had been so proud to work for issued an endless stream of lies, the effect of his disgrace and expulsion was to make him want to regain the approval of Stalin and the party. There were now two Avdeyenkos—two psyches inside one mind. The former self remained even as the new one grew alongside it. The former self was the writer of public reputation; the new self, which knew the truth about Stalin and the party machine, was sure to become the *zek* revealed to him by the now executed Yagoda. The vaunted White Sea and Volga canals were part of the semiotic system that fed his own construction of self. This can explain why Avdeyenko, instead of breaking with the party, focused on regaining its goodwill even as he saw it to be a monstrous creation. We can also imagine that Avdeyenko had to hide from himself the fact that he was choosing his obedient writer self over his truthful *zek* self. So he continued to regard the Communist Party as an honor group and still felt the need to demonstrate that he shared its code.[40] And he was, after many years, allowed back into the party. Avdeyenko's meteoric rise and precipitous fall were not opposite phenomena, nor were they the illogical contradiction they appeared to him to be. They were a calculated continuum of psychological manipulation, one from which he could never wrench free.

Fadeyev, who was expected to parrot Zhdanov and Stalin, wavered between adopting their tone of disgust and trying to mitigate Avdeyenko's plight. He intimated that he would purge the Writers' Union, but offered, "It is difficult to criticize Avdeyenko; he doesn't understand anything" (*PT*, 27). Stalin mocked Fadeyev's hemming and hawing,[41] but Fadeyev carried out Stalin's instruction to have Avdeyenko expelled from the Writers' Union. In September he read the presidium his report on "The Soviet Writer's Moral Character" ("Moralny oblik sovetskogo pisatelia") (*PT*, 42), using Stalin's language but trying to remove its stigma: Stalin had called Avdeyenko a junk peddler; Fadeyev depersonalized it, referring to junk (*barakholstvo*) in the Writers' Union and using that word to characterize Avdeyenko's screenplay.[42] Avdeyenko, evicted from his apartment and left to his own devices to support his wife and baby son, returned to his roots, becoming a worker in the Donbass coal mines.[43] He had at least escaped the identity of *zek*.

Now a spate of plays and films were banned, in some cases by Stalin personally and in others at Agitprop's recommendation. The authors were often grilled before the Central Committee secretaries. The banned plays included Anatoly Glebov's *Frankly Speaking* (*Nachistotu*), Valentin Katayev's *The Little House* (*Domik*), Kozakov's *When I'm Alone* (*Kogda ia odin*), and Leonov's *The Blizzard* (*Metel*) (*PT*, 36–37). As with Avdeyenko, the punishment for these four authors did not progress beyond opprobrium, banned works, and lost income. But the children's writer Yan Larri, who had been taking the precaution of sending chapters of his new science fiction novel to Stalin, was arrested, and the NKVD also came for Semyon Gekht, who had defended Platonov in the *Literary Critic* affair (*PT*, 42).

The Central Committee secretaries were displeased with Fadeyev and his deputies for not having noticed the harmfulness of the banned plays. The Writers' Union presidium had actually praised some of them for the very traits that Stalin and Zhdanov found objectionable. While the Central Committee secretaries were deciding to ban Leonov's *The Blizzard*, the Writers' Union presidium was considering nominating it for a Stalin Prize.[44] The presidium also praised *The Little House*: "When you go to the theater to see a comedy," said one member, "you know in advance that the hero will be an office worker . . . that once again the *meshchanstvo* [petty bourgeoisie] will be satirized, and once again the whole thing will be paraded before us."[45] Others agreed, noting that "it's boring to watch a comedy in which it's clear from the very start who the positive and negative characters are" and that Katayev's play was good because "depending on the situation, [the protagonist] may show positive or negative attributes, so that we can't apply a simple standard to him."[46]

The secretaries imagined that Fadeyev and his deputies had failed to discover the harmful works because their time was taken up with Litfond matters. They took Litfond away from the Writers' Union and placed it under the Arts Committee.[47] This appears to have been another instance of refusing to see what was plainly before them. Countless times they had heard writers explain that literature could not thrive under ideological formulas. It is also true, however, that some officials felt Litfond doled out generous financial aid to undeserving writers and that some writers had gamed the system by manipulating the generous provision that allowed any writer who was too ill to work to receive payments from Litfond for up to four months a year.[48] From this perspective, removing Litfond from the Writers' Union was the principled and economically sound thing to do. But adopting this view also allowed the secretaries to ignore the real reason for the Writers' Union's approval of works they found inadmissible.

With Stalin personally behind the new campaign, Fadeyev increasingly sided with the party secretaries against his own presidium. When twenty-two writers wrote to Zhdanov urging publication of a long-delayed poetry collection by Tikhon Churylin, *Pravda* published their letter, but Fadeyev refused to go out on a limb for Churylin and even sank his request for Litfond assistance (*PT*, 44–45).

A memo from Fadeyev to Stalin, Zhdanov, and Shcherbakov shows him trying to carve out an intellectual position that would square his literary beliefs with party strictures. The memo concerns an article by the old intelligentsia writer Vikenty Veresayev against censorship.[49] Fadeyev's analysis is an intellectual argument with himself, an exercise in justification—of both the party and himself. "Instances of editorial caprice really are common at journals and publishing houses. Everywhere you find unintelligent, semiliterate people who, feeling that they are backed by the government and immune from punishment, warp and maim manuscripts." But Fadeyev finds a way to attack Veresayev for saying what he himself has essentially just acknowledged: Veresayev's characterization, says Fadeyev, contains "a hidden idea—to discredit editors as workers in Soviet government service, as executors of our government's policy, as people who stand guard over the interests of the state."

Veresayev cannot say out loud that he is "yoked" by Glavlit and the political requirements of our journals and publishing houses, and he hides behind the stylistic and artistic side of the question. And the overall tone of his article is a howl over "freedom of the press" in the bourgeois sense. (*PT*, 55–56)

Was not Veresayev's "hidden idea" the same as Fadeyev's lament to Pavlenko, that something was holding him back? Did he or did he not notice this?

Fadeyev did not deny that good literary manuscripts were ruined. By confining the blame to individual editors, he could assure himself of a salutary censorship.[50] When Fadeyev sees overzealous editors, they are acting on their own accord; when Veresayev sees them, he is attacking the state. It was another fifteen years before he could bring himself to place the blame on the party's leaders and therefore on the party itself—and then it would mean suicide. When we come to Fadeyev's suicide note, we will want to recall this memo. They are companion pieces that substitute an apparently plausible explanation for a horrifying truth he does not want to face—that he was serving not a noble cause but its monstrous corruption.

Germany's surprise invasion on June 22, 1941, suddenly made the enemy-hating culture that Stalin stoked necessary and organic.[51] Pasternak's famous remark, shocking on a first hearing, that "the war came as a breath of fresh air," expresses the immediacy of a collective sense of mission. Some 1,200 writers went to the front. Nearly 1,000 of them were from the regional branches; 230 of Moscow's 800 members were doing military service in early 1942.[52] Writers served in combat, as political instructors, and as correspondents for military newspapers and the general press.[53] Their reports boosted the morale of Red Army soldiers as well as that of starving siege victims listening to Leningrad radio in freezing apartments.[54] The Red Army newspaper, *Krasnaia zvezda*, with reporting by Ehrenburg, Vasily Grossman, Simonov, Pavlenko, Surkov, Tolstoy, and Yevgeny Gabrilovich, was read avidly as a candid source of war news.[55] Those who stayed behind, either because of their age or their exceptional literary talent, were evacuated, mostly to Alma-Ata, Chistopol, Kazan, Kuibyshev, Sverdlovsk, Tashkent, or Ufa, where they wrote with a new urgency in support not of a propaganda war but of a war for national survival (*PT*, 64).

The Writers' Union military commission, headed by Pavlenko, was supposed to coordinate writers' contributions to the war effort and assign writers to the various fronts, where they would serve as correspondents.[56] However, turf wars and general confusion hampered the commission's exercise of authority. When writer correspondents showed up at their assignments, the military commissar would often try to tap them as cooks and combatants.[57] Lobansky, the commission's secretary, noted with exasperation that the writer correspondents in Stalingrad were "Comrades Rud, Kats, and Kalalayevsky" and asked, "Are these people known in the literary community?"[58] Frustrated that the posters, leaflets, songs, and one-act plays that writers produced at the commission's behest often were rejected by the publisher or the Arts Committee, Lobansky told the presidium, "I myself do not see the point of continuing this work."[59]

The Writers' Union struggled to arrange food packets, meal service, and evacuations for its members and their families. As the Germans advanced rapidly toward Moscow, its writers were hurriedly evacuated, most of them boarding eastbound trains on October 14 and 15. On the sixteenth, a day of panic among those still remaining, Fadeyev, whose job it was to oversee the evacuation, boarded a train himself. Several writers filed a formal complaint, asserting that he left before all writers had been evacuated. Fadeyev strenuously denied culpability, insisting that the five writers had failed to evacuate through their own fault—for example, by bringing more luggage than could fit on the train. Unwilling to jeopardize his own departure, Fadeyev instructed Kirpotin and the Foreign Commission's Mikhail Apletin to deal with those who were left. Kirpotin, who had orders to evacuate with his family to Chistopol and to oversee the writers there, instead traveled twenty-five hundred kilometers further on to the greater safety and desirability of Tashkent. Once there, he persuaded Fadeyev to put him in charge of its Writers' Union branch. Fadeyev soon regretted agreeing to this, complaining of older-generation writers "who overcame their bourgeois prejudices only to get them back now."[60]

The presidium managed to resume meetings in January 1942. Among its first discoveries was that the union had lost track of most of its membership. Even after many writers returned to Moscow that spring,[61] and Writers' Union operations grew more orderly, there were plenty of opportunities for abuses, especially in the restaurant. When no one was looking, hungry or unscrupulous writers and staff took advantage of the restaurant's unsecured cash receipts. Simonov owed the restaurant 74,702 rubles, prompting one presidium member to rage that he had turned the cash register into his private office.[62] This amount paled in comparison with the 173,160-ruble debt "for vodka and wine" run up by a restaurant stockroom worker. Other staff of the restaurant and accounting office ran up less-egregious illegitimate debts.[63]

In 1943 the presidium met regularly every two weeks, reviewing the quality of the military publishing house (Voenpechat) and assuring that writers were contributing amply to it. It arranged readings for individual writers and discussed their work in a supportive way.[64] It surveyed the quality and output of literature from the union republics, nominated Stalin-prize candidates, and recommended material assistance for destitute writers.[65]

The presidium also continued to admit new members recommended by the selection committee. At its first meeting of 1943 it accepted 25 of 120 applications and deferred action on the rest (until publication of the applicant's first book or until a presidium member could read a published book and make a recommendation). It also elevated twelve candidate members to full membership and deferred two others.[66] The admissions process was compromised, however, as regional officials unconnected to the Writers' Union, apparently trying to help impoverished residents survive, sometimes granted admissions on their own authority.[67] In 1942, 96 members were admitted and 54 rejected; in 1943, 97 were admitted and 84 rejected; in March 1944 the selection committee received orders to be stricter. Statistics for the next few years reflected this: in 1944, 64 were accepted and 71 rejected; in 1945, 24 were accepted and 23 rejected; in 1946, 36 were accepted and 36 rejected.[68]

Political considerations also played their part. The prominent literary historian and Pushkinist Mikhail Beliayev, who had been arrested during the academic historians' affair of 1929–31 and survived the Solovki labor camp, was a candidate member seeking full membership. This future founder of Leningrad's Pushkin museum had published some seventy works and was recommended by Lenin's personal secretary (and Averbakh's father-in-law), Vladimir Bonch-Bruyevich. The entire presidium abstained.[69]

Prewar censorship guidelines now yielded to the imperative of lifting the national spirit.[70] With Zhdanov taken up with seeing Leningrad through the siege, propaganda oversight passed to Shcherbakov, who oversaw the wartime press as chief of the newly created Soviet Information Bureau (Sovinformbiuro). Agitprop officials reported to him, and he also became the gatekeeper of Stalin's mail.[71] On a case-by-case basis, Shcherbakov allowed material normally considered trivial or defamatory, such as private lives and emotional stress. In 1942 he indulged Simonov's love poetry, restoring a publisher's cuts. Another work that landed on Shcherbakov's desk was Aleksandr Dovzhenko's story of a soldier's love affair, "Unforgettable" ("Nezabyvaemoe"). He blocked publication but approved it for a radio broadcast (*PT*, 72). Love lyrics by Aseyev, Selvinsky, and others also passed censorship in the early war years (*PT*, 70).

These allowances were a strictly tactical maneuver, but most writers interpreted them as a sign of a new benevolence.[72] What they read in the press seemed to confirm their supposition. A financial decision was made to suspend *Literaturnaia gazeta*, but to writers it seemed that a source of media harassment was being eliminated. Ehrenburg's eagerly awaited reportage in *Krasnaia zvezda*, detailing German military strengths, Soviet losses, and the heroism of Jews was understood as a policy shift toward truthful writing.[73] But Ehrenburg's pieces were the exception, and Stalin reviewed them before publication.

Those who misread the new pragmatism included Ehrenburg's colleagues on the Jewish Anti-Fascist Committee (JAFC), one of five antifascist fund-raising committees operated via the Soviet Information Bureau.[74] Most of the JAFC's leading members belonged to the Writers' Union or collaborated with writers. Its head was Solomon Mikhoels of the Moscow Yiddish theater; Writers' Union members included Ehrenburg, Grossman, and the Yiddish-language writers Itsik Fefer, Markish, David Bergelson, David Hofstein, and Lev Kvitko. Shcherbakov's deputy at the Soviet Information Bureau, Solomon Lozovsky, was also a member.[75] The JAFC's most notable effort was a visit by Mikhoels and Fefer to Allied capitalist countries, including the United States, to raise funds from wealthy Jewish donors. Its members, however, saw the JAFC as a mark of the party's increased attention to Yiddish culture (a misunderstanding that was uncovered after the war, when party officials expressed anger over the JAFC's continued activism in publishing articles abroad and seeking government aid for needy Soviet Jews).[76]

Fadeyev, too, felt free to unlock his inner liberal. Visiting Leningrad in the spring of 1942, he read the latest chapters of Aleksandr Tvardovsky's *Vasily Tyorkin* to a group of writers remaining in the blockaded city. He included Platonov in a list of authors of important war stories (startling, given his gratuitous harassment of Platonov two years earlier).[77] He slammed the rising star Boris Gorbatov for work that was subliterary; the "new generation of Soviet readers," declared Fadeyev, were too sophisticated for that (*SF*, 829). He supported Shostakovich, still under a cloud, for a Stalin Prize, first class, praising his "newness and diversity."[78]

During three months in blockaded Leningrad he wrote *Leningrad during the Blockade* (*Leningrad v dni blokady*), describing what he witnessed and learned from the city's residents. Shcherbakov demanded that he moderate his description of the harsh living conditions and omit some of the battle episodes. Fadeyev appealed to Zhdanov, who was himself living through the siege and might appreciate an accurate description (*AFPD*, 115). Journal publication was denied, depriving it of its immediacy; the book was published in 1944 after the siege had been lifted.

Fadeyev's most important effort during the war was his novel *The Young Guard*. It closely followed the true story of a youth partisan detachment in the Donbass. Its characters were based on real *komsomoltsy* (Young Communists); Fadeyev learned everything he could about his teenage heroes, studying their letters and interviewing their families. For the first time since *The Rout*, he had found a literary labor of love. He described his state of mind in a letter of November 1944 to the poet Margarita Aliger, with whom he was intimate:

Whenever it was necessary to choose between work and an ephemeral social obligation, like the many years of fruitless "leadership" of the Writers' Union, between work and an obligation to my family or a friend . . . it always . . . happened that my [literary] work came second.

. . . [Writing] is the truest, largest, strongest, most deeply sincere thing I can do for people. And I had to step over everything and do it, so that it does not perish in my soul both for myself and for people. (*FP* 1973, 216)

Three times in this letter Fadeyev invokes God, always in the context of self-analysis and misery at the thought of his failure as a writer. "I have often felt and feel guilty toward god and people, but I never felt the main thing—guilt toward my talent, which doesn't belong to me. I treated my talent with the same lack of respect that Chekhov famously condemned." He confesses to a weak will. And he confides that, although he had been released from his duties to work on *The Young Guard*, for months he could get nothing done because of "an increasingly sharp mental contradiction [*dushevnoe protivorechie*] and my complete inability—given my character—to live under a mental contradiction" (*FP* 1973, 215).

I felt guilty . . . before Tikhonov and Polikarpov for not working at the union, before Kovalchik and Novogrudsky for not working at the newspaper, etc., etc. So I felt guilty before the whole world, and all the more so the more I grew convinced that these people . . . and institutions . . . were happy to see me as guilty and condemn me. And meanwhile I gave all of myself, because my character is that way, to whatever matter (except unfortunately for my main one), sparing no effort . . . with all my soul and talent, mercilessly burning myself at both ends. (*FP* 1973, 217)

The secretaries had been receiving complaints about Fadeyev. In September 1941 Lozovsky, noting that Fadeyev was in the habit of disappearing for days at a time, recommended he be replaced. The Party Control Commission determined that the disappearances were drunken binges, during which he would not return home for days on end and, on at least one occasion, staying at the apartment of an actress.[79] These episodes were common knowledge among writers, who complained that while intoxicated Fadeyev would delegate duties to others. Fadeyev was given a warning, but Lozovsky's recommendation was not followed. Instead, Shcherbakov kept Fadeyev in Chistopol for the first months of the war, shackled to the Writers' Union's wartime newspaper, *Literature and Art* (*Literatura i iskusstvo*) and ignoring his request to serve at the front as a correspondent or political instructor.

As the war continued, Agitprop officials joined the chorus of dissatisfaction with Fadeyev. Some of this was surely the result of client-patron relationships that pitted Malenkov's client Aleksandrov against Fadeyev. Agitprop faulted Fadeyev for a lax leadership style, citing his failure to follow orders to "take measures" to improve literary criticism, allowing presidium meetings to proceed in an "undirected" fashion, and failing to exercise any influence over writers' literary production (*PT*, 75). As to this last point, if there was one matter on which many writers had no quarrel with Fadeyev, this was certainly it. But hard-line communist writers like Vishnevsky and Nikulin wanted Fadeyev to step down. More liberal writers had their own complaints. Aseyev was outraged by what he described as Fadeyev's lack of respect toward writers (*PT* 44, 52).

It seems fair to assume that what lay behind the drinking bouts was in large part the "mental contradiction" Fadeyev described to Aliger, the now tormenting divide between truth and authority. His RAPP comrade Bezymensky, with whom he had long ago fallen out, confronted Fadeyev with his two selves. "Dear Aleksandr Aleksandrovich," wrote Bezymensky, "For a long time now I've not been able to make up my mind (nor do I have the right) to call you Sasha, although sometimes I very much want to." Bezymensky reminded Fadeyev of their idealism in the early days of RAPP:

> You, too, made friends with people you weren't supposed to make friends with, and often did what you weren't supposed to do, those twenty years ago . . . You were very fine, Sasha, which is something I can't say for Aleksandr Aleksandrovich . . . You went against the current and wrote "Against the Current" . . . You have remained an excellent writer, even though you have not managed to unwrap what life placed within you—in part with the help of the October [RAPP] group . . . I am writing this letter to *you*, not to the secretary of the Writers' Union presidium. You're intelligent, you know what I mean. I sincerely wish you health and flourishing. But there are different ways of flourishing. You understand the way I intend it.[80]

These were not just the sentiments of an embittered former friend. Vera Panova, in an otherwise friendly exchange with Fadeyev in 1946, in which the two complimented each other on their latest fiction, wrote, "Back then [in 1925] you were young, slim, and—so they say—kinder than you are now" (*AFPD*, 257).

The NKVD's *seksoty* toward the end of the war reported a variety of feelings among writers, from unhappiness at being allied with countries whose long-term agenda was the Soviet Union's destruction, to hope that Allied pressure would lead to democratizing changes. The journalist P. B. Krasnov reportedly declared that a Soviet victory would leave him with just one option—suicide (*VKI*, 494). But many writers were sanguine. The critic L. Poliak celebrated poets for throwing off the "iron chains" they had worn before the war.[81] Eikhenbaum voiced similar optimism. "Many people think criticism is a particular field whose main purpose is to establish how to write and what to write about," he wrote. "[Such critics] did appear among us, and thank God they have disappeared!"[82]

Even as these sunny claims were being printed, however, prewar controls were being quietly reinstituted. This process had begun as soon as the tide of war turned with the victory at Stalingrad. Much of it was directed at distinguishing between a virtuous Soviet Union and a villainous other. In 1943, *International Literature* (*Internatsionalnaia literatura*), the only place where Soviet readers could read European literature in translation, was discontinued.[83] That December, the Central Committee passed three resolutions intended to prevent "harmful" literature from appearing in magazines.[84] The Jewish editor of *Krasnaia zvezda*, David Vadimov (Ortenberg), was dismissed. *The Black Book* (*Chernaia kniga*), a compendium of wartime Jewish testimonies collected by Ehrenburg and Grossman, was denied publication.[85] The JAFC was disbanded. Earlier still, in the spring of 1943, Fadeyev wrote to Vishnevsky of "slavish bowing before everything foreign" and a new policy to "sharpen the question of the Russian people's national pride" (*FP* 1973, 204–5). All these developments presaged further campaigns to come in 1946 and 1949.

As the party secretaries tried to ensure docility, they discovered a new source of rebellion at the Literary Institute. By now, Gorky's brainchild had about 115 students, and its faculty included many nonparty writers, among them Selvinsky, Shklovsky, Aseyev, Osip Brik, and Zelinsky.[86] Six students had been arrested in 1941–42, and the leaders were coming to see the institute as a breeding ground of dissent.[87] Their unease turned to alarm in 1943, when it emerged that some 250 people had read a diploma work submitted to the creative writing department and described as a neobaroque alternative to socialist realism. The author was Arkady Belinkov; the supervisor was Shklovsky; the title, "A Rough Draft of Feelings" ("Chernovik chuvstv"), was suggested by Zoshchenko; and the department chair was Selvinsky (*TPS*, 1:476–77). Belinkov was arrested in January 1944. Another student, Genrikh Elshtein, who wrote a novel called *Eleven Doubts* (*Odinnadtsat somnenii*), was arrested in April.

Agitprop informed Shcherbakov that 24 percent of the institute's students were Jewish, as were 100 percent of its anti-Soviet students (*TPS*, 1:478–79). Shcherbakov, warning of a "neobaroque challenge to socialist realism," translated this phrase for the other Central Committee secretaries: the neobaroque, he explained, was based on Selvinsky, and it targeted socialist realism in the person of Simonov, now a top Writers' Union deputy (*TPS*, 1:477).[88] The secretaries passed a resolution on July 26, 1944, to shutter the institute.

Simonov, to his credit, defended the institute (although not the offending students) to Stalin, who annulled the resolution (*TPS*, 1:479). Stalin's taking counsel with Simonov shows the fluctuations that were occurring in the Writers' Union leadership. Fadeyev had pleaded to be relieved of his duties in order to devote full time to writing *The Young Guard*. He stepped away in January, describing this move as a leave of absence. This may have been true; however, to the many complaints over his alcoholism must be added his antagonistic relations with Agitprop. Although Agitprop stood above the Writers' Union in the party chain of command, Fadeyev behaved with an arrogance that provoked its officials, causing them to feel that his relationship with Stalin was such that he need not bow to them (*TPS*, 1:474). In memos to the leadership in September and December of 1943, Aleksandrov, Yegolin, and their colleague Aleksei Puzin blamed Fadeyev for allowing the publication of "anti-Soviet" works by Zoshchenko and Selvinsky, and also for bringing incompetent and "politically dubious" people onto the staff of *Literature and Art*.[89]

In a replay of the team model that had existed under Gorky and Shcherbakov, the nonparty Tikhonov took over for Fadeyev, while Malenkov's client Polikarpov, formerly Aleksandrov's deputy at Agitprop, joined the Writers' Union secretariat.[90] Some writers saw what this meant. Chukovsky predicted that Tikhonov would be a "purely decorative figure," while Polikarpov would "bring order, fine us, curse us, etc."[91] It also seems clear that when Stalin needed to reach beyond Polikarpov and actually hear from a writer, he turned to Simonov, not Tikhonov.

Stavsky, meanwhile, was among the war dead. Even here, however, his impulsive nature had a role. After taking part in an exchange of fire between Russian and German snipers, he was heading back to his command post and couldn't resist a quick detour across an open field for a proud look at some German tanks that had been disabled by the Russian snipers. Trotting across that open field, he made an easy target for a lingering German sniper (*AFPD*, 129).

Literaturnaia gazeta resumed publication in October 1944, another sign of resurgent orthodoxy. Its new editor was Surkov, who we recall was launched on the ladder of careerism when Mekhlis entrusted him with rebutting Bukharin at the First Writers' Congress. Also on the editorial board were Gorbatov, Sobolev, Samuil Marshak, Polikarpov, and the ideology official Vadim Kozhevnikov, who reminded everyone that the job of literary critics was to tell writers "what attitude they should adopt to the reality they observe."[92]

Under Polikarpov's scrutiny, writers in the presidium were back to fighting and begging. In the first part of 1946, party and nonparty writers alike called for his removal as well as Surkov's. Aseyev, Gerasimova, Karavayeva, and Vishnevsky stated bluntly that the leaders and supervisors of literature had no credibility with writers.[93] Vishnevsky, who did think the union should be headed by a party official, was appalled at Polikarpov's sneering.[94] The mood at presidium meetings was pugnacious. Where once Shklovsky and Pilniak were the lone voices challenging Shcherbakov, now a critical mass in the room clashed repeatedly with Polikarpov and Surkov. Shklovsky, declaring to Polikarpov that "in the people's court and the municipal court you will be vindicated, but in the court of talent you will be accused,"[95] found plenty of support to fill the gap left by the liquidated Pilniak. Gerasimova unmasked the claim that the Writers' Union was a "creative organization" and offered proposals for turning it into one.[96] She began with the same recommendation Pilniak had urged on Shcherbakov a dozen years earlier: editorial boards needed to consist of writers "who are respected by writers and have literary taste." Many of those present supported her, finding that Surkov's *Literaturnaia gazeta* compared unfavorably with its prewar predecessor in shying away from publishing anything that might provoke a rebuttal.[97] Even worse was that *Literaturnaia gazeta* never defended any of the writers in whose name it was supposed to speak.

SHKLOVSKY: After such a great year [1945] and the place the Soviet Union now has in the world, how does *Literaturnaia gazeta* manage to be such a boring paper!

POLIKARPOV: Such boring writers. What have you discovered that *Literaturnaia gazeta* overlooked?

SHKLOVSKY: I discovered the Serapion brothers and LEF.

VOICE FROM THE FLOOR: And then they were undiscovered.

SHKLOVSKY: I would rather die with LEF than live with you.[98]

Others pointed out that book reviews described all books in the same way:

GRIGORY BROVMAN: . . . the lack of an aesthetic approach to a work makes all writers alike . . . There are four articles (by [Mark] Gelfand, Subotsky, [Natalia] Chetunova, and Libedinsky) of four decent books by [Valentin] Ovechkin, [Petro] Vershigora, [Lazar] Lagin, and [Boris?] Leonidov . . . you can't even tell what the authors of these books wrote—poetry, prose, drama, or water polo . . . Chetunova begins with the remark that Lagin's book is "far from perfect"—

CHETUNOVA (*interrupting*): The editor wrote that, I didn't write it.

BROVMAN: . . . Libedinsky writes vaguely that there are defects. But he doesn't tell us what kind of book it is, or where its originality lies . . . It is wrong . . . to try to "level" these four authors.[99]

Surkov responded not as a writer arguing with colleagues but by adopting the contemptuous posture that party officials—here Mekhlis especially comes to mind—often used toward cadres. The newspaper, he remarked, was only as good as the submissions it received. He threw a line from Gogol at them: "Don't blame the mirror if your face is crooked."[100] His hearers shot back with a list of worthy titles ignored by the press and therefore unknown to the public: Ovechkin's *Greetings from the Front* (*S frontovym privetom*), Leonov's *The Taking of Velikoshumsk* (*Vziatie Velikoshumska*), Gorbatov's *The Unvanquished* (*Nepokorennye*), Vershigora's *People with a Clear Conscience* (*Liudi s chistoi sovestiu*), and Tvardovsky's *Vasily Tyorkin*, which Fadeyev had championed during the war.[101] A discussion of Tvardovsky's *The House by the Road* (*Dom u dorogi*) found Polikarpov in the minority, and it was published over his objections.[102]

Having served at the front, writers chafed at being cut off from all news about fellow writers in the Allied countries.[103] Writers wanted to know, but did not know, what their colleagues in the United States, Britain, and France were working on. They wanted to know, but did not know, the reaction in capitalist countries to their own books. Access to the Writers' Union Foreign Commission, which contained such information, was denied even to members of the presidium. (This policy dated to the Great Purge, and the original head of the Foreign Commission, the Europe-friendly Koltsov, had been arrested in 1938.) In place of *International Literature*, they had to be content with *Friendship of Nations* (*Druzhba narodov*), which covered only the Soviet nationalities.[104] The writers tried a pragmatic but fruitless argument: the only way to fight imperialism was to know what was being said by the other side.[105]

An April 1946 party group meeting to discuss literary criticism turned into a complaint session on Polikarpov.[106] News of this reached the Politburo from multiple sources, including Agitprop's official in attendance, N. Maslin. The long-serving deputy editor of *Znamia*, the poet and scholar Tarasenkov, complained that Tikhonov stood aside as Polikarpov assumed the role of an "all-powerful dictator," that he had unleashed a "terror regime" at *Literaturnaia gazeta*, and that nothing of the kind had been seen "even under the notorious Averbakh" (*PT*, 112). The Writers' Union presidium voted to relieve Polikarpov of his duties, and even though the vote lacked enforcement power, the Politburo removed Polikarpov a week after Maslin's report, on April 9.

This was a strategic move, not a rebuke of Polikarpov. Under party auspices he went on to attend the Higher Party School (Vysshaia partiinaia shkola) and then the Academy of Social Sciences (an institution of the Central Committee). Like Shcherbakov before him, Polikarpov cycled back to literary oversight. In 1955 he was once again a Writers' Union secretary, simultaneously heading Agitprop (*PT*, 114), as Shcherbakov had done.

The presidium tussles and Polikarpov's removal were a sideshow to intrigues among party secretaries maneuvering through Agitprop. Denis

Babichenko has argued that the infamous August 1946 resolution disgracing Zoshchenko and Akhmatova was an accidental result of the rivalry between Zhdanov and Malenkov.[107] Let us review the evidence.

The resolutions of December 1943, intended to strengthen ideological rectitude, made Agitprop's three top officials each personally responsible for oversight of a particular journal. *Novy mir* was assigned to Aleksandrov, *October* to Pyotr Fedoseyev, and *Znamia* to Puzin.[108] Concerned about the scope of these duties, which increased both their workload and their political vulnerability, these three officials proposed relinquishing their oversight of the other eight periodicals under their purview. The Central Committee secretaries acceded to this request, with the result that those eight publications could now send each issue to press based solely on approval from the censorship office (*PT*, 95). Among the eight were two published in Leningrad, *Zvezda* and *Leningrad*; and since Aleksandrov's crew could no longer be held responsible for them, Malenkov could work through Aleksandrov to uncover ideological laxness and pin it on Zhdanov as head of the Leningrad *gorkom* and *obkom* (*PT*, 96, 129).

The ink was barely dry on the resolutions when Zoshchenko came under attack for *Before Sunrise* (*Pered voskhodom solntse*). Aleksandrov and Yegolin, who had earlier accused Fadeyev of promoting it, now made it the subject of another memo to the secretaries, denouncing *October*, the journal that published it.[109] At this point, Zhdanov had the chief of the Leningrad *gorkom* propaganda department compose a letter purportedly by Zoshchenko's indignant readers for the *gorkom*'s newspaper *Leningradskaia pravda* (*Leningrad pravda*). He revised the *gorkom* secretary's draft, explaining, "[We must] strengthen the *attack* on Zoshchenko, who must be thoroughly pecked so that not even a wet spot remains of him"; but he softened the draft's criticisms of the Leningrad Writers' Union (*PT*, 79; emphasis in original).

Did Zhdanov go after Zoshchenko because *Before Sunrise*, with its introspective psychologizing, offended him?[110] Perhaps. But in more than a decade as Leningrad party secretary, Zhdanov allowed Zoshchenko's appointments in the Leningrad literary establishment.[111] The bogus letter could be explained as an attempt to defend himself against accusations of failing to control Leningrad's literary establishment.[112] Disorder in the Leningrad Writers' Union would be laid at Zhdanov's door, but a single errant writer did not reflect on a party boss, who in any case could show resolve by blacklisting him. So in early 1944, Zhdanov may have sought to distance himself from Zoshchenko while putting the Leningrad Writers' Union branch in a better light. Meanwhile, the party secretaries were subjecting all literary magazines to scrutiny. They replaced *Znamia*'s entire editorial board that August and appointed Vishnevsky its editor.

Zhdanov's position vis-à-vis Malenkov likely was weakened by the death of his brother-in-law and ally Shcherbakov two days after the German surrender. It was April 1946 when Stalin, finally heeding Fadeyev and others who argued that there were too few quality submissions to fill the pages of so many journals, drew up a list of potential candidates for elimination. He ranked Moscow's *Novy mir* as the worst, followed by Leningrad's *Zvezda* (*PT*, 117). In an attempt to save *Zvezda*, the Leningrad Writers' Union proposed a new editorial board to the *gorkom*. The proposed board included Zoshchenko, who two years after the flap over *Before Sunrise*, was beginning to receive favorable notices in the Leningrad press.[113] At the end of July *Zvezda* reprinted a story of his, "Aventures of an Ape" ("Prikliucheniia obezyany"), that had appeared a few years earlier in the children's magazine *Murzilka*. *Zvezda*'s editor, Vissarion Sayanov, reasoned that since the story had already passed censorship, it could be republished (*PT*, 125).

This train of events unexpectedly turned Zoshchenko into a pawn in the Malenkov-Zhdanov chess game. The *gorkom* approved *Zvezda*'s new editorial board without seeking Agitprop's approval, perhaps because it had been removed from Agitprop's docket by the 1943 resolutions. Zhdanov was unaware of the *gorkom*'s action, but Malenkov got wind of it and prepared to attack the *gorkom* for overstepping its authority. He worked through Aleksandrov, who with Yegolin compiled a report detailing errors in *Zvezda* and *Leningrad* (*PT*, 121). Zhdanov received it on August 7 along with an urgent summons to appear at the Central Committee *orgbiuro* in Moscow two days later. The editorial boards of *Zvezda* and *Leningrad*, the head of the Leningrad Writers' Union branch, and the Leningrad *gorkom* all had to rush to this meeting. Malenkov, as *orgbiuro* chair, presided.[114] He seized on the Leningrad *gorkom* for bypassing Agitprop. Zhdanov, who was hearing the facts for the first time, tried to shift the blame to the literary intelligentsia while disassociating himself from the *gorkom*'s actions.[115]

Stalin was less interested in the *gorkom* than in the Writers' Union. He closely questioned Aleksandr Prokofiev, the poet who headed the Leningrad branch and served on *Zvezda*'s editorial board. Prokofiev made a brave defense of writers, particularly Akhmatova, noting that "sorrow is found in the Soviet person, too" (*PT*, 124). He and Boris Likharev, the editor of *Leningrad*, admitted to all the faults Stalin found but pleaded to keep that journal open. Writers should be treated gently, said Prokofiev; their sensitive natures were easily wounded. Improvement depended upon criticism, rejoined Stalin (*PT*, 128). As in other meetings with officials who were not part of the inner decision-making group, Stalin began with reasonable arguments. Then he gave a scolding to Tikhonov, Fadeyev, and Vishnevsky and accused Zoshchenko of shirking during the war. That last accusation made its way into the Central Committee resolution one week later.[116]

The August 1946 resolution, then, was the culmination of nearly three years of officials' dissatisfaction with literature, fruitless attempts to bring it under control, and Politburo infighting. Malenkov's scheme to weaken Zhdanov by bringing down the Leningrad *gorkom* led elsewhere when Stalin proved to be more interested in the Writers' Union, and the result was a resolution crushing literature. Zhdanov's August 16 speech defaming Zoshchenko and Akhmatova to an assembly of Leningrad writers repeated word for word much of Stalin's language at the *orgbiuro* meeting.[117] If this interpretation is correct, Zhdanov was saved at Zoshchenko and Akhmatova's expense. Another possibility is that the resolution was Zhdanov's idea, which he presented to Stalin, intending to shore up his position vis-à-vis Malenkov. Either way, literature suffered at the hands of this political intrigue.[118] When it came to the elimination of substandard journals, the ax fell on *Leningrad*, the journal of the Leningrad branch of the Writers' Union, which had not even been on Stalin's list. *Novy mir*, the top candidate for elimination on Stalin's list and widely considered the dumping ground of literature, escaped mention entirely.

For writers hoping for postwar liberalization and high on their success in having gotten rid of Polikarpov, the August 1946 resolution came as a shock. They had attempted to meet Agitprop halfway, suggesting as Polikarpov's replacement the head of the Writers' Union party group, Ivan Gutorov, citing the respect he commanded as a war veteran with an interest in literature.[119] Instead of respectful negotiation, the writers got the August resolution crippling their literary life and describing their best writers as "alien" to the Soviet people.[120] The resolution also pronounced the Politburo's definitive answer to two decades of pleading to be nurtured: friendly relations between writers and editors were against party interests because they sheltered writers from needed criticism (*PT*, 135). *Zvezda* survived only under extraordinary oversight: it was to be edited by Yegolin and overseen by the Leningrad *obkom* chief, Pyotr Popkov. To Aleksandrov fell the fraught responsibility of making sure the resolution was properly implemented (*PT*, 135).

Fadeyev was now brought back with a title that mirrored Stalin's, "general secretary."[121] It was another bit of co-opting flattery. The position of chair (*predsedatel*), which had been created for Gorky and gone unoccupied since his death, was finally officially eliminated. It was no longer needed, since the roles of both Gorky and Shcherbakov would be played by Fadeyev's two selves. An enlarged, twelve-member secretariat was appointed by the presidium, rather than the plenum as stipulated by the statutes. Serving on it as Fadeyev's deputies were Simonov, Vishnevsky, Tikhonov, and Korneichuk, Stalin's favorite who also represented the Ukrainian branch.[122]

Fadeyev's first duty as general secretary was holding a vote to expel Akhmatova and Zoshchenko, two writers whom he cared about, in an act that would plunge them into poverty.[123] The once animated tone of his private notebooks now yielded to dry lists for the public statements he would have to make, with columns, headings, and subheadings, as if in preparation for an exam. In one column, "Akhmatova. Zoshchenko," and opposite their names, Zhdanov's formulas: "Servility to the West." Underneath that, another heading: "Why they are dangerous." Another notation has the ring of self-indoctrination: "Pushkin was not an advocate of art for art's sake."[124] The reward for this hateful work soon came in the form of a longed-for Stalin Prize, first class, for *The Young Guard*.

The writers who back in January had called for Surkov to be removed from *Literaturnaia gazeta* now got their wish. The bad news was that his replacement was Yermilov. During the war he had served under Polikarpov on the central radio committee, where he was in charge of literary broadcasts.[125] Now he controlled a major press outlet for the first time since RAPP. His success in getting *Literary Critic* shut down positioned him well for this promotion, but that mischief-making had deeper repercussions. It had flagged literary criticism as an area of concern, and in 1946 the leaders requested a follow-up assessment and concluded that there had been no improvement. They decided that literary criticism belonged inside Agitprop. This appears to explain the creation of *Culture and Life* (*Kultura i zhizn*) in the summer of 1946 as an organ of Agitprop. Most of its articles were written by Agitprop officials, who did not hesitate to employ unsubstantiated accusations found in denunciations sent to their bosses, the Central Committee secretaries.[126]

Yermilov identified a new opponent in Simonov, now in charge of *Novy mir*, the journal that had escaped extinction only because it was of no use to either Malenkov or Zhdanov in their rivalry. Simonov's first issue took risks with stories by Dovzhenko and Platonov.[127] Just when close editorial nurturing had been declared off limits, Simonov showed signs of being a mentor to talent. Yermilov blasted him, declaring that Platonov's story "Ivanov's Family" ("Semya Ivanova"), which concerned a woman's extramarital affair while her husband was away at war, dishonored the Soviet family.[128]

The simultaneous rise of Yermilov and Simonov reminds us that hardline and liberal cadres could be advanced simultaneously. Yermilov, having destroyed his rivals, emerged as the main prose critic in the postwar years. Yet the main poetry critic of these years was Tarasenkov, who risked keeping books by arrested writers in his home library.

Stalin worked to form the liberal young Simonov into a malleable cadre. A year after graduating from the Literary Institute, he had staked out a permissive view of socialist realism with his article "On the Right to the Lyric" ("O prave na liriku").[129] By 1946 the thirty-one-year-old was the recipient of three Stalin Prizes (at least one of them proposed by Stalin himself) and one of the rarefied elite who had visited the United States, Britain, and France with official delegations.[130] Through such trips, Stalin was advancing an agenda

beyond diplomacy. For these cushy missions he selected people he was courting, co-opting, and also subtly seeding with fear, since a trip to a capitalist
country could later morph into a charge of espionage. Flush with new leadership posts at *Novy mir* and the Writers' Union secretariat, Simonov was
being set up to temper his liberal instincts, hedged in by honors, travels, and
a dacha—the same factor of "being bought" that had so disgusted Shaginian
that she tried to leave the Writers' Union in protest. There is another point to
be made as well. Things were going well for Simonov, and successful people
tend to trust political and social structures. Simonov deserves much credit for
pushing the envelope at *Novy mir*. By his own admission, however, he underestimated the risks he was taking. A relative newcomer, enjoying Stalin's favor,
he had yet to grasp the magnitude of the danger.[131]

    Simonov could feel that he had company in his liberalism. The literary
critics Abram Derman and Iosif Yuzovsky had daringly challenged the canon
and the means of its formation (*PT*, 91). At the Writers' Union's ninth plenum in February 1944, Derman complained that works that had won Stalin
Prizes were above criticism (*PT*, 89). The party literary critic Isai Lezhnev
pointed out that the party pressed writers for new works, only to then condemn anything "fresh" (*PT*, 100). Even Vishnevsky after the war called for
the party to "give us artistic freedom" (*PT*, 104). At a meeting of the Writers'
Union party group in August 1945, Shaginian called for fiction about provincial officials' thievery while the local population went hungry (*PT*, 102).
And *Znamia* (before Vishnevsky took over) printed a positive review of Dovzhenko's work, even as he refused to make required changes to his story
"Ukraine in Flames" ("Ukraina v ogne") (*PT*, 82, 84).

    The presidium in 1947 saw contentious disagreements. "I don't want
to read about the revolution through the eyes of a bourgeois adolescent girl,"
one writer objected when Sobolev recommended publication of *Stepping
into Life* (*Vstuplenie v zhizn*) by E. Sheremeteva.[132] Someone else charged
that the mind-set of a bourgeois character reflected the mind-set of the author. Sobolev replied simply, "I don't read literature that way."[133] Gorbatov,
Gerasimova, and Tarasenkov invoked Chekhov as proof that a narrator may
demur or make only indirect comment. This was essentially the same argument as the one that had been made by *Literary Critic* before Yermilov engineered its demise. Tarasenkov seized on comments purportedly made by Stalin to the effect that his personal preference ran to the Chekhovian model.[134]

    Writers also argued for the right to express themselves freely not just
at closed meetings but in public. They especially wanted to be able to discuss
Red Army soldiers' condition during the war, the privation in rural areas
after the war, and the privileging of ideology over artistry in canonical works.
They wanted the canon to include Yevgeny Dolmatovsky's narrative poem
The Leader (*Vozhd*), about Soviet forces' long retreat in the first part of the

war; Aleksei Kapler's "Letters of Lieutenant L. from Stalingrad" ("Pisma leitenanta L. iz Stalingrada"), describing the miserable condition of Soviet troops; Emmanuil Kazakevich's *Two Men in the Steppe* (*Dvoe v stepi*), about the emotional attachment between a Soviet soldier sentenced to be shot and the soldier assigned to guard him; Viktor Nekrasov's debut novel, *In the Trenches of Stalingrad* (*V okopakh Stalingrada*), which exposed deficiencies in the Soviet military machine; and Vera Panova's *The Factory* (*Kruzhilikha*), which included a talented but power-hungry party boss.

Literaturnaia gazeta's criticism of these latter two novels was hotly contested in the Writers' Union. *In the Trenches of Stalingrad*, which followed a demolition squad in the run-up to the Battle of Stalingrad, contained descriptions of insufficient manpower and matériel in the Soviet war effort, along with hints at Soviet injustices. It appeared in *Znamia* on the eve of the August 1946 resolution. Yermilov ran a critical review,[135] but other orthodox communists like Gorbatov and Subotsky, who had been at the front, loved the book.[136] Gorbatov led the discussion in Fadeyev's absence. Those present were evenly divided over the novel. When the Chuvash playwright P. Osipov complained that harmful ideas expressed by negative characters received no counterweight, Gorbatov replied that "the counterweight is the Soviet reader—who is not as big a fool as all that."[137] The group agreed to instruct *Literaturnaia gazeta* to publish other opinions about Nekrasov's novel.

Yermilov subjected *The Factory* to a series of attacks, ensuring discussion of it in the Writers' Union and apparently hoping to bring down not just Panova but everyone involved.[138] The Writers' Union discussion was led by Subotsky, whose openness to Nekrasov's novel did not extend to civilian plots. Subotsky and Boris Lavrenyov complained that it was unclear where Panova stood in regard to her characters. But others praised this authorial reticence. "The people in our novels and stories are deprived of personalities, which have been replaced by a plus sign or a minus sign," declared Georgy Munblit.[139] L. Pitersky, making the point that there were no purely good or bad people in real life, took a swipe at Subotsky and Lavrenyov:

And those heroes who today have called on authors to portray only the positive—well, I am afraid that these same heroes, who have spoken today in favor of the good personality traits that the heroes of a novel are supposed to have, in their own homes yell at their servants as used to be done in the old days, and we do not therefore consider them to be bad people.[140]

The novel's seven defenders outnumbered its five opponents.[141] Concluding the discussion, Subotsky turned to Munblit: "The fact that for a long time now in your writings and utterances you have ignored our literature's charge to give people a communist upbringing is known to us."[142]

Nekrasov's and Panova's novels went on to win Stalin Prizes. Stalin himself backed *The Factory* for a second-class prize, trumping the prize committee, which under Fadeyev's leadership had shied away from recommending it.[143] Fadeyev's refusal to endorse it hurt him among writers, especially after Stalin's surprise approval. Yermilov, too, came out the loser, once more a pawn in Stalin's game. Stalin had let his cadres argue the hard line so that he could shine as the liberal. Their reward for trying to please him was to be exposed for what they were—cowardly (Fadeyev) or vengeful (Yermilov). Belonging to the honor group meant enduring public humiliation for its benefit. The fact that they repeatedly did so, sometimes with foreknowledge and sometimes unwittingly, was what made them useful to Stalin and surely explains why they repeatedly escaped arrest.

The literary policy that Fadeyev and Yermilov were so dutifully upholding indeed remained the party policy. The prizes, along with one for Vershigora's *People with a Clear Conscience*, were seemingly remarkable victories for creative expression, but in the long view they were. insignificant blips, minor concessions that Stalin could well afford as he prepared the next blow.

Fadeyev's Choice

THE STALIN PRIZES for Panova's, Nekrasov's, and Vershigora's books resulted from the persistence of a minority of writers who time and again singled them out for praise. Thanks to them, *In the Trenches of Stalingrad* and *The Factory* became part of the Soviet literary canon. This did not lessen the effect of the August 1946 resolution. Even assuming the scapegoating of Zoshchenko and Akhmatova was the result of Malenkov's intrigue against Zhdanov, a literary offensive of some sort would have happened regardless, a necessary rebuff of writers' expectations of a freer literature. One could argue that each concession necessitated a compensatory crackdown. It seems likely, however, that even before the prizes, Stalin had in mind a series of new offensives. Foreign policy, including increasing tensions with the former Allies, also affected literary policy, especially after the United States signaled a more interventionist stance with the Truman Doctrine on March 12, 1947.

The August resolution contained the seeds for offshoots in the years to come. One of its accusations against Akhmatova and Zoshchenko was that of "servility to the contemporary bourgeois culture of the West" (*VKI*, 588). This formula was not entirely new; Stalin had used it privately as soon as the tide of war began to turn in 1943, saying that foreign literary works were harmful to Soviet readers.[1] Upon announcement of the Truman Doctrine, he activated this formula, using it against Soviet intellectuals, whom he now chastised for a culture of self-abasement (*dukh samounichizheniia*). The brunt of the Cold War frenzy, which in the United States fell upon the movie industry, in the Soviet Union fell on the party's foremost ideological tool, literature. The next round of targets were writers and academics who had written on anything foreign.

Stalin primed his top literary cadres with his characteristic mix of authoritative instruction, generous offers of resources, and veiled threats. On May 13, 1947, he called Fadeyev and his two top deputies, Simonov and Gorbatov, to a meeting in his office with Zhdanov and Molotov.[2] Simonov wrote a detailed account of this meeting in his diary the next day; and he reproduced that diary entry for his 1979 memoir, interspersing it with hindsight reflections. He has credibly been accused, most notably by Leonid Batkin, of refusing to acknowledge his self-interested pursuit of the spoils of power.[3] Flush with his three Stalin Prizes and the luxury of foreign travel, the thirty-one-year-old Simonov was speeding on his way to three more Stalin Prizes and a spot on the Central Committee.[4] Let us examine the psychological semiotics of Simonov's account.

The May 1947 meeting was Simonov's first time in an intimate meeting with Stalin and his first time in Stalin's office.[5] He noted in his diary the manner in which Zhdanov, Molotov, and Stalin each greeted them (Molotov was friendly and welcomed them back from England; Stalin shook their hands in a "businesslike" way), and where each person was seated vis-à-vis Stalin. Molotov sat closer to Stalin than did Zhdanov; the three writers were directed to seats on the opposite side of the table from Molotov and Zhdanov, not directly across from them, however, but further down, at a greater distance from Stalin's place at the head of the table.[6] Arrived at the inner sanctum of power, the writers were made to know through the semiotics of the long rectangular table that they were mere visitors.

Stalin's purpose in this meeting was to instruct his cadres on his new campaign, but he opened the meeting with an unrelated topic, calculated to disarm them. He began by addressing requests Fadeyev had made for increased Writers' Union support staff and honoraria and improved living conditions. The Politburo, said Stalin, had rejected any increase in honoraria. Fadeyev pushed back and won a concession: Stalin would have a commission study the matter. He turned to Zhdanov to recommend members for it. Zhdanov proposed himself, to which Stalin replied, "That's very modest of you," provoking general laughter. Stalin then declared that Fadeyev, Simonov, and Gorbatov should be on the commission. Fadeyev proposed including the minister of finance. Stalin acceded with an air of magnanimity: "If *you* want, he can be on it. And here's who else—Mekhlis." Stalin watched his cadres' reaction, adding, "But he'd immediately drive you all out, huh?" Everyone "burst out laughing."[7]

The cadres' multilayered laughter expressed three contradictory meanings. It signaled their appreciation of the leader's witticism, their willingness to debase themselves in laughing at their own expense, and a reflexive denial of the witticism's hidden menace (their excessive guffaw). It is not hard to imagine, however, that the unmistakable innuendo of Stalin's "huh" (*a* in Russian) was mitigated by the thrill of sharing a laugh with the leader and Politburo officials. This high was topped off when Stalin handed them another victory, approving a large increase in support staff (from 70 to 122, across all the Writers' Union branches) and overruling Zhdanov, who objected that it would cost too much.

These matters seemed to be the sole reason for the meeting, and when Stalin seemed about to end it, Simonov felt disappointed, wishing it had been longer. Stalin had his cadres where he wanted them. Fadeyev could feel proud that he had been firm—and successful—in expressing principled disagreement with Stalin. All three writers could feel that they had a pair of victories in their pocket. They may even have felt they owed Stalin something—should he ask—in return for his benevolence.

Now Stalin turned to his real agenda: a culture of "self-abasement" among intellectuals. He gave this characterization a veneer of historical credibility, dating it to Peter the Great's employment of German engineers. Handing Fadeyev a typescript, he ordered him to read it aloud. Fadeyev began reading, while Stalin paced back and forth behind him. Trying to avoid the discourtesy of sitting with his back to Stalin, Fadeyev read the entire four pages while twisting halfway around in his chair; Simonov and Gorbatov followed suit.[8] At the conclusion of this exercise in squirming before authority, Stalin made his next pronouncement: someone should write a novel contrasting intellectuals' self-abasement with the healthy patriotism of the Russian folk.[9]

Simonov the memoirist recalls that Stalin had been observing their reactions to what Fadeyev was reading—an accusation against two cancer researchers who had shared their work with American colleagues. He recalls, too, how uneasy he felt while Fadeyev read. We can imagine that Simonov was all too aware that he, too, belonged to the intelligentsia with its culture of self-abasement; but he says only that there was a "note of danger" in the intense way Stalin watched them. Apparently satisfied that the letter had produced an effect, Stalin did not ask their opinion. Simonov writes, "Now, many years later, remembering that moment, I am grateful to him."[10] This twisted gratitude hardly sounds like a memoirist's dissimulation. So great was Simonov's relief that it expanded into a warm feeling toward the hangman for stopping at brandishing the rope. Yes, Batkin is right that Simonov the memoirist refuses to acknowledge that he followed orders in exchange for privilege, but this does not make the emotional bonding a fiction. In a variation on Stockholm syndrome, Simonov formed a bond with his emotional captor that held firm even after thirty years.

Stalin then moved on to another topic, which Simonov feared to commit to paper, noting in his diary simply, "[Stalin] next took up a question that I cannot write about here."[11] He finally described it in 1979; I shall attempt to disentangle his recollection from his commentary. As the cadres were digesting the implications of self-abasement, Stalin fed them more: from now on, *Literaturnaia gazeta* would include coverage of politics and foreign affairs. This might not have mattered much had Stalin not further declared that the paper would now be considered "unofficial." It would be exempt from clearing its articles with the Foreign Ministry—so it could adopt a harder line than the official one.[12] And Stalin gave his cadres a heads-up: the party occasionally might even find it necessary to admonish *Literaturnaia gazeta* for incorrect views.

This putative opposition within the party-controlled media gained Stalin several advantages. There was the appearance of a free press. The party could adopt the more moderate stance, disavowing the "unofficial" hard-line view even as it was widely disseminated and implanted in the popular imagination. This deniability fed people's belief that many arrests were mistakes made by the security services unsanctioned by Stalin. And the new *Literaturnaia gazeta* would reach more readers through increased staff, circulation, and frequency of publication. Stalin's scenario also made good use of Yermilov, unrivaled at harassment journalism, yet also the perfect whipping boy. This time, at least, he was told the reasoning behind an apparently illogical policy. Having not been invited to the meeting, however, he was made to know his place.

Stalin was essentially telling his cadres that the party needed a straw man and would employ *Literaturnaia gazeta* for that purpose. Batkin argues that as veteran spin doctors, Simonov and Fadeyev could not have been surprised at Stalin's move. Possibly; but Stalin did not take this for granted. He took care to preempt any flickering moral scruples. You must understand, Stalin told them, that some situations cannot be handled through official channels; in those instances, *Literaturnaia gazeta* would have to "help" the party. This line of reasoning appealed to the cadres' party loyalty as well as their communist self-image. It also mitigated any distaste they might have for the cynical use to which *Literaturnaia gazeta* was being put, by implying that these uses would only be occasional. It was much easier to accept a questionable action as a rare occurrence than as a general policy. Stalin was offering his cadres a customized version of the package with which he had lured Gorky back from Italy in 1932—a philosophical argument that could make them feel that they were acting on principle even as they accepted the trappings of privilege.

The cadres could also tell themselves that they were using their prestigious office to help deserving writers. As the Kremlin meeting was ending, Simonov worked up the courage to ask Stalin's permission to publish ten stories by Zoshchenko in *Novy mir*. Stalin replied that since Simonov thought they should be published, he should publish them, and then the Politburo would read them. Simonov thus had complete freedom to make an incorrect publishing decision that might expose him to arrest; but remarkably, he did not even perceive the implicit threat in Stalin's remark. Recalling the incident thirty years later, he allowed for the possibility that Stalin might have intended a veiled threat. Thirty years on, he prefers to give Stalin the benefit of the doubt.[13]

In 1950, Simonov replaced Yermilov at *Literaturnaia gazeta*. He already knew his marching orders. Simonov the memoirist recalls how, over and over, he mentally revisited the conundrum of a purportedly unofficial paper, "out of an inner and also professional need."[14] He seems to be admitting, without a trace of embarrassment, that he was guided by Stalin's scheme. "The struggle," he writes, "soon took on various misshapen/ugly [*urodlivye*] forms."[15] In half a sentence, he fleetingly admits that he, too, wrote ugly things that he regrets, and then he leaps to his own defense: Stalin's idea was essentially sound. The question, Simonov explains, was not whether to refuse to fight self-abasement but whether to do it in a principled or a rude way.

If he was being principled, why did he write "ugly" things? Was Simonov eager to convince himself that Stalin's idea was sound because he was not prepared to oppose it? Simonov evades these questions. But the "inner need" that he felt alongside his professional duty points directly to ethical reservations that kept resurfacing and that he kept having to suppress. It is odd, therefore, that the memoirist also writes that Stalin "spoke [about the new *Literaturnaia gazeta*] enthusiastically; he liked the fact that we liked the idea, one felt that he wanted to instill in us the resolve to go about all these questions involving this future newspaper more boldly and freely."[16] Does the memoirist mean that his younger self in Stalin's office truly liked Stalin's idea? Or was he only pretending to like it? Does the older Simonov continue to admire Stalin's gift for inspiring his cadres with a misbegotten resolve? Were the memoirist willfully dissembling, he would see this inconsistency and cover it over. Simonov appears not to notice it. It is another example of our readiness to convince ourselves of what we want to believe. Alliance with power turns out to be the story of co-option. When Stalin suggested that self-abasement should be a topic for a novel, Simonov had unthinkingly mused aloud that it was more suited to a play and promptly found himself cornered into writing one. Stalin read the manuscript and instructed Simonov to change the ending. Simonov did as he was bidden and won another Stalin Prize.[17] His memoir suffers from the same psychological block to self-examination found in Avdeyenko's memoir (and appearing again in Fadeyev's suicide note). But there is every sign that even as he knowingly traded honesty for privilege, his awe of Stalin was genuine, and that even in 1979, when the fear had evaporated, he remained in his thrall.

As in the past, the Russian literary classics were made to serve as banners for the new campaign. Pushkin, Tolstoy, and Dostoevsky were now garbed in Russian purity,[18] and the first victims were literary scholars who had documented these authors' knowledge of European literature. At the Writers' Union's eleventh plenum a month later, Fadeyev sacrificed the Pushkin scholar Isaak Nusinov, and the head of the Gorky Institute of World

Literature, Vladimir Shishmarev, a member of the Academy of Sciences.[19] Shishmarev was removed from his position but escaped arrest. Nusinov, a member of the JAFC, was arrested two years later, by which time the campaign was focused on Jewish intellectuals, and died under interrogation. Over the next months, scholars including Dolinin, Eikhenbaum, Tomashevsky, and Aleksandr Slonimsky were attacked for work they had done on Dostoevsky and Tolstoy prior to the policy of linking these literary giants to the revolution.[20] Agitprop officials were also caught. Kirpotin, whose popular biography of Pushkin had fallen afoul of Stalin's evolving concept of Pushkin in 1937, now came under fire for his work on Dostoevsky, and Aleksandrov, who had written a history of European philosophy, was replaced as Agitprop chief by Mikhail Suslov.[21]

Fadeyev and Simonov, dutifully leading the charge, suddenly found themselves among its victims. Simonov's new novel *Smoke of the Fatherland* (*Dym otechestva*) and Fadeyev's *The Young Guard*, which besides winning a Stalin Prize had been adapted for the stage and was playing in theaters, were now criticized for failing to show the party's leading role in the victory over Germany.[22] As Derman had said, Stalin Prize books were above criticism, unless the critic was Stalin, who is reported to have summoned Fadeyev to his dacha. Fadeyev was shown into the study, where he found Stalin at his desk reading Chekhov. Stalin greeted Fadeyev with a question. "You, Comrade Fadeyev, who are you?" Fadeyev responded that he was a writer, to which Stalin replied, "You're shit, Comrade Fadeyev, not a writer. Chekhov, now he was a writer."[23] The comparison with Chekhov was purely for effect: when Stalin finally articulated his complaint, it was not that *The Young Guard* was aesthetically inferior to Chekhov but that it made the party out to be superfluous.

Fadeyev spent three years rewriting *The Young Guard*. As in 1932, he accepted his shaming and tried to show that he understood how to correct his errors. Did he realize that the point was not in correcting errors but in being shamed? Nothing he did could ward off future shaming. There would always be another pretext. By the time Fadeyev was done, the historical Oleg Koshevoi, who lost his life defending his country, had been memorialized as a literary hero who understood, as Katerina Clark has put it, "the need to subordinate his individual initiative and even his sense of what is right to the judgment of the collective."[24] Clark points out that Fadeyev was not allowed to have autonomy over his own text; we can add that rewriting the novel must have driven home to Fadeyev that he was not allowed to have autonomy over his own self. Like his refashioned Koshevoi, he followed the party in everything, including the moral imperative to decide right and wrong. At the height of the Great Purge he had defended himself against a denunciation with the words, "I never lost my Bolshevik independence in my actions and judgments" (*AFPD*, 66). His rewriting of *The Young Guard* made it impossible for him to maintain this self-image. Surely this was what Stalin intended.

Yermilov, who had faulted *The Young Guard* in *Literaturnaia gazeta*, made a show of enthusiasm when Fadeyev showed him the revised manuscript.[25] He told Fadeyev that he had noticed the lack of party guidance in the original version and had decided that the youthful partisans had so thoroughly internalized party values that they had no need of instructions. But now he saw that including the party's guidance improved the novel. Yermilov knew better than anyone: there is an argument to support whatever position we decide to adopt. Innate feeling, personal courage, and morality stemmed from the party's wise guidance. So Fadeyev had nothing to regret.

As the literary campaign progressed, it began to be affected by another branch of foreign policy as Stalin worked out his stance toward the fledgling state of Israel and, by extension, his domestic policy on Soviet Jews. Jews and other non-Russian nationalities had enjoyed government subsidies since the birth of the Soviet Union, with support for newspapers, literature, theater, and school instruction in their own languages. Lenin and Stalin, as nationalities commissar, reasoned that the surest way to transmit Soviet values to the non-Russian nationalities would be through their own languages. Once those values had been internalized, the national cultures would no longer have any reason to exist.[26] The creation of the JAFC during the war was similarly focused on a short-term goal. By the late 1940s, Stalin no longer had any use for Yiddish culture; and when his hopes of cultivating Israel as an ally were disappointed, Soviet Jews, as natural supporters of the Jewish state, came to seem a potential threat. Mikhoels's assassination in January 1948 was the preface to the execution four years later of the JAFC's other most prominent members, excepting Ehrenburg.

The intersection of overseas diplomacy with literary rivalries played out in the theater world, which since August 1946 had suffered from its own party resolution analogous to the one on literature. Only virtuous characters could appear on stage. This plot-killing instruction produced what became known as the no-conflict era in drama, and liberal theater critics, led by Yuzovsky and Aleksandr Borshchagovsky, head of the literary department at the Red Army Theater, challenged it. They had a trump card—the support of Agitprop. The officials there who had undermined Fadeyev five years earlier were gone, but the new crew under Dmitry Shepilov (and with Boris Riurikov in charge of the arts section) was equally hostile (*TPS*, 2:72). For them, a challenge to the literary establishment offered a way to bring down Fadeyev.

The allied forces of Agitprop and the liberal critics seized their moment at an assembly of the All-Russian Theater Society on November 29,

1948.[27] Borshchagovsky gave the major address and used it to decry the "no conflict" repertoire. He stunned the hall by taking aim at the untouchable trophy playwright Anatoly Sofronov. Agitprop warned Yermilov against printing any criticism of Borshchagovsky, and Yermilov dared not disobey (*TPS*, 2:76).

Fadeyev struck back, rounding up his own allies: Malenkov, Polikarp Lebedev, who headed the Arts Committee, and G. M. Popov, head of the Moscow *gorkom* since Shcherbakov's death (*TPS*, 2:76). Fadeyev also forwarded to Stalin, on December 10, 1948, a denunciation he had received alleging an enemy group of Jewish theater critics inside the Writers' Union and the All-Russian Theater Society.[28] Its author, a journalist named Anna Begicheva, may have written it at the behest of Fadeyev or his supporters. The battle continued on December 15 at the Writers' Union's twelfth plenum, where Fadeyev upheld the hard line and was met with dissent from Yuzovsky and others.[29]

Stalin, upon reading Begicheva's denunciation, found it convenient to meld his literary policy with his Jewish policy. "Servility to the West" could easily be tilted toward Soviet Jews, who typically had family contacts outside the Soviet Union. The first arrests of writers on the JAFC began immediately after the plenum—Fefer, Bergelson, Markish, Kvitko, and Lozovsky. Stalin also had Agitprop use Begicheva's denunciation as a basis for a case against the theater critics. This instruction marked an abrupt end to Agitprop's support for them. Shepilov and company produced a memo noting that of the nine critics on the board of the theater society's critics' division, "only one is a Russian."[30] This memo provided the material for a *Pravda* article on January 28, 1949, that launched the culminating phase of Stalin's campaign.[31] Stalin selected two people to write it—the veteran *Pravda* staffer David Zaslavsky and Fadeyev.[32] Like Fadeyev's 1931 piece against Platonov, this article accused its targets of wearing masks (RAPP's old battle cry to "tear off the masks" proved durable). Seven theater critics were described as an "antipatriotic group," including Yuzovsky, Borshchagovsky, and the same Gurvich whom Yermilov had assigned to defame Platonov in his vendetta against *Literary Critic*.[33]

Possibly Fadeyev instigated the Begicheva denunciation and then showed his vindictiveness by entrusting the anticosmopolitan campaign to the vengeful Sofronov. Or he may have been the unwitting recipient of Begicheva's denunciation, forwarded to him by the security services, and then delegated the dirty work to Sofronov because he had no taste for it himself. Those who take this latter view believe that he regretted doing so when he saw Sofronov's alacrity in accumulating victims.[34] Either way, these years saw Fadeyev's complete moral degradation, the horrifying if logical endgame in his evolution from entitled young communist to alcoholically assisted butcher's minion.

Mikhoels, Gurvich, Kvitko, and Altman were his friends. We have seen the pattern before. In 1939 he tried to help Akhmatova; in 1946 he implemented her undue punishment. In the fall of 1948, Fadeyev appears to have underestimated the threat. He apparently tried to protect Kvitko, pushing for the early release of his book in press, arranging a literary anniversary gathering even though it had already been celebrated, and proposing him for a Stalin Prize.[35] By the time Fadeyev wrote Stalin's article, Kvitko had already been arrested. At conferences in New York and Paris in the spring of 1949, worried foreign colleagues repeatedly asked Fadeyev about rumors that members of the JAFC had been arrested. Fadeyev assured them that all was well.[36]

Altman, an old friend of Fadeyev's, had been named in the Agitprop memo but escaped mention in the January *Pravda* article, perhaps shielded by Fadeyev.[37] At a meeting some months later, Fadeyev listened to Sofronov accuse Altman of acquiring his post at the State Yiddish Theater in order to spy on the Soviet Union. Fadeyev knew this was false since he himself, at Mikhoels's request, had prevailed upon an unwilling Altman to take the post in 1947. Perhaps afraid of becoming the third member of a cooked-up spy ring, Fadeyev did not defend his friend. He went home and sent the Politburo a denunciation accusing Altman of double-dealing.[38]

Shaming articles relied on the methodology of innuendo. Fadeyev and Zaslavsky's article used code words understood to mean Jews, like "bourgeois" and "cosmopolitan," making it easy to deny antisemitism. Other articles hinted at Jewish origins by including the family surname in parentheses following the nom de plume. Pseudonyms had been widespread among Russian revolutionaries since the nineteenth century; never had the papers written, "Gorky (Peshkov)" or "Stalin (Dzhugashvili)." In conversation with his cadres, Stalin professed disapproval of this journalistic practice, asking, why do it? why fan antisemitism?[39] As we have seen, however, Stalin had openly shown Fadeyev and Simonov that he could play the double game of disseminating an attitude through the press and then disavowing it. Was he now playing them for naïfs who would believe that he personally disapproved of media practices and yet could not prevent them? Or was he schooling them in the master strategy of deniability and dissimulation? His manner offered his cadres whichever education they were suited for. A Mekhlis would grasp the strategy and learn to wield it himself; a Stavsky would take the leader's word at face value and still do useful work. Fadeyev and Simonov were quick learners.

Fadeyev was almost certainly privy to the secret executions in August 1952 of fourteen JAFC members, including some of his friends.[40] Still he showed his party credentials with a new memo a few days later. Plays by arrested Jewish dramatists like Lev Sheinin, Mikhail (Isidor) Makliarsky, and

L. Rozner were still playing in theaters—a potential sin that could be laid at his door. Perhaps that is why he urged banning the plays for the sake of the public's "ideological health."[41] He gave a second reason as well: the playwrights' families were collecting performance royalties. He knew that they depended on that income.

Was he protecting his privilege, his freedom, or his life? By now the three were inseparable. He was ensnared in the triple-identity spectrum once dangled before Avdeyenko: writer, chekist, *zek*. It was now clear how insidious the identity of writer was. It did not come with a clearly inked outline distinguishing it from alternative—or was it alternate?—identities. Its edges were ugly and smudged where the security agent had leaked in. A public identity as a writer required compromising more than literary ideals; it required compromising one's humanity.

Simonov faced his own dilemmas. Ordered by Malenkov to denounce critics at Writers' Union assemblies, he pondered and found justification for obeying: he would be in a position to limit the damage. If he refused to denounce, someone else would—Sofronov most likely—and there would be many more casualties.[42] This argument, discovered and rediscovered by countless intellectuals who found themselves in this bind, is persuasive to the point of seduction, because there is almost always some truth to it. Borshchagovsky, too, accepted it when Simonov forewarned him that he would have no choice but to attack him at the next meeting. (Simonov proceeded to deliver an unstintingly incriminating speech.)[43]

The cadre's argument with himself thus concludes with a felicitous solution that allows other questions to go unanswered. If the party-ordered attacks are so upsetting, why keep siding with the party? What does it mean to identify with a party that does such things? Burying these questions was a mechanism of more than physical survival. Avoidance was essential to a virtuous self-image. By the logic that Simonov hit upon now (and that Fadeyev had likely reached when he succeeded Stavsky as head of the Writers' Union), a party order to redefine some number of writers as spies and traitors could be executed by a cadre who was a moderate. This line of thought did not account for the extraordinary force of pressure from above; nor for wild-card denunciations that would further fan the flames; nor for political vulnerabilities that might cause the moderate cadre to reconsider just how moderate he was willing to be. Simonov discovered these facts of life upon learning that he had been denounced for bringing Jews onto the staff of *Novy mir*, and because his two earlier marriages were to Jewish women. He dismissed the Jews at *Novy mir* and compiled a list of Jewish writers whose Writers' Union membership he recommended revoking.[44]

For Yermilov, who used *Literaturnaia gazeta* as a battering ram, it probably helped that apart from Fadeyev and Libedinsky he had no friends in the literary world, eliminating any hand-wringing over personal betrayals. He was rewarded for his good offices in 1948 with a dacha.[45] Unexpectedly, however, his desire to solidify his position brought his tenure at *Literaturnaia gazeta* to an abrupt end in early 1950. Apparently hoping to gain favor with Stalin, and without alerting Fadeyev, he ran an article against Panfyorov (another former Litfront opponent) and surreptitiously had it distributed to the delegates at the Writers' Union's thirteenth plenum, which was then in session.[46] Angered at being blindsided, Fadeyev alluded to his displeasure at the plenum in his concluding address. Publishing the closing address of plenums was part of *Literaturnaia gazeta*'s mandate, but Yermilov was not about to be party to his own shaming. He strategically omitted part of Fadeyev's speech.[47]

Fadeyev now acted to remove Yermilov, hoist on his own petard. If the trigger was Yermilov's impudence, the larger need was to restore civility to *Literaturnaia gazeta*. As it happened, Fadeyev was growing closer to an energetic advocate for a more honest literature—Tvardovsky, whose narrative poem *Vasily Tyorkin* (1945) Fadeyev admired. Fadeyev now convinced Simonov to give up *Novy mir* for *Literaturnaia gazeta*, and Tvardovsky took over *Novy mir*.[48] Yermilov, who was said to be freed up to work on his scholarship, was squirreled away into a research post at the Gorky Institute of World Literature, where he wrote books on Gogol and Dostoevsky and received some rather poor solace in the form of a Stalin Prize (second class) for a book on Chekhov.[49] He was left to console himself with "Chernyshevsky's eternally true words that he who strokes everyone's fur and is hated by no one loves no one but himself!" With a liturgical flourish, he envisioned his foes (*nedrugi-supostaty*) barred from the kingdom of heaven.[50]

Having neutralized Yermilov and advanced Tvardovsky and Simonov, Fadeyev engineered a second job exchange. He removed Sofronov from the Writers' Union secretariat, taking the hunt for cosmopolitans away from Sofronov and handing it to Surkov, who turned over to Sofronov his job as editor of *Ogonyok*.[51]

This swap, however, would have its own consequences. Fadeyev, his liver destroyed by drink, began having frequent hospitalizations, and at these times Surkov took over the Writers' Union's day-to-day operations. The highly ambitious Surkov was now well positioned for advancement when the right time came.

Fadeyev's estrangement from Yermilov and his growing friendship with Tvardovsky occurred in the context of two antithetical literary trends. One was the anticosmopolitan campaign; the other was the optimism, inspired by victory over Germany, that emboldened writers to pivot socialist realism toward a greater honesty. Between these two poles, Fadeyev in these years experienced intensified conflict between his liberal inclinations and obedience to party directives. Fadeyev actively supported Tvardovsky's efforts to publish Grossman's *For a Just Cause* (*Za pravoe delo*), suggesting changes to make it acceptable and even editing the manuscript himself.[52] He was thrilled with Tvardovsky's *Distance beyond Distance* (*Za daliu dal*), which dared to articulate the need for honesty. But he urged Tvardovsky to remove or soften its satirical exposé of an editor who ruins manuscripts with his cuts, and he copied Zhdanov's language of August 1946 to make his point—the poem could be exploited by "enemies" and "the bums of literature" (*AFPD*, 321). It was January 1953; Stalin was preparing his next harassment campaign, a case against Kremlin doctors. Fadeyev was torn in two directions. There had to be a way to harmonize them. He wrote to Tvardovsky,

> You need precision, there cannot be any ambiguity [in *Distance beyond Distance*]. For in the contemporary historical situation, the writer has an enemy who is more dangerous [than editors who censor manuscripts] because he reigns in all countries except the countries of our bloc, and in our country takes the form of *Trotskyism*—the carrier of illusory *bourgeois* "freedom," "freedom" from the dictatorship of the working class, "freedom" from communists with their supervision of laborers, "freedom" from the communist worldview, from the party of communists, from their leading figures, including from their editors . . . [one page omitted]
>
> The words "from the leadership in our clan" are *especially ambiguous*: whose *our* is meant? Writers'? But this isn't written for writers! The Soviet people's? The party's? It is ambiguous!
>
> Since I am convinced that it was not your intention to flirt with all manner of dung, you do not see these places (and *only* these places, for the rest of it is true) with sufficient clarity or have insufficiently thought them out politically . . .
>
> This is what I wanted to tell you from my heart and my reason (*AFPD*, 321–23; emphasis in original).

Once again invoking the Plekhanovite impossibility of freedom in the march of history, Fadeyev tried to use reasoning to reconcile the feelings of his subjective self with his objective intellectual commitment, but the unity between heart and reason was illusory. Where Tvardovsky had been doubly courageous, both in his own work and in standing up for the work of others, Fadeyev's courage, if ever he could find it, was immediately riven by his cadre self. His indignant or perhaps reproachful cry, "It is ambiguous!" had a deep-seated root reaching back to the memory of the night in Stalin's office when he received his instructions to defame Platonov. Stalin had found Platonov's stories double-voiced. Nor was Fadeyev's hedging confined to *Distance beyond Distance*. When *For a Just Cause* was attacked in the press in February, he reversed himself and joined the chorus of criticism (*AFPD*, 325).

He was working on his own novel, *Ferrous Metallurgy* (*Chernaia metallurgiia*). Like *The Young Guard*, it was based on a true incident, in this case a struggle in the metal industry between innovative engineers and entrenched conservatives who acted to block them. It is exactly the topic of Vladimir Dudintsev's blockbuster novel *Not by Bread Alone* (*Ne khlebom edinym*), which appeared after Stalin's death. In this sense, *Ferrous Metallurgy* appears to be part of the postwar wave of interest in finding ways to expose the myths of socialist realism and continue what had been started by Panova and others. According to one report, however, it was Stalin who suggested the topic.[53] It is even possible that he may have wished to show Fadeyev his "liberalism." Fadeyev, determined to write a book with national impact, chose a suitably weighty topic, the process of turning iron ore into steel.[54]

From the hospital, where he was being treated for alcoholism and cirrhosis, Fadeyev implored Surkov to shoulder a larger burden of Writers' Union duties so that he could devote himself to *Ferrous Metallurgy*: "Not to allow me to complete my novel right now would be the same as forcibly delaying childbirth, preventing childbirth. But I will simply perish as a person and as a writer, just as a woman in labor would perish under the same conditions" (*AFPD*, 152).

> I have thoroughly studied the life, daily routine, and production of nine of the most important metallurgy plants in the east and south of the country, I have read an unimaginable amount of brochures by production innovators, I have mastered the biographies of such major Russian metallurgists as Anosov, Chernov, Pavlov, Baikov, Bardin, mastered the biographies of Dzerzhinsky, Kuibyshev, Ordzhonikidze, which will be shown in my novel. I have put into my novel the best of everything that I have thought and felt in a lifetime of fifty years; the novel contains my whole soul, my whole heart. You of all people should know that I do not write in cold blood. (*AFPD*, 151)

This novel, Fadeyev assured Surkov, would be his best ever. "I do not have the right to false modesty; it will literally be a gift to the people, to the party, to Soviet literature" (*AFPD*, 151). The balloon of vanity would soon burst. After three years of research, he finally got to the bottom of the metallurgists' dispute:

The people who were right turned out to be not the "innovators" (for they were inflated, false innovators), but the "routinists" (for they turned out to be simply honest and knowledgeable people) . . . Those who at that time were proclaimed enemies (specifically in the field of metallurgy and in that postwar stage of development) turned out simply to have been slandered. (*FP* 1973, 581)

Again he found himself rewriting an entire novel. For years now he had been a literary industry, with graduate students (the few who chose to specialize in Soviet literature) writing their dissertations on him, and readers showering him with two thousand pages of admiring letters.[55] He even had an ode written to him by a Chinese communist enthusiast.[56] But to Simonov he confided that he was a literary "bankrupt."[57] The time wasted on *Ferrous Metallurgy*'s false premise was bad enough, but unbidden recollection of his own similar behavior in slandering "proclaimed enemies" like Altman and Boris Dairedzhiev must have been worse. And if the novel's topic was really suggested to him by Stalin, then Fadeyev could not have avoided the conclusion that he had been duped. It went beyond a single novel. Thinking that he was fashioning himself a communist, he had let the puppet master Stalin fashion him.[58]

Three weeks after Stalin's death on March 5, 1953, the Politburo declared a prisoner amnesty. Within weeks, the first Gulag survivors began showing up on the streets of Moscow. They were a seemingly endless stream that swelled with each passing month, some one and a half million people in all.[59] Nationwide, the number of returned writers was about five hundred.[60] For Fadeyev, each encounter with a returnee was an encounter with his own conscience. There were old opponents and former friends—Fadeyev's old RAPP comrades Shushkanov and Makaryev, the "vulgar sociologist" Pereverzev, and the "neobaroque" Literary Institute student Belinkov. Gekht, who had stood up for Platonov, reappeared, as did Aleksandr Gladkov, who in 1937 had made mental note of Fadeyev's immunity to political accusations. Altman, released in 1953 after six months in prison, returned home a wreck and died within two years. Yaroslav Smeliakov, one of the Jewish writers whose family Fadeyev had sought to deprive of income, reappeared, as did Gronsky, after sixteen years in the Gulag. A new phrase now entered the language: "illegally repressed." With it, the nation's collective conscience haltingly and painfully began a process of restoration.

Rehabilitation was granted by petition. Fadeyev was inundated with requests from returnees and the families of the dead for character references in support of their petitions. He was supporting rehabilitations—usually posthumous—of the very writers whose arrest warrants he had countersigned. Libedinsky, who had deep affection and sympathy for Fadeyev, listened to his friend tell him, "as if justifying himself," of the many rehabilitation letters he had written.[61] To his friend the filmmaker Esfir Shub, Fadeyev confided that some of his hospitalizations were on his own initiative, a way to avoid difficult conversations. Some of his past deeds he managed to forget, whether through indifference, a drunk-muddled brain, or a psychological survival mechanism. He took offense at the cold greeting given him by the Jewish film director Leonid Trauberg, until Shub, who was Trauberg's colleague and herself Jewish, gently reminded him of the humiliation and impoverishment Trauberg had endured during the anticosmopolitan campaign. Fadeyev expressed regret that he had forgotten—he would have made a point of stopping to talk (*AFPD*, 343–44).

More and more requests crossed his desk. He supported the rehabilitations of friends and colleagues from whom he had tried to distance himself after their arrests. He wrote for old RAPP comrades arrested in 1937–38, including Selivanovsky, Bespalov, and Kirshon.[62] In the end he wrote five hundred support letters.[63] But he refused to write one for Averbakh, citing his closeness to Yagoda (*AFPD*, 200). Whatever role Fadeyev had played in Averbakh's arrest was his most closely guarded secret. Writing for Selivanovsky and Kirshon, he named those they had worked with in the RAPP leadership, including himself, but he made sure never to include Averbakh's name in the same list with his own. If he felt the need to mention Averbakh, he walled him off in a separate sentence (*AFPD*, 198–200). He was uncharacteristically circumspect in his support for Kirshon, in whom there was his own "bullet"; he pointed out that Kirshon had resisted RAPP's dissolution with Averbakh, as if alluding to his own rectitude, and wrote guardedly that the facts "allow one to think" that Kirshon's arrest had been incorrect. Writing for Kirshon brought Fadeyev to a brink he refused to face.

Gronsky tried to make him face it. When asked to write a character reference for Averbakh, Gronsky, who was vigorous in helping clear the names of the dead, told the investigator that he would write one only if the RAPP leaders also did so, or even if only Fadeyev did so. Gronsky, like many others, was sure Fadeyev, Yermilov, and Libedinsky had all denounced Averbakh.[64] Were Fadeyev now to say he believed Averbakh had been illegally repressed, he would be implicating himself, and this was what Gronsky wanted. Averbakh could have been rehabilitated without Fadeyev's testimony; the word of Gronsky and others would have been enough. But Gronsky was not going to let Fadeyev off the hook. Told that Fadeyev, Yermilov, and Libedinsky had all refused to write on behalf of Averbakh, Gronsky did likewise. Averbakh was rehabilitated in 1961 based on testimony from Surkov and Sutyrin.[65]

Dignified recommendations to the rehabilitation commission, anguished and defensive confessions to friends and colleagues, correspondence with friends returned from the Gulag, urgent instructions to his deputies, impassioned briefs to the Central Committee secretaries—these were the writings of Fadeyev's last years. They are a hybrid genre of self-justification and confession, laced with a horror that nothing can be undone.

Two months after Stalin's death, Fadeyev came out of the literary closet—but only to the party leadership and his communist deputies at the Writers' Union. He was obeying party rules that kept disagreements behind closed doors. The moment of opportunity came at an inconvenient time, when he was in the hospital and Surkov was in charge. Fadeyev urged Surkov to relieve writers of union work so that they would have time to write, arguing that this was essential for the future of literature. The quality of fiction was "lower than at any time since the advent of Soviet power," yet "the two or three dozen writers" capable of providing a literary example to the next generation "are up to their ears in every kind of work except for creative writing, although . . . *without their example no new young talents or geniuses can develop naturally*, just as there could not have been Pushkin without Derzhavin, Lomonosov, Griboyedov, Zhukovsky, and Batiushkov" (*AFPD*, 150; emphasis in original). Talented young writers were overloaded with service from the beginning of their careers, leaving them no time to develop as artists. Until this changed, he told Surkov, no amount of shuffling the pieces on the "chessboard of our so-called literary supervision" would help (*AFPD*, 151).

Showing his cards to Surkov was a colossal miscalculation. Some fifteen years earlier, Surkov himself had complained bitterly about the dismal condition of Soviet literature and the party's failure to bring forth any literary talents from the working class. Now, however, he calculated that the party secretaries were not about to open any literary floodgates, and he took advantage of Fadeyev's misplaced confidence to advance himself. He sent a copy of Fadeyev's letter to Pyotr Pospelov, the former *Pravda* editor who was now the Central Committee secretary in charge of ideology. To Khrushchev, Surkov wrote that Fadeyev had given a "panic assessment" of Soviet literature. His view had been jaundiced by alcoholism, illness, and depression; when he recovered he would change his mind. Surkov got Simonov and Tikhonov to join him as signatories (*AFPD*, 152). Had Fadeyev brought these two relative liberals into his confidence, they might have sided with him. But Fadeyev would have believed it a breach of party code to show these thoughts to the nonparty Tikhonov, even though he had spent two years as the Writers' Union's nominal leader.

The secretaries and the Politburo, although they had acted quickly in granting amnesty and discarding Stalin's fabricated doctors' plot,[66] took the hard line on literature, siding with Surkov. His argument was surely more to their liking than was Fadeyev's, and Fadeyev was already compromised in their eyes—he was nothing but a depressed alcoholic. So it was already too late when in August, sensing that the time was right following Lavrenty Beria's execution, Fadeyev sent the first of three lengthy memoranda to Khrushchev and Malenkov, urging reforms.[67] The memos take the form of directives or expert opinion, but they are essentially a desperate plea to reverse the entire literary policy that he had dedicated his whole career to serving.

In his first memo, he told the secretaries what they needed to hear— Soviet literature was wretched and party supervision was to blame. The tsars' Russia, for all its repression, had seen an enviable literature, while the Soviet Union had only Mayakovsky. Endless criticism and self-criticism replaced the reading and writing of books; prizes were awarded to substandard literature while the press pumped out "daily akathistos hymns . . . on the familiar theme that Soviet literature and art are the most advanced in the world" (AFPD, 155, 159). The ironic reference to "akathistos hymns" turns the party's sacralized language against itself and edges toward acknowledgment of what recent scholarship has identified as political religion. "Haven't we overdone our 'guardianship' duties?" Fadeyev asked. "Aren't we getting [writers] unaccustomed to independent thought, to a sense of ownership of their own work, of which they are not only the creators but also the directors; aren't we teaching them to glance fearfully over their shoulders at the bureaucrat functionaries whose knowledge of literature is immeasurably inferior to theirs, but who have been placed above them by virtue of their position in the government hierarchy?" (AFPD, 155).

Having stated the problem in his first memo, he suggested solutions in the second. This memo was harder to write, because the problem was insoluble: how to permit creative freedom without forfeiting party control. Unwilling to locate the blame in the party itself, he points to the "immeasurably inferior" bureaucrats in the Ministry of Culture (which was outside the party chain of command). Solution: remove the ministry from literary supervision and have the party oversee literature directly (AFPD, 160). He points to the August 1946 party resolution on literature as more effective than the companion resolutions on cinema and theater, which were issued not by the party but by the government with its deadening "administrative methods." Even if we grant that he is trying to calculate his argument to appeal to the secretaries, it is shocking to find him crediting the August resolution with an "upsurge and flowering" in literature (AFPD, 161). He is back to the very policies he is trying to change.

Recognizing that the party will never surrender its role as ideological supervisor, Fadeyev advocates tossing out coercive methods and using persuasion instead. And if persuasion did not always work? His answer unraveled his argument:

Any serious ideological worker knows that . . . the state cannot yet completely dispense with the application of coercive methods. It is indisputable, however, that the main methods of the party and the government in directing literature . . . are and must be persuasion and training. (*AFPD*, 161)

Coercion does not work, but we need to use coercion. Fadeyev cannot be clear because that would mean throwing out the party's leading role. He wriggles out of that problem by declaring that coercion is a necessary evil that will fall away once all writers voluntarily adopt the communist view. This was much like the argument once advanced by Lukács in *Literary Critic*. Fadeyev had denounced it then. Now he grasped at it desperately. It was a compromise born of misery, an attempt to preserve his belief in the party as a sacred font of truth. The logic twists its way to the sore spot, and finally he names it. When directives are handed down from on high, writers and "even the cadres who lead them" feel that they must accept the decision "against their own conscience" (*AFPD*, 162). Here we have, in his own words, his admission—carefully depersonalized—that he put the party before his conscience. Aligning one's subjective self with the party was a misplaced notion; conscience would not be denied.

Fadeyev received no response to his memos. Here was a fresh insult— three decades as the top literary cadre and he did not even warrant a reply, much less an audience. Having no personal connection to either Khrushchev or Malenkov, Fadeyev managed an appointment with Pospelov, unaware that Surkov had gotten to him first. Pospelov drily turned the conversation to Fadeyev's drinking problem. But however one views the memos, they were not alcoholic ravings.

Apart from Surkov and later, Simonov, Fadeyev told not a soul about his letters to the leadership. This sense of party discipline was exactly why Stalin had chosen him to lead the union. It had already been his moral undoing; now it turned out to be his political undoing, because it prevented him from gathering allies. Gorky had been similarly marginalized, conducting Writers' Union business by correspondence and in one-on-one interactions. By refusing to share his thoughts even with like-minded friends like Tvardovsky, who was using *Novy mir* to publish the vibrant literature Fadeyev argued for in his memos, he reduced himself to one lone voice when he could have led an entire force. Surkov did understand the power of alliances. As head of the Writers' Union party group, he garnered opposition to Fadeyev. Supported by the Central Committee secretaries, Surkov's faction blocked Fadeyev from giving the keynote speech at the Writers' Union's fourteenth plenum in October 1953 (*AFPD*, 179).

Tvardovsky, too, understood the power of alliances. He turned *Novy mir* into a movement of reformist writers. The December 1953 issue carried Vladimir Pomerantsev's thunderbolt article "On Sincerity in Literature" ("Ob iskrennosti v literature").[68] Tvardovsky realized that by branding the journal, he could maximize the impact of the work it carried. Under an identifiable *Novy mir* brand, these pieces gained a permanent place in literary life, and the public knew where to go for interesting reading. As Stalin had marketed the Writers' Union in 1932, and as he had extended the reach of *Literaturnaia gazeta* during the anticosmopolitan campaign, so Tvardovsky acted now, on his own initiative and without seeking permission.

"On Sincerity in Literature" became a battleground as *Literaturnaia gazeta*, now in the hands of Agitprop's Riurikov, unleashed the full force of its outrage on Pomerantsev, and Moscow University students gathered to defend him. In June, Riurikov, Surkov, Simonov, and Polevoi assembled the students to deliver a scolding.[69] Tvardovsky, although unaware of Fadeyev's memos to the secretaries, counted on Fadeyev's support (*AFPD*, 329, 330). Fadeyev, who attended closed meetings where he could express himself without breaching communist etiquette, still had a chance to influence the leaders, this time with the momentum of a growing movement behind him. Pomerantsev's ideas were in line with his own recommendations to the secretaries.

Perhaps he felt crushed by the secretaries' contempt. Perhaps he bristled at the idea of allying himself with the nonparty upstart Pomerantsev. He parried Tvardovsky's plea for help, citing his diminished role in the Writers' Union and his need to work uninterrupted on *Ferrous Metallurgy*: thinking about literary politics was bad for his health and his novel. He warned Tvardovsky against making the same mistake he had made—getting sucked into administrative work that gave him no time to write. One's own creative work was so much more important than these "tempests in a teapot." Fadeyev was sure that Tvardovsky would act "courageously and according to his conscience." Tvardovsky must obey the party. And if the party decided wrongly, it didn't really matter so much (*AFPD*, 328–39).

In this letter we hear a completely different Fadeyev from the writer of the policy memos. There his reference to conscience suggested division between personal belief and party obligation; but when he writes to Tvardovsky, the fissure is closed up and "conscience" belongs to the party. Caught between the imperatives of literary reform and party discipline, he chooses the latter. Conscience was simple. It meant obedience to the party. So he intimated to Tvardovsky, but of course it was not simple. Reducing the struggle for literature to a "tempest in a teapot"—deciding that an important matter is unimportant—is a classic mechanism for coping with cognitive dissonance. He was still struggling to forge one conscience out of two masters. Similarly disingenuous was his equation of Tvardovsky's fight for literary honesty, which he belittled as "administrative" work, with his own Writers' Union duties. His letter to Tvardovsky reads as a lesson in how to make a cowardly action look credible. Fadeyev had once complained to Andreyev of too many journals that were all alike. But he would not endorse Tvardovsky's lone-wolf action taken without party consent.

Pravda mobilized its favored cadres for bullying, Yermilov and Surkov,[70] as the party secretaries were still trying to decide what to do with *Novy mir*. Pospelov urged that Yermilov be made editor. When Pospelov called *Tyorkin in the Other World* (*Tyorkin na tom svete*) a "slander of Soviet reality," Fadeyev agreed.[71] Tvardovsky was removed in July 1954. Fadeyev counseled him against protesting: if Tvardovsky, a "son of the party," were to do that, he would be doomed to "spiritual apostasy" (*AFPD*, 332).

Yermilov did not get the post. Simonov got his old job back. He had closed ranks behind Surkov and was sounding more and more Stalinist. Once there, however, he continued Tvardovsky's work, publishing Dudintsev's *Not by Bread Alone*, the novel that succeeded where *Ferrous Metallurgy* had failed.[72] For once, the cadre's argument with himself proved true: by taking the hard-line view, I will at least be able to limit the damage; and maybe I can even do some good.

In this fraught standoff between reformers and Stalinists, between Gulag survivors and their betrayers, the Writers' Union held its second congress in December 1954. Twenty years had gone by since the grand first congress. Mass murder and the passage of time had changed the union's makeup. Most Writers' Union members were now Soviet born. From 2,200 members in 1934, the organization had grown to 3,700, only 10 percent of whom had been in the original group.[73] If we use Shentalinsky's estimate of 1,500 members who had perished in the Gulag (thus not counting the 500 who survived) and Babichenko's calculation of 400 killed in wartime military service, then in those two decades the Writers' Union added not 1,300 members but 3,200 members. To this number we must add perhaps as many as another 500 to replace the 500 writers who survived the Gulag, many of whom would not have been reinstated in the union by December 1954.

There was now a steady stream of graduates from the Literary Institute. Ideologically suspect writers eliminated in the terror had been replaced with others more likely to be conformist, if only because more likely to see literature as a pragmatic career choice rather than a calling. More than 90 percent of the 738 delegates to the congress had begun their literary careers after 1917, an accurate reflection of the total membership; many of them had joined the union after the war.[74]

By the measure of pure numbers, Stalin's strategy for building a cadre of writers was a resounding success. The Writers' Union's closed distribution network of privileges assured a ready supply of new members, who received both literary and ideological training at the Literary Institute. Gorky's legacy had grown from humble evening and correspondence courses into a full-time, five-year higher education degree.[75] The unspoken trade-off between upward mobility and individual authority, exposed by the indignant Shaginian in 1936, was on a firm footing. Nearly one-third of Writers' Union members had the privilege of living in Moscow, and most of the rest enjoyed the comparatively high standard of living in other major cities.[76] Membership would more than double throughout the next decades, reaching 9,500 in 1986.[77]

Fadeyev sought permission from the secretaries to publicly express his program for literary reform in his opening address (*AFPD*, 213). The secretaries responded by giving his job to Surkov. At the first congress, Surkov had fulfilled the party assignment of refuting Bukharin. Now he ascended the podium triumphantly to deliver the opening address. Fadeyev was not among the eleven other writers who delivered formal addresses. He could speak only in the discussion period, and even then he was instructed to soften his views. The congress was the public unveiling of Fadeyev's demotion.

Surkov set out to deflate the excitement over the most talked-about books, Ehrenburg's *The Thaw* (*Ottepel*) and Panova's *Seasons of the Year* (*Vremena goda*). Claiming not to dispute their right to show "the darker side of life," he denounced them for "soul building" (*dusheustroitelstvo*)— separating the hero's life from the larger social cause (*VSP*, 27–28).

Surkov's address and the new career pragmatism of the membership were not enough to prevent an extraordinarily contentious congress as writers declared that a vibrant literature could come only with individual voices and self-expression (*VSP*, 345). They demanded that book reviews and prizes reward literary merit, not works that belonged "outside literature." They wanted the Writers' Union's mission to be literary creativity and not social messaging. They wanted relief from the ubiquitous positive hero. They wanted satires that could show Soviet imperfections. They wanted their leaders and editors to stand up for them instead of knocking them down.

Many speeches took on an ad hominem flavor. Writers' literary and personal relationships were tightly intertwined. They drank together and read one another their work; their children played together; they were married to each other and divorced from each other; sometimes they were in-laws; and even if they were none of these, they still might have a child together, like Fadeyev and Aliger. With these long histories that had played out in an ethos of fear and compromise, they now called one another to account.

Several speakers voiced no confidence in their leaders, singling out Fadeyev, Surkov, and the most recent editors of *Literaturnaia gazeta*, Yermilov, Simonov, and Riurikov (*VSP*, 282, 377). Aliger blamed the inhospitable literary atmosphere on the Writers' Union, where discussion was routinely cut off by "an official fist coming down on the table" (*VSP*, 282). The Latvian party writer Vilis Lācis, without naming names, pointed out that the union leaders had never abandoned cliquishness and "chieftanism" (*vozhdism*) and called out "the hypocritical and sanctimonious repudiation of one's own opinions." If Fadeyev mentally excused this subordination of personal opinion in the name of a greater communist good, Lācis had another take on it: it was a bourgeois survival.[78] Ehrenburg commented that Mayakovsky's official exaltation was "painful for [his] contemporaries and friends, who have not forgotten how difficult his creative path was" (*VSP*, 145). This was a clear allusion to Mayakovsky's suicide—and writers' perception of it as a literary act in the face of RAPP's goading. This trail, too, led to Yermilov and Fadeyev.

Simonov, too, came in for ridicule. Sholokhov exposed him as an illustration of an unhealthy practice: the writer who was spoiled by winning literary prizes prematurely. Writers who were ruined in this way, said Sholokhov, could not teach their younger colleagues; and the result would be an end to literature. All that could be learned from Simonov was how to write quickly and diplomatically. Sholokhov advised Simonov to take more time over his writing before someone noticed that the emperor had no clothes (*VSP*, 377). This flourish was greeted with laughter and applause. What Sholokhov left out, of course, was Stalin, the one who had used the prizes to manipulate and co-opt his young cadre. Writers spoke as freely as they did because Stalin was dead, but nearly two years after his death they dared not blame him.

They did, however, shame hack Stalin Prize winners like Anatoly Surov and Semyon Babayevsky. Berggolts declared that the prize for Surov's *The Green Street* (*Zelenaia ulitsa*) set a precedent for ever lower-quality drama, and Veniamin Kaverin envisioned a future in which "the appearance of a Surov is not even imaginable."[79] Writers called for recognition of other works instead— Grossman's *For a Just Cause*, Kazakevich's *A Friend's Heart* (*Serdtse druga*), Svetlov's "The Grenade" ("Grenada"), and Vershigora's *People with a Clear Conscience* (*VSP*, 169, 345). (That Vershigora's memoir, which had won a second-class Stalin Prize, was nonetheless felt to be insufficiently recognized is further evidence that despite the prize the book was not widely promoted.) They wanted an end to the practice of preselecting works for praise and condemnation (*VSP*, 376). Fix criticism, declared Aliger, and you fix literature. Novice critics, she asserted, needed to be able to make mistakes without fear of ruining their career.

Fadeyev's chance to speak came on the ninth day. He adopted a tone of collegiality and communist modesty, but he was facing his colleagues as a defendant before a jury. He thanked them for their criticisms and agreed that the Writers' Union should be run more democratically. He apologized for betraying *For a Just Cause*: "To this day I regret that I showed weakness when in my article about the novel supporting not only what was correct in the criticism of it I also called the novel ideologically harmful" (*VSP*, 511). The applause that met this statement was less an appreciation of this admission than a collective verdict that he had betrayed Grossman. Fadeyev's apology was striped with self-justification: Grossman had in fact made some mistakes, *Novy mir* had published mistaken work, and Pomerantsev had attempted to divert Soviet literature from its honorable mission. Fadeyev did more than tone down his recommendations to the party leadership; he jettisoned them. He was back to the hard line. Soviet literature's primary mission was to argue against its ideological opponents (mostly outside the Soviet Union); cosmopolitans and other enemies remained a force. Much later, on the eve of his suicide, he explained himself to Yermilov: "I didn't want to be in league with . . . all manner of low-minded people [*obyvateli*]—malcontents—especially during the writers' congress" (*AFPD*, 214).

He opposed *Novy mir* and Aliger's call for diverse opinions: "Different opinions can't all be right. In ancient times there was a saying: 'If one has to choose between two evils, then one incorrect viewpoint is better than two correct ones'" (*VSP*, 510). This stunning conclusion echoes his remark to Tvardovsky that it was not really so important if the party leaders took a wrong view. It is the voice of desperation: he would rather be wrong than acknowledge the party's betrayal and his complicity in it. His epiphany on reading Dante's *Inferno* in 1934 had endured. Those who could not choose a side were not even worthy of hell.

In its construction, Fadeyev's speech employs a template used so widely that it can be considered as a genre. Disputes with official policy were placed deep in the middle of a speech, framed by platitudes that provided a facade of acceptability and a hedge against the more daring proposals. Ehrenburg's frame, for example, included passing mention of enemies. Even official addresses closely following the party line employed this structure. Surkov in his opening address needed to raise the awkward subject of poor literary quality, so he embedded that part of his speech in a frame proclaiming literature's value, aspirations, and advances. The more controversial a speaker's proposals were, the greater the amount of space given to the frame.[80]

Fadeyev's speech is a variation on this genre. His frame, rather than being a hedge for an unorthodox proposal, reaffirms party orthodoxy. As such, it is a wall of justification for his actions at the head of the Writers' Union. He invoked the bulwarks to which he always turned for reassurance—partymindedness and the Plekhanovite critique of freedom in the progression of history. Yet even these principles were of dubious structural integrity—hence the need to prop them up by invoking the threat of enemies. The middle of his speech with its stingy acknowledgment of error is dwarfed by the oversized frame. This was his final recitation of his communist credo before his deconstruction of it in his suicide note.

Yermilov calculated differently. He made no mention of enemies, building his frame instead upon the theme of Tolstoyan love and applying it to the critic's métier. This was transparently self-serving hypocrisy. Hiding behind the passive voice, he asserted that criticisms (he meant his own excessively harsh ones, but avoided saying so) of works by Kazakevich, Grossman, Ehrenburg, Panova, and Perventsev were made out of love for the author's previous works (*VSP*, 469).

The congress passed three resolutions that ostensibly improved writers' lot: (1) a broader, more forgiving definition of socialist realism; (2) a new charter outlining greater democracy; and (3) the reestablishment of writers' access to foreign literature. The first resolution affirmed that socialist realism comprised a wide variety of individual literary viewpoints and styles. The effect of this declaration was no more than a squeak, however, since it was dwarfed by a much lengthier reaffirmation in the same document of literature's ideological mission (*VSP*, 590–92). The new charter increased the size of the secretariat to nineteen, ostensibly a democratizing measure but really meaningless since the party continued to instruct the Writers' Union through Agitprop, and before long Polikarpov would simultaneously be Writers' Union first secretary and the responsible Agitprop official. (Although delegates had criticized the Writers' Union leaders, only Berggolts had had the temerity to locate the problem in Agitprop.) Writers came away with one real gain—a new journal dedicated to foreign literature, *Inostrannaia literatura* (*Foreign Literature*).[81]

It is hard to know whether Fadeyev clung to his communist identity as the last thing remaining to him as a literary "bankrupt," or whether he was merely keeping up appearances. An exchange of letters between him and Yermilov a year after the congress reads as an epistolary embrace after the distance that had sprung up between them since Yermilov's removal from *Literaturnaia gazeta*. They warmly reaffirmed their bond, their "like-mindedness," their sworn party duty, and their mutual affection. Alluding to their "disagreement" (*razmolvka*), Fadeyev characterized it as minor. He attributed their estrangement to the pervasive stress under which they lived:

I knew that in some way your life was *very similar* to mine. And I knew that given that life, if we were to have frequent contact we would not only not help each other but also drag each other "down." After all, we are not only like-minded in literature, we are also old friends, accustomed to absolute frankness, a sincerity going beyond Pomerantsev's . . . and we would not have been able to avoid talking about the most difficult thing that attended our life in those years, because it, that life, was difficult. We would not have been able, no matter how much we might have tried, to keep from bringing down that weight on each other, and we felt this from a distance and more or less uncon-sciously avoided each other. (*FP* 1973, 598; emphasis in original)

The put-down of the outsider Pomerantsev is unmistakable. "When it comes to people like you and me," wrote Fadeyev, "even though we have lost much physical and emotional energy . . . if need be we can fight against anyone we need to" (*FP* 1973, 598).

On the same day that he wrote these words, he received a letter that tested his understanding of party duty. It was from his old RAPP friend Ma-karyev. Makaryev and Fadeyev had once done party work together in Rostov; Makaryev had followed in Fadeyev's footsteps as each of them got their big break joining the RAPP secretariat in Moscow; together they had handed out judgments on writers as "one of us" or "not one of us." "Dear Sasha," wrote Makaryev,

A few days ago I returned from a place that not everyone returns from.

I would very much like to see you and tell you of many things that you would find interesting and necessary both as a writer and as a member of the Central Committee, and simply as a human being. But [my wife] has told me that you are ill and in the hospital.

I am troubling you for the following reason.

After nineteen years of life in semifantastical conditions—I am now fully rehabilitated. Of course I was guilty of nothing even nineteen years ago, of nothing, and never, in spite of all the investigation's "methods," did I admit any guilt—but of course for the outside world I am not guilty only after being rehabilitated. Therefore I did not write to you and am writing only now (*AFPD*, 297–98).

Makaryev asks Fadeyev to support his reinstatement in the party:

I can tell you . . . that in the very complicated circumstances of these two de-cades I conducted myself like a communist—at least that's how it seems to me . . .

When I was under interrogation I was questioned about you for half a month. I think I can ask you for ten minutes in return . . . [several lines omitted]

I myself am not, of course, . . . the same Vanka Makaryev you knew but a sick and mutilated old man.

Well, that's enough, all kinds of things happen in this the best of worlds! I send you sincere greetings.

Good health to you!

The letter is signed "Your I. Makaryev."

The polite closing lines are surely a reason why at least one scholar considers this letter evidence that Makaryev still preserved warm feelings for Fadeyev (*AFPD*, 298). But "I think I can ask you for ten minutes in return" implies reproach and perhaps a sneer at the idea that a debt calculated in weeks of torture might be settled by a few minutes at a writing desk. The half month of interrogation about Fadeyev raises two possibilities. If Fadeyev had denounced Makaryev, or if, as some have suggested, Fadeyev gave the NKVD Makaryev's letters to him, then Fadeyev was to blame for his friend's fate.[82] If Fadeyev did not denounce Makaryev, then Makaryev's stoicism in refusing to implicate him could have saved Fadeyev from arrest.[83] This makes it difficult to read the first part of the letter as nothing beyond a natural desire to inform Fadeyev of the horrors of the criminal-justice system. What is it that Fadeyev needs to know not just as a writer and Central Committee member but also as a human being? The word *chelovek* means both "person" and "human being." Makaryev's phrasing seems to point toward humanity.

Makaryev's letter is dated November 12, 1955. On November 15, Fadeyev wrote three letters: one to the Party Control Commission supporting Makaryev's reinstatement, one to Makaryev, and one to Makaryev's wife, Raisa. These letters display the intertwining strands of self-justification and confession that spun out endlessly in Fadeyev's public statements. To Makaryev he wrote as follows:

Dear Vania!

Your letter, of course, greatly agitated me, as did Raia's telegram. Much that is precious and good is connected with our life in the past, and especially in the Rostov period, which I generally recall as one of the brightest periods in my life. Of course we will see each other not just for a "discussion," but we will see each other in general once I leave the hospital and to the end of our days. (*FP* 1973, 604)

Fadeyev's use of the word "discussion" (*beseda*), in quotation marks, is layered with a complex multivoicing. Makaryev did not use this word. With it, Fadeyev acknowledges that he will have to hear Makaryev out and respond. At the same time, the quotation marks undercut the discussion's gravity. "Discussion" thus becomes a lexical gesture holding two opposite meanings. It will be serious (discussion), but their renewed friendship will render that exchange unimportant ("discussion"). It is another variation on the double-edged genre of confession as self-justification that marked the last three years of Fadeyev's life.

I hope I do not have to tell you that I, too, had no doubt of your innocence; back then and later, when talking with Libedinsky, Valia Gerasimova, and Yermilov, we considered it a "mistake" resulting from false testimony or slander. Now, of course, we understand that it wasn't a mistake but a crime among many other similar crimes of those years and later. A few months ago the military procuracy asked me to give you a character reference and I gave it right away. I have a copy of it and I will show it to you.

His prompt response to the procuracy's request counts in Fadeyev's eyes as evidence of active advocacy. Yet he was only responding to an outside initiative. So long has he been cowed that reactivity has come to feel like proactivity. He promises to write the reinstatement recommendation that very day (he kept the promise). In closing, he repeats his assurance of resuming their friendship:

> We will talk about all kinds of other matters when we see each other, and afterward we will also talk about nonmatters. My cordial greetings to Raia, and give her the enclosed note from me.

> I press your hand warmly.
> A.

Raisa Makaryeva had earlier appealed to Fadeyev for additional living space for their family of five living in a single room. Fadeyev had asked her for documentation, which she provided; after some time went by with no further news, she gave up on him and informed his secretary in a frosty tone that Fadeyev need not pursue the matter further (*AFPD*, 202). He now wrote to Raisa explaining why he had been unable to procure a second room. He has an unbelievable workload; each year for the past four years he has spent several months in the hospital being treated for his liver, his heart, and more recently a degenerative nerve condition in his legs; every year he is obliged to make several trips "both abroad and to various metallurgical districts of the country for work on [his] new novel"; Raisa's housing is therefore one of many matters that he has been unable to pursue as energetically as he would like. Fadeyev then offers the kind of autobiographical character reference important in party membership applications and rehabilitation petitions.[84] As Makaryev's claim to have always behaved in a manner befitting a communist seems to quote from his rehabilitation petition, Fadeyev offers Raisa a similar character reference:

> A particular character trait of mine—especially now as I approach old age—can be said to be that I am both "conscientious" and "keep things in memory," and that no matter how long a matter, be it small or large, may drag on, I will definitely fulfill it if possible.

He tries to smooth the awkwardness with a humorous description of his reaction on hearing from his secretary of Makaryeva's anger:

Being familiar with Raisa Grigoryevna's character over the course of many years, I understood that the second room had already been taken away and that Raisa Grigoryevna had put both my secretary and me in the category of "insolent bureaucrats." Never mind, I thought, let me take the blame, at least it will give Soviet power some breathing space. But now, after the fact, I have to tell you that in taking on what was for me a natural obligation to help, I knew perfectly well that my intervention would not meet with success. In my whole time "in power" I had to intercede many dozens of times on various housing matters with the people who decide these things. And never, not once did I succeed, except for a single occasion in the Kuntsevo district when I was able to gain a resolution for a veterinarian from Odintsov to have a plot of land in Odintsov itself on which to build a house. When my own family grew larger, for long years I could not get an improvement in my living conditions until in the late 1940s Korneichuk and Vanda Vasilyevskaia asked comrade Stalin himself to do it for me. (*AFPD*, 203)

After two pages building as ironclad an alibi as possible, Fadeyev inadvertently undermines it: "Having now fully had my say, partly to justify myself and partly out of repentance . . ." The urge to penitence makes its way unbidden into his self-characterization, even though he has so carefully immured himself from guilt.

Fadeyev clearly tried to give his letter a warm tone, show regard for Makaryeva, and demonstrate that his position and privilege have never changed his feelings for his friends. But behind the intentionality we hear unintentional rings as well. "Giving Soviet power some breathing space" sounds like a good-natured willingness to take the blame in service of a cause he still believes in (perhaps not considering that the Makaryevs may not). By now, however, he was confronting the dark reality of having been positioned for an entire career as a hollow authority figure, and his letter is a genial pose. Here is the ending: "I wish you all the best in the world and I do not preclude fighting in future [*v dalneishem*] for a change in your housing situation. Maybe it will turn out to be my second victory on this front" (*AFPD*, 203–4).

His letters to the Makaryevs continue the genre of self-justification infused with confession, an attempt to mitigate the shame, a shame that now came from within and not from the party.

Fadeyev spent more than half his final six months in the hospital. He missed the Twentieth Party Congress, which he was to have attended with Surkov and Sholokhov, the other Central Committee members of the Writers' Union (*AFPD*, 209). There, the arguments Fadeyev had made in his confidential memos were made much more bluntly by Sholokhov. Party bureaucracy wrecked literary talent, proclaimed Sholokhov, and the writer whose talent had suffered most was Fadeyev:

> We robbed Fadeyev of fifteen of the best years of his creative life, and as a result we have neither a general secretary nor a writer . . .
> But all Fadeyev needed was to be freed up from his union duties for a few years, and in a short time he created a splendid work about the Krasnodon young guard. Perhaps unlike any of us novelists, Fadeyev possesses a marvelous ability to write about youth in a deep and stirring way, and this aspect of his great talent is on full view in *The Young Guard*.
> A few years went by, and he again disappeared as a writer and again became a bureaucrat . . . Was there really no party member of lesser talent who could have been given the administrative housekeeping?[85]

Sholokhov's assessment, made in such a triumphal and sensitive venue, is all the more startling in the context of the two men's long history of mutual dislike, dating to the RAPP years when Fadeyev stonewalled the publication of *The Quiet River Don*.[86]

When the congress voted for the next Central Committee slate, Fadeyev was demoted to candidate member. This was inevitable given his diminished role in the Writers' Union; it was nonetheless one more in the string of insults by the party to its cadre.

On the congress's final day, Khrushchev gave his famous "secret speech" behind closed doors, exposing Stalin's crimes. Thirty years after RAPP's injunction to "tear off the masks," Khrushchev tore off Stalin's own. The final straw that Fadeyev had reached for to prop up the teetering image of his honor group had collapsed. There were no internal enemies. There was no honorable leader. The honor was draining away from the honor group itself.

Stalin had been the party. The party's break with Stalin showed the corrosiveness of the party conscience Fadeyev had grafted onto his own. His shame spread ever wider as word of Khrushchev's speech, although not reported in the media, spread like wildfire and unleashed a nationwide psychological upheaval expressed in recriminations, self-examination, and a creeping recognition of ubiquitous complicity. On a Sunday afternoon in May, in the Peredelkino dacha that had been one of the instruments of his co-option, Fadeyev, fifty-four, did away with himself.

Earlier that day Fadeyev tended to routine business matters, and the day before he sent a telegram confirming that he would submit an essay "in about ten days." Some of his friends cited this telegram to suggest that his suicide was a spur-of-the-moment decision that could have been prevented. But his behavior in the days prior suggests otherwise. He sought out his closest friends. To Yermilov he sent carbon copies of his secret memos to the party secretariat: "I want you to read them *all*" (*AFPD*, 212; emphasis in original). He visited with the Libedinskys and also with Shub, telling her that his liver was "touch and go," but that his mental condition was worse: he was under a psychiatrist's supervision, feeling urges to throw himself under a train (*AFPD*, 343). In a phone call with his sister on the day he killed himself, he mentioned having had many distressing conversations with writers (*AFPD*, 18).

Disagreement persists over whether Fadeyev did away with himself out of remorse or over the loss of his stature. This is a false opposition. Human actions frequently result from multiple factors. Fadeyev's shrunken status coincided with his public shame; and this time the shame was not of the party's manufacture. It was his own. Slezkine describes this condition, shared by many Bolsheviks, by paraphrasing Yury Trifonov: conscience "keeps flaring up and cooling off."[87]

He shot himself in bed, muffling the sound with pillows.[88] He left a note. It was addressed to the Central Committee. His wife was away on tour; he was discovered by his thirteen-year-old son Misha, who in later life recalled his pain on learning that "there was no note for us."[89] The note was not for his loved ones but for the honor group that for decades had insulted him even as it co-opted him, making the insult that much worse. He meant it for Khrushchev, Malenkov, and Pospelov, into whose hands it would be delivered.

I see no possibility of going on living, because art, to which I have given my life, has been ruined by a self-confidently ignorant party leadership and is now beyond repair. The best literary cadres . . . have been exterminated or have perished thanks to the criminal connivance of those in power; the best literary people have died prematurely; anyone else with even the slightest ability to create anything of true worth has died short of attaining forty or fifty years of age.

Literature—that holy of holies—has been given over for shredding to bureaucrats and the most backward elements of the people, and the "highest" tribunals, like the Moscow conference or the Twentieth Party Congress ring out with a new slogan like a hunter's cry to his dog—tallyho!

Bemoaning the literary genocide, Fadeyev erases Stalin as its author. By generalizing the guilt ("self-confidently ignorant party leadership," "criminal connivance of those in power," "bureaucrats," "backward elements of the people"), he sidesteps Stalin's role and escapes his own culpability. Using the passive voice, he avoids naming Stalin at all. These rhetorical techniques were the tools of his trade, and he made full use of them. The cause of his suicide is not his own behavior but the party's destruction of literature.

The murderer is not Stalin but the honor group that betrayed its trust. The magnitude of that betrayal merits twelve repetitions of words for destruction and death. Here we can recall Fadeyev's rebuttal of Veresayev's attack on censorship. Fadeyev defended censorship by locating the blame for lackluster literature elsewhere (in overzealous editors). The suicide note, too, exhibits Fadeyev's trademark arguing away of the core problem.

The note employs two tonalities. The vocabulary of destruction is in dialogue with a sacralist register that testifies to what has been destroyed. The only thing left of literature, the "holy of holies," is a handful of writers who have preserved a "sacred flame" of creativity. "Sacred," a designation once reserved for the party, has now come loose and attached itself to art, literature, and creativity. What Fadeyev has painstakingly concealed, however, worms its way back in, as implicit suggestion enters into Bakhtinian dialogue with explicit statement:

> Literature—that highest fruit of the new order—has been humiliated, trampled, ruined. The self-satisfaction of the nouveaux riches [who betray] the great Leninist teaching even when they pay homage to it, to that teaching, has led me to completely mistrust them, for one can expect from them even worse than from the satrap Stalin.

Now Fadeyev names Stalin, with the appropriately disapproving epithet "satrap," but he glides over it quickly, even comparing him favorably to the current leaders. As Stalin is now bracketed and beside the point, so Fadeyev's own conscience is also bracketed, safely outside the web of intersecting guilts—Stalin's, the secretaries', his own. He seems not to notice that he, too, is one of the "nouveaux riches" whom he disparages, a son not only of the Communist Party but also of the Soviet aristocracy.

He revisits his humiliation at the orgkomitet plenum after RAPP's demise, which we saw in chapter 2, as if Stalin had had nothing to do with it:

> After Lenin's death, we were brought down low and treated as schoolboys, made into nonentities, threatened with ideology, and told that this was "party-mindedness."

Ignoring Stalin, Fadeyev instead reserves a rhetorical register of righteous indignation for Malenkov, Pospelov, and Khrushchev: "And now, when everything could have been corrected, there is the primitivism and ignorance—with a repulsive dose of smugness—of those who should correct all this." After lamenting the premature deaths of fifteen hundred writers, he still manages to write that "everything could have been corrected"—another bid to clear himself of blame.

Alternating speech registers contrast the party bosses' fatuity with his own ideals. His scornful indignation toward the bosses gives way to a style of exaltation when he describes his youthful idealism. The word "freedom," which for so long he had enclosed in quotation marks to denote its fraudulence, now appears without quotes, elevated.

> What a sense of freedom and the wide world my generation had when it entered literature in Lenin's lifetime, what uncontainable forces we had in our soul and what splendid works we created and could still have created!

Freedom and party mindedness remain antipodes but have exchanged values. In contrast to the passive voice with which he sidestepped Stalin's warping effect on him, now the active voice marks a pre-Stalinist moment of free agency. Most other instances of active voice also occur outside of Stalin's lifetime ("I do not see the possibility of going on living," "art, to which I have dedicated my life," "my life as a writer loses all meaning," "I request to be buried next to my mother"). Fadeyev's active idealism in embracing communism and his final resolve to end his life mark the only times in his professional life when he was a fully active, autonomous agent. They are the frame for captivity to Stalin, a blurred muddle of reaction replacing action, manipulability replacing agency, and obedience corseted by fear, all of it justified by the inexorable march of history.

The description of his earnest teenage commitment continues in an elevated style and then reverts to righteous indignation, part of a continuing alternation between these two tonalities:

> Made for a great literary contribution in the name of communism, bound to the party, the workers, and the peasants from sixteen years of age, endowed by god with an unusual talent . . . I was full of the highest thoughts and feelings that can be born only of the people's life united with the splendid ideas of communism.
>
> But I was turned into a draft horse, my whole life long I trudged along under the weight of untalented, unjustified, innumerable bureaucratic tasks that could have been done by anyone. (*AFPD*, 215–16)

Again he leaves unsaid that it was Stalin who used him in this way.

The alternation of exaltation and bitterness segues into a funeral oration. His self-eulogy must be in the conditional mood, narrating not the life he lived but the life that could have been.

> When I take stock of my life, it is unbearable to recall the whole collection of cries, exhortations, sermons, and just plain ideological flaws that rained down

on me—of whom our glorious nation would have been right to be proud on the strength of the authenticity and inner modesty of my profound communist talent.

The letter ends with a crescendo into spiritual exaltation with liturgical overtones: "With greatest joy [*s prevelikoi radostiu*], as at deliverance [*izbavlenie*] from this heinous existence, where nastiness, lies, and slander rain down upon you, I depart this life."

The moment of death, exalted as a joyous movement from "this life" to a better one, evokes the Orthodox worship service. The intensifying prefix *pre-* and the word *izbavlenie* are both prominent in Orthodox texts; Fadeyev's phrase "this heinous existence" evokes "this earthly existence," another liturgical formulation. With these rhetorical elements, Fadeyev unstitches the liturgical subtext from Bolshevik propaganda and restores it to the relationship between human and God. Like the faithful worshipper who gladly forsakes earthly existence in order to join God, the cadre joyfully leaves behind his corroded existence within the party. He flees to rejoin his mother and return to the values he learned from her. And it is to God (in lowercase, following Soviet practice) that, earlier in the letter, he attributes his literary talent.

The letter, however, does not quite close on this note of exaltation. As he prepares to sign it, he is again overcome by the feeling of indignity: "The last hope was to at least tell this to the people who lead the state, but for three years now, in spite of my requests, they cannot even receive me." In its concluding obsession with insult, Fadeyev's suicide note mirrors the one written a quarter of a century earlier by Mayakovsky, who could not wrench free of RAPP's coercion even in his last thoughts.

Suicide notes are a final word. But the party snatched away even this prerogative. The secretaries took the last word for themselves, crafting a story to cover up a suicide that would cause it endless embarrassment. Fadeyev had died of alcoholism (*AFPD*, 3, 340). It was the ultimate insult.

His shocked friends sought answers. Shub described Fadeyev as "psychically defenseless," adding, "It is impossible to live year after year in an unsettled personal state" (*AFPD*, 345). Yet she persisted in believing that he acted at a "fateful moment" that could have been averted had family and friends been more attentive (*AFPD*, 345). Gerasimova thought otherwise. Fadeyev committed suicide because his sense of communist obligation had led him to act against human conscience (*AFPD*, 306). To her sober understanding, Libedinsky added an emotional note: "Poor Sasha, he did sentry duty his whole life, and it turned out that what he was guarding was the john!"[90] With no record of Yermilov's reaction, we may wonder if his spiteful outburst of 1935 might have come back to haunt him: "Let them commit suicide."

Fadeyev's suicide note contains no confession. It was not for the secretaries, awash in their own guilt, to be his judges. And yet Fadeyev had made a private thumbnail confession. Fittingly, it was to a man of great probity, Kornei Chukovsky, that he made it: "What a scoundrel I am."[91]

Self-Definition after Stalin

WHAT BECAME OF the Writers' Union—and writers themselves—afterward? The year of Fadeyev's suicide, 1956, exposed a fault line in party policy and society itself, one that mirrored Fadeyev's own inner divide. Khrushchev's exposure of Stalin's crimes was followed by Soviet tanks crushing an anticommunist uprising in Hungary, with a death toll in the thousands, a wave of summary arrests, and, in the following years, an estimated four hundred executions.[1] The Soviet leaders had decided that de-Stalinization was not to mean democratization.

How to de-Stalinize without democratizing the Writers' Union became a policy conundrum as a small number of determined writers, at great risk to themselves but no longer fearing arrest, defied censorship and found ways to bring readers their prohibited works. The second half of the Writers' Union's existence was defined by a struggle between a cohort of courageous writers and a hard-line establishment seeking a means to control them short of Stalin-style arrests.

The "sixties generation" who broke into print during the Thaw had a new perspective on self-definition. Unlike their elders, they saw themselves as heirs—"products"—not only of the revolution but also of the terror.[2] Many of those who became figures in the "young poetry" and "young prose" movements, like Vasily Aksyonov and Yury Trifonov, had as children lost their parents to the Gulag. The 1950s and early 1960s saw nationwide debate over collective and individual responsibility for mass arrests.[3] This national meditation on conscience helped writers take back the mantle of moral leadership that was their prerevolutionary heritage. Acts of defiance by writers seeking to publish in any way they could—in the press, underground, or by having their manuscripts smuggled abroad—played out against the leadership's anxious attempts to devise effective controls for a post-Stalin era.

Pomerantsev's essay on the need for sincerity in literature was soon followed by sincere fiction, and *The Thaw* and *Not by Bread Alone* were especially influential in stimulating discussion of individual complicity in the terror. Meanwhile, the Literary Institute was graduating a new generation of writers, and the Writers' Union in 1956 opened a new journal as a platform for this rising generation. It was the brainchild of Valentin Katayev (whom we last saw restraining Stavsky in 1937),[4] and its title, *Youth* (*Yunost*), had a special ring at that moment, conveying a sense of energy and a call to action. *Yunost* joined *Novy mir* as a home for alternatives to socialist realism. Its budding writers wrote not about grand achievements but about young people's private lives. Heroic biography, the backbone of communist identity and socialist realism, was fading as the new generation turned to critical distance and self-deprecating irony. Gone were the idealism that had characterized the first decades of the revolution, the culture of self-transformation, and with them fiction's corollary emphasis on narrating biography. A critical mass of writers followed Pomerantsev's lead, considering socialist realism, as Solzhenitsyn later put it, "a solemn pledge to abstain from truth."[5] And hanging over the Writers' Union for every writer to contemplate were the compromised biographies of the writers who most personified it, Gorky and Fadeyev.

The reformist energy bursting from *Novy mir* and *Yunost* sparked a fervent counterreaction from writers intent on preserving their reputations. They clung to the imagined master biography of the exemplary Bolshevik, as well as the heroic biographies they had created for themselves. Two years after Khrushchev's secret speech, Agitprop and the Writers' Union under Surkov made two moves to thwart the movement for creative freedom. One of these was aimed at a single novel and its author; the other was a structural change to prevent breaches of literary orthodoxy. The "Pasternak affair" of 1958 unfolded just as the Writers' Union created a new branch to represent the Russian Republic.

Let us consider the structural change first. Before 1958, the RSFSR was the only one of the fifteen union republics without its own Writers' Union branch. The reason seems clear: the Writers' Union consisted primarily of writers who wrote in Russian, which was the primary language of Soviet literature and the lingua franca of the Soviet Union. These realities supported a mind-set of Russian hegemony, so that the Writers' Union's central office was equated with the RSFSR. There were, however, regional branches within the RSFSR—Leningrad, Kuibyshev, Orenburg, Ryazan, Sverdlovsk, Vladivostok, Voronezh, and other cities. By far the largest and most liberal was the Moscow branch, home to the most vocal reformers, including Pomerantsev, Ehrenburg, Dudintsev, Tvardovsky, the contributors to the almanacs *Literary Moscow* (*Literaturnaia Moskva*) and *Pages from Tarusa* (*Tarusskie stranitsy*), and many of the most promising young writers.[6] The Russian Republic branch was devised as an ideological counterweight to the threat posed by the Moscow branch, which now became a subordinate entity within it. The idea seems to have come from Sobolev, longtime chair of the

Writers' Union's selection committee. To maximize the number of conservative and compliant members, admission standards were kept low.[7]

The other signal literary event of 1958 was the Nobel Prize for literature awarded to Pasternak, one year after the surprise publication in Italy of his forbidden novel *Dr. Zhivago*. Pasternak had submitted his manuscript to *Novy mir* and other journals in the spring of 1956. When no one would publish it, he had it smuggled out of the Soviet Union. Not since Zamiatin's and Pilniak's works thirty years earlier had a forbidden book seen publication on the outside. Pasternak's conscious decision to seek publication abroad went to the heart of literary identity and personal ethics—and not only his own. It presented an enormous question for each of his contemporaries to answer for themselves. What if the only way to reach readers was to become a scofflaw, risk harming oneself and one's family, alienate colleagues, neighbors, and the reading public, endure a ruined reputation, and possibly be banished from one's homeland? Eventually, many of the country's best writers would decide to accept these consequences.

Pasternak's wrenching decision did not fully solve the problem. His most essential readers—Soviet readers—still could not read the book. Now it was clear that censorship's target was not only writers. It was equally readers. There was a bitter irony in having recognition come from readers outside Russia who had not suffered through the events that inspired the novel, and who could not even read it in its own language.

The Soviet press branded Pasternak a traitor and confirmed much of the public in that opinion. Having given both his hero, Yury Zhivago, and the revolution an unacceptable biography, Pasternak was made to decline the Nobel and was swiftly expelled from the Writers' Union. Some writers found excuses to miss the expulsion meetings,[8] and the Literary Institute's open letter denouncing Pasternak was signed by only a third of its students as the rest gave the slip to the administrators making the rounds for signatures.[9]

The person most responsible for the harassment campaign against Pasternak was apparently Surkov, who responded to Khrushchev's request for advice by describing Pasternak as undeserving of any leniency.[10] For the rest of its existence, the Writers' Union remained under the control of the Stalinist old guard, like Surkov, or erstwhile literary liberals, like Fedin, whose actions were now dictated by the need to protect the high position they had attained. Fedin's and Simonov's retreat into self-protection can be seen in *Novy mir*'s rejection letter to Pasternak, signed by its entire editorial board: "As people who take a position diametrically opposed to yours, naturally we take the view that there can be no question of publishing *Dr. Zhivago* in the pages of *Novy mir*."[11] The wording was provided by Agitprop—almost certainly by Polikarpov, who, having been removed from his Writers' Union post in 1946 to mollify angry writers, was now in a position of even greater literary oversight. In giving the letter such a highly personalized tone, Polikarpov was binding Simonov and Fedin. What they were signing went beyond rebuffing a manuscript. It was a personal profession of an implicit "position" that could be understood only as a party vow, and it forever placed them in opposition to Pasternak and his literary heirs.

Surkov's advice was disastrous. The Politburo was unprepared for the storm of international outrage over Pasternak's clearly forced refusal of the prize. Khrushchev and his colleagues learned the hard way that in their rivalry with the capitalist democracies, they would need to find a path between hard controls and progressive social image. The party now had a self-image problem of its own, created by its responses to Hungary and Pasternak. Khrushchev replaced Surkov with Fedin.

While remaining a firm brake on writers, the Writers' Union did take steps to end the flagrant disregard of its statutes that had prevailed under Stalin. It held congresses regularly every five years and revised its statutes, specifying in greater detail how the governing bodies would operate. The Third Writers' Congress in 1959 eliminated the presidium, which had never operated according to the statutes, and increased the secretariat to about thirty members, incorporating representatives from each of the union republics.[12] To distance itself from the irregularities of the Stalin years, the union also started numbering its plenums anew, starting in 1959 with what it called the first plenum.[13]

If the "first thaw" ended with the Pasternak affair, a "second thaw" was ushered in with the Twenty-Second Party Congress in October 1961, which moved to wipe Stalin's image from the public eye with a decree removing his body from its place alongside Lenin in the mausoleum and his name from the city that symbolized Soviet heroism, Stalingrad.[14] With Khrushchev intent on furthering de-Stalinization, the time was ripe for the next literary breakthrough. It was not an act of defiance but a special arrangement with Khrushchev himself. Tvardovsky, now back at the helm of *Novy mir*, brought him Solzhenitsyn's manuscript of *A Day in the Life of Ivan Denisovich* (*Odin den Ivana Denisovicha*), in a shrewd move born of a hunch of good chemistry between its fictional hero and the Soviet leader. With Khrushchev's approval, *Novy mir* in November 1962 published the first description ever of life in the Gulag.

This victory sparked a backlash. The book's revelations, and the public's hunger to read it, dismayed the party leadership, which organized a series of face-to-face confrontations meant to shame and demoralize the liberal intelligentsia. A triumphal avant-garde art opening at the Manege across from the Kremlin was derailed by a visit from the Politburo, whose officials strafed the artists with slurs and invective. Three months later, on March 7, 1963, the Kremlin hosted a conference for some two thousand writers and intellectuals, making sure that reformers would be outnumbered by hard-liners. The keynote speaker was Stalin's favorite, Vasilevskaia, who with her writer husband, Korneichuk, topped the official literary elite. She used her speech to cast as suspicious two of the leading literary lights of the younger generation, Aksyonov and Andrei Voznesensky.[15]

Yermilov, too, joined the battle. This cadre who had averted the Gulag through Stalin's backhanded patronage was once again tucked away in a sleepy research post at the Gorky Institute of World Literature, this time alongside Gronsky, who since returning from the Gulag had become one of his many accusers. Yermilov took on Ehrenburg, whose *People, Years, Life* (*Liudi, gody, zhizn*) had for three years been appearing serially in *Novy mir*. Ehrenburg identified a code of silence through which everyone was respon-sible for abetting the terror, and he acknowledged that his own participation in that code made him complicit in the culture of arrest and therefore in the deaths of innocent people. His willingness to point the finger at himself pro-voked spirited public discussion and introspection. His memoir, along with *Dr. Zhivago* and Solzhenitsyn's books, was instrumental in giving people a framework and vocabulary for reflecting upon Stalin's repressions.[16]

Yermilov now wrote in *Izvestiia* that there had been no code of si-lence but simply people who believed in Stalin, and he claimed that there were many instances of people defending someone "who they were sure was not an enemy."[17] This argument of course was meant to reflect on Yermilov himself, as though he had always acted on good intent. His implication, as Kozlov has pointed out, was that since he had acted out of communist dedi-cation, he was more honorable than Ehrenburg, who by his own admission did know of abuses but kept silent. Invoking Tolstoy's famous profession of conscience, "I cannot keep silent," he cast Ehrenburg as its cowardly antith-esis. In a cynical bid to appear as a reformer, he included praise for *A Day in the Life of Ivan Denisovich*. Kozlov has discerned the Stalinist subtext of Yermilov's declaration that "Ehrenburg simplifies the tragedy." It was a tacit reference to a *Pravda* smear article of 1945 headlined "Comrade Ehrenburg Simplifies."[18]

Like Fadeyev, Yermilov had written to the party leaders advocating greater literary freedom (*AFPD*, 212). It is important to recall, too, his private reactions before 1937 to the degradation of literature at the hands of ide-ology and to the party's capricious volte-face judgments, as in the campaign against Shostakovich. With the moment of possibility finally arrived, he was too morally compromised to join the reformers because the battle for litera-ture was also about ethics. Yermilov's cheering the exposure of Stalin's crimes and joining the chorus of horror at the mass arrests was a gambit for public consumption. In the Stalin years, the lover of literature had allowed himself to be strangled by the power-seeking cadre; in the Thaw years, Yermilov remained a Stalinist (while trying to disguise that fact) not out of conviction but because to reassess that era would have meant confronting his own culpability, one so enormous that it would have destroyed his sense of self. Kozlov makes a similar point about a reader who composed a closely argued philippic against Pasternak: "His protest . . . was so furious because it was a desperate defense of his own emotional and intellectual stability."[19]

Many readers saw through Yermilov's argument and responded indignantly.[20] Among writers he was already an outcast. One story goes that a sign in front of his dacha, BEWARE OF MEAN DOG, attracted a bit of graffiti scratched in with a nail: UNSCRUPULOUS, TOO. (The sign quickly disappeared.)[21] The members of the Academy of Sciences reportedly refused to confirm his nomination in 1955.[22] Upon his death in November 1965, the Writers' Union arranged a ceremony for its most dependable critic; not a single writer showed up.[23]

Yermilov lived long enough to have the satisfaction of seeing reform stamped out and the old guard resurgent. For this he might have credited Fedin, who as a young writer had crafted his identity in the Serapion Brotherhood's creed of literary independence. As Writers' Union head, he now was tested by other writers' pursuit of that same independence, especially in the notorious trials of Iosif Brodsky, Andrei Sinyavsky, and Yuly Daniel. In 1964, the twenty-three-year-old Brodsky was tried on a charge of parasitism. Brodsky listed his occupation as poet, but the court refused to recognize him as one since he was not credentialed—he had not attended the Literary Institute and did not belong to the Writers' Union. He was sentenced to exile and hard labor. The next year, Sinyavsky and Daniel received labor-camp sentences for having their critiques of Soviet power published abroad. The argument used against them in court (where one of the prosecution witnesses was Yudin) was taken from Stalin's playbook: showing Soviet shortcomings played into the hands of the country's enemies—in effect, treason. Like Surkov before him, Fedin advocated harsh measures, even when there was little or no pressure to do so. Reportedly, when Brezhnev asked Fedin whether Sinyavsky and Daniel might be dealt with through the Writers' Union instead of a court trial, Fedin said no.[24] It is hard to understand such advice as anything but vengefulness.

The young writers who had broken into print during the Thaw now found that no journal or publishing house would touch them. But banned writers and hungry readers sought one another out. Book lovers with typewriters and carbon paper brought underground works to intelligentsia readers, and samizdat, the literary underground, was born. Solzhenitsyn's description of the underground writer reminds us of Bourdieu's pure artist: "The underground writer's enormous advantage is the freedom to write as he likes: he needs to keep neither censors nor editors in his mind's eye, nothing confronts him except his material, nothing hovers anxiously over him except the truth."[25] The vibrancy of the underground force field highlighted the anemia of literary journals and bookstores. Samizdat works began to appear abroad, smuggled out at the initiative either of the author or of anyone with a carbon copy. Foreign publishers could print any of these works without the author's permission, because the Soviet Union was not a signatory to the Universal Copyright Convention.

A decade of public and private soul-searching had bred a segment of readers who were skeptical of the Soviet press. More important perhaps in the eyes of the Soviet leaders, European intellectuals sympathetic to the Soviet Union were scandalized by the literary trials. Sinyavsky and Daniel's trial became public knowledge in October 1965, a month after it had ended. As the regime was facing condemnation from its own intelligentsia and the outside world, it suddenly received validation from an improbable quarter: that year's Nobel Prize went to Sholokhov. Like Fedin and Simonov, Sholokhov had become a reliable loyalist, making his Nobel a triumph for the party and an important redress of the Pasternak affair. The Nobel committee, intentionally or not, injected itself into the Soviet national reconsideration of individual, collective, and state accountability. Pasternak's and Sholokhov's awards were followed by Solzhenitsyn's in 1970 and Brodsky's in 1987. These awards were cause for reflection upon individual agency, both as a contribution to an ethical society and as an essential factor in literary greatness. These writers joined their countryman Ivan Bunin, who received the Nobel in emigration in 1933, as the Writers' Union's orgkomitet was doing its work.

The trial of Sinyavsky and Daniel had raised the specter of renewed arrests of writers, but the international outcry caused party leaders to seek other means to neutralize troublemakers. One of these was psychiatric institutionalization. Those subjected to this abuse included Valery Tarsis, whose candid report to Stavsky in 1937 on the dysfunction in the Kiev union branch we saw in chapter 4. In 1962–63 Tarsis, who had circulated his work in samizdat, spent seven months in a psychiatric hospital at Khrushchev's order. Later he was stripped of his citizenship.

The party leaders also sought more moderate means of controlling willful writers. By 1967 five stages of corrective action had been defined: (1) a warning, (2) a severe warning, (3) a public rebuke, (4) a reprimand noted in the record, and (5) a severe reprimand with warning noted in the record.[26] As the dissident and human rights movements took shape, there were writers who resisted all these measures. They were expelled from the Writers' Union and usually had their citizenship revoked. Those expelled and publicly disgraced with shame biographies were in fact the most principled and courageous writers of their era: Lidiia Chukovskaia, Aleksandr Galich, Efim

Etkind, Naum Kozhavin, Vladimir Maksimov, Yevgeny Popov, Feliks Svetov, Georgy Vladimov, Vladimir Voinovich, Viktor Yerofeyev, and the Ukrainian literary critics Ivan Dziuba and Mykola Lukash. Nekrasov, too, was among them, three decades after his *In the Trenches of Stalingrad* helped spark a movement for literary honesty. The emigration of writers who were stripped of Soviet citizenship or who made their own choice to leave divided Soviet Russian literature into that published at home and that published in Western outlets like the journals *Grani, Kontinent* in Germany and Ardis Publishing in the United States.

While the five-stage warning system was being developed, the Writers' Union had to field another challenge. In May 1967, just days before the Fourth Writers' Congress was to open, delegates received an open letter from Solzhenitsyn. He called on the congress to abolish censorship and require the Writers' Union to defend its members from persecution. It was not only individual writers who needed protection, he argued, but the whole of Russian literature, which was failing to live up to its past. Describing the confiscation of his manuscript of *In the First Circle* (*V kruge pervom*) by the security organs (in the year of the Sinyavsky-Daniel trial), he enjoined his colleagues to support the publication of *Cancer Ward* (*Rakovy korpus*) and his other banned works.[27]

Solzhenitsyn had submitted *Cancer Ward* to *Novy mir*. Tvardovsky, caught between the author and the Central Committee secretaries, countered Solzhenitsyn with restraining arguments such as he himself had once received from Fadeyev (and he experienced similarly snide treatment from the secretaries as had Fadeyev).[28]

The dynamic between Solzhenitsyn, the congress organizers, who refused to put the letter on the agenda, and Writers' Union members suggests that the force field in which most literary business was transacted remained quite stable in spite of the underground. Eighty-five writers, or 6 percent of the Writers' Union membership, signed an open letter supporting Solzhenitsyn. Another fifteen writers sent Solzhenitsyn private letters of support,[29] bringing the total number of his supporters to about 7 percent. This number—one hundred—is remarkably similar to the number of writers who were the main targets of censorship in the 1930s. How many others secretly agreed with him is another question. The Moscow branch's prose section recommended *Cancer Ward* for publication, but the RSFSR branch recommended against it and refused Solzhenitsyn's requests to disavow defamatory rumors about his military service.[30]

Solzhenitsyn's letter quickly became a cause célèbre outside the Soviet Union, prompting the Writer's Union secretariat to meet with him and Tvardovsky. Fedin, Surkov, Korneichuk, Riurikov, and Simonov were all on the secretariat at this time. Both sides appear to have approached the meeting as a negotiation. Solzhenitsyn had a card to play. *Cancer Ward* was already circulating in samizdat; if it were not published at home, one of the samizdat copies could easily find its way to a Western publisher, and the capitalist democracies would score another victory, pointing to yet another example of the USSR's restrictions on creative freedom. Solzhenitsyn's point was that samizdat had made it impossible to control where a manuscript ended up.

The only one of the secretaries to recommend publishing it—with major cuts—was Simonov. He also favored having the Writers' Union publicly repudiate the false rumors about Solzhenitsyn, and he was alone in this as well. He joined his colleagues in adamantly opposing publication of *In the First Circle*.[31]

Since the security services had confiscated the manuscript of *In the First Circle*, and since it was clear that the Writers' Union secretaries had read it, the connection between the Writers' Union and the security apparatus was exposed. This linkage was made clearer still in the meeting's bizarre aftermath. The manuscript was sent to Germany. Only the KGB could have sent it, because there were no samizdat copies. The party leaders were building a case against Solzhenitsyn as a traitor. He was expelled from the Writers' Union in 1969. The Soviet Union joined the copyright convention in 1973. This act was taken not to protect Soviet writers but to protect the party from the embarrassment of having any more banned works appear in the West. Solzhenitsyn was deported the following year. An open letter in *Pravda* against Solzhenitsyn and the dissident physicist Andrei Sakharov was signed by thirty-one writers, including Surkov, Sofronov, and Aleksandr Chakovsky, but painfully also Fedin, Sholokhov, Simonov, and Tikhonov.[32]

Solzhenitsyn's demand that the Fourth Congress take up the question of the Writers' Union's obligation to act as advocate for its members did not go entirely unheeded. A new charter approved by the Fifth Congress in 1972 contained a provision allowing for the Writers' Union to be dissolved by a resolution of the congress.[33]

The Thaw generation now tried to bring samizdat literature aboveground. Five writers solicited contributions for a literary almanac to be published without a censorship process. When the Writers' Union refused to lend its support, they presented the manuscript, *Metropole* (*Metropol*), and its twenty-three authors at a public opening. The volume's preface stated, "All who wish to [read this book] are invited to do so with a clear conscience."[34] For their own act of conscience, the editors and contributors were condemned by the authorities, and several of them eventually emigrated.

Thirty years after Fadeyev's memos to the party leadership, a new generation of leaders under Mikhail Gorbachev reached the same conclusion. In 1986, as Gorbachev and his head of Agitprop, Aleksandr Yakovlev, were proclaiming glasnost, the Writers' Union held its eighth and final congress. By now the membership had reached 9,561, about half of whom wrote in Russian. The proportion of members with higher education had increased to 80 percent. Not everyone, therefore, had gone through the Literary Institute, and writers still complained that standards were too low.[35]

Fifty-two percent of members had begun their literary activity after 1954. This group, whose literary beginnings dated to the Thaw or after, might be expected to be a groundswell of liberalism. The Thaw generation proudly defined themselves as *shestidesiatniki* (the sixties generation), invoking the 1860s generation that challenged the tsars' repression. However, members older than fifty accounted for 65 percent, a number that could suggest a strong base of conservatism. Just under 60 percent of members belonged to the Communist Party or Komsomol.[36]

Gorbachev and Yakovlev counted on the younger demographic in reaching out to writers to renegotiate the alliance that had been Stalin's essential prop beneath the Writers' Union. They offered political reform and literary renewal. The promise of the Thaw was revived as *Novy mir* under Sergei Zalygin set about publishing as many formerly suppressed works as it could, by Akhmatova, Grossman, Zamiatin, and others. *Ogonyok* under Vitaly Korotich regularly published revelations of literary politics under Stalin.

As liberal writers took Gorbachev's outstretched hand, the Writers' Union secretaries dug in their heels. Its first secretary, Georgy Markov, cast his lot with Gorbachev's Politburo opponents.[37] In the ensuing battle, the Moscow organization, home to two thousand Writers' Union members,[38] recovered its independent status and immediately granted membership to Tatyana Tolstaya, whose application had been turned down by the RSFSR branch. The Leningrad organization also gained independence.[39] These changes became irrelevant when the Soviet Union wrote itself out of existence in December 1991.

Gronsky passed away at the age of ninety in August 1985 on the eve of glasnost and perestroika. He was more successful than Yermilov in refurbishing his reputation. When the Gulag nightmare ended, Gronsky had returned to the project of communist autobiography, beginning with his own rehabilitation petition. This autobiographical character reference was a pragmatic necessity, the only way to regain entrance to society at even the most basic level of obtaining living quarters and an income.[40] For Gronsky, the petition was also the first step in the larger project of reclaiming and reliving his Bolshevik biography. In public lectures glorying over his years at Stalin's side, and in personal conversation recounting his labor-camp experiences, he projected an image of himself as decisive and effective, the result of Bolshevik forging. Thus begins his self–character reference for rehabilitation:

Imprisonment did not break me either physically or morally. I came out of the camps a convinced communist just as I was before, just as you knew me. I came out entirely healthy and fit for work. Solid, revolutionary party temper-ing gave me the strength to endure and overcome the ordeal.[41]

Gronsky's pride in surviving the Gulag was indeed tied to his com-munist identity, which he had embraced as a young man and for which he had suffered imprisonment under tsarist rule. But more than this, Gronsky managed, in his own mind, to integrate his camp experience with his Bolshe-vik character. His account of himself as an effective agent of camp reform during his time inside the Gulag was published by another camp survivor, the historian Anton Antonov-Ovseyenko, to whom he told his story.[42] In this way, Gronsky successfully added another chapter to his communist auto-biography, wiping away the image of degraded weakness attached to being a prisoner and substituting a strong-hero identity.

Gronsky reestablished his reputation by Bolshevizing his prison ex-perience. But even the most impassioned defense of life as a *zek* was in-sufficient to sustain a self-image as a Bolshevik of achievement. For this Gronsky also had to depend on his status during the time when he enjoyed Stalin's favor. This meant recalling and revalidating his actions from that time, not only to himself but publicly. These self-validating reminiscences included, for example, his pride in his ability to "sniff out" enemies like Mirsky, who "smelled of counterrevolution."[43] Such characterizations are not wholly consistent with the mission he took upon himself to aid the reha-bilitation of numerous terror victims. Preserving one's belief in Soviet com-munism given the mass arrest of innocents meant acknowledging Stalin as an abuser who usurped the cause. But Gronsky still needed Stalin in his autobiography.

In some way, Gronsky smoothed out the wrinkle caused by sewing to-gether his glory days with Stalin and his work to rehabilitate the illegally re-pressed (starting with his brawling brother-in-law poet Vasilyev) (*RT*, 292–93). Unlike Fadeyev, he does not appear to have done so in order to assuage a guilty conscience. The fact of having himself been wronged somehow wiped out his own guilt. Not to be forgotten is Gronsky's instigation of Kliuev's hor-rible death. Had Gronsky not been arrested, he would have done the cadre's bidding and continued as a perpetrator of the regime's excesses. His own long stint as a *zek*, however, by turning him into a victim, endowed him with a kind of moral authority. The aura that accrued to him he could reattach to his continuing belief in Stalinism, and he exited life a firm communist of the Stalinist persuasion. In 1937, in 1954, and presumably through the mid-1980s, Gronsky could feel that his personal identity, the party's identity, and the country's identity constituted a united front. Conscience, the universal moral guide that is supposed to unite all humanity, turns out, disturbingly, to be different for each one of us.

To live under political repression is to be in some way constantly aware of one's conscience, even when that awareness takes the form of denial. When we argue with that inner voice; when we win the argument with it; even when we repress it, we are not free of it. The writers who burst the boundaries of socialist realism after Stalin did so however they could, and their writings saw daylight in a haphazard confusion of ways, spilling out of the liberal journals into the literary underground and leaking beyond the borders of the country itself. The artistic and moral imperatives reasserted themselves, not only for the writers who left their homeland but also for those who remained. What mattered was taking ownership of one's own conscience, resolving never to delegate it to anyone, whether a leader, an honor group, or a cherished cause. More than politics, more even than love, conscience is the deepest part of our identity.

Notes

INTRODUCTION

1. Akishina, *Povsednevnaia zhizn' sovetskikh pisatelei*, 118.

2. Mandelstam, *Hope Against Hope*, 135.

3. Shentalinsky, *Arrested Voices*, 187; Maksimenkov, *Sumbur vmesto muzyki*, 236.

4. Khlevniuk, *Politbiuro*, 65–68; cited in Clark, *Moscow, the Fourth Rome*, 81.

5. Fitzpatrick, *Commissariat of the Enlightenment*, 2; Clark, *Moscow, the Fourth Rome*, 29; but Clark also acknowledges that Stalin "took over stewardship of culture" for much of the 1930s (9).

6. The party began to make reference to the "Soviet writer" as early as 1924; see Schull, "Ideological Origins," 480. "Cliquishness" was used commonly in the period when the Writers' Union was being organized; see, for example, *SLNE*, 121.

7. Slezkine, *The House of Government*, 852–55.

8. Clark, *Moscow, the Fourth Rome*, 350.

9. Bourdieu, *The Rules of Art*, 9. For applications of Bourdieu's theory across the non-Russian Soviet republics, see Jurguteinė and Satkauskytė, *Literary Field*.

10. Clark, *Moscow, the Fourth Rome*, 245.

11. *ONI* 1: 215.

12. Including 553 candidate members; *VSP*, 79. But in 1946 Vishnevsky casually cited a figure of 5,000; see Protokoly (presidium and secretariat; Jan. 19–June 30, 1946), RGALI, f. 631, op. 15, ed. khr. 768, l. 24.

13. Shentalinsky, *Arrested Voices*, 6. RAPP, the largest literary group before the creation of the Writers' Union, claimed to have five thousand members, although this list may have been padded with names of factory workers whose recruitment into literature was a product of wishful thinking. Antonov-Ovseenko, *Vragi naroda*, 290, gives a figure of six hundred repressed writers.

14. Batkin, "Son razuma," 47.

15. The point is made in Rayfield, *Stalin and His Hangmen*, 110.

16. Fromm, *Psychoanalysis and Religion*, 35–40.

17. Halfin, *Terror in My Soul*, 51–52.

18. Clark, *Moscow, the Fourth Rome*, 103–4; see also Fitzpatrick, *Everyday Stalinism*, 71–75.

19. Clark, *Moscow, the Fourth Rome*, 56.

20. Getty, *Pragmatists and Puritans*, 14, states that officials of the Party Control Commission alienated party members with their imperious manner.

21. Clark, *Moscow, the Fourth Rome*, 58, 77.

22. Hellbeck, *Revolution on My Mind*, 86; cited in Clark, *Moscow, the Fourth Rome*, 223.

23. Clark, *Moscow, the Fourth Rome*, 158, 162.

24. Slezkine, *House of Government*, 847, 857.

25. Hellbeck, *Revolution on My Mind*, 410n51.

26. Slezkine, *House of Government*, 847.

27. Slezkine, *House of Government*, 850.

28. See Bion, *Experiences in Groups*, 63–66; Markus and Kitayama, "Cultures and Selves"; Taylor, *Pride, Shame, and Guilt*, 56.

29. Bourdieu, *The Rules of Art*, 7–8.

30. Paperno, "What Can Be Done," 567.

31. Naiman, "On Soviet Subjects," 311.

32. On Stalin's reading of new literary works, see Ermolaev, *Censorship in Soviet Literature*, 35, 39, 40, 72. On his involvement in literature in the 1930s, see "K istorii partiinoi politiki," and Gronskii, *Iz proshlogo . . . Vospominaniia*, 136–62; for the 1940s, see Kapitsa, "Eto bylo tak," and Levonevskii, "Istoriia 'Bol'shogo bloknota.'" Clark, *Moscow, the Fourth Rome*, 9, writes that Stalin "took over stewardship of culture" for much of the 1930s. Maksimenkov, *Sumbur vmesto muzyki*, 52, points out that Stalin gave literature his personal attention even when he delegated authority in matters such as the economy and defense.

33. Libedinsky, "O Fadeeve," 248.

34. Markus and Kitayama, "Cultures and Selves"; Tajfel and Turner, "Social Identity Theory"; Taylor, *Pride, Shame, and Guilt*, 26.

35. Garrard and Garrard, *Inside the Soviet Writers' Union*.

36. Lekmanov, *Zhizn' Osipa Mandelshtama*, 206.

37. *MMN*, 268.

38. Shentalinsky, *Arrested Voices*, 198.

CHAPTER ONE

1. Shentalinskii, *Raby svobody*, 54.

2. K. Tomas, "Za konsolidatsiiu kommunisticheskikh sil proletarskoi literatury," *Pravda*, Dec. 4, 1929; cited in Brown, *Proletarian Episode*, 262.

3. Libedinskaia, "Takaia vot istoriia," 268. On Soviet suicides, see Pinnow, *Lost to the Collective*, and Grigorii Chkhartishvili, *Pisatel' i samoubiistvo*.

4. With the exception of E. N. Permitin, noted in Sheshukov, *Neistovye revniteli*, 282.

5. Brown, *Mayakovsky*, 353; Jangfeldt, *Mayakovsky*, 548; Vatulescu et al., *The Svetlana Boym Reader*, 61.

6. Jangfeldt, *Mayakovsky*, 505.

7. The term "national Bolshevism" was Riutin's; see Brandenberger, *National Bolshevism*, 6.

8. Shentalinskii, *Prestuplenie bez nakazaniia*, 504.

9. Or more accurately, VAPP (Vsesoiuznaia assotsiatsiia proletarskikh pisatelei, the All-Union Association of Proletarian Writers). This name was dropped after 1927 in favor of the name RAPP, which had previously denoted a single regional group within VAPP. To avoid confusion, I use the name RAPP to refer to the national association. Under party auspices it organized regional branches where it could, including in Siberia, the North Caucasus, Ukraine, and Azerbaijan.

10. Zhukov, *Fadeev*, 330.

11. Fadeyev, *Materialy i issledovaniia* (1984), 419.

12. Plekhanov's characterization, as cited in Gregor, *Totalitarianism and Political Religion*, 93.

13. The confluence of party duty and literary aesthetics is articulated in Simonov, *Izbrannoe*, 2:387.

14. Kozlov, *Readers*, 279.

15. Maguire, *Red Virgin Soil*, 87, 397–402.

16. Schull, "Ideological Origins," 475.

17. *VKI*, 56; see also Brown, *Proletarian Episode*, 43–45.

18. Beginning in 1920, communist groups like Proletkult, Kuznitsa, and LEF, even while maneuvering to become the leader of literature, had disputed the party's right to control their literary program. Schull, "Ideological Origins," 471, notes Proletkult's attempt in 1920 to gain independence from the Commissariat of Enlightenment. The resistance to the 1925 resolution was led by Ilya Vardin and Semyon Rodov; see *MMN*, 46–52, and Brown, *Proletarian Episode*, 48–49.

19. *MMN* 48, 58, 167; Sheshukov, *Neistovye revniteli*, 297.

20. Sheshukov, *Neistovye revniteli*, 323, 335; *FP* 1973, 62. Sutyrin had previously headed the Zakavkazsky *kraikom* press section.

21. The term "cadres" in reference to RAPP is Averbakh's; see his speech to the first plenum of the Writers' Union *orgkomitet* in *SLNE*, 116; on the "purity" of Marxist literature, see 140. The "literary cell" reference was made by Fadeyev; see his speech in *SLNE*, 125.

22. Fadeyev did not have sole control over *October* but was chief editor at various times.

23. Sheshukov, *Neistovye revniteli*, 331; note also *SLNE*, 131. Among the nonparty figures whom RAPP attacked were Anna Akhmatova, Eduard Bagritsky, Andrei Bely, Aleksei Chapygin, Ehrenburg, Sergei Esenin, Konstantin Fedin, Gorky, Leonid Leonov, Aleksandr Malyshkin, Osip Mandelshtam, Mayakovsky, Boris Pasternak, Pilniak, Mikhail Prishvin, Sergei Sergeyev-Tsensky, Shaginian, Viacheslav Shishkov, Mikhail Sholokhov, Aleksei Tolstoy, Zoshchenko, and critics like Eikhenbaum, Pereverzev, Shklovsky, Vikenty Veresayev, and Voronsky.

24. Sheshukov, *Neistovye revniteli*, 300.

25. A. K. Voronskii, *Literaturnye portrety* (Moscow: Federatsiia, 1929), 279–80; cited in Sheshukov, *Neistovye revniteli*, 265–66. For Voronsky these were not negative features.

26. Slezkine, *The House of Government*, 954.

27. Sheshukov, *Neistovye revniteli*, 279. Litfront, for example, promoted Bezymensky's drama in verse, *The Shot (Vystrel)*, whose schematic characters the Onguardists derided as facile markers of "good" and "bad."

28. Sheshukov, *Neistovye revniteli*, 302; "Opiat' o 'masse' i lichnosti," *NLP*, no. 17 (1928): 14. Kirshon made a similar charge during the feud among RAPP leaders in 1932; see *VP*, 314–15.

29. See social identity theory on in-group and out-group models in Tajfel and Turner, "Social Identity Theory." The authors also note that as the sense of interdependency increases, so does group members' tendency to treat members of the outgroup as undifferentiated members of a group rather than as individuals (279). On group belonging in the Soviet context, see Adler, *Keeping Faith*, 27.

30. Serebrianskii, "Novaia li zemlia?," 174.

31. Usievich, "Za chistotu Leninizma," 177.

32. Yermilov's characterization in *Pravda*, Mar. 9, 1930; cited in Brown, *Mayakovsky*, 359.

33. *SLNE*, 67, 68, 155. On Voronsky's rejoinders to RAPP's attacks, see Maguire, *Red Virgin Soil*, 409–10.

34. Schull, "Ideological Origins," 482. The largest member groups were VAPP, the All-Russian Union of Writers (Vserossiiskii soiuz pisatelei or VSP), formed by intelligentsia writers in 1920 to defend their interests), and the All-Russian Society of Peasant Writers (Vserossiiskoe obshchestvo krestianskikh pisatelei, or VOKP); smaller groups like Kuznitsa, LEF, Pereval, and the Constructivists were also included. Brown, *Proletarian Episode*, dates FOSP's inception to December 27, 1926.

35. On Voronsky's removal, see Maguire, *Red Virgin Soil*, 183–85. Yermilov edited *Young Guard* from 1926 to 1928. Fadeyev edited *October* in 1929–32, with Yermilov and Stavsky on the editorial board; from at least 1930, *Red Virgin Soil* was edited first by Fadeyev and then Yermilov.

36. "Ob obsluzhivanii knigoi massovogo chitatelia," Dec. 28, 1928, in *VKI*, 88. On the April support, see Brown, *Proletarian Episode*, 53.

37. Including Mikhail Bakhtin, Budantsev, Abram Efros, Eikhenbaum, Konstantin Fedin, Sergei Gorodetsky, Vsevolod Ivanov, Veniamin Kaverin, Mikhail Kozakov, Mayakovsky, Pereverzev, Pilniak, Andrei Platonov, Prishvin, I. Rudin, Shklovsky, Aleksei Tolstoy, Semyon Utkin, Nikolai Zabolotsky, Yevgeny Zamiatin, Zoshchenko, and others. On the trials as part of Stalin's bid to destroy the opposition, see Khlevniuk, *Politbiuro*, 34.

38. L. Maksimenkov, "Meierkhol'd and His World (1929–1940)" (lecture, University of Toronto, Mar. 2007).

39. Shentalinsky, *Arrested Voices*, 160.

40. Zhukov, *Ruka sud'by*, 28.

41. Halfin, *Terror in My Soul*, 47–48, 223.

42. Sheshukov, *Neistovye revniteli*, 280.

43. Makarov and Makarova, *Vokrug "Tikhogo Dona,"* suggests that with collectivization dominating the news, the depiction of the Red Army's brutal putdown of the Cossack insurrection could have been seen as an Aesopian criticism of dekulakization. The halt in publication was unrelated to accusations of plagiarism; at Sholokhov's insistence, RAPP formed a commission (headed by Stavsky) to investigate and found the accusation groundless. RAPP's published exoneration can be found in *TS*, 375.

44. Sholokhov, *Pis'ma*, 54.

45. Kolodnyi, *Poety i vozhdi*, 267–68. Stalin's letter is dated July 9, 1929.

46. In *LG*, Oct. 7, 1929, quoted in *TS*, 397.

47. Sheshukov, *Neistovye revniteli*, 327.

48. "Gazeta pisatelei," *LG*, Apr. 22, 1929. Tellingly, the first issues of *Literaturnaia gazeta* do not list members of an editorial board.

49. Shklovskii, "Perepiska pisatelei," *LG*, Apr. 22, 1929.

50. Eikhenbaum, *Moi vremennik*, 59.

51. Chukovskii, *Dnevnik, 1901–1929*, 430.

52. The VSP, one of the main constituent groups within FOSP.

53. "Chto takoe soiuz pisatelei?" 1–3, and "Ko vsem chlenam Vserossiiskogo soiuza pisatelei," 2–3. See also *TS*, 386. It is unclear whether this action was an order from outside or taken at RAPP's initiative.

54. Platonov, "Usomnivshiisia Makar"; *SF*, 815–16.

55. Fadeyev told a friend that Platonov's story had "slipped by him," a comment that suggests that he had not read it and that either the issue had already been submitted for censorship approval before his appointment or that the decision to publish it was made in Fadeyev's absence by a subordinate editor, perhaps Vsevolod Ivanov, the fiction editor. This supposition is reinforced by Fadeyev's further remark that, as a result of the flap over "Makar," *October*'s editorial

board was afraid to make any decisions without him. See A. Fadeev, "Literatura i zhizn'," in *Sobranie sochinenii v 7-i tomakh* (Moscow: Khudozhestvennaia literatura, 1959–61), 4:304.

56. Averbakh, "O tselostnykh masshtabakh i chastnykh Makarakh," *Oktiabr'*, no. 11 (1929): 164–71; *NLP*, nos. 21–22 (1929): 10–17; *Pravda*, Dec. 3, 1929, reprinted in *APVS*, 256–65.

57. Seifrid, *Andrei Platonov*, 11. The two coauthored the satirical *Central Black Earth* (*Che-Che-O*).

58. Platonov, "Pervyi Ivan," 159–68.

59. Seifrid, *Andrei Platonov*, 137, citing Vladimir Vasilev, *Andrei Platonov* (Moscow: Sovremennik, 1982), 132, says the trip was funded by *Red Virgin Soil*. *APVS*, 281n, suggests it was Federatsiia.

60. Viacheslav Polonskii, "Moia bor'ba na literaturnom fronte." The incident is described slightly differently in Browning, *Boris Pilniak*, 33.

61. *APVS*, 284. Three other internal reviews are also published on 282–84.

62. Maksimenkov, *Sumbur vmesto muzyki*, 245.

63. Maksimenkov, *Sumbur vmesto muzyki*, 245.

64. Sheshukov, *Neistovye revniteli*, 267.

65. Sheshukov, *Neistovye revniteli*, 260.

66. Sheshukov, *Neistovye revniteli*, 275–88; Efim Dobin, "Rozhdenie geroia Iu. Libedinskogo," *LG*, May 12, 1930, and the following issue.

67. Sheshukov, *Neistovye revniteli*, 289–90.

68. Sheshukov, *Neistovye revniteli*, 322–23. The opponents, Aleksandr Bezymensky, Anna Karavayeva, Aleksandr Serafimovich, and the journalist Taras Kostrov were outvoted by Yermilov, Fadeyev, Kirshon, Libedinsky, Selivanovsky, Shushkanov, and Sutyrin.

69. See, for example, Libedinskii, "Neskol'ko slov o Pereverzeve," 17–22, and Georgii Gorbachev, "Raskol v pereverzevtsakh," 185–206. The Pereverzevites included Communist Academy professors Bespalov, Valery Druzin, Mikhail Gelfand, Aleksandr Zonin, S. R. Babukh, Ulrikh Fokht, [Viktor?] Kin, Gennady Pospelov, and Vasily Sovsun. Their Litfront allies included Georgy Gorbachev, Bezymensky, Semyon Rodov, and Vishnevsky.

70. "Protsess Prompartiia i literatura," 45. Those mentioned were Jack Althausen, Konstantin Fedin, Yury Olesha, Boris Pilniak and Ilya Selvinsky.

71. Brown, *Proletarian Episode*, 214. See, for example, Kor, "Ne poputchik, a soiuznik ili vrag," 39–40.

72. "Kakoi nam nuzhen pisatel'?" *NLP*, no. 6: 32–46.

73. "Kakoi nam nuzhen pisatel'," *NLP*, nos. 20–21 (1931): 59; cited in Dobrenko, *Making of the State Writer*, 379.

74. "Kakoi nam nuzhen pisatel'," *NLP*, nos. 20–21 (1931): 59; cited in Dobrenko, *Making of the State Writer*, 380.

75. His response can be found in *APVS*, 286–87.

76. Polonsky did not believe Fadeyev's claim that he had not been the one to approve the story. He thought that Fadeyev printed the story in an attempt to raise the quality of *Red Virgin Soil* to what it had been under Voronsky; see *APVS*, 272.

77. Fadeev, "Ob odnoi kulatskoi khronike," 209.

78. Halfin, *Terror in My Soul*, 52.

79. Stalin's comment to Molotov and others, "you are blind like kittens," points up another effect of his brand of charisma: infantilization. Compare Stalin's image to Hitler's "Führer myth [of] piety, devotion, and steadfastness" described in Koonz, *The Nazi Conscience*, 22.

80. On the history of this phrase, see Brown, *Proletarian Episode*, 82–84.

81. Fadeev, "Ob odnoi kulatskoi khronike," 206.

82. *FP* 1973, 45. An abbreviated version of this letter appeared as a story after Fadeyev's death: "O liubvi," *Iunost'*, no. 9 (1957), and in *Komsomol'skaia pravda*, Sept. 8, 1957.

83. A follow-up article, A. Selivanovskii, "V chem 'somnevaetsia' Andrei Platonov," *LG*, June 10, 1931, says nothing about doubt in spite of its title. Selivanovsky likely consulted Fadeyev's piece while working on his own assignment.

84. Fadeev, *Sobranie sochinenii* (Moscow: Khudozhestvennaia literatura, 1971), 410.

85. Erenburg, *Liudi, gody, zhizn'* 3:127; cited in Torchinov and Leontiuk, *Vokrug Stalina*, 511. Fadeyev's mother was not a member of the Communist Party.

86. Yermilov to Fadeyev, Apr. 19/20, 1935. Yermilov's letters to Fadeyev are housed in RGALI, f. 1628, op. 2, ed. khr. 712, ll. 97–171 (letters dated before Mar. 12, 1936), and ed. khr. 713, ll. 1–23 (letters dated from Mar. 12, 1936). Further citations are given by date in the text.

87. Fadeyev, *Sobranie sochinenii v 7-i tomakh*, 7:109–11; cited in Kiseleva, *Fadeev-Khudozhnik*, 5; emphasis in original. The letter, to Pavlenko, is dated Oct. 24, 1936.

88. Platonov, "Mne eto nuzhno ne dlia 'slavy,'" 175.

89. *Gor'kii i sovetskie pisateli*, 313. Gorky's reply is dated September 18, 1929.

90. *Gor'kii i sovetskie pisateli*, 314.

91. Platonov, "Mne eto nuzhno ne dlia 'slavy,'" 177. The letter is dated July 24, 1931.

92. Platonov, "Mne eto nuzhno ne dlia 'slavy,'" 177.

93. Platonov, "Mne eto nuzhno ne dlia 'slavy,'" 178.

94. Galushkin, "Andrei Platonov—I. V. Stalin—'Literaturnyi kritik,'" in *SF*, 816.

95. Platonov, "Mne eto nuzhno ne dlia 'slavy,'" 180.

96. Platonov, "Mne eto nuzhno ne dlia 'slavy,'" 180. The letter is dated May 23, 1933.

97. Platonov, "Mne eto nuzhno ne dlia 'slavy,'" 183.

98. Dobrenko, *Making of the State Writer*, 226.

99. Shentalinsky, *Arrested Voices*, 257; Gronskii, *Iz proshlogo . . . Vospominaniia*, 22.

100. M. Gor'kii, "Esli vrag ne sdaetsia—ego unichtozhaiut," *Pravda*, Nov. 15, 1930, and M. Gor'kii, "Esli vrag ne sdaetsia—ego istrebliaiut," *Izvestiia*, Nov. 15, 1930; cited in Yedlin, *Maxim Gorky*, 191. Gorky's feuilleton, in particular its title, became an instant icon of Soviet culture, invoked by Stalin during World War II and used as the title of a film (in a different context) more than fifty years later, *Esli vrag ne sdaetsia . . .* (directed by Timofei Levchuk, 1982). On Stalin's use of the phrase, see Stalin, *O velikoi otechestvennoi voine sovetskogo soiuza*, 86–87.

101. For this and other utopian influences on Gorky, see Agursky, "Occult Source of Socialist Realism," 247–72. Gorky's utopianism knew no bounds. He imagined Soviet science achieving human immortality; see Agurskii, "Velikii eretik," 61, and Gorky's brief allusion to victory over death in A. M. Gor'kii, "O temakh," in *Sobranie sochinenii v 30-i tomakh*, 27:106. Stalin played to Gorky's utopianism, agreeing to fund the immortality project through an important research center, the Institute of Experimental Medicine, founded in 1890 by Prince Oldenburgsky; see Basinskii, "Stalin, Gor'kii, i bessmertie." Stalin reorganized the institute; see "Fifty Years of Soviet Experimental Biology and Medicine."

102. Quoted in Vaksberg, *Murder of Maksim Gorky*, 193. On Gorky's religious thought more generally, see Agurskii, "Velikii eretik."

103. Halfin, *Terror in My Soul*, 12. Kotkin, *Magnetic Mountain*, 226, notes, "Much like Christianity's message regarding the circumstances of life in the next world, Marxism-Leninism in power appeared to embody the triumph of the underdog, and the historical vanquishing of injustice—but here, in this world."

104. Brodskii, *Solovki*, 320; Solzhenitsyn, *Gulag Archipelago*, 62–63.

105. Gorky, *Selected Letters*, 324.

106. Kotkin, *Magnetic Mountain*, 231.

107. Festinger, *Theory of Cognitive Dissonance*; Christopher T. Burris, Harmon-Jones, and Tarpley, "By Faith Alone"; van Veen, Krug, Schooler, and Carter, "Neural Activity."

108. Rayfield, *Stalin and His Hangmen*, 215–16.

109. Rayfield, *Stalin and His Hangmen*, 216.

110. Gorky, *Selected Letters*, 302.

111. Shentalinsky, *The KGB's Literary Archive*, 203–4.

112. The 5,000 figure was stated by Fadeev; see *MMN*, 662.

113. Garrard and Garrard, *Inside the Soviet Writers' Union*, 241.
114. Sheshukov, *Neistovye revniteli*, 299.
115. Dobrenko, *Making of the State Writer*, 324–25, 331.
116. Kurilov, "Gor'kii i Vechernii rabochii literaturnyi universitet (VRLU)," 268.
117. Dobrenko, *Making of the State Writer*, 332.
118. Dobrenko, *Making of the State Writer*, 332.
119. V. P. Stavskii, "Zapisnaia knizhka," 1924–1935, RGALI, f. 1712, op. 2, ed. khr. 56, l. 2.
120. Dobrenko, *Making of the State Writer*, 369.
121. Dobrenko, *Making of the State Writer*, 370.
122. Dobrenko, *Making of the State Writer*, 326; V'iugin, *Politika poetiki*, 122.
123. See, for example, "Privetstvie vtoromu plenumu pravleniia RAPP'a. Tapp'u nado pomoch'," *NLP*, no. 18 (1929): 1.
124. Tucker, *Stalin in Power*, 70; for an example of RAPP's appropriation of this term, see A. Selivanovskii, "Sistema koshek (O poezii N. Zabolotskogo)," *NLP*, no. 15 (1929): 32. RAPP's plenums are described in "K plenumu pravleniia RAPP," *NLP*, no. 15 (1929): 1–3, and "Rezoliutsiia plenuma pravleniia RAPP po dokladu tov. L. Averbakha," *NLP*, no. 9 (1931): 1–6.
125. Sheshukov, *Neistovye revniteli*, 305. Panfyorov's group had its own artistic platform and included Vladimir Bil-Belotserkovsky, Boris Galin, Boris Gorbatov, Vasily Ilyenkov, Yakov Ilyin, Aleksandr Isbakh, G. Kish, Ioann Novich, Lev Ovalov, and Mikhail Platoshkin. In a blow to the Onguardists, the much-admired Serafimovich supported Panfyorov's group.
126. Sheshukov, *Neistovye revniteli*, 306.
127. Sheshukov, *Neistovye revniteli*, 303.
128. Sheshukov, *Neistovye revniteli*, 308–9. The *Pravda* article appeared on Nov. 24, 1931.
129. See Averbakh, "O perestroike RAPP," 6–13; L. Averbakh, "Za leninskuiu partiinost' tvorcheskogo metoda," 172.
130. See the excerpt from his speech to writers in October 1932 in *ONI* 1.
131. Averbakh, "Za leninskuiu partiinost'," 172. Besides Trotsky and Voronsky, Averbakh named G. Lelevich, Ilya Vardin, Pereverzev and his adherents, those who had challenged RAPP for control of the proletarian literary magazine *Growth* (Aleksandr Bek, Lidiia Toom, and the Georgian literary critic Platon Kikodze), and various groups, including Kuznitsa, LEF, and Litfront. See also "Kruzhok rabochei kritiki 'Rost'," 19–20.
132. Averbakh, "Za leninskuiu partiinost'," 169–70.
133. Averbakh, "Za leninskuiu partiinost'," 172.
134. Petr Pavlenko, "Tvorcheskaia diskussiia v VSSP," 141.
135. An allusion to the adolescent protagonist of *The Minor* (*Nedorosl*) by Denis Fonvizin (1744–1792).

136. Pavlenko, "Tvorcheskaia diskussiia v VSSP," 142.

137. Pavlenko, "Tvorcheskaia diskussiia v VSSP," 145.

138. Pavlenko, "Tvorcheskaia diskussiia v VSSP," 142, 148.

139. Vaksberg, *Murder of Maksim Gorky*, 307–8, makes a case for Gorky's involvement in approaching Kirov about this possibility.

140. Makarov and Makarova, *Vokrug "Tikhogo Dona,"* 96–99.

141. Reportedly, Stalin remarked that the novel's third volume would appeal to émigré White Guards, and Sholokhov passed this test by countering that they would have poor satisfaction indeed, since the novel portrayed their defeat. Fadeyev had ignored a June 3 letter from Gorky urging publication; see Sholokhov, *Pis'ma*, 66. Ermolaev, *Mikhail Sholokhov*, 31, confirms the July meeting date.

142. Sheshukov, *Neistovye revniteli*, 316. *MMN*, 128, refers to an archival document suggesting Averbakh may have known about the dissolution as early as January and even been involved in brainstorming it.

143. Sheshukov, *Neistovye revniteli*, 318.

144. Sheshukov, *Neistovye revniteli*, 314–15; see also V'iugin, *Politika poetiki*, 128.

145. Sheshukov, *Neistovye revniteli*, 337.

146. "K istorii partiinoi politiki," 149.

147. "K istorii partiinoi politiki," 149; Ivan Gronskii, "Vospominaniia ob A. M. Gor'kom," Sept. 21, 1963, AG, MoG-3-25-5, l. 17.

148. Sheshukov, *Neistovye revniteli*, 337.

149. Ivan Gronskii, "Stenogramma besedy na temu 'Gor'kii i Stalin' i 'Gor'kii i kul't lichnosti'," Sept. 28, 1963, AG, MoG-3-25-6. Gronsky gives Stalin's words as a direct quote, although presumably he was giving them as he remembered them thirty-one years later.

150. Shentalinsky, *Arrested Voices*, 261.

151. Tucker, *Stalin in Power*, 212.

CHAPTER TWO

1. Sheshukov, *Neistovye revniteli*, 317.

2. Sheshukov, *Neistovye revniteli*, 320. A RAPP leadership meeting on May 2, 1932, included Averbakh, Benito Buachidze, Fadeyev, S. Fridman, Mikhail Luzgin, Makaryev, Selivanovsky, Mark Serebriansky, Stavsky, and Aleksei Surkov.

3. As phrased in Subotskii, "O khode perestroiki literaturnykh organizatsii," 169; see also Iudin, *Ob ustave soiuza sovetskikh pisatelei*, 25–32, and "K istorii partiinoi politiki," 144.

4. "Iz protokola № 107 zasedaniia Orgbiuro TsK VKP(b)," *MMN*, 139; *NLP*, nos. 13–14 (May 1932): 2.

5. *MMN*, 139, gives the complete list. The claim about Fadeyev is made in *MMN*, 93.

6. *NLP*, nos. 13–14 (May 1932): 2. The presidium's other members were Gronsky, Kirpotin, Panfyorov, Malyshkin, Leonov, Tikhonov, and candidate members Pavlenko and Aseyev. In the fall of 1932 and the summer of 1933, the *orgkomitet* came to include Gorky (chair), Stetsky (Agitprop's chief), Averbakh, Aseyev, Makaryev, Panfyorov, Pavlenko, Serafimovich, Stavsky, Subotsky, Yermilov, and Yudin.

7. *NLP*, nos. 13–14 (May 1932): 2, reported the following composition of the RSFSR (Rossiiskaia Sovetskaia Federativnaia Sotsialisticheskaia Respublika) *orgkomitet* (the composition of the all-union *orgkomitet* was announced in August). From the VSSP, Leonov, Pavlenko, Malyshkin, Nikolai Ognyov, Ivanov, Vladimir Lidin, Inber, and Lidiia Seifullina. From RAPP, Averbakh, Kirshon, Fadeyev, Aleksandr Bezymensky, Aleksandr Serafimovich, Panfyorov, Stavsky, Fyodor Gladkov, Illesh, and Sholokhov. From Pereval, Ivan Katayev, Boris Guber, and Nikolai Zarudin. From ROPKP (Rossiiskaia Organizatsiia Proletarsko-Kolkhoznykh Pisatelei), Semyon Podyachev, Aleksei Demidov, Pyotr Zamoisky, Aleksei Dorogoichenko, Ivan Shukhov, Efim Permitin, Ivan Makarov, Ivan Batrak, Andrei Semyonov. From LOKAF (Literaturnoe Obyedinenie Krasnoi Armii i Flota), Leonid Degtiarev, Ivan Novikov-Priboi, Selvinsky, and Vladimir Lugovskoi. Also included were Nikolai Aseyev, Afinogenov, Vladimir Bakhmetyev, Feoktist Berezovsky, V. N. Bill-Belotserkovsky, Ivan Zhiga, Slonimsky, Tikhonov, Konstantin Fedin, and Mikhail Chumandrin.

8. Antonov-Ovseenko, *Vragi naroda*, 171. The Cheka was the political police.

9. Service, *Stalin*, 263–64, observes that Stalin "surrounded himself with persons such as Molotov and Kaganovich who shared his assumptions, and he promoted others who could be trained to internalize them (or to go along with them out of ambition or fear)."

10. *SLNE*, 52–53. The reported number of factory circles in Moscow increased from 62 (of which only 28 were active), to 116 (of which 79 were active). Whether the *orgkomitet* really increased the number of literary circles or was counting circles that already existed was questioned by Kirshon; see *SLNE*, 196.

11. *SLNE*, 190; Dobrenko, *Making of the State Writer*, 339.

12. *VKI*, 182. In fact the resolution, while referring to a single institute, gave rise to two, one offering an academic program and the other a research facility. The academic program was located at 25 Tverskoi Boulevard (Herzen House) and was initially called the Moscow Evening Workers' Literary University. In 1936 its name was changed to the A. M. Gorky Literary Institute (Literaturny Institut imeni A. M. Gorkogo). The research institute, located at 25a Povarskaia ulitsa, was originally named the Maxim Gorky Literary Institute (Literaturnyi

Institut imeni Maksima Gor'kogo); in August 1934 it was renamed the Maxim Gorky Institute of Literature (Institut Literatury imeni A. M. Gor'kogo); in 1938 it was given its present name, the Maxim Gorky Institute of World Literature (Institut Mirovoi Literatury imeni A. M. Gor'kogo), when the theoreticians at *Literaturnyi kritik*, who argued for connections between Soviet literature and European, or "world literature," were influential.

13. Dobrenko, *Making of the State Writer*, 342.

14. Dobrenko, *Making of the State Writer*, 325.

15. *PVSSP*, 663. The first ninety writers were admitted on May 13, 1934; see Fleishman, *Boris Pasternak*, 167, and Smith, *D. S. Mirsky*, 355.

16. Dobrenko, *Making of the State Writer*, 395–96.

17. These figures come from putting together the information Yudin supplied to Zhdanov and those he gave in his public report at the first congress. One hundred three belonged to the Komsomol and 438 were party members; see *PVSSP*, 663, and *ONI* 2: 248.

18. *PVSSP*, 663, gives the following membership figures: RSFSR 1,535, Ukraine 206, Georgia 158, Belorussia "about 100," Armenia 90, Azerbaijan 79, Turkmenia 26. Altstadt, *Politics of Culture*, 200, gives the figure for Azerbaijan on January 1, 1937, right before the purge reached that branch as 65.

19. On Germany, see Barbian, "Literary Policy," 167–70. Since each German state had its own culture ministry, the creation of the central Propaganda Ministry in 1933 caused turf wars; see Steinweis, *Art, Ideology*, 63–64. Culture officials like Alfred Rosenberg, although shunted to minor posts, got Goebbels to take a harder line by accusing him of laxity. Steinweis, *Art, Ideology*, 34–41, notes that officials from various agencies, often with warring agendas, intervened in literary policy. Other organizations like Strength through Joy, the National Socialist Culture Community, and the German Art Society also fought for control; even the Economics Ministry insisted on a role in the arts. The Reich Culture Chamber was itself created to prevent the Nazi trade union organization, the German Labor Front, from wresting control of culture workers from the Propaganda Ministry; see Barbian, "Literary Policy," 166.

20. Hitler had to insist on this in the face of opposition from officials like Goering; see Steinweis, *Art, Ideology*, 33. Steinweis also notes that the law establishing the culture chambers was passed with difficulty, over the objections of several ministers (42).

21. Steinweis, *Art, Ideology*, 62.

22. Steinweis, *Art, Ideology*, 40; Barbian, "Literary Policy," 180. Clinefelter, *Artists for the Reich*, 101, notes that Hitler did personally select works for the Great German Art exhibitions, but only because he was appalled by so many of the submissions.

23. Steinweis, *Art, Ideology*, 44.

24. Clinefelter, *Artists for the Reich*, 60.

25. Barbian, "Literary Policy," 172–73, 177.

26. Steinweis, *Art, Ideology*, 43.

27. Barbian, "Literary Policy," 180.

28. Ermolaev, *Censorship in Soviet Literature*, 77, notes that from 1932 to 1941 the censorship eliminated from literary works deprecatory remarks about the intelligentsia.

29. *VKI*, 755. The *orgkomitet* itself first met on May 26, 1932.

30. Sheshukov, *Neistovye revniteli*, 314.

31. Bourdieu, *The Rules of Art*, 82.

32. Bourdieu, *The Rules of Art*, 83.

33. Eikhenbaum, *Moi vremennik*, 58.

34. "Obespechim vse usloviia tvorcheskoi raboty literaturnykh kruzhkov," *LG*, May 23, 1932, contains the first printed mention of the term.

35. And is largely corroborated by Shentalinskii, *Raby svobody*, 347.

36. Dobrenko, *Making of the State Writer*, 357.

37. Troyat, *Gorky*, 22.

38. Gorky to Shcherbakov, Feb. 19, 1935, AG, PG-rl 55-1-5, l. 2; Gor'kii, "K proektu programm dlia litkruzhkov," 1935, AG, LSG 9-18-2, l. 1.

39. The idea of transformation was not, of course, the exclusive province of socialist realism and its adherents. For a discussion of avant-garde artists' embrace of transformation through Bolshevism, see Groys, *Total Art*, 19–23. Groys points out the irony that avant-garde artists, by insisting on a close connection between politics and art, paved the way for socialist realism.

40. Gorky, *Selected Letters*, 315–16.

41. Zhukov, *Ruka sud'by*, 151.

42. Dobrenko, *Making of the Soviet Writer*, 361.

43. Fitzpatrick, *The Cultural Front*, 5.

44. Yedlin, *Maxim Gorky*, 132.

45. Yedlin, *Maxim Gorky*, 193.

46. *SL*, 158. Ogryzko, "Gromila sovetskoi literatury," asserts that it was Yermilov who recommended including "Session on Laughter"; but Averbakh got in trouble for it; see *MMN*, 224.

47. Vaksberg, *Murder of Maxim Gorky*, 286.

48. Dobrenko, *Making of the State Writer*, 401, notes that the censorship was directed mainly at some one hundred old intelligentsia writers, including Shaginian, Leonov, Fedin, Aleksei Tolstoy, Pavlenko, Aseyev, and Selvinsky.

49. Dobrenko, *Formovka sovetskogo chitatelia*, 116–23.

50. Dobrenko, *Formovka sovetskogo chitatelia*, 103, 110–11.

51. "Postanovlenie Politburo TsK VKP(b) o likvidatsii monopol'nykh prav teatrov na postanovku p'es," *VKI*, 185. The resolution listed Konstantin Trenev's *Liubov Yarovaia*, Afinogenov's *Fear (Strakh)*, Kirshon's *Bread (Khleb)* and *The Rails Are Humming (Relsy gudyat)*, and Gorky's *Yegor Bulychev*. The di-

rectorate's chair was Abel Yenukidze, head of the Central Executive Committee; the other members were Voroshilov, Andrei Bubnov (the head of Narkompros [Narodny komitet prosveshcheniia]), Shmidt, and Aleksandr Smirnov. Afinogenov's and Kirshon's plays made it onto the list despite their unwillingness to accept RAPP's demise.

52. *SLNE*, 23. These included Fadeyev's *The Rout*, Panfyorov's *Whetstones*, Sholokhov's *Virgin Soil Upturned* (*Podniataia tselina*), Leonov's *Skutarevsky*, Vsevolod Ivanov's "Journey to a Nonexistent Country" ("Puteshestvie v stranu, kotoroi net"), and Tikhonov's "War" ("Voina").

53. "K istorii partiinoi politiki," 151, 163.

54. Usievich, "Za chistotu Leninizma," 170. Usievich was Feliks Kon's daughter and had traveled with Lenin on the armored train that carried him back into Russia in 1917 courtesy of the Imperial German Army high command.

55. "V plenu burzhuaznogo literaturovedeniia," *LG*, Aug. 23, 1932; cited in Fadeev, *Materialy i issledovaniia*, 510–12, which also refers to a similar article in a Smolensk newspaper. Fadeyev defended himself in A. Fadeev, "Nebol'shoe pouchenie," *LG*, Sept. 17, 1932.

56. Sheshukov, *Neistovye revniteli*, 318–19.

57. Yermilov's speech of October 1932 in *SLNE*, 181, and Yermilov to Fadeyev, Sept. 11, 1932, show that one month before that speech, Yermilov and Fadeyev had not broken with Averbakh.

58. "Soiuznik ili vrag, i gde u nas glavnaia opasnost'," *LG*, Oct. 11 and Oct. 17, 1932; "Khudozhestvennaia literatura i voprosy kulturnoi revoliutsii," *LG*, Oct. 23, 1932; "Zadachi marksistsko-leninskoi kritiki," *LG*, Oct. 23, 1932; and "O sotsialisticheskom realizme," *LG*, Oct. 29 and Nov. 11, 1932.

59. Koonz, *The Nazi Conscience*, 13.

60. Mosse, *Nazi Culture*, xxiv.

61. Personal communication with Lidiia Libedinskaia, Moscow, May 1997. Fadeyev himself used to tell this story to close friends.

62. Sheshukov, *Neistovye revniteli*, 326.

63. Fadeyev, "Khudozhestvennaia literatura i voprosy kul'turnoi revoliutsii," *LG*, Oct. 23, 1932.

64. For example, Taylor, *Pride, Shame, and Guilt*, 85, notes, "The person [in a shame culture] . . . accepts [the authority's] verdicts as correct and binding. What the authority pronounces to be wrong must not be done."

65. Etkind, "Soviet Subjectivity."

66. For analysis of these group behaviors, see Markus and Kitayama, "Cultures and Selves," 423, 425, and Tajfel and Turner, "Social Identity Theory," 283–84.

67. *SLNE*, 9. The uncorrected transcript of Gronsky's address in *MMN*, 169, makes harsh statements omitted in the published transcript; for example, "hostile parts of the intelligentsia" that had existed until recently. Gronsky had no qualms

about catapulting Kliuev into exile and his manuscripts into oblivion with a single telephone call to Yagoda at the OGPU; see Shentalinsky, *Arrested Voices*, 198.

68. Ronen, "Inzhenery chelovecheskikh dush," 393–94. Similarly, Zhdanov's description in 1946 of Akhmatova as "half nun, half harlot" was a paraphrase from Eikhenbaum's 1923 book, *Anna Akhmatova*, where it was not used in a negative sense; see Any, *Boris Eikhenbaum*, 258.

69. *ONI* 2: 247. Later she did join the Writers' Union.

70. *SLNE*, 195. When, in response to these cries of indignation, a voice from the floor suggested that he could be reeducated, another voice called out that he would be reeducated "at his grave" (161). Only Aleksandr Tarasov-Rodionov dared to point out that RAPP's leadership did nothing to help Klychkov reeducate himself (176). Klychkov's speech momentarily unified communist writers, who defended themselves and RAPP as well.

71. Antipina, *Povsednevnaia zhizn' sovetskikh pisatelei*, 188. On Althausen's unusual biography, see Rina Lapidus, *Young Jewish Poets Who Fell as Soviet Soldiers in the Second World War* (London: Taylor and Francis, 2014), 8–30.

72. Antipina, *Povsednevnaia zhizn' sovetskikh pisatelei*, 183–89.

73. Fleishman, *Pasternak v tridtsatye gody*, 131–32. The epigram is printed in *RT*, 41: "O, muza, segodnia vospoi Dzhugashvili / sukina syna. / Uporstvo osla i khitrost' lisy / sovmestil on umelo. / Narezavshi tysiachi tysiach petel', / nasiliem k vlasti probralsia. / Nu chto zh ty nadelal, kuda ty zalez?—rasskazhi mne, / Seminarist nerazumnyi."

74. Fleishman, *Pasternak v tridtsatye gody*, 134–35; Gor'kii, *Neizdannaia perepiska s Bogdanovym*, 295–96.

75. Sarnov, *Stalin i pisateli*, 31.

76. Ruder, *Making History for Stalin*, 87–88; Ruder notes that after Yagoda's arrest most copies of the volume were removed from public circulation and placed in special repositories.

77. Writers' laudatory letters to Yagoda following their canal trip can be found in *MMN*, 260–61. Gorky's closeness to the Sverdlov family may explain his benevolent attitude toward Averbakh. In 1932, when journals were reorganized and given new editorial boards, Averbakh was left out; see "Iz protokola 115 zasedaniia sekretariata TsK VKP(b)," June 22, 1932, in *MMN*, 144. Gorky, however, included Averbakh in various projects.

78. Ruder, *Making History for Stalin*, 48.

79. Ruder, *Making History for Stalin*, 50.

80. Avdeenko, *Nakazanie bez prestupleniia*, 24, 30.

81. Fadeev, "Literatura i zhizn'," in *Sobranie sochinenii v 5-i tomakh*, 4:124.

82. Platonov, "Mne eto nuzhno ne dlia 'slavy,'" 180–81.

83. As to how Alymov, a prisoner who was put to work building the canal, also came to be one of the authors who contributed to the 1933 volume, see Gnetnev, "Belomorkanal."

84. Avdeenko, *Nakazanie bez prestupleniia*, 102–3.
85. Avdeenko, *Nakazanie bez prestupleniia*, 104–5.
86. Avdeenko, *Nakazanie bez prestupleniia*, 111–12.
87. Avdeenko, *Nakazanie bez prestupleniia*, 179.
88. Bion, *Experiences in Groups*, 94.
89. Nikita Khrushchev, Speech to 20th Congress of the C.P.S.U., Nikita Khrushchev Reference Archive, https://www.marxists.org/archive/khrushchev/1956/02/24.htm.
90. Avdeenko, *Nakazanie bez prestupleniia*, 133.
91. "Postanovlenie SNK RSFSR 'O stroitel'stve "gorodka pisatelei,"'" *SL*, 162–63. Berelowitch, "Peredelkino," 203.
92. Berelowitch, "Peredelkino," 206.
93. Gorky to Nikolai Nakoriakov, Feb. 24, 1936, RGALI, f. 631, op. 15, ed. khr. 136, l. 4.
94. Marchenkov et al., *Ulitsa Kachalova*, 6/2, 75.
95. Muzei-kvartira A. M. Gor'kogo, Moscow, explanatory notes inside the residence.
96. Torchinov and Leontiuk, *Vokrug Stalina*, 487.
97. Berelowitch, "Peredelkino," 205–6. Lovell, "Making of the Stalin-Era Dacha," cites 1.5 million rubles allotted for the first thirty dachas, which was followed by additional funding for further dacha construction (2 million rubles in 1936 for dachas outside Moscow and Leningrad).
98. Berelowitch, "Peredelkino," 207. The Nashchokina building was ready in 1933; the Lavrushinsky building around 1937.
99. Berelowitch, "Peredelkino," 209.
100. Blium, *Sovetskaia tsenzura*, 275.
101. Lobov and Vasil'eva, *Peredelkino*, 529, 533.
102. *RT*, 230–31.
103. Lobov and Vasil'eva, *Peredelkino*, 34; Torchinov and Leontiuk, *Vokrug Stalina*, 486.
104. Lobov and Vasil'eva, *Peredelkino*, 117.
105. Lobov and Vasil'eva, *Peredelkino*, 115.
106. Lobov and Vasil'eva, *Peredelkino*, 59.
107. M. Gor'kii, "Po povodu odnoi diskussii," *LG*, Jan. 28, 1934. Gorky used the phrase against Panfyorov again (this time *slovesnyi brak*) while the congress was in session; see M. Gor'kii, "Otkrytoe pis'mo A. S. Serafimovichu," *LG*, Feb. 14, 1934. The third installment of *Whetstones* was praised in B. Reznikov, "Novye liudi kolkhoznoi derevni (O tret'ei knige *Bruskov* F. Panferova)," *Pravda*, Jan. 13, 1934, 4; cited in Fleishman, *Pasternak v tridstatye gody*, 158.
108. Rubtsov, *Alter ego Stalina*, 59.
109. M. Gor'kii, "O boikosti," *LG*, Feb. 28, 1934; cited in Fleishman, *Pasternak v tridstatye gody*, 159.
110. See Vaksberg, *Murder of Maksim Gorky*, 301–2; this is also the under-

standing of the museum staff at Riabushinsky House. Yedlin, *Maxim Gorky*, 206, does not describe this variant but notes what appear to be various attempts to cover up the circumstances of Max's death.

111. On May 15; see *ONI* 2: 245.

112. Taubman, *Khrushchev:*, 77–78. On the Kirov assassination, see Knight, *Who Killed Kirov?*.

113. Robin, *Socialist Realism*, 10, cautions against retrojecting the events surrounding Kirov's assassination onto the writers' congress, which took place in a more relaxed atmosphere. But Stalin often thought ahead, and it seems clear that the congress was part of a longer-term strategy.

114. On February 22; see Fleishman, *Pasternak v tridtsatye gody*, 131, 160.

115. Fleishman, *Pasternak v tridtsatye gody*, 161.

116. By contrast *Pravda*, which had been purged of oppositionists in November 1930, remained so; see Rubtsov, *Alter ego Stalina*, 62.

117. See Smith, *D. S. Mirsky*, 267; Fleishman, *Pasternak v tridtsatye gody*, 186.

118. *PVSSP*, 700. Some of the more notable nonparty delegates to the congress, besides Gorky, were Avdeyenko, Aseyev, Babel, David Bergelson, Chukovsky, Efros, Eisenstein, Ehrenburg, Fedin, Itzik Fefer, Olga Forsh, Yevgeny Gabrilovich, Yury German, Kuzma Gorbunov, Ivanov, Ilyin, Ilya Ilf, Inber, Veniamin Kaverin, Lev Kassil, Katayev, Nikolai Kharitonov, Semyon Kirsanov, Lev Kvitko, Mikhail Kozakov, Boris Kornilov, Boris Lavrenyov, Leonov, Vladimir Lidin, Vladimir Lugovskoi, Perets Markish, Samuil Marshak, Nikolai Nikitin, Lev Nikulin, Aleksei Novikov-Priboi, Olesha, Pasternak, Konstantin Paustovsky, Pilniak, Nikolai Pogodin, Prishvin, Panteleimon Romanov, Aleksandr Romm, Boris Romashov, Vissarion Saianov, Seifullina, Selvinsky, Sergeyev-Tsensky, Shaginian, Maria Shkapskaia, Shklovsky, Yevgeny Shvarts, Slonimsky, Leonid Sobolev, Mikhail Svetlov, Tikhonov, Tolstoy, Konstantin Trenev, Tretyakov, Aleksandr Tvardovsky, Tynianov, Iosif Utkin, Vikenty Veresayev, Iosif Yuzovsky, Zazubrin, Zelinsky, and Zoshchenko. Ehrenburg and Tikhonov, who served as liaisons to Western organizations, may have remained nonparty at the party's own behest; see Krasnov, *Vvedenie v konstitutsionnoe pravo*, 36. Utkin, although listed as nonparty, had built his career through the Komsomol, in which he held important posts.

119. Ruder, *Making History for Stalin*, 86.

120. *VKI*, 236, 762. See also Makin, "Nikolai Kliuev."

121. Others, including Klychkov, did intercede for him, and he was later transferred to Tomsk.

122. Dobrenko, *Making of the State Writer*, 374–75; *PVSSP*, 235–36.

123. Hellbeck, *Revolution on My Mind*, 302.

124. Pavlenko, on hearing from Tikhonov of the ideas he planned to put forth in his formal address, advised him to stick with approved formulations; see P. A. Pavlenko, "Iz pisem k drugu (N. S. Tikhonov)," *Znamia*, no. 4 (1968): 135; cited in Fleishman, *Pasternak v tridtsatye gody*, 186.

125. Rayfield, *Stalin and His Hangmen*, 222.

126. Gorky, *Selected Letters*, 295; *PVSSP*, 574.

127. See Robin, *Socialist Realism*, 20–25; and Fleishman, *Pasternak: tridt-satye gody*, 203–15.

128. *PVSSP*, 479–503. He attacked Russian Formalism as an example of the latter. This was unfair, but a necessary exercise in self-protection.

129. Medvedev, *Nikolai Bukharin*, 84; cited in Robin, *Socialist Realism*, which argues that Bukharin would not have perceived the applause as dangerous.

130. *PVSSP*, 524, 537, 549, 557; see also *VKI*, 230–31.

131. *VKI*, 231–32. The letter is undated; the editors date it Aug. 31–Sept. 1, 1934. Zhdanov shared Gorky's view that communist writers' speeches were inferior to those of nonparty writers; see *VKI*, 231.

CHAPTER THREE

1. *VKI*, 238.

2. *MMN*, 295n. Stalin was biding his time until he could do away with Kamenev. Chukovskii, *Dnevnik, 1930–1969*, 117, refers to reports that Kamenev was considered for a major address at the writers' congress. In the meantime, Kamenev was listed as a member of the Writers' Union board and the presidium, although there is no indication of his participation.

3. Maksimenkov, *Sumbur vmesto muzyki*, 26.

4. Lekmanov, *Zhizn' Osipa Mandelshtama*, 182.

5. See, for example, *AFPD*, 66.

6. Maksimenkov, *Sumbur vmesto muzyki*, 172.

7. Steinweis, *Art, Ideology*, 55.

8. Steinweis, *Art, Ideology*, 60, 63.

9. After 1935, political and censorship decisions were made by the ministry. To ensure that the chambers implemented these decisions, Goebbels appointed Hinkel to purge, restaff, and restructure them. Hinkel, who joined the SS at this time, used SS officers as chamber staff, increasing the information flow between the security police and the chambers. In 1938 Hinkel dismantled the theater-management agencies, which had remained outside NSDAP control. See Steinweis, *Art, Ideology*, 51–63.

10. Shentalinsky, *Arrested Voices*, 212.

11. Dmitry Marchenko headed the party group until 1936; see *SF*, 878. [Osip] Reznik was the Writers' Union *partbiuro* secretary beginning in the summer of 1944; see Tsentral'nyi arkhiv obshchestvennykh dvizhenii Moskvy, f. 8131, op. 1, ed. khr. 1a, l. 1. Vishnevsky and Fyodor Gladkov also appear to have served in this capacity.

12. Marchenkov, *Ulitsa Kachalova 6/2*, 78, cites the figure of forty thousand correspondents in Gorky's lifetime.

13. Shentalinsky, *Arrested Voices*, 246.

14. Shentalinsky, *Arrested Voices*, 268. On Marianna Gerasimova, who was married to Libedinsky, see *MMN*, 380.

15. *PVSSP*, 716–18. See also Matlock, "'Governing Organs,'" 382.

16. Minutes and transcripts of all presidium meetings from its inception in September 1934 until Gorky's death nearly two years later show that Gorky was never present. See Stenogramma (presidium; Nov. 19, 1934), RGALI, f. 631, op. 1, ed. khr. 51; Protokol no. 3 (presidium, Jan. 23, 1935), RGALI, f. 631, op. 15, ed. khr. 11; Stenogramma (presidium and secretariat; Mar. 31, 1935), f. 631, op. 15, ed. khr. 13; Stenogramma (presidium; Oct. 15, 1935), f. 631, op. 15, ed. khr. 17. Shcherbakov chaired all these meetings. He also chaired meetings of the secretariat (as was proper): See Protokol i stenogramma (secretariat; Oct. 29, 1934), RGALI, f. 631, op. 1, ed. khr. 49; Protokol no. 5 i stenogramma (Apr. 19, 1935), f. 631, op. 15, ed. khr. 3; Stenogramma (secretariat; Sept. 16, 1935), RGALI, f. 631, op. 15, ed. khr. 5. Shcherbakov kept Gorky informed by letter of decisions made by the presidium and secretariat. His letters to Gorky are housed in Rossiiskii gosudarstvennyi arkhiv sotsial'noi i politicheskoi istorii (hereafter RGASPI), f. 88, op. 1; copies of them are housed in AG, f. 1330/6. Gorky's letters to Shcherbakov are located in AG, f. 1330/6, no. PG-rl 55. Portions of the correspondence are published in "Pis'ma A. M. Gor'kogo A. S. Shcherbakovu," *Istoricheskii arkhiv*, no. 5 (1960): 11–22, and in Gor'kii, *Sobranie sochinenii v 30-i tomakh*, 30:366–67, 370–71, 374, 381–84, 386–87, 389–90, 396–97.

17. *LG* reported the act as though it were business as usual; see Matlock, "'Governing Organs,'" 391.

18. Maksimenkov, *Sumbur vmesto muzyki*, 26; *VKI*, 248.

19. This was not the only time that Stalin placed, as a temporary measure, in an important and visible position someone he mistrusted and intended eventually to bring down. Tucker, *Stalin in Power*, 283, observes that Stalin acted in this manner with regard to Bukharin and Radek after the Seventeenth Party Congress.

20. Shcherbakov to Gorky, Nov. 17, 1934, AG, KG-17, 90-4-2, l. 1; Shcherbakov to Gorky, Oct. 1935, AG, KG-P 90-4-14, l. 2; Shcherbakov to Gorky, Oct.–Nov. 1934, RGASPI, f. 88, op. 1, ed. khr. 482, l. 16; Shcherbakov to Gorky, Jan. 11, 1935, RGASPI, f. 88, op. 1, ed. khr. 486, ll. 7, 9; Shcherbakov to Gorky, Feb. 1936, RGASPI, f. 88, ed. khr. 504, l. 1; Shcherbakov to Gorky, Nov. 21, 1934, RGASPI, f. 88, op. 1, ed. khr. 484.

21. On Gorky's reaction to politically motivated favoring of certain writers, see his letter to Stalin in Gorky, *Selected Letters*, 352–53.

22. Dobrenko, *Making of the State Writer*, 364; see also Clark, *Petersburg*, 286–88.

23. Shcherbakov to Gorky, Oct.–Nov. 1934, RGASPI, f. 88, op. 1, ed. khr. 482, l. 16; Shcherbakov to Gorky, Nov. 21, 1934, RGASPI, f. 88, op. 1, ed. khr. 484, ll. 1, 2.

24. Gorky to Shcherbakov, AG, PG-rl 55-1-21, l. 1.

25. Kotkin, *Magnetic Mountain*, 215.

26. Stenogramma (presidium: Nov. 19, 1934), ll. 2–27.

27. Stenogramma (presidium: Nov. 19, 1934), ll. 32–33.

28. Stenogramma (presidium and secretariat; Mar. 31, 1935), l. 25.

29. A. P. Platonov, "Takyr'," *Krasnaia nov'*, 9 (1934): 82–94. Platonov had managed to get included in a writers' brigade that traveled to Turkmenistan; see "Platonov v Srednei Azii."

30. Goncharov and Nekhotin, *Andrei Platonov v dokumentakh*, 857.

31. See, for example, Ermilov, "Uchenik gimnazii Shklovskogo," 16–30.

32. I. V. Stalin, "Golovokruzhenie ot uspekhov," *Pravda*, Mar. 2, 1930.

33. Clark and Dobrenko, *Soviet Culture and Power*, 258, 303. As a party member, Gorelov outranked the nonparty Tikhonov.

34. One *seksot's* report mentions such occasions as if they were criminal acts, naming the Leningrad poets Pavel Karaban, Vladimir Narbut, Igor Postupalsky, Boris Turganov, and the Ukrainian writers Aleksandr Kopylenko, Petro Panch, and Leonid Pervomaisky; see *VKI*, 312–14. Narbut, to whom Mandelshtam recited his Stalin epigram, and Postupalsky were accused of Ukrainian nationalism and arrested in 1937.

35. Stenogramma (presidium and secretariat; Mar. 31, 1935), l. 7.

36. Shcherbakov to Gorky, Jan. 11, 1935, AG, f. 1330/6, KG-P 90-4-4; Gorky to Shcherbakov, AG, f. 1330/6, PG-rl 55-1-23.

37. D. I. Zaslavskii, "Literaturnaia gnil'," *Pravda*, Jan. 20, 1935.

38. D. I. Zaslavskii, "Zametki chitatelia. Po povodu zamechanii A. M. Gor'kogo," *Pravda*, Jan. 25, 1935.

39. Chukovskii, *Dnevnik, 1930–1969*, 122.

40. A. M. Gor'kii, "Literaturnye zabavy," *Pravda*, Jan. 24, 1935; cited in Chukovskii, *Dnevnik, 1930–1969*, 481–82.

41. F. Panferov, "Otkrytoe pis'mo," *Pravda*, 28 Jan. 1935.

42. Rubtsov, *Alter ego Stalina*, 89.

43. "Pis'ma A. M. Gor'kogo A. S. Shcherbakovu," 21.

44. Tomoff, *Creative Union*, 104–5, reports a similar occurrence in the newly formed composers' union in 1947, when leading composers repeatedly approached Agitprop to have unqualified members removed but were consistently rebuffed.

45. Stenogramma (presidium and secretariat; Mar. 31, 1935), ll. 2–4.

46. Dobrenko, *Making of the State Writer*, 341.

47. Stenogramma (presidium and secretariat; Mar. 31, 1935), l. 4.

48. "Pis'mo A. A. Surkova A. S. Shcherbakovu" [ne rannee 1936 g.], RGALI, f. 1712, op. 1, ed. khr. 64, l. 2 verso.

49. Protokoly nos. 37–38 i stenogrammy (secretariat and presidium; Sept. 19–Dec. 6, 1947), RGALI, f. 631, op. 15, ed. khr. 816, l. 49.

50. "Fedor Ivanovich Panferov"; Yermilov to Fadeyev, June 7, 1937, ll. 61, 62. *Whetstones* appeared from 1928 (book 1) through 1937 (book 4).

51. Yermilov to Fadeev, Dec. 4, 1936, l. 39.

52. Perkhin, "Polemika M. Gor'kogo s A. Avdeenko," 146. See also Kirpotin, *Nachalo*, 162–63.

53. Cited in Maksimenkov, *Sumbur vmesto muzyki*, 257. Arkadyev was executed in mid-1937.

54. Shcherbakov to Gorky, Oct. 15, 1935, AG, f. 1330/6, KG-P 90-4-13, l. 2.

55. RGALI, f. 631, op. 15, ed. khr. 17, l. 3.

56. Gorky to Shcherbakov, Oct. 1935, AG, PG-rl 55-1-18, l. 1.

57. *SL*, 207. For Soviet views on suicide in the 1930s, see Pinnow, *Lost to the Collective*, 234–35, 239–42.

58. Khrushchev, *Khrushchev Remembers*, 171–72. Khrushchev's assertion that Shcherbakov was transferred from the Writers' Union at Gorky's request is incorrect.

59. Shaginian applied during a recheck of party cards that caused a freeze on new admissions from January 1933 through November 1936; see Getty, *Origins*, 58. She became a party member in 1942.

60. Gor'kii, *Sobranie sochinenii v 30-i tomakh*, 30:366.

61. *VP*, 45. Pearl Buck was not a missionary but the daughter of missionary parents.

62. *VP*, 176–84. See also Brown, *Proletarian Episode*, 156.

63. Yermilov to Fadeyev, Feb. 3, 1936.

64. Fleishman, *Boris Pasternak*, 269.

65. Maksimenkov, *Sumbur vmesto muzyki*, 19.

66. *VKI*, 290. Clark and Dobrenko, *Soviet Culture and Power*, 246, notes significant public support for Shostakovich following the *Pravda* attacks.

67. Maksimenkov, *Sumbur vmesto muzyki*, 45. The article is "Sumbur vmesto muzyki," *Pravda*, Jan. 28, 1936. Shostakovich's ballet *Bright Stream* (*Svetlyi ruchei*) was also disgraced; see "Baletnaia fal'sh," *Pravda*, Feb. 6, 1936.

68. *VKI*, 289. Other casualties of the policy shift were Prokofiev's planned *The Lenin Cantata* (*Cantata o Lenine*), Bedny and Tairov's *Epic Heroes* (*Bogatyri*), Bulgakov's *Molière* (*Molyer*) (which played for seven performances in 1936), and Eisenstein's *Bezhin Meadow* (*Bezhin Lug*). *Bezhin Meadow* was denied on March 5, 1937; see Maksimenkov, *Sumbur vmesto muzyki*, 241. On *Epic Heroes*, see Dubrovsky, "Chronicle."

69. Stenogramma (3rd plenum; Feb. 14, 1936) RGALI, f. 631, op. 15, ed. khr. 119, l. 80.

70. *PVSSP*, 578–97; RGALI, f. 631, op. 15, ed. khr. 119, ll. 81, 87.

71. Stenogramma (3rd plenum; Feb. 14, 1936), RGALI, f. 631, op. 15, ed. khr. 118, ll. 30–33.

72. Halfin, *Terror in My Soul*, 31.

73. Stenogramma (3rd plenum; Feb. 14, 1936), RGALI, f. 631, op. 15, ed. khr. 118, l. 83.

74. Stenogramma (3rd plenum; Feb. 14, 1936), RGALI, f. 631, op. 15, ed. khr. 118, ll. 66–68.

75. Stenogramma (3rd plenum; Feb. 14, 1936), RGALI, f. 631, op. 15, ed. khr. 118, l. 83.

76. Stenogramma (3rd plenum; Feb. 15, 1936), RGALI, f. 631, op. 15, ed. khr. 120, l. 38.

77. RGALI, f. 631, op. 15, ed. khr. 120, l. 46.

78. Stenogramma (3rd plenum; Feb. 15, 1936), RGALI, f. 631, op. 15, ed. khr. 120, l. 46.

79. Stenogramma (3rd plenum; Feb. 14, 1936), RGALI, f. 631, op. 15, ed. khr. 118, l. 81.

80. Stenogramma (3rd plenum; Feb. 14, 1936), RGALI, f. 631, op. 15, ed. khr. 118, l. 85.

81. Maksimenkov, *Sumbur vmesto muzyki*, 60, 68–71.

82. Maksimenkov, *Sumbur vmesto muzyki*, 243.

83. Maksimenkov, *Sumbur vmesto muzyki*, 81. Kerzhentsev had held high positions in the diplomatic service and as Molotov's deputy. Earlier he had been a Menshevik; Maksimenkov suggests that this may have been a reason why he now received this job (65). A party worker with a compromised past might be more aggressive in advocating the general line in proof of his loyalty.

84. Maksimenkov, *Sumbur vmesto muzyki*, 79–80, 301–2, notes that Kerzhentsev formulated legislation and submitted it to the Politburo and had status equal to that of a Politburo member.

85. Maksimenkov, *Sumbur vmesto muzyki*, 101–6, argues that Kerzhentsev was likely its author.

86. Shcherbakov to Gorky, Feb. 28, 1936, AG, f. 1330/6, no. KG-17 90-4-18, l. 1. Lewin, *Making of the Soviet System*, 238, notes that "coming down hard" as an "example to others" was commonly employed by the leadership in confronting infighting and red tape.

87. Protokol No. 2 i stenogramma (presidium; Feb. 27, 1936), RGALI, f. 631, op. 15, ed. khr. 67, l. 6a.

88. Tucker, *Stalin in Power*, 273, notes that in 1934 Stalin ordered dachas built for top NKVD officials to ensure their loyalty and cooperation in carrying out arrest orders for the Old Bolsheviks.

89. Protokol No. 2 i stenogramma (presidium; Feb. 27, 1936), l. 4.

90. Protokol No. 2 i stenogramma (presidium; Feb. 27, 1936), ll. 8–9.

91. Protokol No. 2 i stenogramma (presidium; Feb. 27, 1936), l. 8.

92. Protokol No. 2 i stenogramma (presidium; Feb. 27, 1936), l. 10.

93. Protokol No. 2 i stenogramma (presidium; Feb. 27, 1936), l. 13.

94. Protokol No. 2 i stenogramma (presidium; Feb. 27, 1936), l. 15.

95. Protokol No. 2 i stenogramma (presidium; Feb. 27, 1936), l. 70.
96. Shcherbakov to Gorky, Feb. 28, 1936, l. 1.
97. Gorky, *Selected Letters*, 366.
98. Getty, *Origins*, 17; "Pobol'she konkretnoi samokritiki," *Pravda*, Mar. 11, 1936; "Za samokritiku," *Literaturnyi Leningrad*, Mar. 20, 1936; Ia. Eidel'man, "Dnevnik diskussii," *LG*, Mar. 15, 1936.
99. Seven Moscow meetings occurred, from March 10 to March 31, and six in Leningrad, from March 25 to April 13. *Literaturnaia gazeta* published partial transcripts of thirty-five out of fifty-one Moscow speeches. Some of the sixteen unpublished speeches were summarized. *Literaturnyi Leningrad* published excerpts from twenty-four out of some forty-five Leningrad speeches. This smaller percentage seems due to Leningrad writers' greater resistance to falling in line.
100. N. Tikhonov, "Budem trebovatel'nyi k sebe," *Literaturnyi Leningrad*, Apr. 20, 1936; O. Forsh, "Razgovor budet delovoi i konkretnyi," *Literaturnyi Leningrad*, Apr. 1, 1936; B. Lavrenev, "Strana zhdet ot nas bol'shogo iskusstva," *Literaturnyi Leningrad*, Apr. 8, 1936; R. Messer, "Preodolenie formalizma," *Literaturnyi Leningrad*, Apr. 20, 1936. Fifteen speakers named colleagues who were supposedly guilty of these sins. The nineteen speeches fully supporting *Pravda* include one by the director of a factory library, as well as Kirpotin's, and also four critics, Anna Beskina, Mikhail Maizel, Lev Tsyrlin, and G. Belitsky. Only Aleksei Tolstoy, Nikolai Zabolotsky, and the literary scholar Viktor Zhirmunsky gave the kind of self-criticism that *Pravda* wanted. The others (Druzin, Nikolai Svirin, Viktor Bespamiatnov, Naum Berkovsky, and Yu. Berzin), while pointing the finger at other writers, did not self-criticize but instead defended themselves against charges of formalism or naturalism. See N. Berkovskii, "Dumat' za sebia, govorit' za vsekh," *Literaturnyi Leningrad*, Mar. 27, 1936; N. Svirin, "Za muzhestvo kritiki," *Literaturnyi Leningrad*, Apr. 1, 1936; Iu. Berzin, "Upreki v formalizme byli osnovatel'ny," *Literaturnyi Leningrad*, Apr. 8, 1936; V. Druzin, "Pafos realisticheskogo masterstva," *Literaturnyi Leningrad*, Apr. 8, 1936; V. Bespamiatnov, "Bol'shoi literature—bol'she trebovaniia," *Literaturnyi Leningrad*, Apr. 20, 1936.
101. Quoted in Ia. Eidel'man, "Dnevnik diskussii," *LG*, Mar. 15, 1936; transcripts of Pasternak's two speeches are in *MMN*, 475–85.
102. "Na obshchemoskovskom sobranii pisatelei, 16 marta," *LG*, Mar. 20, 1936.
103. Ia. Eidel'man, "Dnevnik diskussii," *LG*, Mar. 15, 1936; "Na obshchemoskovskom sobranii pisatelei. 16 marta," *LG*, Mar. 20, 1936; "Na obshchemoskovskom sobranii pisatelei. 19 marta," *LG*, Mar. 27, 1936; "Na obshchemoskovskom sobranii pisatelei. 26 marta," *LG*, Mar. 31, 1936; "Na obshchemokovskom sobranii pisatelei. 31 marta," *LG*, Apr. 5, 1936. Unlike *LG*, *Literaturnyi Leningrad* printed sizable excerpts from even the most outspoken addresses. It was shut down the following year.
104. "Na obshchemoskovskom sobranii pisatelei. 19 marta. 23 marta," *LG*,

Mar. 27, 1936; "Na obshchemoskovskom sobranii pisatelei. 26 marta," *LG*, Mar. 31, 1936.

105. B. M. Eikhenbaum, "Zhizn' ushla v storonu ot formalizma," *Literaturnyi Leningrad*, Apr. 1, 1936; K. Fedin, "Ne snizhat' urovnia svoego iskusstva," *Literaturnyi Leningrad*, Apr. 8, 1936; M. M. Zoshchenko, "Literatura dolzhna byt' narodnoi," *Literaturnyi Leningrad*, Apr. 20, 1936; M. Kozakov, "Narodnost' i kritika," *Literaturnyi Leningrad*, Apr. 20, 1936; N. Nikitin, "Nekhvataet voli k druzhbe," *Literaturnyi Leningrad*, Apr. 20, 1936.

106. "Dnevnik diskussii," *Literaturnyi Leningrad*, Mar. 27, 1936; "Dnevnik diskussii," *Literaturnyi Leningrad*, Apr. 8, 1936.

107. *Literaturnyi Leningrad*, Mar. 20, 1936.

108. Tikhonov, "Budem trebovatel'ny k sebe."

109. Gronsky was at *Novy mir*, Panfyorov at *October*, Vishnevsky at *Znamia*, and Libedinsky at *Zvezda*.

110. *SL*, 216. Also taking part in this meeting were Boris Agapov, Gennady Fish, Ivan Katayev, Lev Ovalov, Konstantin Paustovsky, Yakov Rykachev, Skosyrev, Sletov, Zarudin. Stavsky gave the opening speech and then left.

111. Gor'kii, *Sobranie sochinenii v 30-i tomakh*, 27:523–28; see also Shentalinsky, *The KGB's Literary Archive*, 269.

INTERMEZZO ONE

1. Hellbeck, *Revolution on My Mind*, 320.

2. Slezkine, *The House of Government*, 833.

3. The exception was *Novy mir*, which Gronsky edited until his arrest in 1937, when Stavsky took over. *Young Guard* was edited by Anna Karavayeva, *October* by Panfyorov, *Znamia* by Vishnevsky, and *Zvezda* by Libedinsky. Bespalov headed the contemporary literature section of Gosizdat khudozhestvennoi literatury.

4. RGALI, f. 1628, op. 2, ed. khr. 712, l. 86. Pilniak stated in March 1935 that the members of *Red Virgin Soil*'s editorial board did not even know what the journal was publishing; see Stenogramma (presidium and secretariat; Mar. 31, 1935), l. 22.

5. Vsevolod Lebedev, *"Detstvo," Krasnaia nov'*, no. 1 (1936): 3–97; see also Yermilov to Fadeyev, Feb. 11, 1936, l. 122.

6. Yermilov to Fadeyev, undated (between Dec. 4, 1936, and June 7, 1937), l. 53.

7. Yermilov, "Literaturnyi dnevnik," *Krasnaia nov'*, no. 3 (1936): 262–67.

8. Yermilov, "Literaturnyi dnevnik," 262.

9. Yermilov to Fadeyev, Dec. 4, 1936, l. 41. Yermilov may have had in mind Stavsky (judging from an earlier remark in the same letter).

10. Service, *Stalin*, 316.

11. Khlevniuk, *Politbiuro*, 144.

12. Yermilov to Fadeyev, Jan. 12, 1935, l. 14; emphasis in original.

13. Yermilov to Fadeyev, Apr. 19/20, 1935, ll. 31–32.

14. Smith, *D. S. Mirsky*, 267 (Gorky's letter to Stalin is dated Aug. 2, 1934); *Pravda*, Jan. 24, 1935; cited in Smith, *D. S. Mirsky*, 268.

15. Yermilov to Fadeyev, undated (after July 1935), l. 68.

16. Yermilov to Fadeyev, undated (before Jan. 31, 1936), ll. 61, 68–69, 80; see Yermilov to Fadeyev, undated letter, RGALI, f. 1628, op, 2, ed. khr. 712, l. 72 on Ravinsky's article defending the Writers' Union against *Red Virgin Soil*.

17. Yermilov to Fadeyev, Apr. 19/20, 1935, l. 31.

18. Yermilov to Fadeyev, Apr. 19/20, 1935, l. 31; emphasis in original.

19. Milgram, *Obedience to Authority*, 8.

20. Yermilov to Fadeyev, Apr. 19/20, 1935, l. 30.

21. Yermilov to Fadeyev, Apr. 19/20, 1935, l. 34.

22. Yermilov to Fadeyev, Apr. 19/20, 1935, l. 35.

23. Yermilov to Fadeyev, Apr. 19/20, 1935, l. 35.

24. Yermilov to Fadeyev, Apr. 19/20, 1935, l. 36. Mekhlis repeated this stunt in an October 1936 article on Tairov's staging of Bedny's *Bogatyri*; see Rubtsov, *Alter ego Stalina*, 90.

25. Yermilov to Fadeyev, Apr. 19/20, 1935, l. 36.

26. Yermilov to Fadeyev, Apr. 19/20, 1935, l. 37.

27. Yermilov to Fadeyev, Apr. 19/20, 1935, l. 37.

28. Žižek, *Sublime Object*, 66.

29. On the recheck of party cards and resulting expulsions after Kirov's murder, see Khlevniuk, *Politburo*, 146–47.

30. Yermilov to Fadeyev, Apr. 21, 1936, ll. 27–28.

31. Yermilov to Fadeyev, Apr. 21, 1936, l. 26; emphasis in original.

32. Halfin, *Terror in My Soul*, 213.

33. Yermilov to Fadeyev, Apr. 21, 1936, l. 26.

34. Yermilov to Fadeyev, Jan. 31, 1936. l. 97.

35. I. Lezhnev, "Litso zhurnala," *Pravda*, Jan. 31, 1936.

36. Yermilov to Fadeyev, Jan. 31, 1936, l. 97.

37. Yermilov to Fadeyev, Jan. 31, 1936, l. 97.

38. Yermilov to Fadeyev, Feb. 3, 1936, l. 106; emphasis in original. Yermilov behaves according to self-discrepancy theory, seeking to bring his "actual self" into line with his "idealized self" or "ought self"; see Higgins, "Self-Discrepancy," 154. When Yermilov finally calmed down, he observed with humorous self-deprecation, "I didn't make a single mistake in all this time except for one—too much emotion!" (Yermilov to Fadeyev, Feb. 21, 1936, l. 154).

39. Lebedev, *"Detstvo"*; L. Nikulin, "Voz'mite v ruki karandash," *Pravda*, Feb. 13, 1936. Nikulin, confronted by Gekht for this slanderous article, reportedly reddened and replied, "I've done worse" (*SL*, 216). Here was a rare point of

agreement between Yermilov and Shklovsky, who had defended Lebedev at the *orgkomitet* plenum in 1932; see *SLNE*, 170.

40. Yermilov to Fadeyev, Feb. 16, 1936, l. 139.

41. Yermilov to Fadeyev, Feb. 3, 1936, l. 146.

42. Yermilov to Fadeyev, Feb. 11, 1936, l. 131; emphasis in original. On the impact of RAPP's dissolution on the proletarian musicians' organization, see Frolova-Walker and Walker, *Music and Soviet Power*, 314–27.

43. Yermilov to Fadeyev, Feb. 11, 1936, l. 131; emphasis in original.

44. Yermilov to Fadeyev, Feb. 11, 1936, l. 131; emphasis in original.

45. Yermilov to Fadeyev, Feb. 16, 1936, l. 147; emphasis in original.

46. Yermilov to Fadeyev, Feb. 16, 1936, l. 146. Yermilov was repeating the prediction in "Muddle Instead of Music" of a more discerning mass reader; see Maksimenkov, *Sumbur vmesto muzyki*, 68. Maksimenkov on p. 15 writes that Fadeyev accepted the *Pravda* line deposing "left art" unreservedly. But his pronouncements in RAPP and his correspondence with Yermilov make clear that his personal opinion was different.

47. Žižek, *Sublime Object*, 73.

48. Yermilov to Fadeyev, Feb. 16, 1936, l. 148.

49. Taylor, *Pride, Shame, and Guilt*, 68.

50. See Žižek, *How to Read Lacan*, on the ego ideal.

51. Yermilov to Fadeyev, Apr. 21, 1936, l. 25.

52. Yermilov to Fadeyev, Feb. 24, 1936, l. 160.

53. Yermilov to Fadeyev, Apr. 21, 1936, l. 31.

54. Yermilov to Fadeyev, Apr. 21, 1936, ll. 33–34; emphasis in original.

55. Yermilov to Fadeyev, Mar. 12, 1936, l. 14.

56. Yermilov to Fadeyev, Mar. 16, 1936, ll. 14–18. Fadeyev, too, wrote a denunciation; see Yermilov to Fadeyev, Mar. 12, 1936, l. 21. Afinogenov was editor of *Teatr i dramaturgiia*.

57. Yermilov to Fadeyev, Mar. 16, 1936, l. 21.

58. Yermilov to Fadeyev, Apr. 24, 1936, l. 22.

59. Yermilov to Fadeyev, Apr. 24, 1936, l. 22.

60. Yermilov to Fadeyev, Apr. 24, 1936, ll. 22–23; emphasis in original.

61. Milgram, *Obedience to Authority*, 9.

62. Yermilov to Fadeyev, undated letter (between Dec. 1936 and June 1937), l. 57; emphasis in original.

63. Ogryzko, "Gromila sovetskoi literatury."

64. Fromm, *Psychoanalysis and Religion*, 77.

65. Yermilov to Fadeyev, Dec. 4, 1936, l. 43.

66. Hellbeck, *Revolution on My Mind*, 288.

67. Hellbeck, *Revolution on My Mind*, 328, 329, 335.

68. Hellbeck, *Revolution on My Mind*, 338.

CHAPTER FOUR

1. *LF*, 26. In a May 3, 1937, memo to the Central Committee secretaries, A. I. Angarov, deputy head of the Central Committee's Department of Cultural Enlightenment, and E. M. Tamarkin, head of its literary sector, wrote, "The secretaries who bear responsibility for the union are Comrades Stavsky, Lakhuti, and Vsevolod Ivanov. In practice, leadership of the union is concentrated in Comrade Stavsky's hands, because Comrade Lakhuti cannot, and Vsevold Ivanov cannot and does not want to busy himself with union matters" (*LF*, 23).

2. These were *Proshli* (1924); *Stanitsa. Kubanskie ocherki*, 3rd ed. (Moscow, 1930); *Razbeg* (Moscow, 1931); *Sil'nee smerti: Krug rasskazov* (Moscow, 1932); *Na grebne* (Moscow: Gospolitizdat, 1934). *Razbeg* and *Na grebne* were reprinted as *Kuban'skie zapisi* (Moscow: Sovetskii pisatel', 1935).

3. Sheshukov, *Neistovye revniteli*, 320.

4. Yezhov took over the NKVD in September 1936, Stavsky the Writers' Union in late August 1936. Yezhov's power began to wane in May 1938, when he was made commissar of water transport, and he was removed as NKVD head in December 1938; Stavsky was eased out of the top job between spring and midsummer of 1938.

5. Maksimenkov, *Sumbur vmesto muzyki*, 61, 79–80, 301–3. Agitprop was run by a series of deputies, Angarov, Shablovsky, and Konstantin Yukov.

6. Maksimenkov, *Sumbur vmesto muzyki*, 23, 301–2.

7. A. I. Melua, comp., *Repressirovannaia nauka*, vol. 2 (St. Petersburg: Nauka, 1994), 77; cited in Torchinov and Leontiuk, *Vokrug Stalina*, 337.

8. Hellbeck, *Revolution on My Mind*, 305.

9. See statistics on this in Lewin, *Making of the Soviet System*, 212.

10. *Sovetskie pisateli*, 4:591. Biographical information on Stavsky also comes from *Kratkaia literaturnaia entsiklopediia*; "V. P. Stavskii," in "Predislovie k opisi," RGALI, f. 1712; and *Vladimir Petrovich Stavsky (1900–1943). Ukazatel' literatury* ([Leningrad]: Lenizdat, 1966), 4–6.

11. Viola, *Best Sons*, 11.

12. Viola, *Best Sons*, 14, 16, states that at the end of the Civil War, the party was an "isolated outpost . . . in alien territory," and that for many workers the lesson of the Civil War was the kulak's ability to threaten the Soviet regime.

13. Viola, *Best Sons*, 11, notes that in recruiting cadres for grain requisitioning, the government looked primarily to the working class as the mainstay of Bolshevik support.

14. Service, *Stalin*, 257.

15. *Sovetskie pisateli*, 4:591.

16. See Viola, *Best Sons*, 14, and Sharlet, "Stalinism," 163.

17. On the 25,000ers, see Viola, *Best Sons*, 3.

18. Huskey, "Vyshinsky, Krylenko," 415, and Sharlet, "Stalinism," 162.

19. Sharlet, "Stalinism," 162–63.

20. Huskey, "Vyshinsky, Krylenko," 415.

21. Sharlet, "Stalinism,"168.

22. Solomon, "Soviet Criminal Justice," 393, 396.

23. Sharlet, "Stalinism," 156.

24. Getty, *Origins*, 118, 126.

25. Viola, "Second Coming," 69–70.

26. See, for example, Vyshinsky and Kareva, *Soviet Socialist Law*, 3; Vyshinsky, *Law of the Soviet State*, 645.

27. V. P. Stavskii, "Tetrad' s dnevnikovymi zapisiami," 1936–1938, RGALI, f. 1712, op. 2, ed. khr. 63, l. 9.

28. Stavskii, "Tetrad'," 1936–1938, l. 11.

29. Stavskii, "Dnevnik," Feb. 14, 1940—ne rannee iiulia 1940, RGALI, f. 1712, op. 4, ed. khr. 9, l. 50.

30. Garros, Korenevskaya, and Lahusen, *Intimacy and Terror*, 237–38.

31. See, for example, V. P. Stavskii, "Dnevnik," Jan. 1, 1938–Apr. 17, 1939, RGALI, f. 1712, op. 4, ed. khr. 8, ll. 17, 38, 41; Stavskii, "Dnevnik," Feb. 14, 1940—ne rannee iiulia 1940, l. 50.

32. Stavskii, "Dnevnik," Jan. 1, 1938–Apr. 17, 1939, ll. 34–37; published in English in Garros, Korenevskaya, and Lahusen, *Intimacy and Terror*, 236–37.

33. Stavskii, "Dnevnik," Jan. 1, 1938–Apr. 17, 1939, l. 38. Rampant theft of dacha construction materials is corroborated in Berelowitch, "Peredelkino," 204. My reading of Stavsky's diary does not support the conclusion in Figes, *The Whisperers*, 281, that Stavsky was "tormented by doubts" and experienced a "loss of faith."

34. Hoffman, *Stalinist Values*, 61.

35. Hoffman, *Stalinist Values*, 61, 67.

36. Gorham, *Speaking in Soviet Tongues*, 59.

37. Stavskii, "Dnevnik," Jan. 1, 1938–Apr. 17, 1939, l. 23. Also in Garros, Korenevskaya, and Lahusen, *Intimacy and Terror*, 229.

38. "Pis'ma Stavskogo Vladimira Petrovicha Fadeevu A. A.," 1925–1940, RGALI, f. 1628, op. 2, ed. khr. 1167, ll. 4–5.

39. Lewin, *Making of the Soviet System*, 218.

40. Stavskii, "Zapisnaia knizhka," ll. 31 verso, 32.

41. Stavskii, "Zapisnaia knizhka," l. 42.

42. *Kratkaia literaturnaia entsiklopediia*, 7:134; RGALI, f. 1712, "Predislovie k opisi," l. 2.

43. *Sovetskie pisateli*, 4:590.

44. Stavskii, "Dnevnik," Jan. 1, 1938–Apr. 17, 1939, l. 55; Garros, Korenevskaya, and Lahusen, *Intimacy and Terror*, 237, 245.

45. Gorky to Shcherbakov, Aug. 1935, AG, PG-rl 55-1-25, l. 1. On one oc-

casion Stavsky watched in disgust as Shcherbakov leafed through novels lying on his desk, hunting for examples of good writing to "teach" Stavsky how to improve. "I see how things are," Stavsky wrote in his diary. "It's nothing but a threshing floor" (Stavskii, "Dnevnik," 1941–1943, RGALI, f. 1712, op. 4, ed. khr. 10, ll. 32–33).

46. Stavskii, "Zapisnaia knizhka," ll. 67–68 verso.

47. Groys, *Total Art*, 45.

48. Kupina, *Totalitarnyi iazyk*, 10.

49. One article repeats these two words, mantralike, six times in fifteen paragraphs; see "Sdelat' vse prakticheskie vyvody" [unsigned], *LG*, Aug. 27, 1936; V. Stavskii, "Ne uspokaivat'sia, usilivat' rabotu," *LG*, Sept. 1, 1936; "O pisatel'skoi etike" [unsigned], *LG*, Sept. 30, 1936. As head of the Writers' Union, Stavsky would have written the front-page lead editorials. Those he accused were Afinogenov, Aleshin, Ivan Katayev, Fridlend (Feliks Svetov), Richard Pikel, and Aleksei Garri; the Armenian writers Simonian, Alazan, and Bakunts; and Vagarshak Ter-Vaganian, who in 1927 had circulated an underground manuscript criticizing Stalin's falsification of history and exposing the personality cult being built around Stalin. On Ter-Vaganian, see Kun, *Stalin*, 234, 235.

The word *chest* also receives emphasis in another lead editorial, "Znamia novoi kul'tury," *LG*, Dec. 1, 1936; see also the reference to *chestnye trudiashchiesia* in "Rech' tov. V. P. Stavskogo," *LG*, Dec. 6, 1936 (Stavsky's speech at the Eighth Congress of Soviets, the precursor to the Supreme Soviet, which adopted the Stalin constitution).

50. "O pisatel'skoi etike," *LG*, Sept. 30, 1936.

51. See Protokoly 18-21 i stenogramma (secretariat; 1937), RGALI, f. 631, op. 15, ed. khr. 160, l. 10. This practice was quite common throughout the 1930s and 1940s. Invited guests might be journal editors or members of the Writers' Union's republic branches involved in the business at hand. Others may have been invited to assure a critical mass that would support motions for expulsion.

52. Maksimenkov, *Sumbur vmesto muzyki*, 216.

53. Protokoly 18-21 i stenogramma (secretariat; 1937), l. 53.

54. Protokoly 18-21 i stenogramma (secretariat; 1937), l. 55.

55. Protokoly 18-21 i stenogramma (secretariat; 1937), ll. 55–56.

56. Protokoly 18-21 i stenogramma (secretariat; 1937), ll. 59–60.

57. Protokoly 18-21 i stenogramma (secretariat; 1937), l. 46.

58. Protokoly 1-2 i stenogrammy (secretariat; Jan. 7–25, 1937), RGALI, f. 631, op. 15, ed. khr. 168, l. 48.

59. Stavskii, "Sdelat' vse prakticheskie vyvody."

60. See, for example, Stenogramma (presidium and secretariat; Mar. 31, 1935), RGALI, f. 631, op. 15, ed. khr. 13, l. 25.

61. The plenum was slightly delayed in order to make the Hall of Columns available for the state funeral on February 21 of Ordzhonikidze, whose suicide

a few days after the conviction of his protégé Piatakov was publicly described as heart failure. See Stenogramma (presidium; Feb. 20, 1937), RGALI, f. 631, op. 15, ed. khr. 169, l. 7, and Getty and Naumov, *The Road to Terror*, 218, 365.

62. See Sandler, "1937 Pushkin Jubilee," 199, and Blium, *Sovetskaia tsenzura*, 169; cited in Sandler, "1937 Pushkin Jubilee," 199.

63. Dubrovsky, "Chronicle," 84; Petrone, *Life*, 120.

64. *VKI*, 218. The Politburo passed three resolutions on memorializing Pushkin: on July 27, 1934, December 15, 1935, and December 29, 1936 (280, 344–46). The heroization of Pushkin was not immediately publicized and was another example of how the party would sometimes leave cadres uninformed; see Dubrovsky, "Chronicle," 88.

65. Any, "Red Pushkin," 382–83.

66. Kirpotin, *Nasledie Pushkina i kommunizm*. See also V. Kirpotin, "Aleksandr Sergeevich Pushkin," *Oktiabr'*, no. 1 [1937]: 5–65 (an excerpt from his book of the same title [Moscow: Khudozhestvennaia literatura, 1937]).

67. Kirpotin, "Aleksandr Sergeevich Pushkin," 16.

68. Stenogramma (Fourth plenum; Feb. 22, 1937, evening session), RGALI, f. 631, op. 15, ed. khr. 179, ll. 17–19.

69. Stenogramma (Fourth plenum; Feb. 22, 1937, evening session), ll. 9–12; Stenogramma (Fourth plenum; Feb. 26, 1937, evening session), RGALI, f. 631, op. 15, ed. khr. 187, ll. 134–58.

70. Getty and Naumov, *The Road to Terror*, 90.

71. Stenogramma (Fourth plenum; Feb. 22, 1937, evening session), l. 59.

72. Stenogramma (Fourth plenum; Feb. 23, 1937, evening session), RGALI, f. 631, op. 15, ed. khr. 181, ll. 83ff.

73. Stenogramma (Fourth plenum; Feb. 22, 1937, evening session), ll. 61–62.

74. Stenogramma (Fourth plenum; Feb. 22, 1937, evening session), l. 61.

75. Stenogramma (Fourth plenum; Feb. 23, 1937, morning session), RGALI, f. 631, op. 15, ed. khr. 180, l. 18. On Stalin's redefinition of Peter the Great as a state builder and part of a "usable past" for the Soviet Union, see Brandenberger, *National Bolshevism*, 47–58.

76. Stenogramma (Fourth plenum; Feb. 23, 1937, morning session), l. 25.

77. Tynianov's reference to Pushkin's "barely sketched out" characters suggests the formalist interest in fragmentation and interruption, and his invitation to the reader to contribute meaning through the act of interpretation implies what Monika Greenleaf has aptly called "the addressee's unforeseeable contribution to the generation of meaning" ("Tynianov, Pushkin, and the Fragment," 281). Dimitri Mirskii, "Problema Pushkina," 101, had similarly argued that Pushkin's aesthetics were "open." Mirsky's article, written before the Politburo resolution on Pushkin but published only after a long delay, was another example of publication that appeared just as a change in party line made it unacceptable. See Platt, "Feast," 126.

78. Stenogramma (Fourth plenum; Feb. 23, 1937, morning session), l. 8.

79. Stenogramma (Fourth plenum; Feb. 22, 1937, evening session), l. 65.

80. Stenogramma (Fourth plenum; Feb. 23, 1937, morning session), ll. 44–45.

81. Stenogramma (Fourth plenum; Feb. 23, 1937, morning session), l. 56. On writers' use of historical analogy to come to terms with the Stalin era, see Clark, *Petersburg*, 192; Smith, "Reach of Modern Life," 93; Trigos, "Exploration"; Bulgakova, "Pushkinskie motivy u Eizenshteina," cited in Smith, "Reach of Modern Life," 105–6.

82. Stenogramma (Fourth plenum; Feb. 23, 1937, morning session), l. 56.

83. Stenogramma (Fourth plenum; Feb. 24, 1937, evening session), RGALI, f. 631, op. 15, ed. khr. 183, l. 35.

84. Stenogramma (Fourth plenum; Feb. 26, 1937, morning session), RGALI, f. 631, op. 15, ed. khr. 186, l. 35; Stenogramma (Fourth plenum; Feb. 26, 1937, evening session), l. 59. *Pravda* and *Izvestiia* criticized Selvinsky on the penultimate day of the plenum. At the plenum, the poet Dmitry Petrovsky denounced both Selvinsky and Pasternak, referring to Pasternak's "Bukharin period" and accusing him of using coded language and being "two-faced"; see Stenogramma (Fourth plenum; Feb. 24, morning session), RGALI, f. 631, op. 15, ed. khr. 182, ll. 64–65.

85. Stenogramma (Fourth plenum; Feb. 26, 1937, morning session), RGALI, f. 631, op. 15, ed. khr. 186, l. 40.

86. Stenogramma (Fourth plenum; Feb. 26, 1937, morning session), l. 39

87. Stenogramma (Fourth plenum; Feb. 26, 1937, morning session), l. 43.

88. "Vyshe revoliutsionnuiu bditel'nost'," *Literaturnyi kritik*, no. 9 (1936): 7, cited in *MMN*, 684. Lominadze had committed suicide two years earlier. Makaryev was also attacked in this article; Brown, *Proletarian Episode*, 224–25, 284, states that most literary professionals who perished when Stavsky headed the Writers' Union had differences with Stavsky or Yudin dating to RAPP, naming Georgy Gorbachev, Anna Grudskaia, Ivan Katayev, Lelevich, Rodov, Selivanovsky, [Igor?] Serebriakov, Tarasov-Rodionov, Ekaterina Troshchenko, and Voronsky.

89. *MMN*, 662. For Averbakh's earlier accusations against Trotskyists, see "Ko vsem chlenam RAPPa," *LG*, July 25, 1930.

90. *MMN*, 683; Protokol no. 6 i stenogramma (presidium; Sept. 1, 1937), RGALI, f. 631, op. 15, ed. khr. 173, ll. 13–18.

91. Protokol no. 6 i stenogramma (presidium; Sept. 1, 1937), ll. 18–19.

92. Petrone, *Life*, 167.

93. See Kun, *Stalin*, 238.

94. Protokol no. 6 i stenogramma (presidium; Sept. 1, 1937), ll. 27–28.

95. Protokol no. 6 i stenogramma (presidium; Sept. 1, 1937), ll. 18, 31–35, 65–66.

96. Protokol no. 6 i stenogramma (presidium; Sept. 1, 1937), l. 18.

97. "Piat' let," *LG*, Apr. 20, 1937; *MMN*, 652.

98. See, for example, Aleksandr Gladkov's description, *MMN*, 652.

99. Maksimenkov, *Sumbur vmesto muzyki*, 7, which also suggests that Stavsky, assiduous in his denunciation of Averbakh in 1932, now accused Fadeyev of having met with Averbakh to reconstitute the RAPP group.

100. According to Kostyrchenko, *Stalin protiv "kosmopolitov,"* 105–6, Stalin protected Fadeyev beginning in 1932.

101. Smith, *D. S. Mirsky*, 266; *MMN*, 624.

102. Smith, *D. S. Mirsky*, 264, citing Vishnevsky's diary entry of Nov. 5, 1935; on possible reasons for Mirsky's arrest, see 260–66.

103. In a letter to Stalin of August 2, 1934, and a *Pravda* article of Jan. 24, 1935; see Smith, *D. S. Mirsky*, 267.

104. Smith, *D. S. Mirsky*, 266, 291.

105. On countersigning of warrants, see Cohen, *An End to Silence*, 115; Mandelstam, *Hope Against Hope*, 355; and Shentalinsky, *Arrested Voices*, 159.

106. See, for example, Fadeyev's reference to an *anonimka* in *AFPD*, 68.

107. Clark, *Moscow, the Fourth Rome*, 231–32.

108. Zolotonosov, *Kak pisateli Leningrada*.

109. Shentalinsky, *Arrested Voices*, 186–87; see generally the chapter on "denunciation as a literary genre," 158–96.

110. Shentalinsky, *Arrested Voices*, 176.

111. Lekmanov, *Zhizn' Osipa Mandel'shtama*, 206; Mandelstam, *Hope Against Hope*, 302.

112. Shentalinsky, *Arrested Voices*, 190.

113. *LF*, 26. Vishnevsky and Pavlenko were two of the worst denouncers. On Vishnevsky's denunciations, see *MMN*, 655. On Fadeyev as Stavsky's deputy, see *AFPD*, 67.

114. Mandel'shtam's tepid ode to Stalin was denied publication (and was later destroyed by Nadezhda and Akhmatova; see Mandelstam, *Hope Against Hope*, 46).

115. Mandelstam, *Hope Against Hope*, 303.

116. E. Polianovsky, "Smert' Osipa Mandel'shtama," pt. 2, *Izvestiia*, May 26, 1992.

117. Polianovsky, "Smert' Osipa Mandel'shtama," pt. 2, dates this meeting "on the eve of 1938"; Mandelstam, *Hope Against Hope*, 353, implies it was later that winter.

118. Mandelstam, *Hope Against Hope*, 354, notes, "We never for a moment thought that Fadeyev's gloom might somehow be connected with M.'s fate and Andreyev's refusal to help—a terrible sentence in itself."

119. Lekmanov, *Zhizn' Osipa Mandel'shtama*, 208.

120. Polianovsky, "Smert' Osipa Mandel'shtama," pt. 2. Lekmanov, *Zhizn'*

Osipa Mandel'shtama, 209, contains the complete text of Stavsky's letter to Yezhov. Mandelstam, *Hope Against Hope*, 356, suggests that the Samatikha stay was an NKVD setup; Gershtein, *Moscow Memoirs*, 354, dismisses the idea. Smith, *D. S. Mirsky*, 233, says Stavsky was "almost certainly" the one who told the NKVD about Mandel'shtam's Stalin poem.

121. Shentalinsky, *Arrested Voices*, 188.

122. "Spetsspravka sekretno-politicheskogo otdela GUGB NKVD SSSR o nastroeniiakh sredi pisatelei," Arkhiv Aleksandra N. Iakovleva, https://www.alexanderyakovlev.org/almanah/inside/almanah-doc/58257.

123. Sholokhov's correspondence with Stalin on the grain crisis is published in Murin, *Pisatel' i vozhd'*, 22–69.

124. On Stalin's systematic arrests of *obkom* and *raikom* secretaries, see Getty, *Pragmatists and Puritans*, 31.

125. Murin, *Pisatel' i vozhd'*, 19. Ermolaev, *Mikhail Sholokhov*, 40, says Yezhov personally interrogated Lugovoi.

126. Ermolaev, *Mikhail Sholokhov*, 41.

127. Murin, *Pisatel' i vozhd'*, 19.

128. Sholokhov, *Pis'ma*, 180.

129. Murin, *Pisatel' i vozhd'*, 72.

130. Murin, *Pisatel' i vozhd'*, 71.

131. Murin, *Pisatel' i vozhd'*, 73.

132. Murin, *Pisatel' i vozhd'*, 73.

133. Murin, *Pisatel' i vozhd'*, 147n31.

134. Murin, *Pisatel' i vozhd'*, 148, 149.

135. Murin, *Pisatel' i vozhd'*, 96–103.

136. Murin, *Pisatel' i vozhd'*, 77.

137. The full text of their report is in Murin, *Pisatel' i vozhd'*, 108–27.

138. Murin, *Pisatel' i vozhd'*, 150.

139. See also the episode in Boeck, *Stalin's Scribe*, 214–15.

140. Medvedev, "The Riddles Grow," 111; cited in Ermolaev, *Mikhail Sholokhov*, 44.

141. Getty, *Origins*, 175, notes that loyalty checks increased in the second half of 1937.

142. Protokoly 18-21 i stenogramma (secretariat; 1937), l. 42.

143. *SL*, 256.

144. *SL*, 262.

145. *SL*, 300, 305.

146. Blium, *Sovetskaia tsenzura*, 48.

147. On the failure to provide guidance for the myriad inexperienced party workers who replaced purged officials, see Petrone, *Life*, 171.

148. Zolotonosov, *Kak pisateli Leningrada*.

149. R. A. Medvedev, *K sudu istorii: Genezis i posledstviia Stalinizma* (New

York: Knopf, 1974), 445; cited in Garrard and Garrard, *Inside the Soviet Writers' Union*, 260. In 1934, the membership was 2,200; in 1936, Gorky used a ballpark figure of 3,000, likely an overstatement but reflecting the continuing admission of new members. In January 1938, Marchenko, the recent head of the *partkom*, estimated Writers' Union arrests (counting beginning in the summer of 1936) at one-third the membership; this included some 50 Literary Institute students, whose arrests he dated from 1935 to 1937; see *MMN*, 733–34. He also claimed that the institute's chief, M. Borsky, who was forced out of his position by scandal, fled to Rostov on the Don, where with Stavsky's help he became deputy head of the *obkom* Agitprop. Altstadt, *Politics of Culture*, 200–201, provides figures for the Azerbaijan branch in line with the upper end of this estimate. Altstadt counts the number of expelled members at 37 percent, the great majority of them also arrested. Seven new members were admitted in 1937, as against 24 expulsions.

150. Stenogramma (presidium; Feb. 20, 1937), ll. 25–27, 35; "Pis'mo A. A. Surkova A. S. Shcherbakovu" [ne rannee 1936 g.], ll. 1–3; *MMN*, 346–49, 732–38; *LF*, 27–33.

151. A. A. Fadeev, "Zapisnaia knizhka," Dec. 16, 1936–May 2, 1937, RGALI, f. 1628, op. 1, ed. khr. 400, l. 38.

152. "Pis'mo A. A. Surkova A. S. Shcherbakovu" [ne rannee 1936 g.], ll. 2–2 verso; f. 631, op. 15, ed. khr. 266, ll. 12–14, 39.

153. Maksimenkov, *Sumbur vmesto muzyki*, 308. Angarov and Tamarkin had also supported Eisenstein when his work on *Bezhin Meadow* had come under fire two months earlier and apparently even after the Central Committee resolution banning the film; see *VKI*, 357–58.

154. See the complaint letter from five Kuibyshev writers and *LG*'s validation of it in *MMN*, 690–92.

155. *AFPD*, 8. It was established by the Stalin constitution to replace the Congresses of Soviets.

156. "Ob oshibkakh partorganizatsii pri iskliuchenii kommunistov iz partii," *Pravda*, Jan. 29, 1938. See also Getty, *Origins*, 186.

157. Maksimenkov, *Sumbur vmesto muzyki*, 288.

158. *SL*, 269–70. Nikitin noted that Stavsky had to ask the secretariat to approve a working vacation for Vishnevsky so he could get relief from nonstop Writers' Union meetings.

159. *Pravda*, Jan. 26, 1938; see also *AFPD*, 56n2.

160. *LF*, 276. The meetings were on March 25, March 27, and April 8.

161. A. Murugov and I. Kaganovich, "God raboty na osnove iiunskogo prikaza," *Sotsialisticheskaia zakonnost'*, no. 7 (1939): 12; cited in Solomon, "Soviet Criminal Justice," 406.

162. Quoted in Garros, Korenevskaya, and Lahusen, *Intimacy and Terror*, 229–30.

163. Stavskii, "Dnevnik," Jan. 1, 1938–Apr. 17, 1939, l. 17.

INTERMEZZO TWO

1. Litvin, *Dnevnik istorika*, 506.
2. Platt, "Feast," 300, 318.
3. Two documents signed by Stalin, Kirov, and Zhdanov were published after the fact. See "Zamechaniia po povodu konspekta uchebnika po istorii SSSR," and "Zamechaniia po povodu konspekta uchebnika po novoi istorii," in *Pravda* and *Izvestiia*, Jan. 27, 1936; cited in *VKI*, 440.
4. Usievich, "Za chistotu Leninizma," 171.
5. A. Mazaev, *O 'Literaturnom kritike' i ego esteticheskoi programme. Stranitsy otechestvennoi khudozhestvennoi kul'tury, 30-ye gody* (Moscow: Gosudarstvennyi Institut Iskusstvoznaniia, 1995), 154–55, cited in Galushkin, "Andrei Platonov," *SF*, 825; Clark, "Germanophone Contributions," 513.
6. *Kratkaia literaturnaia entsiklopediia*, s.v. "Literaturnyi kritik."
7. Clark, "Germanophone Contributions," 515.
8. Clark, *Moscow, the Fourth Rome*, 168.
9. Clark, *Moscow, the Fourth Rome*, 179. The Comintern entity that oversaw foreign literature, MORP (International Association of Revolutionary Writers), was discontinued. Clark writes that the Foreign Commission had more power than VOKS, the official outlet for cultural ties with other countries.
10. *SF*, 818, citing a *Pravda* article of August 8, 1936.
11. For example, Platonov, "Bessmertie," 114–28, and Platonov, "Fro," 129–45; see also *MMN*, 520. Lukács included the protagonist of "Bessmertie" in a list of heroes from Soviet classics, alongside Levinson in Fadeyev's *Razgrom*; see *APVS*, 329.
12. In *Znamia*, no. 4 (1937): 276; cited in *APVS*, 329.
13. *APVS*, 345. For a discussion of this story in the context of Soviet subjectivity, see Naiman, "On Soviet Subjects," 314.
14. Platonov's story did not make it into the volume it was intended for; it appeared in 1940 in the journal *Industriia sotsializma* under the title "Zhizn' v semeistve"; see *MMN*, 520.
15. *MMN*, 515. Also defending Platonov were Gekht and Sergei Malakhov, who as a referee for Sovetsky pisatel had recommended at least one of Platonov's stories for publication.
16. Clark, "Germanophone Contributions," 527.
17. Clark, *Moscow, the Fourth Rome*, 166.
18. A. A. Fadeev, "Zapisnaia knizhka," Mar. 18, 1938–Nov. 8, 1939, RGALI, f. 1628, op. 1, ed. khr. 404, ll. 7–8.
19. Clark, "Germanophone Contributions," 525; "Stenogramma vystuplenii aspirantov i studentov pri zhurnale 'Literaturnyi kritik' v Institute Istorii, Filosofii i Literatury, Apr. 2–14, 1939, RGALI, f. 631, op. 15, ed. khr. 360, ll. 8–22.
20. V. Ermilov, "O vrednykh vzgliadakh 'Literaturnogo kritika,'" *LG*,

Sept. 10, 1939; V. Ermilov, "O nekotorykh literaturno-khudozhestvennykh zhurnalakh," *Bol'shevik*, no. 11 (1939): both cited in *APVS*, 425.

21. The Administration of Propaganda and Agitation, as it was now called, was headed at this moment by Zhdanov; Aleksandrov headed its propaganda department.

22. *SF*, 822. The offending journal was *Kniga i proletarskaia revoliutsiia*.

23. Another factor in Yermilov's victory may have been the Soviet tilt away from internationalized ideology in 1939, after the victory of Franco and the end of the Popular Front in France; see Clark, *Moscow, the Fourth Rome*, 308.

24. Both actions were taken in a resolution of the Central Committee *orgbiuro* of November 26, 1940; printed in *VKI*, 463.

25. Naiman, "On Soviet Subjects," 314.

CHAPTER FIVE

1. Shentalinsky, *Arrested Voices*, 193.
2. Shentalinsky, *Arrested Voices*, 159; Cohen, *An End to Silence*, 115.
3. Berelowitch, "Peredelkino," 204.
4. On Bilimenko and Nerezov, see *AFPD*, 25.
5. Ivanov, *Dnevniki*, 42.
6. Lewin, *Making of the Soviet System*, 222.
7. *AFPD*, 17. Erenburg, *Liudi, gody, zhizn'*, 127, states, "Fadeyev was a bold but disciplined soldier; he never forgot the prerogative of the commander in chief. For him that commander in chief was Stalin."
8. Lekmanov, *Zhizn' Osipa Mandel'shtama*, 176.
9. Fadeev, *Sobranie sochinenii v semi tomakh* (Moscow: 1971), 126; cited in Kiseleva, *Fadeev-Khudozhnik*, 4–5. The letter is dated October 24, 1936; emphasis in original.
10. Kiseleva, *Fadeev-Khudozhnik*, 7–8.
11. *LG*, Aug. 11, 1940; cited in *APVS*, 427.
12. Rubtsov, *Alter ego Stalina*, 83–84.
13. "Aleksandr Aleksandrovich Fadeev," Khronos: Vsemirnaia istoriia v Internete, ed. Viacheslav Rumiantsev, www.hrono.ru/biograf/Fadeyev.html.
14. A. A. Fadeev, "My nepobedimy," *LG*, Feb. 1, 1937; cited in Brown, *Proletarian Episode*, 225.
15. A. A. Fadeev, "Zapisnaia knizhka," Jan. 5–26, 1937, RGALI, f. 1628, op. 1, ed. khr. 401, l. 20.
16. *VKI*, 424. The presidium members were Gerasimova, Karavayeva, Valentin Katayev, Fedin, Pavlenko, Sobolev, Tolstoy, Vishnevsky, Vasily Lebedev-Kumach, Aseyev, Sholokhov, Korneichuk, Mashashvili (Alio Mirtskhulava), and Yanko Kupala.
17. These figures are arrived at by comparing *VKI*, 424, and *PT*, 15.
18. "Pravlenie Soiuza Sovetskikh Pisatelei," May 4–July 29, 1939, RGALI,

f. 631, op. 15, ed. khr. 408, ll. 17–19; "Perepiska s uchrezhdeniiami," Jan. 20–Dec. 21, 1939, RGALI, f. 631, op. 15, ed. khr. 415, ll. 3, 5, 6.

19. Boborykin, *Aleksandr Fadeev*, 334.

20. See Protokol i stenogramma (presidium and poetry section; Nov. 22, 1938), RGALI, f. 631, op. 15, ed. khr. 266, l. 39.

21. Ermolaev, *Censorship in Soviet Literature*, 58–59.

22. Kozlov, *Readers*, 175.

23. Tvardovsky's characterization in *AFPD*, 304; see also Ermolaev, *Censorship in Soviet Literature*, 39.

24. "Perepiska s uchrezhdeniiami," Jan. 20–Dec. 21, 1939, l. 16.

25. "Perepiska s uchrezhdeniiami," Jan. 20–Dec. 21, 1939, l. 16.

26. Zhukov, *Ruka sud'by*, 114.

27. "Pis'ma Fadeeva A. A. v TsK i drugie," 1931–1956, RGALI, f. 1628, op. 2, ed. khr. 433, l. 8.

28. Slezkine, *The House of Government*, 954.

29. From 1942 through 1946, the union added 317 new members; see Protokoly nos. 37–38 i stenogrammy (secretariat and presidium; Sept. 19–Dec. 6, 1947), l. 47. Using the statistics in *PT*, 111 and 117, that 400 writers were killed in the war and that in 1946 the Writers' Union reached 2,760 members, I arrive at 2,843 members at the outbreak of war in 1941.

30. Stenogramma (expanded presidium; Jan. 25–27, 1942), RGALI, f. 631, op. 15, ed. khr. 576, l. 4.

31. Fadeyev, *Sobranie sochinenii v piati tomakh*, 5:487.

32. "Pravlenie Soiuza Sovetskikh Pisatelei," May 4–July 29, 1939, ll. 1–9. The poem, by Aleksei Platonov, was published in *Literaturnyi sovremennik*, no. 20 (1938).

33. Protokol (presidium; Nov. 11, 1939), RGALI, f. 631, op. 15, ed. khr. 351, l. 8.

34. Protokol no. 16 (presidium; May 10, 1940), RGALI, f. 631, op. 15, ed. khr. 443, l. 4.

35. "Perepiska s uchrezhdeniiami," Jan. 20–Dec. 21, 1939, l. 10; Protokol no. 15 (presidium; Mar. 21, 1940), RGALI, f. 631, op. 15, ed. khr. 442, ll. 1–2.

36. "Perepiska s uchrezhdeniiami," Jan. 20–Dec. 21, 1939, l. 10.

37. This included the Writers' Union's own publications *Novy mir*, *October*, *Red Virgin Soil*, *Znamia*, and *Zvezda*; see *PT*, 16–18, and *MMN*, 840–42. According to Maksimenkov, *Sumbur vmesto muzyki*, 301, Agitprop's restructuring dated to August 1938. Probably the transition was begun then and the resolution passed upon completion of the new structure a year later. After Kerzhentsev's removal, the Arts Committee was broken into separate agencies for music, film, and architecture; they were overseen by the new Upravlenie Propagandy i Agitatsii TsK. In addition, a republic Arts Committee was established within the RSFSR (297–98).

38. Avdeenko, *Nakazanie bez prestupleniia*, 201.

39. Avdeenko, *Nakazanie bez prestupleniia*, 213. Stalin employed a similar tactic on other occasions, notably at Selvinsky's November 1943 *prorabotka* described in *PT*, 86–88. On Selvinsky's troubles in these years, see Shrayer, *I Saw It*, 140–62.

40. On internalizing the values of one's oppressor, see Adler, *Keeping Faith*, 21.

41. Avdeenko, *Nakazanie bez prestupleniia*, 215.

42. The episode is described in *PT*, 25–30. Ruder, *Making History for Stalin*, 65, states that Avdeyenko's and Fadeyev's sons were friends, but that Fadeyev nonetheless denounced Avdeenko. He was reinstated in the Writers' Union in 1945, and in the party in 1955; see "Aleksandr Avdeenko: Biografiia," People SU, http://www.people.su/1915.

43. Avdeenko, *Nakazanie bez prestupleniia*, 247.

44. *PT*, 33–34, suggests this may have saved Leonov from becoming the first victim of the campaign.

45. Protokol no. 15 (presidium; Mar. 21, 1940), l. 9.

46. Protokol no. 15 (presidium; Mar. 21, 1940), ll. 8, 15.

47. *PT*, 38–39.

48. Protokol no. 9 i stenogramma (presidium; Feb. 7, 1940), RGALI, f. 631, op. 15, ed. khr. 437, l. 43.

49. *PT*, 55. The memo is dated May 7, 1941.

50. This was a common argument. Aseyev made it in a 1943 letter to Stalin, but presumably out of diplomacy and self-protection—he did not necessarily believe that party policy was blameless; see *PT*, 85–86.

51. Adler, *Keeping Faith*, 109.

52. Stenogramma (expanded presidium; Jan. 25–27, 1942), l. 4.

53. In January 1943 the head of the Writers' Union military commission, Lobansky, provided the following (incomplete) breakdown of 306 writers assigned to various outlets: central army press and *apparat*, 40; central navy press and staff, 23; central general political press, including radio, TASS, and Soviet Information Bureauburo, 50; various front newspapers, 39; army, corps, and divisional press, 104; fleet press (probably air force), 36; Stenogramma (presidium; Jan. 29, 1943), RGALI, f. 631, op. 15, ed. khr. 611, l. 4. See also *PT*, 64.

54. Ehrenburg, *The War 1941–45*; Stenogramma (presidium; Jan. 29, 1943), l. 5. Writers who saw combat included Afinogenov, Boris Dairedzhiev, Fadeyev, Fish, Yevgeny Gabrilovich, Arkady Gaidar, Emanuil Kazakevich, Zakhar Khatzrevin, Kirsanov, Yury Krymov, Boris Lapin, Lidin, Surkov, Tarasov, Tvardovsky, Utkin, and Vishnevsky. Writers who served as war correspondents included Liusia Argutinskaia, Ehrenburg, Ilya Frenkel, Savva Golovanivsky, Gorbunov, Vasily Grossman, Isbakh, Vadim Kozhevnikov, Levin, Libedinsky, Mikhail Matusovsky, Petrov, Platonov, Selvinsky, Sholokhov, Stavsky, and the expelled Avdeyenko.

55. Ehrenburg, *The War 1941–45*, 53–55.

56. The wartime military commission (*voennaia komissiia*) replaced the de-

fense commission (*oboronnaia komissiia*). Its members in January 1943 were Pavlenko (chair), Shchipachev (deputy), Lobansky (secretary), Raisa Azarkh, Lavrenev, Leites, Libedinsky, Lev Oshanin, Nikolai Panov, Aleksei Simukov, Lev Slavin, Sergei Vashentsev, and Yury Veber; see Protokoly nos. 1–25 (presidium; 1943), RGALI, f. 631, op. 15, ed. khr. 608, l. 11.

57. Stenogramma (presidium; Jan. 29, 1943), l. 8.

58. Stenogramma (presidium; Jan. 29, 1943), l. 6.

59. Stenogramma (presidium; Jan. 29, 1943), l. 7.

60. Stenogramma (expanded presidium; Jan. 25–27, 1942), l. 25.

61. Antipina, *Povsednevnaia zhizn' sovetskikh pisatelei*, 248; *PT*, 65–66.

62. Protokoly nos. 1–25 (presidium; 1943), ll. 55, 63.

63. Protokoly nos. 1–25 (presidium; 1943), ll. 61–62.

64. Protokoly nos. 1–25 (presidium; 1943), ll. 23, 23 verso.

65. Protokoly nos. 1–25 (presidium; 1943), ll. 23–25. Pyotr Grigoryevich Skosyrev presided in Fadeyev's absence.

66. Protokoly nos. 1–25 (presidium; 1943), ll. 1–3.

67. Protokoly nos. 37–38 i stenogrammy (secretariat and presidium; Sept. 19–Dec. 6, 1947), l. 47.

68. Protokoly nos. 37–38 i stenogrammy (secretariat and presidium; Sept. 19–Dec. 6, 1947), l. 48. The head of the commission in 1948 was the nonparty Leonid Sobolev.

69. Protokoly nos. 1–25 (presidium; 1943), ll. 46–51. Bonch-Bruyevich's daughter Yelena, Averbakh's wife, was also in the Gulag at this time.

70. See, for example, Shcherbakov's comment in Brandenberger, *National Bolshevism*, 180.

71. Rubenstein, *Tangled Loyalties*, 202, 207; *PT*, 81, 86.

72. Clark and Dobrenko, *Soviet Culture and Power*, 348–49.

73. Rubenstein, *Tangled Loyalties*, 191. Their publication was perhaps another instance of the special status accorded to Ehrenburg, who also wrote for the Allied press services that published in American, British, and French newspapers. But *Krasnaia zvezda*'s editor, David Vadimov (Ortenberg), himself a Jew, also took risks in deciding against censoring Ehrenburg's reports before Stalin reviewed each issue.

74. Its formation was an uneasy negotiation between Jewish Bund leaders and the Soviet government; see Montefiore, *Stalin*, 560, and "Dokladnaia zapiska G. F. Aleksandrova," Fond Aleksandra N. Yakovleva.

75. Of the fifteen committee members who were tried in secret in 1952, only Lozovsky resisted confession under torture. See Rubenstein, *Stalin's Secret Pogrom*, 10.

76. "Dokladnaia zapiska G. F. Aleksandrova," Fond Aleksandra N. Yakovleva.

77. A. Fadeev, "Otechestvennaia voina i sovetskaia literatura," in Fadeev, "Literatura i zhizn'," 4:331.

78. A. A. Fadeev, "Iz vystuplenii na zasedaniiakh Komiteta po Stalinskim Premiiam, Dec. 30, 1940–Feb. 10, 1953, RGALI, f. 1628, op. 3, ed. khr. 3, l. 7. This was in April 1945. On this prize, see Tomoff, *Creative Union*, 209, 240. Why the Writers' Union chief should have been placed in charge of the music prizes is another question.

79. *PT*, 67. In 1949 Dmitry Shepilov (deputy director of Agitprop in the military) wrote to Malenkov that these episodes occurred four or five times a year; see RGASPI, f. 17, op. 132, ed. khr. 224, l. 65.

80. RGALI, f. 631, op. 15, ed. khr. 608, ll. 6–8. The letter is dated December 12, 1942. Fadeyev's response, in which he reproaches Bezymensky for fixating on personal feuds when the nation's survival was at stake, is published in *Vokrug Fadeeva*, 60–61.

81. L. Poliak, "O liricheskom epose Velikoi Otechestvennoi voiny," *Znamia*, nos. 9–10 (1943); cited in *PT*, 97.

82. B. M. Eikhenbaum, "Pogovorim o nashem remesle," *Zvezda*, no. 2 (1945): 108.

83. Sherry, *Discourses*, 70.

84. Two are published in *VKI*, 507–8. On the third, see *PT*, 90.

85. Rubenstein, *Tangled Loyalties*, 217.

86. *TPS*, 1:479. I extrapolate the number 115 from figures given for 1944 in *TPS*, 1:479.

87. *TPS*, 1:476; Kostyrchenko, *Stalin protiv "kosmopolitov,"* 106–7.

88. *TPS*, 1:477.

89. They meant Zoshchenko's *Before Sunrise* and Selvinsky's *Who Did Russia Sing to Sleep* (*Kogo baiukala Rossiia*). A February 10, 1944, resolution of the Central Committee secretariat called Selvinsky's poem a slander against the Russian people and relieved Selvinsky of his duties as a war correspondent; *TPS*, 1:475. This decision was reversed when Selvinsky produced a poem praising Stalin; *TPS*, 1:475–76.

90. Volkov, "Za kulisami," 46, notes Polikarpov was Malenkov's client. Polikarpov had also been head of the radio committee during the war; see "V soiuze sovetskikh pisatelei SSSR," *Literatura i iskusstvo*, Jan. 22, 1944. *AFPD*, 129–30, states that on January 19, 1944, the Writers' Union presidium voted Tikhonov *predsedatel* while simultaneously appointing Polikarpov secretary. Meeting minutes give Polikarpov's title as secretary of the board (*sekretar pravleniia*). Berzer, "Stranitsy starogo kalendaria," 186, and Garrard and Garrard, *Inside the Soviet Writers' Union*, 87, refer to Polikarpov as the union's *orgsekretar*.

91. Clark and Dobrenko, *Soviet Culture and Power*, 381.

92. Protokol no. 1 i stenogramma (presidium; Jan. 17, 1946), RGALI, f. 631, op. 15, ed. khr. 767, l. 97.

93. Protokoly (presidium and secretariat; Jan. 19–June 30, 1946), ll. 3, 15.

94. Protokoly (presidium and secretariat; Jan. 19–June 30, 1946), l. 23.

95. Protokol no. 1 i stenogramma (presidium; Jan. 17, 1946), l. 53.

96. Protokoly (presidium and secretariat; Jan. 19–June 30, 1946), l. 8.

97. Protokol no. 1 i stenogramma (presidium; Jan. 17, 1946), l. 39.

98. Protokol no. 1 i stenogramma (presidium; Jan. 17, 1946), ll. 34–35, 52–54.

99. Protokol no. 1 i stenogramma (presidium; Jan. 17, 1946), ll. 34–35.

100. Protokol no. 1 i stenogramma (presidium; Jan. 17, 1946), l. 19.

101. Protokol no. 1 i stenogramma (presidium; Jan. 17, 1946), ll. 60, 85–86.

102. Protokoly (presidium and secretariat; Jan. 19–June 30, 1946), l. 13. The minutes record only that "the participants in the discussion gave the poem a high rating" and list the following contributors: Vladimir Aleksandrov [Keller], Ivan Gutorov, Mikhail Isaakovsky, Aleksandr Kovalenkov, Leites, Petrovsky, Polikarpov, Reznik, Sobolev, Tarasenkov, Tikhonov, and Tvardovsky himself. See also Berzer, "Stranitsy starogo kalendaria," 187.

103. Protokol no. 1 i stenogramma (presidium; Jan. 17, 1946), ll. 77–79.

104. Clark, *Moscow, the Fourth Rome*, 190. It began publication in 1939.

105. Protokoly (presidium and secretariat; Jan. 19–June 30, 1946), l. 22; protokol no. 32 i stenogramma (presidium; Aug. 18, 1947), ed. khr. 814, l. 70.

106. *PT*, 113. See also letters from presidium members Aseyev, Gerasimova, Karavaeva, and Vishnevsky urging Polikarpov's removal in Protokoly (presidium and secretariat; Jan. 19–June 30, 1946), ll. 3, 13, 14, 23.

107. *PT*, 124–31; Volkov, "Za kulisami," 44–49.

108. *PT*, 90. This resolution was passed on December 2.

109. *PT*, 74. The memo triggered a Writers' Union meeting at which Fadeyev did his party duty, criticizing Zoshchenko and then defended having done so: "We are writers—what are we? We are not sycophants in our government, we answer for our government." But Forsh and Marshak stood up for Zoshchenko. See *PT*, 76.

110. This is suggested in V'iugin, *Politika poetiki*, 311–12.

111. Volkov, "Za kulisami," 45.

112. Volkov, "Za kulisami," 46.

113. Yury German's article in *Leningradskaia pravda*, July 6, 1946; cited in *PT*, 121.

114. Memoirs of this meeting are in Kapitsa, "Eto bylo tak," 136–49, and Levonevskii, "Istoriia 'Bol'shogo bloknota,'" 193–97.

115. Volkov, "Za kulisami," 44–45; V. I. Demidov and V. A. Kutuzov, *Poslednii udar*, in V. I. Demidov and V. A. Kutuzov, comps., *Leningradskoe delo*, 51; cited in *PT*, 119, 133.

116. The meeting is described in *PT*, 124–31.

117. Volkov, "Za kulisami," 49.

118. Malenkov managed at least a partial victory; see Hahn, *Postwar Soviet Politics*, 45.

119. Protokoly (presidium and secretariat; Jan. 19–June 30, 1946), ll. 14,

15; protokola i stenogramma (party group; Jan. 28–Mar. 27, 1946), Tsentral'nyi arkhiv obshchestvennykh dvizhenii Moskvy, f. 8131, op. 1, ed. khr. 3, l. 4.

120. "Postanovlenie orgbiuro TsK VKP(b) o zhurnalakh *Zvezda* i *Leningrad*," *VKI*, 587–88.

121. *VKI*, 603; "Sobranie aktiva Leningradskoi partiinoi organizatsii," *LG*, Aug. 24, 1946.

122. The members at large were Boris Gorbatov, Leonov, and six writers from the non-Russian republics: I. G. Semper (Estonia), Andrei Upit (Latvia), Antanas Venclova (Lithuania), Simon Chikovani (Georgia), Musa Aibek (Uzbekistan), and Yakub Kolas (Belorussia). See "V prezidiume pravleniia soiuza sovetskikh pisatelei SSSR," *LG*, Sept. 7, 1946.

123. "Rezoliutsiia prezidiuma pravleniia soiuza sovetskikh pisatelei SSSR ot 4 sentiabria 1946 g.," *LG*, Sept. 7, 1946; see also *Peterburgskii zhurnal*, nos. 1–2 (1993): 34–36. Despite Fadeyev's public denunciation of Akhmatova and Zoshchenko at the time of the 1946 party resolution, they both turned to him for help; see *AFPD*, 13.

124. A. A. Fadeev, "Zapisi o sovetskoi literature," 1946–1947, RGALI, f. 1628, op. 1, ed. khr. 429, ll. 3, 5.

125. Ogryzko, "Gromila sovetskoi literatury."

126. *PT*, 118. See, for example, B. Riurikov, "Vrednaia kontseptsiia professora B. Eikhenbauma," *Kul'tura i zhizn'*, Oct. 20, 1946.

127. A. Platonov, "Sem'ia Ivanova," *Novyi mir*, nos. 10–11 (1946); cited in Simonov, *Izbrannoe*, 2:370.

128. Kormilov, lecture, Dec. 8, 2004.

129. In *LG*, Dec. 28, 1939; cited in Clark, *Moscow, the Fourth Rome*, 331.

130. The prizes were for *A Guy from Our Town* (*Paren' iz nashego goroda*) (1942, first class), *Russian People* (*Russkie liudi*) (1943, second class), and *Days and Nights* (*Dni i nochi*) (1946, second class).

131. Simonov, *Izbrannoe*, 2:371, 394.

132. Protokoly nos. 5–22 (secretariat; Jan. 31–May 16, 1947), RGALI, f. 631, op. 15, ed. khr. 808, l. 54.

133. Protokoly nos. 5–22 (secretariat; Jan. 31–May 16, 1947), ll. 53, 58.

134. Stenogramma (prose section; Jan. 9, 1948), RGALI, f. 631, op. 20, ed. khr. 32, l. 25.

135. S. Nagornyi, "Chelovek na voine," *LG*, Dec. 21, 1946.

136. Gorbatov served as a war correspondent and Subotsky as assistant to the military procurator; arrested in 1937, he had been released in 1940.

137. Protokol no. 31 i stenogramma (presidium; Dec. 26, 1946) RGALI, f. 631, op. 15, ed. khr. 779, l. 58.

138. See, for example, A. Ivich, "Liudi dobrye," *LG*, Dec. 24, 1947.

139. Stenogramma (prose section; Jan. 9, 1948), l. 62.

140. Stenogramma (prose section; Jan. 9, 1948), l. 82.

141. Stenogramma (prose section; Jan. 9, 1948), l. 82.

142. Stenogramma (prose section; Jan. 9, 1948), l. 107.

143. Ehrenburg, *Post-War Years, 1945–1954*, 46. Other possible reasons for the prize are offered in Dunham, *In Stalin's Time*, 176–83, and Svirskii, *Na lobnom meste*, 68–69.

CHAPTER SIX

1. See Fadeyev's use of this language in a letter to Vishnevsky in *FP* 1973, 204–5.

2. Simonov, *Izbrannoe*, 2:383–84.

3. Batkin, "Son razuma," 22.

4. Batkin, "Son razuma," 17–18, 44.

5. Simonov, *Izbrannoe*, 396.

6. Simonov, *Izbrannoe*, 2:378.

7. Simonov, *Izbrannoe*, 2: 380.

8. Simonov, *Izbrannoe*, 2:384.

9. Simonov, *Izbrannoe*, 2:386.

10. Simonov, *Izbrannoe*, 2:386.

11. Simonov, *Izbrannoe*, 2:387.

12. Simonov, *Izbrannoe*, 2:388. Protokol no. 32 i stenogramma (presidium; Aug. 18, 1947), ed. khr. 814, ll. 1–12, corroborates Simonov's account.

13. Simonov, *Izbrannoe*, 2:394.

14. Simonov, *Izbrannoe*, 2:387.

15. Simonov, *Izbrannoe*, 2:385.

16. Simonov, *Izbrannoe*, 2:390.

17. For *Someone Else's Shadow* (*Chuzhaia ten'*) (1950, second-class prize); see Simonov, *Izbrannoe*, 2:407–8.

18. See, for example, the words of N. F. Belchikov in Levitt, *Russian Literary Politics*, 167.

19. "XI plenum pravleniia soiuza sovetskikh pisatelei SSSR. Literatura posle postanovleniia TsK VKP(b) ot 14-ogo avgusta 1946 goda o zhurnalakh 'Zvezda' i 'Leningrad'. Doklad general'nogo sekretaria SSP SSSR tov. A. Fadeeva," *LG*, June 29, 1947. In the 1930 literary debates, Nusinov had defended Pereval and criticized RAPP's harassment politics and its low level of argumentation. His denunciation of the Pereverzev school, however, gave RAPP a momentary boost. See Sheshukov, *Neistovye revniteli*, 263, 271.

20. "Za bol'shevistskuiu partiinost' v sovetskom literaturovedenii," *LG*, Jan. 10, 1948. On the criticism of Kirpotin's book, see Any, "Red Pushkin," 384.

21. Figes, *The Whisperers*, 492.

22. "'Molodaia gvardiia' na stsene nashikh teatrov," *Kul'tura i zhizn'*, Nov. 30, 1947; N. Maslin, "Zhizn' vopreki . . . ," *Kul'tura i zhizn'*, Nov. 30, 1947;

"'Molodaia gvardiia' v romane i na stsene," *Pravda*, Dec. 3, 1947; "Roman 'Molodaia gvardiia' i ego instsenirovki," *LG*, Dec. 7, 1947; all cited in Swayze, *Political Control*, 273.

23. Lobov and Vasil'eva, *Peredelkino*, 61.

24. Clark, *The Soviet Novel*, 163.

25. "Kritikovat' smelo i otkryto," *LG*, Dec. 7, 1947; Yermilov to Fadeyev, Oct. 6/7, 1951.

26. Martin, *The Affirmative Action Empire*, 5.

27. Cosponsored by the Writers' Union and the Arts Committee; see *TPS*, 2:75.

28. Figes, *The Whisperers*, 494.

29. Swayze, *Political Control*, 59.

30. "Agitprop TsK VKP(b)—v sekretariat TsK VKP(b) s proektom postanovleniia o bor'be s kosmopolitizmom v teatral'noi kritike," Fond Aleksandra N. Iakovleva, http://www.alexanderyakovlev.org/fond/issues-doc/68607. The memo is dated January 23, 1949.

31. "Ob odnoi antipatrioticheskoi gruppe teatral'nykh kritikov," *Pravda*, Jan. 28, 1949, http://www.ihst.ru/projects/sohist/books/cosmopolit/100.htm.

32. Gromova, *Raspad*, 253; Borshchagovskii, *Zapiski balovnia sud'by*, 4, 74, 221.

33. Also named were Grigory Boiadzhiev, Yefim Kholodov, [Leonid] Maliugin, and Yakov Varshavsky.

34. *TPS* 2:77, alleges that the denunciation was instigated by "Fadeyev's side." An archival document is cited, but it is unclear if it refers specifically to this statement or only to Begicheva's history of writing denunciations. Figes, *The Whisperers*, 494, suggests that Fadeyev received the denunciation without foreknowledge and that he was happy to have Sofronov do the dirty work. Simonov, *Izbrannoe*, 447, thinks that Fadeyev did not foresee how far-reaching the consequences would be. For transcripts and an account of infighting and accusations of cosmopolitanism in the Writers' Union's Leningrad branch, as well as Fadeyev's role there, see Zolotonosov, *Gadiushnik*, 24–118.

35. Gromova, *Raspad*, 240–41.

36. Fadeyev was following the playbook. When the American singer Paul Robeson visited Moscow and repeatedly insisted on seeing Fefer, Fefer was whisked out of his Lubianka cell and over to Robeson's hotel room, and then back again. See Rubenstein, *Stalin's Secret Pogrom*, 47–49.

37. Names in a draft list could be removed or added as patronage or vengeance came into play. Boris Laskin was included in Begicheva's denunciation but was omitted from both the Agitprop memo and the *Pravda* article (protected perhaps by Simonov, his relative by marriage). Ehrenburg's and Zaslavsky's names were removed from a list of JAFC members marked for arrest. Figes, *The Whisperers*, 495–96, suggests that Fadeyev may have proposed their removal to Stalin.

38. Gromova, *Raspad*, 257–58; *VKI*, 657–59; cited in Galina Belaia, "Slu-chai Fadeeva," *Voprosy literatury*, no. 2 (2005), http://magazines.russ.ru/voplit /2005/2/be3-pr.html. In the same memo, Fadeyev denounced theater critic and former Litfront member Dairedzhiev.

39. Simonov, *Izbrannoe*, 471. Similarly, Hitler, before consolidating power, would go for long stretches without any public mention of Jews, while reaffirming his Jewish policy in private communications or in coded language understood by the Nazi faithful; see Koonz, *The Nazi Conscience*, 105–6.

40. Mandelstam, *Hope Against Hope*, 355.

41. *VKI*, 682. Fadeyev alludes to thirteen theater artists, of whom he names, besides Sheinin, Makliarsky, and Rozner, Leonid Khait, Vadim Kozin, Yaroslav Smeliakov, and M. Ulitsky.

42. Figes, *The Whisperers*, 498–99.

43. Gromova, *Raspad*, 263.

44. Figes, *The Whisperers*, 499.

45. Lobov and Vasil'eva, *Peredelkino*, 537.

46. V. V. Ermilov, "O durnom sochinitel'stve," *LG*, Feb. 1, 1950; Vladimir Ognev, "Vremia Simonova," *LG*, Apr. 22, 2009, https://lgz.ru/article/N17 —6221—-2009-04-22-/Vr%D0%B5mya-Simonova8602/.

47. Compare "Zakliuchitel'noe slovo A. Fadeeva," *LG*, Feb. 11, 1950 with the account in Viacheslav Ogryzko, "Bor'ba za vlast'," *Literaturnaia Rossiia*, Oct. 1, 2015, https://litrossia.ru/item/8255-plata-za-vlast.

48. On the exchanges between Fadeyev and Tvardovsky, see *AFPD*, 313–14, and Simonov, *Izbrannoe*, 447.

49. Ermilov, *A. P. Chekhov*, and Ermilov, *Dramaturgiia Chekhova*. On the Stalin prizes, see Ogryzko, "Gromila sovetskoi literatury."

50. Yermilov to Fadeyev, undated [not before mid-Oct. 1952], l. 149. The exclamation point was Yermilov's own addition.

51. Simonov, *Izbrannoe*, 447.

52. *AFPD*, 279–80, 314. The story appeared in *Novyi mir*, nos. 7–10 (1952).

53. Cohen, *An End to Silence*, 118.

54. Boborykin, *Aleksandr Fadeev*, 327–28.

55. These readers' letters to Fadeev (dating from 1938–1954) are in RGALI, f. 1628, op. 1, ed. khr. 619–37.

56. Lu Li, "My privetstvuem Vas, tov. Fadeev! Stikhotvorenie," Sept. 30, 1949, RGALI, f. 1628, op. 1, ed. khr. 1423, ll. 1–3.

57. Figes, *The Whisperers*, 589.

58. I agree with Brandenberger, *National Bolshevism*, 7, that designating Stalin a puppet master ignores the important roles of other key figures in policy decisions. But when it came to persuading and fashioning cadres Stalin had specifically chosen for their manipulability—first and foremost Fadeyev—the puppet master characterization is apt.

59. Dobson, *Khrushchev's Cold Summer*, 25, 51. The amnesty decree was issued Mar. 27, 1953.

60. Shentalinsky, *Arrested Voices*, 6.

61. Iu. Libedinskii, "Moia posledniaia vstrecha c A. A. Fadeevym," May 14, 1956, RGALI, f. 1628, op. 2, ed. khr. 1425, l. 7.

62. *AFPD*, 64, 68, 204–5 (on Nerezov); 67, 196 (on Katayev); 183; 198–99 (on Selivanovsky and Kirshon).

63. Zhukov, *Fadeev*, 292; no documentation is included, but if roughly five hundred writers returned, the figure makes sense.

64. *RT*, 298–300; Lobov and Vasil'eva, *Peredelkino*, 59. Gronsky also accused Bezymensky, Sergei Mikhalkov, Simonov, and Usievich of having written denunciations of Averbakh.

65. Artizov et al., *Reabilitatsiia*, 353.

66. Dobson, *Khrushchev's Cold Summer*, 25.

67. The letters are published in *AFPD*, 154–69.

68. V. Pomerantsev, "Ob iskrennosti v literature," 218–45.

69. Kozlov, *Readers*, 51, 53, 79–80.

70. V. Ermilov, "Za sotsialisticheskii realizm," *Pravda*, June 3, 1954; Aleksei Surkov, "Pod znamenem sotsialisticheskogo realizma," *Pravda*, May 25, 1954, both cited in Kozlov, *Readers*, 73.

71. On July 7, 1954; see *AFPD*, 330, and Kozlov, *Readers*, 75.

72. Vladimir Dudintsev, "Ne khlebom edinym," *Novyi mir* 1954, no. 8:31–118, no. 9:37–188, no. 10:21–98, cited in Kozlov, *Readers*, 88. The ending had to be changed before the novel could be published.

73. Of the 3,695 members, 553 were candidate members. The second congress approved new statutes eliminating candidate membership, but apparently existing candidate members retained their union membership. See Garrard and Garrard, *Inside the Soviet Writers' Union*, 241.

74. Kovalev et al., *Ocherk istorii russkoi sovetskoi literatury*.

75. *Bol'shaia sovetskaia entsiklopediia*, s.v. "Literaturnyi institut," http://dic .academic.ru/dic.nsf/bse/104020/Literaturnyi.

76. ENI Sholokhova, "Rech' na XX s"ezde KPSS," http://feb-web.ru/feb /sholokh/texts/sh0/sh8/sh8-317-.htm.

77. Garrard and Garrard, *Inside the Soviet Writers' Union*, 241.

78. *VSP*, 112. A writer of some popularity in his native Latvia, Lācis served on the Council of Ministers of the Latvian SSR and, although a lifelong communist, had curried favor with the interwar authoritarian leader of Latvia, Kārlis Ulmanis.

79. *VSP*, 170, 345. Berggolts provoked noise and laughter by saying that Simonov had claimed Surov's play had "blazed a new trail in literature," and Sofronov that the play had "made him grow wings."

80. On speeches as a genre with predictable party-minded frames, see Yurchak, *Everything Was Forever*.

81. *VSP*, 593. For an analysis of *Inostrannaia literatura* and the earlier *Internatsionalnaia literatura*, see Sherry, *Discourses*, 67–140.

82. Valerii Yakovlevich Vakulenko, "Pochemu zastrelilsia Fadeyev," http://www.literatura.kg/articles/?aid=1236. This is not the only case in which Fadeyev has been alleged to have used his correspondence with a close RAPP friend to protect himself. Lidiia Libedinskaia categorically refuted the suggestion that in 1937 Fadeyev entered Libedinsky's apartment when only the servant was home, searched Libedinsky's desk for the letters Fadeyev had written him, and removed them (personal communication, May 1997). That accusation is made in Svirskii, *Na lobnom meste*, 84. For evidence that Fadeyev denounced Makaryev, see Boeck, *Stalin's Scribe*, 262.

83. Makaryev's interrogation about Fadeyev brings to mind Mandelstam's assertion that some writers were sent to the Gulag on charges of belonging to a conspiracy headed by Fadeyev and Tikhonov (*Hope Against Hope*, 316).

84. How petitioners reclaimed their right to self-definition is discussed in Dobson, *Khrushchev's Cold Summer*, 203–7, and Adler, *Keeping Faith*, 70–106.

85. "Rech' na XX s"ezde KPSS," Fundamental'naia elektronnaia biblioteka. Russkaia literatura i fol'klor, http://feb-web.ru/feb/sholokh/texts/sh0/sh8/sh8-317-.htm. By now, however, Sholokhov too was thoroughly co-opted; see Boeck, *Stalin's Scribe*, 178-182.

86. In fact, Sholokhov did also decry Fadeyev's power lust and authoritarian handling of Writers' Union affairs.

87. Slezkine, *The House of Government*, 977.

88. Libedinskaia, "Takaia vot istoriia," 268.

89. "Literaturnoe Peredelkino. Aleksandr Fadeev," Rossiia—kul'tura, https://tvkultura.ru/video/show/brand_id/27632/episode_id/1184499/video_id/1157622/.

90. Libedinskaia, "Takaia vot istoriia," 268.

91. Chukovskii, *Dnevnik 1930–1969*, 211. Fadeyev was referring to his censure of *Za pravoe delo*; but there is reason to believe he sought out Chukovsky to unburden himself more generally.

EPILOGUE

1. Lendvai, *One Day*, 151, 215; 119–25 contain an account of the Kremlin decision to proceed with the invasion.

2. Kozlov, *Readers*, 187.

3. Kozlov, *Readers*, gives an excellent discussion of this debate.

4. Gladilin, *Making and Unmaking*, 46.

5. Solzhenitsyn, *Oak and the Calf*, 8.

6. Garrard and Garrard, *Inside the Soviet Writers' Union*, 199.

7. Gladilin, *Making and Unmaking*, 87.

8. "Iskliucheniia iz soiuza pisatelei SSSR Borisa Pasternaka," Mul'tiurok, Marat Bopyshevich Baltabaev, https://multiurok.ru/blog/iskliuchieniie-iz-soiuza -pisatieliei-sssr-borisa-pastiernaka.html.

9. Kozlov, *Readers*, 128.

10. Garrard and Garrard, *Inside the Soviet Writers' Union*, 140.

11. "Pis'mo chlenov redkollegii zhurnala 'Novyi mir' B. Pasternaku," *LG*, Oct. 25, 1958, http://vivovoco.astronet.ru/VV/PAPERS/LITRA/PASTERNAK-58 /PAST3.HTM.

12. *Chetvertyi s"ezd pisatelei*, 259, lists twenty-eight secretaries. Solzhenit-syn, *Oak and the Calf*, 175, mentions that in 1967 the Writers' Union secretariat had forty-two secretaries; this may include branch secretaries.

13. *Chetvertyi s"ezd pisatelei*, 258.

14. Gladilin, *Making and Unmaking*, 90–91; Kozlov, *Readers*, 154–55.

15. Gladilin, *Making and Unmaking*, 107.

16. Kozlov, *Readers*, 208.

17. Vladimir Ermilov, "Neobkhodimost' spora: Chitaia memuary I. Eren-burga 'Liudi, gody, zhizn',' " *Izvestiia*, Jan. 30, 1963; cited in Kozlov, *Readers*, 187.

18. Kozlov, *Readers*, 189.

19. Kozlov, *Readers*, 130.

20. Kozlov, *Readers*, 191.

21. Svirskii, *Na lobnom meste*, 105. This was not the only witticism whose humor relied on a role reversal between a harmless dog and a vicious Yermilov ready to bite.

22. Ogryzko, "Gromila sovetskoi literatury."

23. Sarnov, "Golos vechnosti."

24. Garrard and Garrard, *Inside the Soviet Writers' Union*, 141.

25. Solzhenitsyn, *Oak and the Calf*, 10.

26. Chukovskaia, *Protsess iskliucheniia*, 51. These were not published in any of the congress proceedings.

27. Solzhenitsyn, *Oak and the Calf*, 460–61.

28. Solzhenitsyn, *Oak and the Calf*, 152–54, 167.

29. Solzhenitsyn, *Oak and the Calf*, 460–61.

30. Solzhenitsyn, *Oak and the Calf*, 462.

31. Solzhenitsyn, *Oak and the Calf*, 470.

32. The letter was published August 31, 1973.

33. *Piatyi s"ezd pisatelei*, 176. The charter also reestablished a smaller, more workable leadership body, called the *biuro*, within the secretariat (175). The *biuro* was the de facto principal organ, and its resolutions were binding. Garrard

and Garrard, *Inside the Soviet Writers' Union*, 81–82, state that the *biuro* was actually formed in 1970.

34. Aksyonov et al., *Metropole*, xx.

35. *Vos'moi s"ezd pisatelei*, 494. About 16 percent of members were women.

36. *Vos'moi s"ezd pisatelei*, 494.

37. Garrard and Garrard, *Inside the Soviet Writers' Union*, 202.

38. Garrard and Garrard, *Inside the Soviet Writers' Union*, 279.

39. Garrard and Garrard, *Inside the Soviet Writers' Union*, 288. The successor to the Writers' Union in the Russian Federation is the International Commonwealth of Writers' Unions. The main successor to the RSFSR branch is the Union of Writers of Russia (Soiuz pisatelei Rossii; 6,991 members in 2004), with Bondarev as its chair. More liberal writers formed a separate organization, the Union of Russian Writers (Soiuz rossiiskikh pisatelei; approximately 3,500 members in 2016; the first secretary was Svetlana Vasilenko). A third organization not to be confused with this one is the Rossiiskii soiuz pisatelei (Russian Union of Writers).

40. Adler, *Keeping Faith*, 19.

41. Dobson, *Khrushchev's Cold Summer*, 80.

42. Antonov-Ovseenko, *Vragi naroda*, 159–94. Here we learn that Gronsky earned the trust of the camp commandant, who placed him in charge of the kitchen and bathhouse, and also that Gronsky wrote to Stalin with suggestions for camp reforms, hoping also to win early release.

43. I. M. Gronskii, "Vospominaniia ob A. M. Gor'kom," IMLI MoG 3-25-5, l. 17. See also Antonov-Ovseenko, *Vragi naroda*, 193–94.

Bibliography

ARCHIVAL SOURCES

Arkhiv Gor'kogo pri Institute mirovoi literatury imeni A. M. Gor'kogo. Lichnyi arkhiv A. M. Gor'kogo.

Rossiiskii gosudarstvennyi arkhiv literatury i iskusstva: fond 631, Soiuz sovetskikh pisatelei SSSR; fond 1628, A. A. Fadeev; fond 1712, V. P. Stavskii.

Rossiiskii gosudarstvennyi arkhiv sotsial'noi i politicheskoi istorii: fond 77, A. A. Zhdanov; fond 88, A. S. Shcherbakov.

Tsentral'nyi arkhiv obshchestvennykh dvizhenii Moskvy: fond 813, Partorgani-zatsiia SSP SSSR, Krasnopresnenskii raion, g. Moskva.

PUBLISHED SOURCES

Adler, Nanci. *Keeping Faith with the Party: Communist Believers Return from the Gulag.* Bloomington: Indiana University Press, 2012.

Agursky, Mikhail. "An Occult Source of Socialist Realism: Gorky and Theories of Thought Transference." In *The Occult in Soviet and Russian Culture*, ed. Bernice Glatzer Rosenthal, 247–72. Ithaca, N.Y.: Cornell University Press, 1997.

———. "Velikii eretik: Gor'kii kak religioznyi myslitel'." *Voprosy filosofii*, no. 8 (1991): 54–74.

Aksyonov, Vasily, et al., eds. *Metropole: Literary Almanac.* New York: Norton, 1982.

Altstadt, Audrey L. *The Politics of Culture in Soviet Azerbaijan, 1920–1940.* London: Routledge, 2016.

Antipina, Valentina. *Povsednevnaia zhizn' sovetskikh pisatelei, 1930-e–1950-e.* Moscow: Molodaia gvardiia, 2005.

Antonov-Ovseenko, Anton. *Vragi naroda.* Moscow: Intellekt, 1996.

Any, Carol. *Boris Eikhenbaum: Voices of a Russian Formalist.* Stanford, CA: Stanford University Press, 1994.

———. "The Red Pushkin and the Writers' Union in 1937: Prescription and Taboo." In *Taboo Pushkin: Topics, Texts, Interpretations*, ed. Alyssa Dinega Gillespie, 378–400. Madison: University of Wisconsin Press, 2012.

Artizov, A., et al., comps. *Reabilitatsiia: Kak eto bylo*. Vol. 2. Moscow: Mezhdu-narodnyi fond "Demokratiia", 2003.

Avdeenko, A. *Nakazanie bez prestupleniia*. Moscow: Sovetskaia Rossiia, 1991.

Averbakh, L. "O perestroike RAPP." *NLP*, nos. 35–36 (1931): 6–13, continued in *NLP*, no. 1 (1932): 1–9.

———. "O tselostnykh masshtabakh i chastnykh Makarakh." *Oktiabr'*, no. 11 (1929): 164–71; *NLP*, nos. 21–22 (1929): 10–17. Reprinted in *APVS*, 256–65.

———. "Za leninskuiu partiinost' tvorcheskogo metoda." *Oktiabr'*, no. 1 (1932): 169–79.

Babichenko, D. L., comp. *"Literaturnyi front": Istoriia politicheskoi tsenzury 1932–1946 gg; Sbornik dokumentov*. Moscow: Entsiklopediia rossiiskikh dereven', 1994.

———, comp. *Pisateli i tsenzory: Sovetskaia literatura 40-x godov pod politiche-skim kontrolem TsK*. Moscow: Rossiia molodaia, 1994.

———, comp. *"Shchast'e literatury": Gosudarstvo i pisateli, 1925–1938; Doku-menty*. Moscow: Rosspen, 1997.

Barbian, Jan-Pieter. "Literary Policy in the Third Reich." In *National Social-ist Cultural Policy*, ed. Glenn R. Cuomo, 155–96. New York: St. Martin's Press, 1995.

Basinskii, Pavel. "Stalin, Gor'kii, i bessmertie." http://gorkiy-lit.ru/gorkiy/biografiya/basinskij-gorkij/stalin-gorkij-i-bessmertie.htm.

Batkin, Leonid. "Son razuma." In *Osmyslit' kul't Stalina*. Comp. Khuan Kobo, 9–53. Moscow: Progress, 1989.

Belaia, Galina. "Sluchai Fadeeva." *Voprosy literatury*, no. 2 (2005): 52–65.

Berelowitch, Alexis. "Peredelkino: Le village des écrivains." In *Moscou 1918–1941: De "l'homme nouveau" au bonheur totalitaire*, ed. Catherine Gousseff, 199–212. Paris: Autrement, 1993.

Berzer, A. "Stranitsy starogo kalendaria." *Voprosy literatury*, no. 12 (1987): 183–94.

Bion, Wilfred. *Experiences in Groups and Other Papers*. London: Tavistock Pub-lications, 1961.

Blium, A. V. *Sovetskaia tsenzura v epokhu total'nogo terrora, 1929–1953*. Saint Petersburg: Akademicheskii proekt, 2000.

Boborykin, V. *Aleksandr Fadeev: Pisatel'skaia sud'ba*. Moscow: Sovetskii pisa-tel', 1989.

Boeck, Brian. *Stalin's Scribe: Literature, Ambition, and Survival; The Life of Mikhail Sholokhov*. New York: Pegasus Books, 2019.

Borshchagovskii, A. M. *Zapiski balovnia sud'by*. Moscow: Sovetskii pisatel', 1991.

Bourdieu, Pierre. *The Rules of Art: Genesis and Structure of the Literary Field*. Trans. Susan Emanuel. Stanford, CA: Stanford University Press, 1995.

Brandenberger, David. *National Bolshevism: Stalinist Mass Culture and the For-mation of Modern Russian National Identity, 1931–1936*. Cambridge, MA: Harvard University Press, 2002.

Bibliography

Brodskii, Iurii. *Solovki: Dvadtsat' let osobogo naznacheniia*. Moscow: Mir iskusstva II, 2008.

Brown, Edward J. *Mayakovsky: A Poet in the Revolution*. Princeton, NJ: Princeton University Press, 1973.

———. *The Proletarian Episode in Russian Literature, 1928–1932*. New York: Octagon Books, 1971.

Browning, Gary. *Boris Pilniak: Scythian at a Typewriter*. Ann Arbor, MI: Ardis, 1985.

Bulgakova, Oksana. "Pushkinskie motivy u Eizenshteina." In *Pushkinskaia konferentsiia v Stenforde, 1999: Materialy i issledovaniia*, ed. David Bethea et al., 472–84. Moscow: OGI, 2001.

Burris, Christopher T., Eddie Harmon-Jones, and W. Ryan Tarpley. "By Faith Alone: Religious Agitation and Cognitive Dissonance." *Basic and Applied Social Psychology* 19 (1997): 17–31.

Chetvertyi s"ezd pisatelei SSSR: 22–27 maia 1967 g; Stenograficheskii otchet. Ed. G. M. Markov et al. Moscow: Sovetskii pisatel', 1968.

Chkhartishvili, Grigorii. *Pisatel' i samoubiistvo*. 2nd ed. Moscow: Zakharov, 2006.

"Chto takoe soiuz pisatelei?" *NLP*, no. 16 (1929): 1–3.

Chukovskaia, Lidiia. *Protsess iskliucheniia: Ocherk literaturnykh nravov*. Paris: YMCA Press, 1979.

Chukovskii, K. I. *Dnevnik, 1901–1929*. Moscow: Sovetskii pisatel', 1991.

———. *Dnevnik, 1930–1969*. Moscow: Sovremennyi pisatel', 1994.

Clark, Katerina. "Germanophone Contributions to Stalinist Literary Theory: The Case of Georgy Lukacs and Michail Lifšic, and Their Roles in *Literaturnyi kritik* and IFLI." *Russian Literature* 63 (2008): 513–32.

———. *Moscow, the Fourth Rome: Stalinism, Cosmopolitanism, and the Evolution of Soviet Culture, 1931–1941*. Cambridge, MA: Harvard University Press, 2011.

———. *Petersburg: Crucible of Cultural Revolution*. Cambridge, MA: Harvard University Press, 1995.

———. *The Soviet Novel: History as Ritual*. Chicago: University of Chicago Press, 1981.

Clark, Katerina, and Evgeny Dobrenko, eds. *Soviet Culture and Power: A History in Documents, 1917–1953*. New Haven, CT: Yale University Press, 2007.

Clinefelter, Joan L. *Artists for the Reich: Culture and Race from Weimar to Nazi Germany*. Oxford: Berg, 2005.

Cohen, Stephen F., ed. *An End to Silence: Uncensored Opinion in the Soviet Union*. New York: Norton, 1982.

Demidov, V. I., and V. A. Kutuzov, comps. *"Leningradskoe delo."* Leningrad: Lenizdat, 1990.

Dobrenko, Evgeny. *Formovka sovetskogo chitatelia: Sotsial'nye i esteticheskie predposylki retseptsii sovetskoi literatury*. Saint Petersburg: Akademicheskii proekt, 1997.

———. *The Making of the State Writer: Social and Aesthetic Origins of Soviet Literary Culture*. Trans. Jesse M. Savage. Stanford, CA: Stanford University Press, 2001.

Dobson, Miriam. *Khrushchev's Cold Summer: Gulag Returnees, Crime, and the Fate of Reform after Stalin*. Ithaca, NY: Cornell University Press, 2009.

"Dokladnaia zapiska G. F. Aleksandrova i zaveduiushchego otdelom vneshnei politiki TsK VKP(b) M. A. Suslova V. M. Molotovu i sekratariu TsK VKP(b) A. A. Kuznetsovu." Fond Aleksandra N. Yakovleva. http://www.alexanderyakovlev .org/fond/issues-doc/69317.

Dubrovsky, A. M. "Chronicle of a Poet's Downfall." In *Epic Revisionism: Russian History and Literature as Stalinist Propaganda*, ed. Kevin M. F. Platt and David Brandenberger, 77–98. Madison: University of Wisconsin Press, 2006.

Dunham, Vera S. *In Stalin's Time: Middle Class Values in Soviet Fiction*. Cambridge: Cambridge University Press, 1979.

Ehrenburg, Ilya. *Post-War Years, 1945–1954*. Trans. Tatiana Shebunina with Yvonne Kapp. London: Macgibbon and Kee, 1966.

———. *The War, 1941–45*. Trans. Tatiana Shebunina with Yvonne Kapp. London: Macgibbon and Kee, 1964.

Eikhenbaum, B. M. *Moi vremennik: Slovesnost', nauka, kritika, smes'*. Leningrad: Izd-vo pisatelei v Leningrade, 1929.

Erenburg, I. G. *Liudi, gody, zhizn'*. 3 vols. Moscow: Sovetskii pisatel', 1990.

Ermilov, V. V. *A. P. Chekhov, 1860–1904*. Moscow: Molodaia gvardiia, 1949.

———. *Dramaturgiia Chekhova*. Moscow: Sovetskii pisatel', 1948.

———. "Uchenik gimnazii Shklovskogo." *NLP*, no. 7 (1929): 16–30.

Ermolaev, Herman. *Censorship in Soviet Literature, 1917–1991*. Lanham, MD: Rowman and Littlefield, 1997.

———. *Mikhail Sholokhov and His Art*. Princeton, NJ: Princeton University Press, 1982.

Etkind, Aleksandr. "Soviet Subjectivity: Torture for the Sake of Salvation?" *Kritika: Explorations in Russian and Eurasian History* 6, no. 1 (2005): 171–86. Project MUSE, doi:10.1353/kri.2005.0004.

Fadeev, A. A. *Materialy i issledovaniia*. Moscow: Khudozhestvennaia literatura, 1977.

———. *Materialy i issledovaniia*. Moscow: Khudozhestvennaia literatura, 1984.

———. "Ob odnoi kulatskoi khronike." *Krasnaia nov'*, nos. 5–6 (1931): 206–9. Reprinted in *APVS*, 272–78.

———. *Pis'ma, 1916–1956*. Moscow: Sovetskii pisatel', 1967.

———. *Pis'ma, 1916–1956*. Moscow: Sovetskii pisatel', 1973.

———. *Pis'ma i dokumenty: Iz fondov Rossiiskogo gosudarstvennogo arkhiva literatury i iskusstva*. Comp. N. I. Dikushina. Moscow: Izdatel'stvo literaturnogo instituta im. A. M. Gor'kogo, 2001.

———. *Sobranie sochinenii.* Moscow: Khudozhestvennaia literatura, 1971.

———. *Sobranie sochinenii v piati tomakh.* Moscow: Khudozhestvennaia literatura, 1959–61.

———. *Sobranie sochinenii v 7-i tomakh.* Moscow: Khudozhestvennaia literatura, 1969–71.

"Fedor Ivanovich Panferov." *Khronos: Vsemirnaia istoriia v Internete.* Ed. Viacheslav Rumiantsev. http://hrono.ru/biograf/bio_p/panferov_fi.php.

Festinger, Leon A. *A Theory of Cognitive Dissonance.* Stanford, CA: Stanford University Press, 1957.

"Fifty Years of Soviet Experimental Biology and Medicine." *Bulletin of Experimental Biology and Medicine* 64, no. 5 (November 1967): 1139–146. https://doi.org/10.1007/BF00790512.

Figes, Orlando. *The Whisperers: Private Life in Stalin's Russia.* New York: Metropolitan Books, 2007.

Fitzpatrick, Sheila. *The Commissariat of Enlightenment: Soviet Organization of Education and the Arts under Lunacharsky, October 1917–1921.* Cambridge: Cambridge University Press, 1970.

———. *The Cultural Front: Power and Culture in Revolutionary Russia.* Ithaca, NY: Cornell University Press, 1992.

———. *Everyday Stalinism: Ordinary Life in Extraordinary Times; Soviet Russia in the 1930s.* New York: Oxford University Press, 1999.

Fleishman, Lazar'. *Boris Pasternak v tridtsatye gody.* Jerusalem: Magnes Press, 1984.

Frolova-Walker, Marina, and Jonathan Walker. *Music and Soviet Power, 1917–1932.* Woodbridge, Suffolk, UK: Boydell Press, 2012.

Fromm, Erich. *Psychoanalysis and Religion.* New Haven, CT: Yale University Press, 1950.

Galushkin, Aleksandr. "Andrei Platonov—I.V. Stalin—'Literaturnyi kritik.'" In *SF,* 815–26.

Garrard, John, and Carol Garrard. *Inside the Soviet Writers' Union.* New York: Free Press, 1990.

Garros, Véronique, Natalia Korenevskaya, and Thomas Lahusen. *Intimacy and Terror: Soviet Diaries of the 1930s.* New York: New Press, 1995.

Gershtein, Emma. *Moscow Memoirs: Memories of Anna Akhmatova, Osip Mandelstam, and Literary Russia under Stalin.* Trans. and ed. John Crowfoot. Woodstock, NY: Overlook Press, 2004.

Getty, J. Arch. *Origins of the Great Purges: The Soviet Communist Party Reconsidered, 1933–1938.* Cambridge: Cambridge University Press, 1985.

———. *Pragmatists and Puritans: The Rise and Fall of the Party Control Commission.* Carl Beck Papers in Russian and East European Studies 1208. Pittsburgh: University of Pittsburgh Center for Russian and East European Studies, 1997.

Getty, J. Arch, and Oleg V. Naumov. *The Road to Terror: Stalin and the Self-*

Destruction of the Bolsheviks, 1932–1939. New Haven, CT: Yale University Press, 1999.

Gladilin, Anatoly. *The Making and Unmaking of a Soviet Writer: My Story of the "Young Prose" of the Sixties and After.* Trans. David Lapeza. Ann Arbor, MI: Ardis, 1979.

Gnetnev, Konstantin. "Belomorkanal: Vremena i sud'by." Rumiantsevskii muzei. Ed. Viacheslav Rumiantsev. http://www.rummuseum.ru/lib_g/belomor26.php.

Goncharov, Vladimir, and Vladimir Nekhotin, comps. *Andrei Platonov v dokumentakh OGPU-NKVD-NKGB, 1930–1945.* In *SF.*

Gorbachev, Georgii. "Raskol v pereverzevtsakh." *Krasnaia nov'*, no. 3 (1930): 185–206.

Gorham, Michael S. *Speaking in Soviet Tongues: Language Culture and the Politics of Voice in Revolutionary Russia.* DeKalb: Northern Illinois University Press, 2003.

Gor'kii, A. M. *Sobranie sochinenii v 30-i tomakh.* Moscow: Gosudarstvennoe izdatel'stvo Khudozhestvennaia literatura, 1949–56.

Gor'kii, M. *Neizdannaia perepiska s Bogdanovym, Leninym, Stalinym, Zinov'evym, Kamenevym, Korolenko.* Vol. 5 of *Materialy i issledovaniia.* Moscow: Nasledie, 1998.

Gor'kii i sovetskie pisateli: Neizdannaia perepiska. Ed. I. I. Anisimov. Literaturnoe nasledstvo, 70. Moscow: Izd-vo Akademii nauk SSSR, 1963.

Gorky, Maksim. *Selected Letters.* Ed. Andrew Barratt and Barry P. Scherr. Oxford: Clarendon Press, 1997.

Greenleaf, Monika Frenkel. "Tynianov, Pushkin, and the Fragment: Through the Lens of Montage." In *Cultural Mythologies of Russian Modernism: From the Golden Age to the Silver Age*, ed. Boris Gasparov, Robert P. Hughes, and Irina Paperno, 264–92. Berkeley: University of California Press, 1992.

Gregor, A. James. *Totalitarianism and Political Religion.* Stanford, CA: Stanford University Press, 2012.

Gromova, Natal'ia. *Raspad: Sud'ba sovetskogo kritika, 40–50-e gody.* Moscow: Ellis Lak, 2009.

Gronskii, Ivan. *Iz proshlogo . . . Vospominaniia.* Moscow: Izvestiia, 1991.

Groys, Boris. *The Total Art of Stalinism: Avant-garde, Aesthetic Dictatorship, and Beyond.* Princeton, NJ: Princeton University Press, 1992.

Hahn, Werner G. *Postwar Soviet Politics: The Fall of Zhdanov and the Defeat of Moderation, 1946–53.* Ithaca, NY: Cornell University Press, 1982.

Halfin, Igal. *Terror in My Soul: Communist Autobiographies on Trial.* Cambridge, MA: Harvard University Press, 2003.

Hellbeck, Jochen. *Revolution on My Mind: Writing a Diary under Stalin.* Cambridge, MA: Harvard University Press, 2006.

Higgins, E. Tory. "Self-Discrepancy: A Theory of Relating Self and Affect." *Psychological Review* 94, no. 3 (July): 319–40.

Hoffman, David L. *Stalinist Values: The Cultural Norms of Soviet Modernity, 1917–1941*. Ithaca, N.Y.: Cornell University Press, 2003.

Huskey, Eugene. "Vyshinskii, Krylenko, and the Shaping of the Soviet Legal Order." *Slavic Review* 46, no. 3/4 (1987): 414–28.

Ivanov, Vsevolod. *Dnevniki*. Moscow: IMLI RAN, 2001.

Iudin, P. *Ob ustave soiuza sovetskikh pisatelei*. Moscow: Gos. izd. Khudozhestvennaia literatura, 1934.

Jangfeldt, Bengt. *Mayakovsky: A Biography*. Trans. Harry D. Watson. Chicago: University of Chicago Press, 2014.

Jurgutienė, Aušra, and Dalia Satkauskytė, eds. *The Literary Field under Communist Rule*. Boston: Academic Studies Press, 2018.

"Kakoi nam nuzhen pisatel'?" *NLP*, no. 6 (1931): 32–46.

"Kakoi nam nuzhen pisatel'." *NLP*, nos. 20–21 (1931): 59.

Kapitsa, Petr. "Eto bylo tak." *Neva*, no. 5 (1988): 136–48.

Khlevniuk, O. V. *Politbiuro: Mekhanizmy politicheskoi vlasti v 1930-e gody*. Moscow: Rosspen, 1996.

Khrushchev, Nikita Sergeevich. *Khrushchev Remembers*. Trans. and ed. Strobe Talbott. Boston: Little, Brown, 1970.

Kirpotin, Valerii. *Nachalo*. Moscow: Sovetskii pisatel', 1986.

———. *Nasledie Pushkina i kommunizm*. Moscow: Gos. izd. khudozhestvennaia literatura, 1936.

Kiseleva, F. *Fadeev-Khudozhnik v zamyslakh i pretvorenii*. Moscow: IMLI RAN, 2001.

"K istorii partiinoi politiki v oblasti literatury (Perepiska I. Gronskogo i A. Ovcharenko." *Voprosy literatury*, no. 2 (1989): 143–66.

Knight, Amy. *Who Killed Kirov? The Kremlin's Greatest Mystery*. New York: Hill and Wang, 1999.

Kolodnyi, Lev. *Poety i vozhdi: Tainy nashego vremeni*. Moscow: Golos, 1997.

Koonz, Claudia. *The Nazi Conscience*. Cambridge, MA: Belknap Press, 2003.

Kor, B. "Ne poputchik, a soiuznik ili vrag." *NLP*, no. 2 (1931): 39–40.

Kormilov, S. I. Lecture given at the MGU *filfak*, December 8, 2004. http://msu-philologist.narod.ru/literature/critique/lectures/Lecture_12.htm.

Kornienko, N. V., ed. and comp. "*Strana filosofov" Andreia Platonova: Problemy tvorchestva*. Vol. 4. Moscow: RAN, Institut mirovoi literatury im. A.M. Gor'kogo, "Nasledie," 2000.

Kostyrchenko, Gennadii. *Stalin protiv "kosmopolitov": Vlast' i evreiskaia intelligentsia v SSSR*. Moscow: Rosspen, 2009.

———. *Tainaia politika Stalina: Vlast' i antisemitizm; Novaia versiia*. 2 vols. Moscow: Mezhdunarodnye otnosheniia, 2015.

Kotkin, Stephen. *Magnetic Mountain: Stalinism as a Civilization*. Berkeley: University of California Press, 1997.

Kovalev, V. A., et al. *Ocherk istorii russkoi sovetskoi literatury. Chast' vtoraia.*

Moscow: Akademiia nauk SSSR, 1955. Reproduced at Biografia.ru, Zhizn' uspeshnykh liudei. http:// www.biografia .ru/ arhiv/ ochlit38 .html.

"Ko vsem chlenam Vserossiiskogo soiuza pisatelei." *NLP*, no. 17 (1929): 2–3.

Kozlov, Denis. *The Readers of Novyi Mir: Coming to Terms with the Stalinist Past*. Cambridge, MA: Harvard University Press, 2013.

Krasnov, M. A. *Vvedenie v konstitutsionnoe pravo s raz"iasneniem slozhnykh voprosov: uchebnoe posobie*. Moscow: Vysshaia shkola ekonomiki, 2018. DOI: 10.17323/978-5-7598-1766-6.

Kratkaia literaturnaia entsiklopediia. Moscow: Sovetskaia entsiklopediia, 1962–78.

"Kruzhok rabochei kritiki 'Rost.'" *NLP*, no. 3 (1931): 19–20.

Kun, Miklós. *Stalin: An Unknown Portrait*. Budapest: Central European University Press, 2003.

Kuniaev, Stanislav, and Sergei Kuniaev. *Rasterzannye teni*. Moscow: Golos, 1995.

Kupina, N. A. *Totalitarnyi iazyk: Slovar' i rechevye reaktsii*. Ekaterinburg: Izd-vo Ural'skogo Universiteta ZUUNTs, 1995.

Kurilov, A. S. "Gor'kii i Vechernii rabochii literaturnyi universitet (VRLU)." *Literaturovedcheskii zhurnal*, no. 29 (2011): 268.

Lapidus, Rina. *Young Jewish Poets Who Fell as Soviet Soldiers in the Second World War*. London: Taylor and Francis, 2014.

Lekmanov, Oleg. *Zhizn' Osipa Mandelshtama: Dokumental'noe povestvovanie*. Saint Petersburg: Izdatel'stvo zhurnala 'Zvezda', 2003.

Lendvai, Paul. *One Day That Shook the Communist World: The 1956 Hungarian Uprising and Its Legacy*. Princeton, NJ: Princeton University Press, 2008.

Levitt, Marcus C. *Russian Literary Politics and the Pushkin Celebration of 1880*. Ithaca, NY: Cornell University Press, 1989.

Levonevskii, Dmitrii. "Istoriia 'Bol'shogo bloknota.'" *Zvezda*, no. 7 (1988): 190–205.

Lewin, Moshe. *The Making of the Soviet System: Essays in the Social History of Interwar Russia*. New York: Pantheon Books, 1985.

Libedinskaia, Lidiia. "Takaia vot istoriia." *Voprosy literatury*, no. 3 (May–June 2000): 253–77.

Libedinskii, Iurii. "Neskol'ko slov o Pereverzeve." *NLP*, no. 19 (1929): 17–22.

———. "O Fadeeve." *Voprosy literatury*, no. 3 (May–June 2000): 236–52.

Litvin, A. L., ed. *Dnevnik istorika S. A. Piontkovskogo, 1927–1934*. Kazan': Kazanskii gos. universitet, 2009.

Lobov, Lev, and Kira Vasil'eva. *Peredelkino: Skazanie o pisatel'skom gorodke*. Moscow: Boslen, 2011.

Lovell, Stephen. "The Making of the Stalin-Era Dacha." *Journal of Modern History* 74, no. 2 (2002): 253–88. https://doi.org/10.1086/343408.

Maguire, Robert A. *Red Virgin Soil: Soviet Literature in the 1920s*. Princeton, NJ: Princeton University Press, 1968.

Makarov, A. G., and S. E. Makarova. *Vokrug "Tikhogo Dona": Ot mifotvorchestva k poisku istiny*. Moscow: Probel, 2000.

Makin, Michael. "Nikolai Kliuev—Prophet of Loss." *Slavic and East European Journal* 49, no. 4 (2005): 591–611.

Maksimenkov, L. V. "Ocherki nomenklaturnoi istorii sovetskoi literatury (1932–1946)." Pt. 1. *Voprosy literatury*, July–August 2003, 212–58.

———. "Ocherki nomenklaturnoi istorii sovetskoi literatury (1932–1946): Stalin, Bukharin, Zhdanov, Shcherbakov i drugie." Pt. 2. *Voprosy literatury*, September–October 2003, 241–97.

———. *Sumbur vmesto muzyki: Stalinskaia kul'turnaia revoliutsiia 1936–1938.* Moscow: Iuridicheskaia kniga, 1997.

Mandelstam, Nadezhda. *Hope Against Hope.* Trans. Max Hayward. New York: Atheneum, 1976.

Marchenkov, A. M., et al. *Ulitsa Kachalova, 6/2.* Moscow: Moskovskii rabochii, 1990.

Markus, Hazel Rose, and Shinobu Kitayama. "Cultures and Selves: A Cycle of Mutual Constitution." *Perspectives on Psychological Science* 5, no. 4 (2010): 420–30.

Martin, Terry. *The Affirmative Action Empire: Nations and Nationalism in the Soviet Union, 1923–1939.* Ithaca, NY: Cornell University Press, 2001.

Matlock, Jack F., Jr. "The 'Governing Organs' of the Union of Soviet Writers." *American Slavic and East European Review* 15 (October 1956): 382–99.

Medvedev, Roy. *Nikolai Bukharin: The Last Years.* Trans. A. D. P. Briggs. New York: Norton, 1980.

———. "The Riddles Grow: A Propos Two Review Articles." *Slavic and East European Journal* 21, no. 1 (Spring 1977): 104–16.

Mezhdu molotom i nakoval'nei: Soiuz sovetskikh pisatelei SSSR; Dokumenty i kommentarii. Ed. Goriaeva, T. M. et al. Vol. 1. Moscow: Rosspen, 2011.

Milgram, Stanley. *Obedience to Authority: An Experimental View.* New York: Harper and Row, 1974.

Mirskii, Dimitri. "Problema Pushkina." *Literaturnoe nasledstvo* 16–18 (1934): 91–112.

Montefiore, Simon Sebag. *Stalin: The Court of the Red Tsar.* New York: Knopf, 2004.

Mosse, George L. *Nazi Culture: Intellectual, Cultural, and Social Life in the Third Reich.* Trans. Salvator Attanasio et al. Madison: University of Wisconsin Press, 1966.

Murin, Iurii, comp. *Pisatel' i vozhd': Perepiska M. A. Sholokhova c I. V. Stalinym.* Moscow: Raritet, 1997.

Naiman, Eric. "On Soviet Subjects and the Scholars Who Make Them." *Russian Review* 60, no. 3 (July 2001): 307–15.

Ogryzko, Viacheslav. "Bor'ba za vlast'." *Literaturnaia Rossiia*, Oct. 1, 2015. https://litrossia.ru/item/8255-plata-za-vlast.

———. "Gromila sovetskoi literatury." *Literaturnaia Rossiia*, Feb. 23, 2015. http://www.litrossia.ru/archive/item/5306-oldarchive.

"Opiat' o 'masse' i lichnosti." *NLP*, no. 17 (1928): 14–16. (Signed with Yermilov's initials).

Paperno, Irina. "What Can Be Done with Diaries?" *Russian Review* 63, no. 4 (October 2004): 561–73.

Pavlenko, Petr. "Tvorcheskaia diskussiia v *VSSP*." *Krasnaia nov'*, no. 1 (1932): 141–48.

Perkhin, V. V. "Polemika M. Gor'kogo s A. Avdeenko (K kharakteristike dukhovnoi programmy kritika)." In *M. Gor'kii. Materialy i issledovaniia*. Vol. 4, *M. Gor'kii i ego epokha*. Ed. V. S. Barakhov et al., 143–49. Moscow: Nasledie, 1995.

Pervyi vsesoiuznyi s"ezd sovetskikh pisatelei, 1934: Stenograficheskii otchet. Ed. I. K. Luppol et al. Moscow, Gosudarstvennoe izdatel'stvo "Khudozhestvennaia literatura," 1934.

Petrone, Karen. *Life Has Become More Joyous, Comrades: Celebrations in the Time of Stalin*. Bloomington: Indiana University Press, 2000.

Piatyi s"ezd pisatelei SSSR, 29 iiunia–2 iulia 1972: Stenograficheskii otchet. Ed. G. M. Markov et al. Moscow: Sovetskii pisatel', 1972.

Pinnow, Kenneth. *Lost to the Collective: Suicide and the Promise of Soviet Socialism, 1921–29*. Ithaca, NY: Cornell University Press, 2011.

Platonov, A. "Mne eto nuzhno ne dlia 'slavy.'" *Voprosy literatury*, no. 9 (1988): 174–83.

———. *Vospominaniia sovremennikov: Materialy k biografii*. Comp. N. V. Kornienko and E. D. Shubina. Moscow: Sovremennyi pisatel', 1994.

Platonov, Andrei. "Bessmertie." *Literaturnyi kritik*, no. 8 (1936): 114–28.

———. "Fro." *Literaturnyi kritik*, no. 8 (1936): 129–45.

———. "Pervyi Ivan." *Oktiabr'*, no. 2 (1930): 159–68.

———. "Usomnivshiisia Makar." *Oktiabr'*, no. 9 (1929): 28–41.

"Platonov v Srednei Azii." *Diletant*. Mar. 11, 2018. https://diletant.media/excursions/39513490/.

Platt, Jonathan Brooks. "Feast in the Time of Terror: Stalinist Temporal Paradox and the 1937 Pushkin Jubilee." PhD diss., Columbia University, 2008.

Platt, Kevin M. F., and David Brandenberger, eds. *Epic Revisionism: Russian History and Literature as Stalinist Propaganda*. Madison: University of Wisconsin Press, 2006.

Polonskii, Viacheslav. "Moia bor'ba na literaturnom fronte. Dnevnik, mai 1920–ianvar' 1932." Zhurnal'nyi zal. http://magazines.russ.ru/novyimi/2008/1/po12.html (accessed July 17, 2013). Duplicated from *Novyi mir*, no. 1 (2008).

Pomerantsev, Vladimir. "Ob iskrennosti v literature." *Novyi mir*, no. 12 (1953): 218–45.

"Protsess Prompartiia i literatura." *NLP*, no. 1 (1931): 45–46.

Rayfield, Donald. *Stalin and His Hangmen: The Tyrant and Those Who Killed for Him*. New York: Random House, 2005.

Robin, Regine. *Socialist Realism: An Impossible Aesthetic*. Trans. Catherine Porter. Stanford, CA: Stanford University Press, 1992.

Ronen, Omri. "Inzhenery chelovecheskikh dush: K istorii izrecheniia." *Lotmanovskii sbornik* 2 (1997): 393–400.

Rubenstein, Joshua. *Stalin's Secret Pogrom: The Postwar Inquisition of the Jewish Anti-Fascist Committee*. New Haven, CT: Yale University Press, 2001.

———. *Tangled Loyalties: The Life and Times of Ilya Ehrenburg*. Tuscaloosa: University of Alabama Press, 1996.

Rubtsov, Iurii. *Alter ego Stalina: Stranitsy politicheskoi biografii L. Z. Mekhlisa*. Moscow: Zvonnitsa-MG, 1999.

Ruder, Cynthia. *Making History for Stalin: The Story of the Belomor Canal*. Gainesville: University Press of Florida, 1998.

Sandler, Stephanie. "The 1937 Pushkin Jubilee as Epic Trauma." In *Epic Revisionism: Russian History and Literature as Stalinist Propaganda*, ed. Kevin M. F. Platt and David Brandenberger, 193–213. Madison: University of Wisconsin Press, 2006.

Sarnov, Benedikt. "Golos vechnosti." Lechaim. http://www.lechaim.ru/ARHIV /141/Sarnov.

———. *Stalin i pisateli*. Vol. 1. Moscow: Eksmo, 2008.

Schull, Joseph. "The Ideological Origins of 'Stalinism' in Soviet Literature." *Slavic Review* 51, no. 3 (Fall 1992): 468–84.

Sed'moi s"ezd pisatelei SSSR: 30 iiunia–4 iiulia 1981; Stenograficheskii otchet. Ed. G. M. Markov et al. Moscow: Sovetskii pisatel', 1983.

Seifrid, Thomas. *Andrei Platonov: Uncertainties of Spirit*. Cambridge: Cambridge University Press, 1992.

Serebrianskii, M. "Novaia li zemlia? (O F. Gladkove)." *Oktiabr'*, no. 8 (1931): 174–81.

Service, Robert. *Stalin: A Biography*. Cambridge, MA: Harvard University Press, 2006.

Sharlet, Robert. "Stalinism and Soviet Legal Culture." In *Stalinism: Essays in Historical Interpretation*, ed. Robert C. Tucker, 155–79. New York: Norton, 1977.

Shentalinskii, Vitalii. *Prestuplenie bez nakazaniia: Dokumental'nye povesti*. Moscow: Progress-pleiada, 2007.

———. *Raby svobody: V literaturnykh arkhivakh KGB*. Moscow: Parus, 1995.

Shentalinsky, Vitaly. *Arrested Voices: Resurrecting the Disappeared Writers of the Soviet Regime*. Trans. John Crowfoot. New York: Free Press, 1993.

———. *The KGB's Literary Archive*. Trans. John Crowfoot. London: Harvill Press, 1995.

Sherry, Samantha. *Discourses of Regulation and Resistance: Censoring Translation in the Stalin and Khrushchev Era Soviet Union*. Edinburgh: Edinburgh University Press, 2015.

Sheshukov, S. I. *Neistovye revniteli: Iz istorii literaturnoi bor'by 20-kh godov*. Moscow: Moskovskii rabochii, 1970.

Shestoi s"ezd pisatelei SSSR: 21 iiunia–25 iiunia 1976 g.; Stenograficheskii otchet. Ed. G. M. Markov et al. Moscow: Sovetskii pisatel', 1978.

Sholokhov, M. A. *Pis'ma*. Moscow: IMLI RAN, 2003.

Shrayer, Maxim D. *I Saw It: Ilya Selvinsky and the Legacy of Bearing Witness to the Shoah*. Boston: Academic Studies Press, 2013.

Simonov, Konstantin. *Izbrannoe*. Vol. 2, *Stikhotvoreniia. Razmyshleniia*. Yekaterinburg: U-faktoriia, 2005.

Slezkine, Yuri. *The House of Government: A Saga of the Russian Revolution*. Princeton, NJ: Princeton University Press, 2017.

Smith, Alexandra. "The Reach of Modern Life: Tynianov's Pushkin, Melancholy and the Critique of Modernity." *Wiener slawistischer Almanach* 61 (2008): 85–108.

Smith, G. S. *D. S. Mirsky: A Russian-English Life, 1890–1939*. Oxford: Oxford University Press, 2000.

Solomon, Peter. "Soviet Criminal Justice and the Great Terror." *Slavic Review* 46, no. 3/4 (1987): 391–413.

Solzhenitsyn, Aleksandr I. *The Gulag Archipelago, 1918–1956: An Experiment in Literary Investigation II–IV*. Trans. Thomas P. Whitney. New York: Harper and Row, 1975.

———. *The Oak and the Calf: Sketches of Literary Life in the Soviet Union*. Trans. Harry Willetts. New York: Harper and Row, 1981.

Sovetskaia literatura na novom etape: Stenogramma pervogo plenuma orgkomiteta Soiuza sovetskikh pisatelei (29 oktiabria–3 noiabria 1932). Ed. L. Subotskii. Moscow: Sovetskaia literatura, 1933.

Sovetskie pisateli: avtobiografii. 5 vols. Moscow: Khudozhestvennaia literatura, 1959–88.

Stalin, I. V. *O velikoi otechestvennoi voine sovetskogo soiuza*. Moscow: Goslitizdat, 1950.

Steinweis, Alan E. *Art, Ideology, and Economics in Nazi Germany: The Reich Chambers of Music, Theater, and the Visual Arts*. Chapel Hill: University of North Carolina Press, 1996.

Subotskii, L. "O khode perestroiki literaturnykh organizatsii." *Oktiabr'*, no. 12 (1932): 169–90.

Svirskii, Grigorii. *Na lobnom meste: Literatura nravstvennogo soprotivleniia (1946–1976 gg.)*. London: Novaya literaturnaya biblioteka, 1979.

Swayze, Harold. *Political Control of Literature in the USSR, 1946–1959*. Cambridge, MA: Harvard University Press, 1962.

Tajfel, Henri, and John C. Turner. "The Social Identity Theory of Intergroup Behavior." In *Political Psychology: Key Readings*, ed. John T. Jost and Jim Sidanius, 276–93. New York: Psychology Press, 2004.

Taubman, William. *Khrushchev: The Man and His Era*. New York: Norton, 2003.

Taylor, Gabriele. *Pride, Shame, and Guilt: Emotions of Self-Assessment*. Oxford: Clarendon Press, 1985.

Tomoff, Kiril. *Creative Union: The Professional Organization of Soviet Composers, 1939–1953*. Ithaca, NY: Cornell University Press, 2006.

Torchinov, V. A., and A. M. Leontiuk. *Vokrug Stalina: Istoriko-biograficheskii spravochnik*. Saint Petersburg: Filologicheskii fakul'tet Sankt-Peterburgskogo universiteta, 2000.

Tret'ii s"ezd pisatelei SSSR. 18–23 maia 1959: Stenograficheskii otchet. Ed. P. Brovka et al. Moscow: Sovetskii pisatel', 1959.

Trigos, Ludmilla. "An Exploration of the Dynamics of Mythmaking: Tynianov's *Kiukhlia*." *Slavic and East European Journal* 46, no. 2 (Summer 2002): 283–300.

Troyat, Henri. *Gorky*. Trans. Lowell Bair. London: Allison and Busby, 1994.

Tucker, Robert C. *Stalin in Power: The Revolution from Above, 1928–1941*. New York: Norton, 1990.

Tvorchestvo i sud'ba Aleksandra Fadeeva: Stat'i, esse, vospominaniia, arkhivnye materialy, stranitsy letopisi. Ed. V. Ia. Savateev et al. Moscow: RAN, Institut mirovoi literatury im. A.M. Gor'kogo, 2004.

Usievich, E. "Za chistotu Leninizma v literaturnoi teorii." *Oktiabr'*, no. 9 (1932): 169–84.

Vaksberg, Arkady. *The Murder of Maxim Gorky: A Secret Execution*. Trans. Todd Bludeau. New York: Enigma Books, 2007.

van Veen, Vincent, Marie K. Krug, Jonathan Schooler, and Cameron S. Carter. "Neural Activity Predicts Attitude Change in Cognitive Dissonance." *Nature Neuroscience* 12 (2009): 1465–75.

Vatulescu, Cristina, et al., eds. *The Svetlana Boym Reader*. New York: Bloomsbury Academic, 2018.

Viola, Lynne. *The Best Sons of the Fatherland: Workers in the Vanguard of Soviet Collectivization*. New York: Oxford University Press, 1987.

———. "The Second Coming: Class Enemies in the Soviet Countryside, 1927–35." In *Stalinist Terror: New Perspectives*, ed. J. Arch Getty and Roberta T. Manning, 65–98. Cambridge: Cambridge University Press, 1993.

V'iugin, V. Iu. *Politika poetiki: Ocherki iz istorii sovetskoi literatury*. Saint Petersburg: Ateleia, 2014.

Vladimir Petrovich Stavskii (1900–1943). Ukazatel' literatury. Comp. E. Stepanova. [Leningrad]: Lenizdat, 1966.

Vlast' i khudozhesvennaia intelligentsia: Dokumenty TsK RKP(b), VChK–OGPU-NKVD o kul'turnoi politike. 1917–1953 gg. Comp. Andrei Artizov and Oleg Naumov. Moscow: Mezhdunarodnyi fond "Demokratiia," 2002.

Vokrug Fadeeva: Neizvestnye pis'ma, zametki i dokumenty. Comp. N. I. Dikushina. Moscow: Literaturnyi Institut, 1996.

Volkov, Vitalii. "Za kulisami." *Avrora*, no. 8 (1991): 42–51.

Vos'moi s"ezd pisatelei SSSR, 24 iiunia–28 iiunia 1986: Stenograficheskii otchet. Ed. G. M. Markov et al. Moscow: Sovetskii pisatel', 1988.

Vtoroi plenum pravleniia Soiuza sovetskikh pisatelei SSSR, mart 1935: Stenograficheskii otchet. Moscow: Gosizdat "Khudozhestvennaia literatura," 1935.

Vtoroi vsesoiuznyi s"ezd sovetskih pisatelei, 15–26 dekabria 1954: Stenogra-fiicheskii otchet. Ed. M. Bazhan et al. Moscow: Sovetskii pisatel', 1956.

Vyshinsky, Andrei Y., ed. *The Law of the Soviet State.* Trans. Hugh W. Babb. New York: Macmillan, 1948.

Vyshinsky, Andrei, and M. Kareva. *Soviet Socialist Law.* Translated by Arthur Prudden Coleman et al. Austin: University of Texas, 1950.

Yedlin, Tovah. *Maxim Gorky: A Political Biography.* Westport, CT: Praeger, 1999.

Yurchak, Alexei. *Everything Was Forever, Until It Was No More: The Last Soviet Generation.* Princeton, NJ: Princeton University Press, 2005.

Zhukov, Ivan. *Fadeev.* Moscow: Molodaia gvardiia, 1989.

———. *Ruka sud'by: Pravda i lozh' o Mikhaile Sholokhove i Aleksandre Fadeeve.* Moscow: Voskresen'e, 1994.

Žižek, Slavoj. *How to Read Lacan.* New York: Norton, 2007.

———. *The Sublime Object of Ideology.* New York: Verso, 1989.

Zolotonosov, M. *Kak pisateli Leningrada radovalis' nachalu Bol'shogo terrora.* 812 Online. http://www.online812.ru/2012/05/18/011/.

Zolotonosov, M. N. *Gadiushnik: Leningradskaia pisatel'skaia organizatsiia; Iz-brannye stenogrammy c kommentariiami (iz istorii sovetskogo literaturnogo byta 1940–1960-kh godov.* Moscow: Novoe literaturnoe obozrenie, 2013.

Index

Ababkov, Ivan, 64
Abakumov, Viktor, 72
Abduction of Europe (*Pokhishchenie Evropy*) (Fedin), 104
"About a Certain Kulak Chronicle" ("Ob odnoi kulatskoi khronike") (Fadeyev and Sutyrin), 31–32
Academy of Social Sciences, 183
Academy of Sciences, 195–96, 230
"Adventures of an Ape" ("Prikliucheniia obezyany") (Zoshchenko), 185
Afinogenov, Aleksandr: expulsion from party, 120–21, 138–40; as living man proponent, 75; and Pasternak, 104; in RAPP, 44; in second plenum, 94–95
"Against the Current" ("Protiv techeniia") (Fadeyev), 18
agency: individual, 231; and "new man," 9–10; vs. obedience, 222; of writers, 5–6, 10, 19, 62
Agitprop (Agitation and Propaganda Department): and Akhmatova, 167; and Avdeyenko, 67; and bannings, 167, 172; and denunciations, 148; and Fadeyev, 4, 157, 159, 166, 178, 181, 197–99; and Gorbachev, 233–34; and Gorky, 54, 73; and Jewish students, 180; in literary policy, 19; and Pasternak, 227–28; and Pomerantsev, 209; and Pushkin, 133, 196; and RAPP, 44–45; and Shcherbakov, 93; and Stavsky, 148, 149–50, 247n149; in structure of Soviet regime, 82–83, 169–70, 176, 184, 274n37; and Writers' Union, 3–4, 83, 183, 226, 247n6; and Yermilov, 198; and Zoshchenko, 184–86
Akhmatova, Anna: banning of, 167; cartoon of, 39; Fadeyev and, 167, 169, 199; and

literary mastery, 91; marginalization of, 51; publication during Thaw, 234; resolution disgracing, 184–87, 191; and Writers' Union membership, 63
Aksyonov, Vasily, 225
Aleksandrov, G., 229
Aleksandrov, Vladimir, 154, 159, 167, 170, 178–81, 184, 186, 196, 272n21
Aliger, Margarita, 99–100, 177–79, 211–12, 213
All-Russian Society of Peasant Writers, 18
All-Russian Theater Society, 197–98
Althausen, Jack, 98, 99, 251n71
All-Union Arts Committee (Vsesoiuzny komitet po delam iskusstv pri SNK SSSR), 100
Altman, Iogann, 134, 136, 159, 199, 204
Alymov, Sergei, 67
"Among Animals and Plants" ("Sredi zhivotnykh i rastenii") (Platonov), 155
Andreyev, Andrei, 93, 110, 111, 120, 124, 149–51, 167, 171, 210
Andreyeva, Mariia, 38
Angarov, A. I., 149, 263n1, 270n153
Anov, Nikolai, 64
Antonov-Ovseyenko, Anton, 235
Apletin, Mikhail, 175
Ardis Publishing, 232
Arkadyev, Mikhail, 91, 257n53
Aseyev, Nikolai: attacks on, 149, 181; at Avdeyenko "grilling," 171; censorship and, 176; and Fadeyev, 166, 179; at first congress, 74; at Literary Institute, 180; and Mayakovsky, 98; payments to, 130; and Pushkin plenum, 134, 136
autobiography, communist: as character reference, 7, 234–35; compromised,

Index

Index

Index

Ferrous Metallurgy (Chernaia metallurgiia) (Fadeyev), 203, 204, 210

Firin, Semyon, 65–69, 75, 133, 170

Flaubert, Gustave, 5, 51–52

force field, literary: literary milieu as, 5–6, 11; Pavlenko role in, 127; and Platonov, 27–28; Samizdat and underground in, 231, 232

For a Just Cause (Za pravoe delo) (Grossman), 202, 203, 212

"For Future Use" ("Vprok") (Platonov), 27–34, 157

Formalism, campaign against, 10, 39–40, 85, 97, 100–105, 109, 120

FOSP (Federation of Organizations of Soviet Writers), 22, 24, 41–42, 240n34, 241n52

foreign policy and literature, 12, 180, 191–92, 197

frames masking sensitive material, 136, 213–14, 222

Frankly Speaking (Nachistotu) (Glebov), 172

freedom: artistic, 88, 105, 117, 188; creative, 226, 233; Fadeyev on, 200, 202, 207, 213, 222; interpretive, 136; of the press, 166, 174; Solzhenitsyn on, 230–31; as threat, 194; Yermilov on, 229

free market, literature in, 51–52, 102

Friend's Heart, A (Serdtse druga) (Kazakevich), 212

Friendship of Nations (Druzhba narodov), 183

Fromm, Erich, 7, 121, 143

From Six Books (Iz shesti knig) (Akhmatova), 167

Frunze, Mikhail, 28

Furmanov, Dmitry, 8

Gabrilovich, Yevgeny, 174

Galich, Aleksandr, 231–32

"Garbage Wind" ("Musornyi veter") (Platonov), 34–35

Garrard, Carol, 11

Garrard, John, 11

Gerasimova, Valeriia, 32, 83, 163, 181–82, 216–17, 223

Gladkov, Fyodor, 7–8, 78, 23, 71, 78, 95–96, 129, 140, 204

glasnost period, 233–34

Glebov, Anatoly, 172

Goebbels, Joseph, 50, 58, 248n19, 254n9

Gorbachev, Mikhail, 233–34

Gorbatov, Boris, 72, 177, 181, 183, 188–93, 293n136

Gorbov, Dmitry, 96

Gorelov, Anatoly, 88, 149, 256n33

Gorky, Maxim: aesthetics of, 53; and Avdeyenko, 69, 91; as board chair of Union, 79, 81–111, 186; children of, 38, 72, 73 cognitive dissonance and rationalizing of, 38; death of, 105, 123, 147; and Dostoevsky, 90; and factory workers, 40; and Fadeyev, 111, 140, 162, 208, 226; and first plenum, 52, 84–85; at first Writers' Congress, 72–79; and Grigoryev, 23; lack of awareness, 78, 88; lavish lifestyle of, 46, 51, 70, 72, 142; and Lenin, 35–37, 45, 54, 116, 158; and Literary Institute, 49, 180, 211; and literary mastery issue, 90–92, 154–55; and Mirsky, 141; and orgkomitet of Union, 45, 47, 80; and Panfyorov, 73, 89–90; and Platonov, 33–36, 158–59; prestige of, 6–7, 50; pseudonym of, 199; and public/private divide, 9; RAPP and, 21, 43; return to Soviet Union, 45–46, 48–49, 194; and secret police, 83; and Shaginian, 94–95, 103; and Shcherbakov, 11, 80–106, 108, 181; and Sholokhov, 43, 246n141; on socialist realism, 53–55; and Stalin, 4–5, 6–7, 11, 34–38, 42–46, 53, 71–73, 78–79, 82, 86, 93, 105–6, 123; on Stavsky, 129; utopianism of, 9, 36–37, 53–54; and Vasilyev, 64–65; and White Sea canal visit, 67, 69; wives of, 38; and Writers' Union establishment, 40, 45, 78–79; and Yagoda, 72; and Yermilov, 43, 66, 78–79, 81, 110, 159. See also specific works

Gorky Institute of World Literature, 121, 195–96, 201, 229, 247n12

Gorodetsky, Sergei, 23, 40

Gosizdat Publishing House, 28, 90

Grani, 232

Great Purge of 1937–38: and apartments, 3, 72; and Foreign Commission, 183; and Fadeyev, 196–97; and Grigoryev, 23; and "Mayakovsky's choice," 14–15; and Onguardists, 15–16; and Shcherbakov, 12; and Sholokhov, 147; and Stalin, 5,

Index

Ingulov, Sergei, 148
Inostrannaia literatura (Foreign Literature), 214
Inside the Soviet Union (Garrard and Garrard), 11
Institute of Red Professors, 16, 48, 81
insult: to Avdeyenko, 171; to Fadeyev, 44, 208, 219–20, 223; to Gorky, 35; by honor group, 220; to Nadezhda Mandelshtam, 71; by RAPP leaders, 61; to Shaginian, 102; to Yermilov, 117–18
International Congress of Writers in Defense of Culture against Fascism, 99
International Literature (Internatsionalnaia literatura), 115, 180
In the East (Na vostoke) (Pavlenko), 143
In the First Circle (V kruge pervom) (Solzhenitsyn), 232–33
In the Trenches of Stalingrad (V okopakh Stalingrada) (Nekrasov), 189, 190, 191, 232
Israel, Soviet Jews and, 197
Ivanov, Vsevolod, 6, 19, 52, 75, 80, 84, 123, 130–32, 162, 277n1
Ivan the Terrible (Ivan Groznyi) (Tolstoy), 71
Izvestiia, 48, 63, 73, 148, 153, 229

Jasieński, Bruno, 45
Jewish Anti-Fascist Committee (JAFC): arrest and execution of members, 199–200, 281n37; disbanding of, 180; members in Union, 176–77
Jews: censorship of, 180, 275n73; executions of, 196, 197, 199–200; Fadeyev and, 24, 180, 198–99, 204, 205; as heroes, 176; Nazis and, 50, 83, 281n39; Soviet attacks on, 180–81, 196–201; Stalin policy on, 197–98; as Union members, 176–77, 200

Kaganovich, Lazar, 44–45, 75–76, 78, 80–81, 93, 141, 149
Kamenev, Lev: arrest of, 109–10; dacha of, 161; and Gorky, 42, 81, 85; and Stavsky, 147; trial of, 119, 121, 123, 163; and Zinovyev, 65, 89, 110
Kanatchikov, Semyon Ivanovich, 24, 25, 29
Kapler, Aleksei, 189
Karavayeva, Anna, 151, 152, 260n3

Katayev, Ivan, 149
Katayev, Valentin: and arrests of writers, 130–32; and Avdeyenko, 171; banning of work, 172–73; and Fadeyev, 166; and Mandelshtam, 143; on Stavsky, 151–52; White Sea Canal trip, 66, 67; and *Youth*, 226
Kaverin, Veniamin, 212
Kazakevich, Emmanuil, 189, 212, 214
Kerzhentsev, Grigory, 97, 100–101, 124, 150, 258n93
KGB, 233
Kharms, Daniil, 104
Khrushchev, Nikita: Fadeyev and, 207–8, 219–20, 221; and Pasternak, 227–28; on Shcherbakov, 85, 257n58; "secret speech" on Stalin's crimes, 14, 219, 225, 226; and Tarsis, 231
"Kirdzhali" (Pushkin), 136
Kirov, Sergei, assassination of, 73, 3, 109–14, 142, 275n29
Kirpichnikov, Vladimir Petrovich. *See* Stavsky, Vladimir (Vladimir Petrovich Kirpichnikov)
Kirpotin, Valery: joint Agitprop/Union role, 47, 86, 166; denunciation of *Literary Critic*, 157–59; and Fadeyev, 157, 175; at first plenum, 55, 74; and RAPP, 44; and orgkomitet of Union, 47, 82; on Pushkin, 133–34, 196; on "subjective idealism," 116, 166, 175, 196
Kirsanov, Semyon, 76, 104, 130, 134
Kirshon, Vladimir: and Afinogenov, 120, 139; arrest of, 137–38; expulsion from Union, 139–40; and Fadeyev, 161–62, 205; at first orgkomitet plenum, 60–63; and Pilniak, 86; and RAPP, 44, 240n28; and Shaginian, 103; and Stavsky, 151
Kliuev, Nikolai, 11, 39, 65–66, 74, 149, 161, 235, 251n67
Klychkov, Sergei: accused of "kulak mentality," 29–30; execution of, 149, 161; at first orgkomitet plenum, 51, 63, 251n70; as peasant, 63, 65; on RAPP, 47
Kolchak, Aleksandr, 17
Koltsov, Aleksei, 16
Koltsov, Mikhail, 5, 8, 183
Komsomol, the, 16, 41, 49, 81, 177, 234
Kon, Feliks, 24, 250n54
Kontinent, 232

Index

symbolism in, 129; Yermilov and, 119,
201. *See also specific works*
Lifshits, Michael, 154, 156, 157
Lifshits, Vladimir, 104
Likharev, Boris, 185
*Literary Contemporary (Literaturnyi
sovremennik)*, 167
Literary Critic (Literaturnyi kritik), 12, 60,
115–16, 208
literary mastery: Akhmatova and, 91;
Bukharin on, 76–78, 91; Gorky on, 40,
90–92, 154–55; vs. ideological credentialing, 91, 96–97; Pasternak and, 75, 91;
Stalin on, 57; and Union membership,
49; Yermilov on, 96, 112, 229–30
Literary Moscow (Literaturnaia Moskva),
226
Literary Study (Literaturnaia ucheba), 40,
48–49, 80
Literature and Art (Literatura i iskusstvo),
178, 181
Literaturnaia gazeta (Literary Gazette):
and Aleksandrov, 159; Fadeyev and, 60,
140, 165; and Gorky, 48–49; and Nekrasov, 189; and Pasternak, 104; and RAPP,
24–26, 29; and Riurikov, 209, 211; and
Simonov, 193–95, 211–12; and Stavsky,
130, 132, 140, 149; and Surkov, 181–82,
187; suspension of, 176; as organ of Writers' Union, 15, 63, 259n99; and Yermilov,
60, 108, 110, 111, 140, 157, 197, 201
Litfront writers' group: arrests of, 137–38;
infighting with RAPP and aftermath, 23–
24, 25, 29, 41, 57, 88, 150, 201, 245n131,
281n38; and literary scene, 18
Little House (Domik) (Katayev), 172
*Living and the Dead, The (Zhivye i mert-
vye)* (Simonov), 8
"living man" theory: Afinogenov and, 75;
Libedinsky and, 29; Onguardists and,
20, 22–23, 98, 159; Platonov and, 156; as
psychological approach to characters, 19,
56; RAPP and, 52, 55; and selfhood, 20;
vs. socialist realism, 52; Trotsky and, 56;
Yermilov and, 159
Lobansky (secretary of Union military commission), 174–75, 274n53
Lominadze, Beso, 137, 267n88
Lozovsky, Solomon, 177, 178, 198, 276n75
Lugovoi, Pyotr, 145, 269n125

Lugovskoi, Vladimir, 134
Lukash, Mykola, 231–32
Lunacharsky, Anatoly, 28, 37, 55

Mahogany (Krasnoe derevo) (Pilniak), 26–
27
Maizel, Mikhail, 138, 142
Makaryev, Ivan, 23, 44, 57, 62, 137, 204,
215–18, 283nn82–83
Makaryeva, Raisa, 216, 217–18
Makliarsky, Mikhail (Isidor), 199–200
Maksimenkov, Leonid, 12
Maksimov, Vladimir, 231–32
Malenkov, Georgy, 159, 170–71, 178, 181,
184–87, 191, 198, 200, 207–8, 220–21
Malraux, Andre, 74
Mandelshtam, Nadezhda, 3, 71, 144,
268n114
Mandelshtam, Osip: denunciation and ar-
rest of, 141, 143, 144, 161; exile of,
11, 74, 82; Fadeyev and, 143–44, 161,
283n83; as forced laborer, 69, 149; and
Novy Mir, 61; as old intelligentsia, 91;
Tolstoy and, 71; Vishnevsky and, 11
Man with a Gun (Chelovek s ruzhyom)
(Pogodin), 139
marketing of ideology, 51–52, 66, 74, 103
Markish, Perets, 104, 177, 198
Markov, Georgy, 234
Markov, Sergei, 64–65, 74
Marshak, Samuil, 181
Maslin, N., 183
Martynov, Leonid, 64–65, 74
Mass, Vladimir, 54, 74
Master and Margarita, The (Bulgakov),
167
Mayakovsky, Vladimir: and Aseyev, 98; 116;
Fadeyev and, 207, 223; and RAPP, 21;
Stalin's elevation of, 97–100, suicide of,
14–15, 212, 223. *See also specific works*
"Mayakovsky's choice," 14–15
Maznin, Dmitry, 113–14
Mekhlis, Lev: and Avdeyenko, 68, 69, 170–
71; belittling of subordinates, 8; denun-
ciations to, 143, 147–48; Gorky and, 87,
89; at *Pravda*, 43, 67, 76, 87, 115–17,
165; and Stalin, 12, 100, 124, 192, 199;
and Stavsky, 152; and Yermilov, 12, 112,
115–16, 120
Melekhov, Grigory, 43, 145

Index

Orlov, V. N., 92, 119
Orthodox Ones, The (*Ortodoksy*) (Tarasov), 141
Osipov, P., 189
Ostrovsky, Nikolai, 8
Our Achievements, 66, 105
Ovalov, Lev, 41
Ovechkin, Valentin, 182, 183

Pages from Tarusa (*Tarusskie stranitsy*), 226
Palę Paryż (*I Burn Paris*) (Jasieński), 45
Pamir writers' group, 64
Panfyorov, Fyodor: and Gorky, 73, 79, 81, 89–90; and *October*, 43; and RAPP, 41; and Stavsky, 147–48; and Tikhonov, 105; and Yermilov, 201
Panova, Vera, 79, 189, 190, 191, 203, 211
"Pao-Pao" (Selvinsky), 55
Paperno, Irina, 9–10, 12
Party Control Commission, 115, 147, 178, 216
party-mindedness, 99
Pashukanis, Yevgeny, 125–26
Pasternak, Boris: on beginning of WWII, 174; Bukharin on, 76–77; debates on, 98–99, 104; and Gronsky, 61; and literary mastery, 75, 91; in NKVD reports, 166; and Nobel Prize, 226–28, 230, 231; and Pushkin plenum, 134, 136, 137. *See also* *Dr. Zhivago* (Pasternak)
Pavlenko, Pyotr, 11, 28, 85, 87, 92, 101, 103, 143–44, 152, 163–66, 174, 254n124, 268n113
"Peacock, The" ("Pavlin") (Sergeyev-Tsensky), 55
People of the First and Second Five-Year Plans, The (*Liudi pervoi i vtoroi piatiletki*) (Gorky), 409
People with a Clear Conscience (*Liudi s chistoi sovestiu*) (Vershigora), 183, 190, 212
People, Years, Life (*Liudi, gody, zhizn*) (Ehrenburg), 229
Pereval writers' group: infighting with RAPP and aftermath, 21, 28–30, 141, 240n34, 280n19; and literary scene, 18, 19; and "Mozart principle," 28–29; and Writers' Union, 48
Pereverzev, Valeryan, 21, 153, 157–58
Pereverzevites: on classics, 21; infighting with RAPP and aftermath, 21, 25, 28–30, 153–54, 245n131, 28n19; and literary scene, 18, 22
Peshkov, Alexei Maximovich. *See* Gorky, Maxim (Alexei Maximovich Peshkov)
Peshkov, Max, 38, 73
Peshkov, Zinovy, 38
Peshkova, Ekaterina, 38
Peshkova, Nadezhda ("Timosha"), 38, 72
Peter the Great, 193
Petrov, Yevgeny, 143
Piatakov-Radek trial, 132–33, 137, 165
Pilniak, Boris: and censorship, 8; at first orgkomitet plenum, 62; as nonparty writer, 6, 19; shamed by RAPP, 23, 26–28
Pitersky, L., 189
Platonov, Andrei: branded as kulak, 58, 61, 66–67, 163, 203; defense of, 155–56, 172, 204, 272n15; and Fadeyev, 177, 198; "For Future Use" controversy, 27–32; literary identity, of, 133, 156–60; as maverick, 13; and RAPP, 26–36; and Yermilov, 33, 66–67, 87–88, 105, 155–60, 187, 198. *See also specific works*
Plekhanov, Georgy, 56, 202, 213
plenums of Writers' Union: first, 84; second, 94–96, 104, 108, 120; third, 97–100, 129; fourth (Pushkin), 133–37, 158
Pogodin, Nikolai, 103, 139
Polevoi, Boris, 209
Poliak, L., 179
Polikarpov, Dmitry: in Agitprop, 214, 227–28; on Akhmatova, 167; belittling of subordinates, 8; in Union secretariat, 181–83, 186, 277n90; and Yermilov, 187
policy, literary: and "below/above" divide, 6; and cadre, 8; and de-Stalinization, 225; enforcers of, 13; Fadeyev and, 180, 190, 213; and foreign policy, 12, 180, 191–92, 197–98; Gorky and, 49, 53, 85, 98; and Jewish policy, 198; and Literary Institute, 49, 180; and literary milieu, 11–12; Stalin and, 10, 19, 41, 53–54, 93–94, 176; Surkov and, 207; Trotsky and, 19; writers' choices regarding, 13; Writers' Union lack of role in, 54
Polonsky, Viacheslav, 27–28, 33, 243n76
Pomerantsev, Vladimir, 209, 213–15, 225–26
Popkov, Pyotr, 186
Popov, Yevgeny, 232

311

Index

Position of the Working Class in Russia
(*Polozhenie rabochego klassa v Rossii*)
(Bervi-Flerovsky), 36–37
Pospelov, Pyotr, 208, 210, 220–21
Possessed, The (*Besy*) (Dostoevsky), 89
Postyshev, Pavel, 45
Pozdyshev (writer), 104
Pravda: automatized language in, 129;
Avdeyenko and, 69, 170, 171; Averbakh
and, 22–23, 27; Gorky and, 73, 80, 89,
105, 111–12; and JAFC arrests, 198–99;
letter against Solzhenitsyn in, 233; *Literary Critic* and, 154, 158; Litfront and,
29; Mekhlis at, 43, 67, 76, 87, 115–17,
165; and RAPP, 14, 41; on self-criticism,
103–4, 134; Shostakovich attack in,
97, 100–101, 103, 107, 134; as Stalin's
mouthpiece, 73; Yermilov and, 116–20,
210, 229
Pribludny, Ivan, 72, 149
Prishvin, Mikhail, 21, 23, 38–39, 60–61, 66,
101, 109
Prokofiev, Aleksandr, 185
Proletkult, 18, 239n18
Prompartiia trial, 22–23, 29, 41, 88
propaganda: through Agitprop agency, 4,
157, 170, 272n21; and automatization,
129; Bolshevik, 6, 223; Soviet vs. Nazi
structures for, 49–50, 58–59, 82–83,
248n19; Stalin and, 59; during WWII,
174, 176, 184
Propaganda Ministry, Germany, 49–50
Provisional Government, 48–49
"psychologism" error, 21
psychology, personal: and "below/above"
divide, 6; of characters, 20; vs. ideology,
154; and public/private divide, 8–12; and
terror, 107–22
psychiatric hospitalization, as alternative to
arrest, 231
public/private divide in selfhood, 8–12
Pushkin, Aleksandr: and Agitprop, 133;
banning of, 21; changing stance on, 195–
96; as classic, 35, 55; plenum on, 133–
37, 158; Stalin and, 196. *See also specific
works*
Puzin, Aleksei, 181, 184

Queen of Spades (*Pikovaia dama*) (Meyerhold), 117
Quiet River Don, The (*Tikhii Don*) (Sholok-

hov), 23–24, 33, 42–43, 109, 145, 149,
147, 165, 219

Radek, Karl, 74, 123, 132–34, 137, 141,
165, 255n19
Radishchev, Aleksander, 53, 85
raikom (district party committee) arrests,
145–47, 150, 165
RAPP (Russian Association of Proletarian
Writers): dissolving of, 15; and emergence of Writers' Union, 12; harassment
politics of, 15–16, 21–35; infighting with
Litfront, 23–24, 25, 29, 41, 57, 88, 150,
201, 245n131, 281n38; infighting with
Pereval, 21, 28–30, 141, 240n34, 280n19;
infighting with Pereverezites, 21, 25, 28–
30, 153–54, 245n131, 28n19; journals
controlled by, 19–20; and "living man"
theory, 19; and Mayakovsky, 14–15; and
Red Virgin Soil, 18–31
Red Army: and Cossack rebellion, 43,
241n43; newspaper of, 24, 174, 197; and
party discipline, 17; "village pacification"
program of, 124–25; in WWII, 174, 188
Red Virgin Soil (*Krasnaia nov*): Anov and,
64; Fadeyev and, 115–16, 119, 243n76;
labeled as errant, 115; as party organ,
167; and RAPP founding, 18–31; Voronsky and, 18–19, 21; Yermilov as editor of,
60, 87, 107–21, 158, 240n5
rehabilitation of prisoners, 38, 66, 68–69,
204, 206, 217, 234–35
Reich Association of Jewish Culture
Leagues, 83
Reich Culture Chamber, 49–51, 82–83,
248nn19–20
Reizin, Semyon, 103, 148
Riurikov, Boris, 197, 209, 211, 232
Riutin, Martermyan, 46, 64
Road to Ocean (*Doroga na okean*) (Leonov), 92
Rodchenko, Aleksandr, 97
Romanov, Panteleimon, 104
"Rough Draft of Feelings, A" ("Chernovik
chuvstv") (Belinkov), 180
Rout, The (*Razgrom*) (Fadeyev), 8, 17–18,
20, 41, 109, 129
Rozental, Mark, 148, 150, 154
Rozhkov, P. D., 150
Rozner, L., 199–200
Ruin (*Razrukha*) (Kliuev), 66

Index

313

Index

denigration by other writers, 129; in establishment of Union, 15,45; and Fadeyev, 7, 15, 45, 62, 88, 128, 140, 149, 151–52, 165, 268n99; as fanatic, 124; and formalism, 39–40; formative experiences of, 124–27; and Gorky, 65, 79, 81, 82; and Great Purge, 7; as head of Union, 100, 124, 130–31, 147–52, 155, 263n1, 265n49; internal division, lack of, 131–32; in Mandelshtam denunciation, 143–44; Mirsky and, 141; and NKVD, 143; and Old Bolshevik show trials, 12, 123–51, 267n88; and orgkomitet of Union, 65, 79, 81, 84–86, 88; and Pamir group, 64; personal papers of, 11; and Platonov, 155; and Pushkin plenum, 134–35; and raikom mass arrests, 145–51; in RAPP, 12, 23, 44–45, 241n43; and self-transformation, 128; and Shaginian, 103; and Shcherbakov, 81–86, 88, 103, 120, 1245, 127, 129–30, 132, 265n45; and Sholokhov, 144–46; Stalin's use of, 124, 140, 152, 165–66, 199; and Tarsis, 231; and terror of Old Bolshevik show trials, 12, 123–51, 267n88; at third plenum, 97–98; and Trotskyists, 129–30, 137–39; "unmasking" by, 124, 130, 151; writing style of, 127–28; and Yermilov, 11, 12, 15, 45, 120, 88, 140, 152, 240n35. *See also specific works*
Stepping into Life (*Vstuplenie v zhizn*) (Sheremeteva), 188
Stetsky, Aleksei: censorship by, 54, 73; and Fadeyev, 110, 111; and First Writers' Congress, 76, 81; as orgkomitet member, 82; and Stalin, 24, 45
Stockholm syndrome, 193
Story of a Real Man, The (*Povest o nastoiashchem cheloveke* (Polevoi), 8
Strict Youth, A (*Strogy iunosha*) (Olesha), 96
Strauss, Richard, 50
"subjective idealism," 116
subjectivity: vs. communist objectivity, 20, 63; Soviet, 160
Subotsky, Lev, 48–49, 87, 103, 108, 148, 149, 182, 189
supply and demand in literature, 91–92
Surkov, Aleksei: and Averbakh, 80; and Fadeyev, 201, 203, 206–8; at first con-

gress, 76–77; on Kirshon, 138; at *Literaturnaia gazeta*, 181–82, 187; and Mandelshtam, 143; as obedient, 166; at Pushkin plenum, 136–37; at presidium meeting, 86–87; and Stavsky, 149; at third plenum, 98, 99; as Union head, 201, 203, 205–13; war reporting of, 174; on working-class writers, 90
Surov, Anatoly, 212, 283n79
Suslov, Mikhail, 196
Sutyrin, Vladimir, 19, 30–32, 205, 239n20
"Svaaker" (Fedin), 61
Sverdlov, Yakov, 16, 38
Sverdlov Communist Institute, 81
Svetlov, Mikhail, 119, 130, 134, 212
Svetov, Feliks, 232

Taking of Velikoshumsk (*Vziatie Velikoshumska*) (Leonov), 183
"Takyr" (Platonov), 156
Tal, Boris, 148
Tale of the Unextinguished Moon, The (*Povest o nepogashennoi lune*) (Pilniak), 28, 141
Tales of Belkin (*Povesti pokoinogo Ivana Petrovicha Belkina*) (Pushkin), 136
Tarasov, Aleksandr, 141, 251
Tarsis, Valery, 148, 231
Tchaikovsky, Pyotr, 54
"That's Good!" ("Khorosho!") (Mayakovsky), 98
Thaw, The (*Ottepel*) (Ehrenburg), 211, 225
Theory of Literature (*Teoriia literatury*) (Tomashevsky), 39–40, 128
They Made It Through (*Proshli*) (Stavsky), 128
Thirty Nights in a Vineyard (*Tridtsat nochei na vinogradnike*) (Zarudin), 55
Ticket to History (*Bilet po istorii*) (Shaginian), 120
Tikhonov, Nikolai: and Fadeyev, 186, 206; at first congress, 73–74, 268n124; and Gorelov, 88; as head of Leningrad branch, 103–4; as nonparty writer, 6, 11, 19, 94, 270n33; and Polikarpov, 183; at Pushkin plenum, 134–36; and Solzhenitsyn 233; and Stalin, 185; as Union leader, 166, 181, 277n90
"To Licinius" ("Litsiniiu") (Pushkin), 133
Tolstaya, Tatyana, 234

Index

Tolstoy, Aleksei, 70–72, 109, 117, 150, 151, 162, 174

Tolstoy, Leo: changing stance on, 195–96; as classic, 20, 23, 35; Fadeyev and, 129, 164, 167; Yermilov on, 108, 214, 229

Tomashevsky, Boris, 39–40, 128

tonalities: in Fadeyev's suicide note, 221–24; in Stalin comments, 30–31

Toward a History of Realism (K istorii realizma) (Lukács), 156

Trauberg, Leonid, 205

Tretyakov, Sergei, 8, 63, 86

Trifonov, Yury, 220, 225

Trotsky, Leon: and Averbakh, 16, 137, 245n131; and Bukharin, 78; edited out, 54; and living man theory, 56; and nonparty writers, 18, 19, 21, 22

Trotskyists: accusation of slander by, 147; and trial of Rightists, 148, 150–51; writers labeled as, 21, 96, 113, 121, 129, 137–38, 141, 144

Truman Doctrine, 191

truth: and absolute language, 30; vs. authority, 7–8, 32, 179; Bourdieu on, 230–31; evidential vs. ideological, 18; Fadeyev and, 164, 174; party as source of, 37, 141, 171–72, 208; pledge to abstain from, 226; and socialist realism, 52–53; and subject, 113

Tsar's Road (Osudareva doroga) (Prishvin), 66

Tsesarsky, Vladimir (?), 147

Tvardovsky, Aleksandr, 177, 183, 201–2, 208–10, 213, 226, 228, 232

Two Five-Year Plans (Dve piatiletki), 35

Two Men in the Steppe (Dvoe v stepi) (Kazakevich), 189

Tynianov, Yury, 6, 55, 134, 136, 143, 267n77

Tyorkin in the Other World (Tyorkin na tom svete) (Tvardovsky), 210

"Ukraine in Flames" ("Ukraina v ogne") (Dovzhenko), 188

"Unforgettable" ("Nezabyvaemoe") (Dovzhenko), 176

Universal Copyright Convention, 231

"unmasking" tactic, 21–22, 124, 130, 148, 150–51, 165

Unvanquished, The (Nepokorennye) (Gorbatov), 183

Upravlenie Propagandy i Agitatsii TsK (Propaganda and Agitation Administration), 170

Ushinsky, Konstantin, 16

Usievich, Elena: and Fadeyev, 111; at first orgkomitet plenum, 60, 62, 63; and Onguardists, 56, 154, 156; and Stavsky, 147–48, 150; as theorist, 13; and Yermilov, 154, 157, 169

Utkin, Semyon, 100, 134

Vadimov, David, 180, 276n73

Vakhtangov, Yevgeny, 54

Vasilyev, Pavel, 11, 64–65, 74, 149, 161, 235

Vasily Tyorkin (Tvardovsky), 177, 183, 201

Veresayev, Vikenty, 173–74, 221

Vershigora, Petro, 182, 183, 190, 212

Vinogradov, Anatoly, 93

Viola, Lynn, 126

Vishnevsky, Vsevolod: aid to Mandelshtam, 11, 143–44, 148; and Babel's arrest, 72; as cadre, 80, 179; denunciations by, 140, 141; and Fadeyev, 179, 180; at first congress, 78; Gorky on, 73; at meetings, 86, 270n158; on Polikarpov, 181–82, 277n106; and presidium of Union, 166, 181–82; as reliable, 28, 85; and secretariat of Union, 150; attack on Shaginian, 102–3; and Stavsky, 166; and Tikhonov, 105; at *Znamia*, 184, 260n109

Vladimov, Georgy, 231–32

Voenpechat, 175

Voinovich, Vladimir, 231–32

Voitinskaia, Olga, 149

voronshchina writers, arrests of, 141

Voronsky, Aleksandr: arrest of, 141; execution of, 149; and Mustangova, 99; and *Red Virgin Soil*, 18, 20, 21, 22, 24, 28, 243n76

Voroshilov, Kliment, 72

VSP (Vserossiisky Soiuz Pisatelei, All-Russian Union of Writers), 41–42

Vyshinsky, Andrei, 126, 169

Wax Figure, The (Voskovaia persona) (Tynianov), 55, 61

We (My) (Zamiatin), 26–27

When I'm Alone (Kogda ia odin) (Kozakov), 172

Whetstones (Bruski) (Panfyorov), 41, 73, 90